YOURS ALWAYS FLEW FURTHER.

DATE DUE

FURTHER. FASTER. SMARTER. SAFER. More effective. More efficient. More powerful. You've always been about making things better. So has Boeing – better technology, a better world, and better careers. If you want your career to fly further, let it take off at Boeing. The job categories listed below include some of the key skills we typically seek.

- Structural Analysis/Design
- Electrical Engineering
- Systems Engineering

- Embedded Software Engineering
- Business and Planning Analysis
- Programmer/Analyst

- Control Systems Engineering
- Ops Analysis
- Avionics

If you would like to view a comprehensive listing of all available positions, please visit: boeing.com/employment/college. Security clearance requirements are indicated in the position listings. U.S. Citizenship is necessary for all positions requiring a security clearance.

Boeing is an equal opportunity employer supporting diversity in the workplace.

Apply at: *boeing.com/employment/college*

BOEING ®
Forever New Frontiers

The media's watching Vault!
Here's a sampling of our coverage.

"For those hoping to climb the ladder of success, [Vault's] insights are priceless."
– *Money magazine*

"The best place on the web to prepare for a job search."
– *Fortune*

"[Vault guides] make for excellent starting points for job hunters and should be purchased by academic libraries for their career sections [and] university career centers."
– *Library Journal*

"The granddaddy of worker sites."
– *US News and World Report*

"A killer app."
– *New York Times*

One of Forbes' 33 "Favorite Sites"
– *Forbes*

"To get the unvarnished scoop, check out Vault."
– *Smart Money Magazine*

"Vault has a wealth of information about major employers and job-searching strategies as well as comments from workers about their experiences at specific companies."
– *The Washington Post*

"A key reference for those who want to know what it takes to get hired by a law firm and what to expect once they get there."
– *New York Law Journal*

"Vault [provides] the skinny on working conditions at all kinds of companies from current and former employees."
– *USA Today*

IDEAS.
INSIGHTS.
PERSPECTIVES.

Everyone's got them. Everyone's welcome.

Blurring the lines between distinctions. Encouraging initiative and creativity. Honoring our differences. These are just a few of the principles that have allowed Oxford Health Plans to foster a workplace community where all people are treated with respect and dignity. And, all people are welcome.

It is our mission to celebrate the diversity of our employees. We believe that the success of our company, employees and, ultimately, our industry relies on new ideas and innovations. This can only be achieved when individuals from unique backgrounds collaborate and share their perspectives and viewpoints. And what we learn from our employees' diverse perspectives, we translate into sound business practices that benefit everyone. Including you.

Now is the time to consider a career with us. Here, you'll thrive in an environment that is diverse, vibrant, exciting and welcoming.

To learn more, please visit our web site at **www.oxfordhealth.com.**

Oxford Health Plans is an Affirmative Action/Equal Opportunity Employer.
Females and minorities are encouraged to apply.

THE VAULT
COLLEGE
CAREER BIBLE

THE VAULT
COLLEGE
CAREER BIBLE

VAULT EDITORS

For information about permission to reproduce selections from this book, contact Vault Inc.150 W. 22nd St. New York, New York 10011-1772, (212) 366-4212.

Library of Congress CIP Data is available.

ISBN 1-58131-283-0

Printed in the United States of America

Acknowledgments

Thanks to everyone who had a hand in making this book possible, especially Kelly Shore, Elena Boldeskou, Kristy Sisko and Joseph Naggiar. We are also extremely grateful to Vault's entire staff for all their help in the editorial, production and marketing processes. Vault also would like to acknowledge the support of our investors, clients, employees, family, and friends. Thank you!

Visit Vault at **www.vault.com** for insider company profiles, expert advice, career message boards, expert resume reviews, the Vault Job Board and more.

VAULT CAREER LIBRARY

ix

Join the Winning Team
it'sallinside
JCPenney
With JCPenney there is a World of Opportunities in a variety of Different Career Paths.
If you:
• Demonstrate a can-do attitude
• Are multi-task oriented
• Take the initiative
• Posses excellent leadership skills
• Have exceptional communication skills
• Display a strong fashion sense
Then we are looking for you!
Qualifications:
• 3.0 G.P.A. preferred
• Undergraduate degree in Business, Marketing, Merchandising and/or strong retail experience will be considered. Plus opportunities in Information Technology.
• Candidates must presently be authorized to work in the U.S. on a full-time basis.
Check with your campus Career Center to see whether a JCPenney Recruiter will be visiting your campus or post your resume on line at:
http://jcpenney.recruitmax.com/candidates

Table of Contents

INTRODUCTION   **1**

THE COLLEGE STUDENT JOB SEARCH   **5**

On-Campus Recruiting and Internships   **7**
On-Campus Recruiting and Internships 7
The Importance of Interning 7
Make Sure You Don't Blow Your Internship 9
How to Take Advantage of Your Internship 10

Resumes   **13**
Sample Resumes 14

Cover Letters   **17**
The Cover Letter Template 17

Interviews   **23**
Getting Ready 23
At the Interview 25
Questions to Expect: The Quality Search 28

Schmoozing/Networking   **31**
Schmoozing to Find a Job Through People 31
Schmoozing to Find a Job When in School 31
Schmoozing to Find a Job Out of School 33

WORKPLACE DIVERSITY   **37**

Overview   **38**

Mentors   **39**
A Crucial Advantage 39
Identifying Potential Mentors 39

Appearance   **45**

Visit Vault at www.vault.com for insider company profiles, expert advice,
career message boards, expert resume reviews, the Vault Job Board and more.

VAULT CAREER LIBRARY   xi

Dealing with Stereotyping   47

Common Stereotypes: Women 48

Common Stereotypes: Minorities 51

Common Stereotypes: Gay Men 53

Employer Directory   55

GRADUATE EDUCATION   59

Considering Graduate School   61

Graduate School: To Go or Not To Go 61

Graduate School Options: Certification vs. a Degree 61

Considering Graduate School? 63

Law School   65

Choosing a Law School 65

Law School Reputation 66

Ask Anna: Time Off Before Taking the Plunge 67

LSAT 101 68

Business School   71

Why the MBA? 71

GMAT 101 72

Graduate Education Directory   75

INDUSTRY OVERVIEWS   77

Accounting   79

Why Accounting? 79

Accounting Uppers and Downers 80

Public vs. Private Accounting 82

The CPA 85

Employer Directory 87

Advertising   89

An Introduction to Advertising 89

Media Options 90

Major Career Paths in Advertising 92

Employer Directory 95

Aerospace & Defense   97

Industry Outlook 97

Employer Directory 101

Banking   105

Investment Banking 105

Commercial Banking 106

Corporate Finance 107

Institutional Sales and Trading (S&T) 109

Research 111

Employer Directory 118

Biotech/Pharmaceuticals   125

The Global Pharmaceutical Industry 125

Departments in a Biotech Company 127

To Lab or Not To Lab? 129

Laboratory Research Careers 130

Non-Laboratory Research Careers 131

How it Comes Together 135

Employer Directory 136

Consumer Products/Marketing   139

Consumer Products/Marketing Industry Overview 139

Marketing and Brand Managers 141

Careers in Marketing 142

What is a Brand? 146

Top 12 Ways to Revitalize a Brand 147

Employer Directory 148

Energy/Oil & Gas   151

Energy Industry History 151

Understanding the New Energy Industry 154

Types of Energy Companies 157

The Oil and Gas Industry 158

Getting Hired 162

Employer Directory 166

Fashion   169

Fashion Design Jobs 169

The Scoop on Design Careers 170

Our Survey Says: Fashion Industry Culture 171

Networking 172

Day in a Life: Assistant Product Manager 174

Visit Vault at **www.vault.com** for insider company profiles, expert advice,
career message boards, expert resume reviews, the Vault Job Board and more.

VAULT CAREER LIBRARY   **xiii**

Day in the Life: Dress Buyer 175

Employer Directory 177

Financial Services and Insurance   181

Brokerage Services 181

A Day in the Life: Credit Analyst 182

Credit Card Services 186

Insurance 189

Insurance Agent 193

Actuary 193

Employer Directory 195

Government and Politics   201

Life on Capitol Hill 201

Why Capitol Hill? 201

Capitol Hill Internships 203

Advocacy Organizations 205

The Staff Assistant 207

The Foreign Service 208

Employer Directory 212

Health Care   215

Health Care Industry Overview 215

Employer Directory 223

High Tech   227

The Scope of High Tech Careers 227

Categories of Tech Professionals 228

Common Positions for Recent College Grads 229

Employer Directory 233

Hospitality and Tourism   237

The Industry of Fun 237

Hospitality Careers 240

Travel Agent 242

Employer Directory 244

Investment Management   247

History 247

Buy-side vs. Sell-side 250

Portfolio Manager Assistant 251

Investment Research Assistant 253

Marketing and Sales 254

Employer Directory 256

Law/Paralegal   259

Corporate Law Basics 259
Areas of Corporate Practice 262
Day in the Life: Junior Corporate Associate 266
Litigation Basics 268
Lawsuits and Trials 269
Day in the Life: Corporate Litigation Associate 270
Day in the Life: Assistant District Attorney 271
Paralegal 273
Employer Directory 275

Management Consulting   279

What is Consulting? 279
Consulting Skill Sets 282
Who Hires Consultants, and Why? 285
Training for Consultants 287
Employer Directory 290

Manufacturing   297

The Engine Driving the Economy 297
Employer Directory 300

Media/Entertainment   303

The Industry 303
The Big Conundrums 307
Creative Assistants 309
Survival Skills for Assistants 310
Employer Directory 313

Nonprofit   315

Nonprofit Uppers and Downers 315
Many Choices 316
Nonprofit Doesn't Mean Money Doesn't Matter 317
The Board of Directors 318
Development Work and Organizations 319
Day in the Life: Peace Corps Volunteer, Senegal 320
Employer Directory 323

Visit Vault at **www.vault.com** for insider company profiles, expert advice,
career message boards, expert resume reviews, the Vault Job Board and more.

VAULT CAREER LIBRARY

xv

Public Relations   325

What is PR? 325

Public Relations History 325

Publicist 329

Employer Directory 331

Publishing   333

The Book Publishing Industry 333

Departments at a Book Publisher 335

Day in the Life: Book Editorial Assistant 336

Day in the Life: Book Publicity 338

Magazine Careers: Working Your Way Up 340

Breakdown of Magazine Assistant Positions .341

Employer Directory 347

Real Estate   349

History of the Real Estate Industry in the United States 349

Industry Trends 351

Residential Real Estate Brokers 352

Tenant Representation 352

Property Management 353

Employer Directory 354

Retail   357

Retail Industry Overview 357

Retail Careers in Fashion 360

Employer Directory 362

Technology Consulting   365

The State of Technology Consulting 365

Day in the Life: IT Consultant 368

Employer Directory 371

Telecommunications   375

Telecom Calling 375

Employer Directory 379

Transportation and Airlines   381

Turbulent Skies for Airlines 383

Carrying the Load 386

Road and Track 388

A Life in Transportation 389

Employer Directory 390

Introduction

Maybe you're facing the end of your college career. Maybe you've already graduated. Either way, you're facing the question you've been asked all your life: What are you going to do when you grow up? Only now, this question is no longer hypothetical. So what are you going to do?

First: relax. Whether you're a college junior, senior, or recent graduate, the world will not end if you don't have a job lined up just yet. Almost everyone has difficulty figuring out what they want to do with the rest of their life, and absolutely everyone goes through the painful process of finding their first real job. You're in good company.

Moreover, after several years of layoffs and hiring freezes, the U.S. job market has finally begun to pick up again. In the spring and summer of 2004, U.S. employers began adding jobs again after many months of net losses in jobs created. According to a survey by the National Association of Colleges and Employers (NACE), employers indicated that they would be hiring nearly 13 percent more new college graduates in 2004 than they had in 2003.

Still, for most first-time jobseekers, finding that first job is never easy. This Vault guide will help you get a leg up on the competitive job search, and will give you an overview of popular industries and careers to help you narrow your career search.

Start with your career center

Whether you're currently enrolled or a recent graduate, your college career center is a good place to start on your job search. Counselors at the career center can often provide help with resumes and interviewing. The center will also usually have job and internship listings, as well as contact information for alumni in your field of interest willing to provide advice to wide-eyed newbies. Remember, you can still use your college career center even if you've graduated.

Narrow your career options

Look for information about day-to-day responsibilities. It's tough to really understand what it's like to work at a job, which is why Vault provides Days in the Life and Q&As for many different occupations. Some of these are included in this book, others can be found in Vault's guides on specific industries or on www.vault.com.

Visit Vault at **www.vault.com** for insider company profiles, expert advice, career message boards, expert resume reviews, the Vault Job Board and more.

VAULT CAREER LIBRARY   1

Don't stress

This said, don't stress out over the choice of your first job. Gone are the days of working 40 years at one job and leaving with a and gold watch. Today's job market is much more fluid – most professionals starting their careers today will work in at least five different industries or functions during their careers.

Good luck!
The Team at Vault

VAULT CAREER LIBRARY

Innovation. Leadership. You.

Join Symbol Technologies in leading the enterprise mobility revolution! Only Symbol combines all three key components of enterprise mobility – the ability to capture, move and manage mission-critical information in real-time, at the point of business activity. Our customers span the globe, and choose to do business with Symbol not only for our peerless technology, but for our dedication to service and constant focus on success.

If you're in search of an exciting career with growth potential, Symbol may have the perfect opportunity for you. For over 30 years, talent as varied as engineers to marketers have found sucess at Symbol. Discover how you can too.

symbol®
The Enterprise Mobility Company ™

Symbol Technologies, Inc. • www.symbol.com
Global Headquarters: One Symbol Plaza, Holtsville, NY 11742-1300

THE COLLEGE
STUDENT
JOB SEARCH

On-Campus Recruiting and Internships

On-Campus Recruiting and Career Fairs

If you want to start your career at a large company, being a college student puts you in a good position to do so. Many major employers recruit college students at targeted campuses. Employers in professional services fields such as accounting, consulting, and investment banking hire large classes of graduating students each year as analysts, while major employers in other industries often hire new grads into management development programs. (These same employers normally hire many juniors as interns. Many students who intern at a company are extended full-time offers after graduation.)

The best place to find out which companies recruit at your school is your career services office. Companies generally visit the campus in the fall to give presentations to interested students; some colleges also hold career fairs, at which HR representatives from these companies collect resumes and speak with students. If you think you might be interested in a company, don't fail to go to these presentations!

If you're interested in a company, make sure you attend all that company's presentations and speak to at least one company representative. Sometimes this rep will be an HR professional, sometimes a manager in the department that is recruiting, and still other times the rep will be a new hire at the company, often an alumnus of your university. Ensure that you get the business card of the representative with whom you connect the most strongly. Then follow up with an e-mail expressing your interest and perhaps making an on-target inquiry or two. This will show your motivation and initiative – and remember, companies want to hire students who are interested in them and motivated to work for them. Don't overdo it, however; writing your new contact every week is overkill.

Later in the fall, these companies hold a first-round of interviews with students on-campus or very near campus, often at the career center. Students who pass the first round then visit the company's offices for a second day of interviews that takes a half-day or full day. The same process is followed for internships, though recruiting for summer internships generally happens at the beginning of the spring semester.

The Importance of Interning

If you're reading this book as an underclassman or early in your senior year, you're in good shape – many college students don't begin thinking about careers until late in their senior year or (gasp) after graduation. If you're one of the early birds, make sure you take advantage of your time by getting experience through a summer and/or school-year internship.

What is an internship?

An internship is a sort of trial run at a company – and one of the best ways to test out a potential career field or employer. Internships can last two weeks or a full year, though most of them are for a three-month period or so. Most internships take place over the summer, though others may occur over the fall or spring

Visit Vault at www.vault.com for insider company profiles, expert advice, career message boards, expert resume reviews, the Vault Job Board and more.

VAULT CAREER LIBRARY 7

semester or of a duration of your choosing. Similarly, the majority of internships are full-time, though some are part-time.

Why do an internship?

You might be tempted just to take a job to earn money. There's nothing wrong with that – but there's so much more right with doing an internship. For example, if you want to break into a field that's tough to crack, like entertainment or advertising or politics, the very best way to get a job in the field is to have interned in it. Not only will you have great experience on your resume, you'll meet plenty of contacts and potential mentors. Similarly, interning at a top company puts you on the fast track to getting a full-time offer from that firm – or one of its competitors! Most large companies are much more likely to hire a former intern than someone "right off the street." Even if you don't end up working for your employer, you'll have some invaluable and difficult-to-obtain experience on your resume.

But I need to get paid!

Don't think that doing an internship means giving up on pay altogether. It's true that many internships are unpaid or only offer college credit – at the same time, these are often small, interesting organizations or companies in glamorous industries. But many others offer some kind of payment, from a stipend or travel allowance to a very generous salary. Others offer interesting perks, including travel and the chance to attend exclusive industry events.

Tips for applying to internships

Let's say you've found an internship that interests you. That's great. The first thing you should do is to follow all the instructions. Here's a short checklist of things you need to do when applying for internships.

Apply by the deadline. A few months before the deadline is even better – a small organization might just take the first qualified intern who applies.

Follow the instructions! If you're asked to provide a writing sample, don't send your photo portfolio. If you're asked to provide a reference, start canvassing your teachers and professors.

Make sure your resume is up to date and thoroughly spellchecked. If you've never written a resume, go to your school career guidance center and ask for help. And ask an experienced professional or two you trust to review your resume. If you are applying for internships in different fields, you may need to have more than one version of your resume highlighting different experience. Ensure that your most current contact information is on the resume.

Don't ignore the cover letter. Make a persuasive case in your cover letter, which should be tailored to each internship, that you really want to intern at the company. Do your research and be specific – and honest – about why the opportunity is right for you. Again, make sure you carefully proofread the cover letter. Let a trusted friend or teacher read it as well.

Follow up. If you're really interested in an internship, there's nothing wrong with a quick call or e-mail a few weeks after the application to let the organization know how interested you are. But don't pepper them with phone calls every day.

Carpe diem. If you're really interested in an internship, but your qualifications aren't quite right, apply anyway and stress your real interest. Many organizations would rather have a truly excited and motivated intern than one that just meets the qualifications on paper.

Take experience over money. You can always earn money. The window of opportunity for internship isn't eternally open. If you're really broke, consider taking a part-time job in order to work at the internship you really want.

Intern anytime

Most companies with internships have formal programs during the summer, when they hire a number of college or high school students. However, many companies also hire during the school year, so if you're starting your senior year, it's not too late to get that all-important professional work experience.

And, even if you've graduated from college, you can still intern to gain experience if you haven't landed a full-time job. We can't stress this enough: if you can manage it financially, interning in a profession in which you have long-term interest is almost always more preferable than taking a paying job that has nothing to do with your interests. If you're a college graduate, this may mean moving home or working a night job for fewer hours and less pay. Years down the road, we're sure you'll agree that it was worth it.

For information on internship programs, refer to the *Vault Guide to Top Internships*, which has information on more than 750 top programs, and check out the Internship Board at www.vault.com for up-to-date listings.

Make Sure You Don't Blow Your Internship

Remember that scene in *Grease* when the Rydell High kids are singing about the summer? Danny "had me a blast," while for Sandy it "happened so fast." It seems a strange comparison, but many summer interns at America's leading companies describe their summers the same way. Not all experiences are quite so rosy, but in any case, young employees get both a feel for their corporate culture and a taste of the work force during the course of these often finely crafted programs. Whether their time is spent doing substantive work that affects the company, or just making Starbucks runs all summer, there is a goal in mind. Summer interns need to spend those precious weeks making a favorable impression in order to get that all-important full-time offer.

Granted, the reason that many summer programs are so carefully organized and lavish is so that interns will want to come back. In many programs, "you have to seriously mess up not to get [an offer]." Much more commonly though, interns are not afforded such leeway, and need to be aware of what it takes to secure a full-time position. First and foremost, while the fate of the company may not hinge on the work interns produce, optimum effort must still be made on assignments. Simply put, no matter if it seems

Visit Vault at **www.vault.com** for insider company profiles, expert advice, career message boards, expert resume reviews, the Vault Job Board and more.

 CAREER LIBRARY

9

insignificant, "whatever work you do, make sure to do a good job," advises one recruiter. Satisfying this requirement may mean punching the clock after the summer sun has disappeared for the night. Most businesses do not take kindly to employees who leave a vapor trail out the door when the five o'clock whistle blows.

Also extremely important are the connections, however informal, made with established employees. This is especially true with mid-level and senior employees who have a say in who gets hired. Those who assume that a stellar academic record and a shiny pair of Ferragamo wing tips are a substitute for engaging conversation may be in for a rude awakening come Labor Day. Successful networking can be accomplished by working for a variety of people or through socialization inside the office. Attendance at company social events, when offered, is an "important way to build personal relationships within the company" as well. Whether cruising the halls or knocking a few back at the local pub, a gregarious persona cannot be discounted – "office wallflowers just will not cut the mustard," says one corporate insider. On the other hand, there are limits; for instance, insiders at Goldman Sachs tell a cautionary tale wherein one investment banking associate who failed to get an offer was snubbed "as a result of excessive brown nosing."

At the same time, summer interns need to be careful about exposing, or more to the point imposing, their personality on their fellow employees. At some companies, for example, "you're not allowed to be rude to anyone – secretaries, the lady in the cafeteria, or whoever it is." Even fast-paced offices with a reputation for "screamers" may be averse to bringing in new people who will perpetuate a harsh culture. "Some summer interns behave completely inappropriately," says a source at a Wall Street firm. "One recent summer associate had a big mouth and she screamed a lot. She made enemies in only eight weeks, including some managing directors."

Of course, even when interns generally play their cards right, one wrong move may stand between them and a job offer. For instance, an insider tells Vault that one would-be full-timer was not asked back to his company after "arguing with a partner at a softball game about what position to play." Another inexplicably turned over an entire assignment to an unqualified subordinate. Perhaps the most extreme example involved an overly enthusiastic intern at one firm who, while on a company retreat, stripped off his clothes and hopped into the hot tub. That's a little too much information!

How to Take Advantage of Your Internship

The internship craze is reaching new heights. Nearly three-quarters of all college students do internships today as compared to 1 in 36 in 1980. These numbers have made many employers a bit uneasy. After all, these employers are, for the most part, getting all this labor for free, or at most a small stipend. Isn't there something a little bit wrong with that? Many employers think so. That won't stop them from taking the sweet deal, but they won't feel good about. That's where you--the intern--come into the picture. The intern has an extremely receptive and grateful audience at his internship, an audience that aims to please. Consequently, if the intern plays his cards well, he or she can do extraordinary things during his two-or-three month stint.

1. Be there first

At most internships, especially those that take place in the summer, the company or organization will have several interns for a particular time period. If possible, arrive a week or so before the other interns. First, you will get more individual attention in the beginning and consequently can establish yourself as the "favorite" intern.

Second, you may be able to get the first pick of the assignments. Third, you may get the first pick of the desks, or wherever they will seat you. Employing this rule to its extremes, interns have been known to use this seemingly simple technique to get the later-arriving interns to become their "pseudo-interns"-- farming out menial tasks to them so they can concentrate on more substantive work.

2. Look around

Once you get inside a company, you should not feel restrained by the department that you're working in- -or even to your assigned supervisor. Figure out what you most want to do in the organization and schmooze the person who does it. A good way to do this is to ask them to lunch. A good line is: "I'm try-ing to absorb as much information as I can in this internship, and what you do seems particular interest-ing. I wonder if you are available for lunch anytime this week." They will almost always say "Yes." When they describe what they do at lunch, try to relate the skills that they employ to skills that you have. For example, if they tell you about the press release they are writing for company X, slip in how that's similar to your college newspaper writing experience. Hopefully, they will then offer you a chance to draft a press release.

If not, try to give them another nudge, but make it gently. "Oh, writing press releases seems like so much fun!" you can add, or something to that effect.

3. Never complain

When you are given menial errands to do, take it in good cheer. No one likes a whiner. If you feel like you must say something, couch it in humor. One State Department intern remembers telling his boss: "Although being a Deputy Assistant Secretary of Photocopying has its moments, I was wondering if I could do more substantive work here." It got his message across – and worked. Remember: As long as you do a few things that look impressive, you won't have to put on your resume that for 99 percent of the time you ran errands and photocopied stuff. So instead of complaining about your menial tasks – or even non-verbally complaining by acting dour--express an interest in doing substantive work, and be specific as possible. Specificity shows interest.

Visit Vault at **www.vault.com** for insider company profiles, expert advice, career message boards, expert resume reviews, the Vault Job Board and more.

V/\ULT CAREER LIBRARY   11

Looking for a job or internship? Take advantage of all of the resources on Vault.com

● **Vault Internship Board and Vault Job Board:** Search thousands of top listings

● **Vault Resume and Cover Letter Reviews:** Rated the "Top Choice" by The Wall Street Journal for resume makeovers.

● **Vault Employer Research:** Read employee surveys, company news and more.

● **Vault Career Advice:** Read more Days in the Life, sample resumes and cover letters, expert career columns and more.

● **Vault Guides:** *Vault Guide to Resumes, Cover Letters and Interviews, Vault Guide to Schmoozing, Vault Guide to Top Internships*

Go to www.vault.com
or ask your bookstore or librarian for other Vault titles.

Resumes

What can you do?

Rule number one: employers don't really, truly care what you did at your last job. They care about what you can do for them. They wonder about your potential for future success working for them. Your resume must answer these questions.

As Shannon Heidkamp, recruiting manager for a division of Allstate Insurance says, "People need to ask themselves 'What value can I offer this prospective employer?'" These before-and-after samples tell potential employers what skills each employee used, what tasks they accomplished, and what honors they garnered – skills, tasks, and honors that can be applied to future jobs. Specific job openings, whether advertised through newspaper ads, Internet sites or inter-office memos, come with specific job descriptions. If you find out about the job through a friend, ask for a copy of the job description. Your job is to meet those requirements by listing your qualifications that most closely meet these prerequisites.

Ten seconds

Studies show that regardless of how long you labor over your resume, most employers will spend 10 seconds looking at it. That's it.

Because of the masses of job searchers, most managers and human resource employees receive an enormous number of resumes. Faced with a pile of paper to wade through every morning, employers look for any deficiency possible to reduce the applicant pool to a manageable number. Thus, your resume must present your information quickly, clearly, and in a way that makes your experience relevant to the position in question. That means condensing your information down to its most powerful form.

So distill, distill, distill. Long, dense paragraphs make information hard to find and require too much effort from the overworked reader. If that reader can't figure out how your experience applies to the available position, your resume is not doing its job.

Solve this problem by creating bulleted, indented, focused statements. Short, powerful lines show the reader, in a glance, exactly why they should keep reading.

Think about how to write up your experience in targeted, clear, bulleted, detail-rich prose.

Visit Vault at **www.vault.com** for insider company profiles, expert advice, career message boards, expert resume reviews, the Vault Job Board and more.

VAULT CAREER LIBRARY 13

Sample Resumes

SANDRA'S READY FOR A POSITION AS A PRIVATE SCHOOL TEACHER

Sandra Pearson
Sandypear@ivillage.com
11 Hillhouse Aavenue
New Haven, Connecticut
06511
(203) 555-8103

Education:

Yale University, New Haven, CT
Bachelor of Arts, May 2005; Double Major
Psychology and History
2001 National Merit Scholar Award
2000 Micehouse National Laboratory Internship

Skills:

Microsoft Word, Excel
Editing and proofreading
Proficient Spanish
Graphic design

Work Experience:

Project Hand in Hand 2005
Consultant to teach adults an accredited course on creating curriculum based on the Multiple Intelligence theory

Toddling On Up 2002-2004
Teacher, day care provider; creator of art curriculum and designer of weekly programs

Yale Greenpeace Office 2004
Distributed information on recycling, made presentations; visited, advised and reorganized locations in the Yale and New Haven Communities

Learning Disabilities Center at Yale 2002
Performed various clerical duties; read onto tapes and copied materials for special needs members of the Yale community

XYZ Vacuums
Sales representative for high-quality vacuum cleaners

Activities:

Kappa Betta Sorority 2003-2005; Social Chair 2004-2005
Community Relations Council 2003-2004
Black Alliance at Yale; Publicity Manager, 2003-2004
Yale Gospel Choir 2002-2005
Black Caucus at Yale; co-founder 2002-2005
Roots Theatre Ensemble; costume designer 2002-2003, actress 2002-2004
Yale Antigravity Society 2004

FARLEY CRAFTILY DISGUISES HIS GAPS IN WORK EXPERIENCE

Farley Suber

345 Fenwick Street   Elton Park, CO 79403   (750) 555-4212

Objective: Seeking an entry-level position in sales or marketing

Education:
Bachelor of Arts in Communication (Public Relations) May 2004
Minor: Business/Liberal Arts
University of Chicago, Chicago, IL
Cumulative GPA: 3.1 out of 4.0

Experience:

LONS Computing Systems
Sales and Marketing Representative
- Applied marketing skills to increase sales of Macintosh computers
- Cultivated client relationships, increasing customer satisfaction and repeat sales
- Placed advertising in magazines including *Men's Health*, *GQ*, and *Wired*
- Wrote press releases on new computer products

Broadway Master Theatre
Marketing Assistant
- Assisted with the planning, creation and distribution of theatrical press releases
- Wrote radio advertisements
- Tracked attendance based on information from reservationists and box office attendants
- Handled photo releases mailings to be distributed to the media sources

Honors and Interests:

- **Senior Honors:** Senior cumulative average of 4.0 out of 4.0
- **Terrence S. Duboff Award:** Award for academic achievement excellence in communications
- **NCAA Division 1 Golfer:** Winner of the Greenview Collegiate Classic 2004, 2nd Place finalist 2004 NCAA MidWest Cup
- **Chi Phi Sigma Fraternity:** Rush Chairman, Scholarship Chairman, Standards Board, Senior Steering Committee

Visit Vault at **www.vault.com** for insider company profiles, expert advice, career message boards, expert resume reviews, the Vault Job Board and more.

VAULT CAREER LIBRARY   **15**

It's what you did, not what your name tag said

Resumes should scream ability, not claim responsibility. Employers should be visualizing you in the new position, not remembering you as "that account assistant from Chase." While some former employers can bolster your resume by their mere presence, you don't want to be thought of as a cog from another machine. Instead, your resume should present you as an essential component of a company's success.

Think broadly

Applicants applying for specific job openings must customize the resume for each position. Many job-hunters, particularly those beginning their careers, apply to many different jobs.

A person interested in a career in publishing, for example, might apply for jobs as a writer, proofreader, editor, copywriter, grant proposal writer, fact-checker, or research assistant. The applicant may or may not have the experience necessary to apply for any of these jobs. But you may have more skills than you think.

When considering the skills that make you a valuable prospect, think broadly. Anybody's who's worked a single day can point to several different skills, because even the most isolated, repetitive jobs offer a range of experience. Highway toll collection, for instance, is a repetitive job with limited variation, but even that career requires multiple job skills. Helping lost highway drivers read a map means "Offering customer service in a prompt, detail-oriented environment." Making change for riders translates as "Cashiering in a high-pressure, fast-paced setting." But unless these toll-booth workers emphasize these skills to prospective employers, it'll be the highway life for them.

Selected history

A lot of things happen in everyone's day, but when someone asks "How was your day?" you don't start with your first cough and your lost slippers. You edit. Resumes require that same type of disciplined, succinct editing. The better you are at controlling the information you create, the stronger the resume will be.

When editing your history to fit the resume format, ask yourself, "How does this particular information contribute towards my overall attractiveness to this employer?" If something doesn't help, drop it. Make more space to elaborate on the experiences most relevant to the job you are applying.

Similarly, if information lurks in your past that would harm your chances of getting the job, omit it. In resume writing, omitting is not lying. If some jobs make you overqualified for a position, eliminate those positions from your resume. If you're overeducated, don't mention the degree that makes you so. If you're significantly undereducated, there's no need to mention education at all. If the 10 jobs you've had in the last five years make you look like a real life Walter Mitty, reduce your resume's references to the most relevant positions while making sure there are no gaps in the years of your employment.

Cover Letters

The Cover Letter Template

Your Name
Your Street Address, Apartment #
Your City, State Zip
Your Email Address
Your (h) PHONE NUMBER
Your (f) FAX NUMBER

Contact's Name
Contact's Title
Contact's Department
Contact's Name
Contact's Street Address, Suite #
Company City, State Zip
Company PHONE NUMBER
Company FAX NUMBER

Date

Dear Ms./Mr. CONTACT,

The first paragraph tells why you're contacting the person, then either mentions your connection with that person or tells where you read about the job. It also quickly states who you are. Next it wows them with your sincere, researched knowledge of their company. The goal: demonstrating that you are a worthy applicant, and enticing them to read further.

The second and optional third paragraph tell more about yourself, particularly why you're an ideal match for the job by summarizing why you're what they're looking for. You may also clarify anything unclear on your resume.

The last paragraph is your goodbye: you thank the reader for his or her time. Include that you look forward to their reply or give them a time when you'll be getting in contact by phone.

Sincerely,

Sign Here

Visit Vault at **www.vault.com** for insider company profiles, expert advice, career message boards, expert resume reviews, the Vault Job Board and more.

VAULT CAREER LIBRARY   17

Date

Placement of the date, whether left justified, centered or aligned to the right, is up to your discretion, but take the time to write out the entry. If you choose to list the day, list it first, followed by the month, date, and year, as follows: Tuesday, July 9, 2004. (Europeans commonly list the day before month, so writing a date only in numbers can be confusing. Does a letter written on 4/7/04 date from April 7, or July 4?)

Name and address

Your name and address on the cover letter should be the same as the one on your resume. Uniformity in this case applies not only to the address given, but the way the information is written. If you listed your street as Ave. instead of Avenue on your resume, do so on your cover letter too.

Your header can be displayed centrally, just like the resume header — including your name in a larger and/or bolded font. But in most cases, the heading is either left justified or left justified and indented to the far right hand side of the page.

If you choose to list your phone number, make sure that you don't list it somewhere else on the page.

Next comes the address of the person you are writing. In many circumstances, you'll have the complete information on the person you're trying to contact, in which case you should list it in this order:

• Name of contact
• Title of contact
• Company name
• Company address
• Phone number
• Fax number

However, in many cases, you have less than complete information to go on. This is particularly true when responding to an advertisement. If you have an address or phone or fax number but no company name, try a reverse directory, such as Superpages (www.superpages.com), which lets you trace a business by either its address or phone number.

When you're trying to get a name of a contact person, calling the company and asking the receptionist for the name of the recipient (normally, though not always, head of HR) may work. But usually, companies don't list this information because they don't want you calling at all. So if you call, be polite, be persistent, ask for a contact name, say thank you and hang up. Don't identify yourself. If you have questions, wait until the interview.

If you don't get all of the info, don't worry. There are several salutations to use to finesse the fact that you've got no idea who you're addressing. Some solutions are:

To whom it may concern: A bit frosty, but effective.

Dear Sir or Madam: Formal and fusty, but it works.

Sirs: Since the workforce is full of women, avoid this outdated greeting.

Omitting the salutation altogether: Effective, but may look too informal.

Good morning: A sensible approach that is gaining popularity.

Format

Unlike the resume, the cover letter offers the writer significant room for flexibility. Successful cover letters have come in various different forms, and sometimes cover letters that break rules achieve success by attracting attention. But most don't. Here are some basic guidelines on what information the body of a cover letter should deliver.

First paragraph

To be successful, this first paragraph should contain:

• A first line that tells the reader why you're contacting them, and how you came to know about the position. This statement should be quick, simple and catchy. Ultimately, what you're trying to create is a descriptive line by which people can categorize you. This means no transcendental speeches about "the real you" or long-winded treatises on your career and philosophy of life.

• Text indicating your respect for the firm's accomplishments, history, status, products, or leaders.

• A last line that gives a very brief synopsis of who you are and why you want the position. The best way to do this, if you don't already have a more personal connection with the person you're contacting, is to lay it out like this:

I am a (your identifying characteristic)

+

I am a (your profession)

+

I have (your years of experience or education)

+

I have worked in (your area of expertise)

+

I am interested in (what position you're looking for)

And thus a killer first paragraph is born.

Visit Vault at **www.vault.com** for insider company profiles, expert advice, career message boards, expert resume reviews, the Vault Job Board and more.

VAULT CAREER LIBRARY   **19**

Middle paragraph(s)

The middle paragraph allows you to move beyond your initial declarative sentences, and into more expansive and revealing statements about who you are and what skills you bring to the job. This is another opportunity to explicitly summarize key facts of your job history. The middle paragraph also offers you the opportunity to mention any connection or prior experience that you may have with the company.

Tell the employer in this paragraph how, based on concrete references to your previous performances, you will perform in your desired position. This does not mean making general, unqualified statements about your greatness such as "I'm going to be the best you've ever had" or my "My energetic multi-tasking will be the ultimate asset to your company."

Comments should be backed up by specific references. Try something along the lines of "My post-graduate degree in marketing, combined with my four years of retail bicycle sales would make me a strong addition to Gwinn Cycles' marketing team."

Or: "Meeting the demands of a full-time undergraduate education, a position as student government accountant, and a 20-hour-a-week internship with Davidson Management provided me with the multi-tasking experience needed to excel as a financial analyst at Whittier Finance."

Many advertisements ask you to name your salary requirements. Some avoid the problem altogether by ignoring this requirement, and this may be the safest route — any number you give might price you out of a job (before you have the chance to negotiate face-to-face at an interview). Alternatively, you might be pegged at a lower salary than you might otherwise have been offered. If you must give a salary requirement, be as general as possible The safest bet is to offer as general a range as possible ("in the $30,000s"). Put the salary requirement at the end of the paragraph, not in your first sentence.

Some cover letter writers use another paragraph to describe their accomplishments. This makes sense if, for example, your experience lies in two distinct areas, or you need to explain something that is not evident on your resume, such as "I decided to leave law school to pursue an exciting venture capital opportunity" or "I plan to relocate to Wisconsin shortly." Do not get overly personal — "I dropped out of business school to care for my sick mother" is touching, but will not necessarily impress employers.

Final paragraph

The final paragraph is your fond farewell, your summation, a testament to your elegance and social grace. This should be the shortest paragraph of the letter. Here, tell your readers you're pleased they got so far down the page. Tell them you look forward to hearing from them. Tell them how you can be reached. Here's some sample sentences for your conclusion.

Thank you sentences:
Thank you for your time.
Thank you for reviewing my qualifications.
Thank you for your consideration.
Thank you for your review of my qualifications.

Way too much:
It would be more than an honor to meet with you.

A note of confidence in a callback:
I look forward to your reply.
I look forward to hearing from you.
I look forward to your response.
I look forward to your call.

Over the top:
Call me tomorrow, please.

Visit Vault at **www.vault.com** for insider company profiles, expert advice, career message boards, expert resume reviews, the Vault Job Board and more.

VAULT CAREER LIBRARY   **21**

Interviews

Getting Ready

Would a seasoned attorney stride into a courtroom on the day of an important case without having considered every angle of the case? Would a professional climber arrive in Kathmandu without provisions and maps of Mount Everest? Nope. If you want to sway the jury or reach the summit, you've got to go into the big event prepared. The same is true of going into an interview. Preparation is an essential part of the interview process and one that is easy to overlook or shortchange.

According to polls, most job candidates spend less than an hour preparing for their interviews. No one is going to make you prepare for an interview, least of all the people who will be asking the questions, so it's up to you to get ready on your own.

Unprepared interview subjects often give poor interviews, says Clift Jones, an account director at Bozell Worldwide Advertising. "One of the biggest mistakes people make is to come in with no agenda. They don't know why they want the job, anything about the unique strengths of the company, or why they'd be a good match. They're eager and little else. It's much more impressive if they've put a lot of thought into what they want from a situation and what they have to offer before they come in."

By preparing for the interview you'll be doing yourself a favor. Remember: more time spent in preparation means less anxiety on the day of the interview. It's a relief to have something relevant to say, a cogent question on your tongue, a collection of stories underscoring specific elements of your prodigious competence, when the interviewer's anticipatory eyes fall on you and it's your turn to speak.

In addition to alleviating pre-interview stress, being prepared has several other benefits:

- It shows the interviewer that you care enough about the position, the company, and the industry to research its current status and future.
- It suggests that once you're hired, your preparation for meetings and assignments will be equally as sound.
- It shows respect for the interviewer and the company he or she works for.
- It provides more opportunities for you and the interviewer to have a meaningful conversation in which you can find common ground.

Research

Research is a vital preparation tool. Over time, companies, like countries, develop distinct cultures and inner languages. In some cases the language of a corporation or industry can become so specialized that an outsider will have trouble understanding it. The job candidate who learns an organization's lingo well enough to speak it during the interview just might, like a long-lost relative, be embraced with a cry of, "He's one of us!" and welcomed into the fold.

Where can someone find this kind of insider knowledge? Vault produces a series of profiles and surveys on organizations that can help the information-hungry interviewee. Other user-friendly, if more compa-

Visit Vault at **www.vault.com** for insider company profiles, expert advice, career message boards, expert resume reviews, the Vault Job Board and more.

VAULT CAREER LIBRARY

23

ny-friendly, sources of information include the packets prepared for a company's stockholders. Any stockbroker will send you these, provided you assure them of your interest in someday purchasing stocks through them. A company's human resources, treasury, or public relations office will be happy to send you an annual report (which will include a company's financial, marketing, and product report), a prospectus (which includes a list of the CEO and major players), or a 10K report (which contains a company's historical and financial information).

Trade magazines, (or "the trades") industry insider magazines, can apprise you of current events, hirings and firings, trends, and other relevant issues. Libraries, career centers, and web sites can also be valuable information-gathering places. Spending a day at the library is an especially good way to get the job search going if you're just starting out.

Perhaps the most direct way of getting the real skinny on a company is to talk to someone who works there. Speaking to someone in a position similar to the one in which you're interested, can give you vital insights into the company's modus operandi and expose some of the rats in its cellar — or executive suites. If you don't know anyone who's had experience at the company, you might ask around to see if you have any less obvious connections to the industry or a parallel field.

As in other areas of the job search, it's a good idea to treat your preparation for the interview as a job. You might, for example, want to keep a notebook for observations on the companies with which you've interviewed. Or, you might collect the information you gather in an interview folder. Not only will this give you some practice — a warm-up in the organizational skills important in any job — but it will also help you focus and take the preparation process a little more seriously. Some especially important things to remember are the names, numbers and extensions of any contacts with whom you've spoken, the dates and times when those contacts occurred, lists of reasons why you're interested in a particular organization, and potential obstacles or drawbacks associated with a company.

Review your resume

Before the interview, your resume is probably going to be the only thing the interviewer knows about you. In most cases, whoever is going to interview you will have that resume close at hand and might even have memorized key elements of it, so it's important you to be totally familiar with what you've written. Take some time to review what you've done and to observe how it's represented. If you haven't updated your resume in a while, you might discover serious omissions. Maybe you've left off an important experience, or maybe you've forgotten about an experience that could take center stage during the interview. If you can't remember something on your resume, your interviewer may think you are lying.

Check the dates of past jobs for any gaps you might be asked to explain. If you were out searching for the last living grizzly bear in Arizona for those few months when you weren't working, spend some time thinking about how you can turn this to your advantage in the interview. Those tracking skills might prove your passion, bravery and tenacity, for example. Just as importantly, this offbeat experience might help you establish a connection with your interviewer and give him or her an insight into your character.

Consider doing some role playing as you review your resume. Try stepping outside yourself and look at your resume hypercritically, as an employer looking to hire you would. Based on your resume, try imagining questions you'd ask yourself and reasons for not hiring yourself. Once you've imagined the on-paper preconceptions this person likely has of you before you meet him, you can come up with an effective plan for exceeding these expectations face to face.

Because computers play such a vital role in the workplace, it's a good idea to review before the interview exactly which programs you know. If you have experience with any of the programs the company uses, you can make an immediate positive impact on the organization. If you're particularly ambitious, you can give yourself this computer advantage by finding out which programs the company uses and familiarizing yourself with them before the interview.

Emotional preparation

Even if you've made yourself into a walking tome of facts and figures, computer programs and trade lingo, you might not make a good impression unless you're emotionally prepared for the interview. In a mad rush to do whatever you have to do to land a job, you may not take the time to ask yourself how you really feel about this job.

The interview is as much a forum for you to find out if the company and the job fit your needs as it is for the company to discover whether or not you're right for them. You may have to give up some aspects of your dream job, but the goal is to sacrifice as little as possible. What do you want from a job? What are you good at doing? What do people compliment you on?

In the ideal situation, the interviewer and the interviewee are equally interested in finding a perfect fit. Look out for yourself. Ask hard questions about work conditions, drawbacks, and low points. If asked tactfully and backed up with research, well-directed questions of this sort won't offend a responsible interviewer. After all, a happy employee is going to be more productive than someone who hates his job.

But if you choose unwisely the first time, don't worry — jobs are no longer forever. People change careers nowadays about as often as their hairstyles. Chances are, even the person who interviews you, if he or she hasn't been living in a cave with blind fish, will understand that you probably won't be with the company for life. Gone are the days of the 1950s "company man" who signed up after college and stayed on until he retired. Nevertheless, choosing a job and career right the first time saves a lot of time and angst.

At the Interview

The meeting and small talk

If you're old enough to be vying for a job that requires a serious interview, you've probably met a lot of people in your life. Extend those social skills to the people in the office. Maintain solid eye contact and a firm handshake. This proven greeting combination implies strength, confidence, competence, and honesty. Consider the alternative: shifty eyes and a limp handshake.

After the initial meeting and a stroll back to the interview room, the next phase of the interview begins — small talk. The interview hasn't officially begun, but make no mistake: your ability to talk about the

Visit Vault at **www.vault.com** for insider company profiles, expert advice, career message boards, expert resume reviews, the Vault Job Board and more.

VAULT CAREER LIBRARY

25

weather is being measured up. The topic of conversation might in fact be the weather, a brief discussion of the latest media frenzy, the game last night, a round or two of the name and geography game. Small talk is meant to relax you, so allow yourself to be relaxed. Remember though, that you're still in an interview and anything you say can be used against you in the decision process. Answer small talk questions briefly, honestly, diplomatically and tactfully. Be witty, but not obscene or clownish.

The main event

At some point, the interviewer will shift to the heart of the matter and begin to ask questions pertaining to the job and your fitness for it. Often these questions will follow a description of the available job and an explanation of the company and what it does.

Often the segue from the small talk session into the more serious portion of the interview will be marked by a description of what the company does. Your interviewer might ask you what you know about the company, and after you give your answer (astute and detailed, due to your extensive research) the interviewer will talk about the company, the job, the industry, their plans for the future. This is a good time to demonstrate your listening skills. Let them see that you're listening and interested and pay attention to what they're saying. Take notes on the notepad you remembered to bring.

Focus

Before anything else is said it might be helpful, here, to dispense an all-purpose interviewing bromide: remember to focus. Once the middle, substance portion of the interview begins, the interviewer is primarily interested in your past job performances and possibly your life performances in as much as they relate to the open job. He or she wants to know how your experience and personality will translate into the available job. For example, when the interviewer says, "Tell me about yourself," they're interested in your work experiences, not the fact that you were born in deepest February when the moon was on the wane, and frost obscured the windowpane. Your interviewer will be thinking of little else except whether or not you will be able to do the job. (This does not mean that you should purge yourself of all personality — it's fine to mention that you like ice fishing — but you should keep your eye on conveying your fitness for the job.)

During the interview you should act like a boxer in the ring. You want to land as many substantive punches as possible. You want every one of your answers to count. If you use up a lot of your time and energy on false punches — statements that fail to focus on the job and why you're a good person to fill it — the interviewer is going to decide you're wasting time. If you feel yourself getting off topic and talking about something that's not really relevant, it's all right to mention this. Your interviewer will appreciate the fact that you reined yourself in — this demonstrates control, maturity, an understanding of the bottom line, and well-developed communication skills.

Honesty

Any lies you tell about your background and accomplishments will come back to haunt you. Similarly, unless you're an experienced actor, any affectations in attitude or manner will be detected by an experienced interviewer. Interview situations are stressful enough; you don't need to add method acting to the mix. Be honest without dwelling on your weaknesses. Be the best version of yourself. Practiced interviewers will appreciate your candor. They'll know they're dealing with an honest person.

Who's doing what for whom? It is better to give than to receive

Often, an applicant will blithely run through a litany of reasons why the position fits his career paths without mentioning what skills, insights, or vision he can bring to the position. It's a good idea to steer clear of this trap. Often when thinking of a position, especially one that is perfect for our career aspirations, we do tend to think about it in terms of what it has to offer us. Your love for the position, however, should not be the focus of the interview. The spotlight, from beginning to end, should shine on the myriad reasons why you'll be indispensable to the company once you're in the position.

Finding common ground and bonding

Employers, being human, will often hire someone they like — someone who reminds them of themselves at the same age, or someone to whom they are connected in whatever way — instead of the person who will perform best in the job. It's far more difficult to turn a friend down for a job than it is to nix someone about whom you have no particular feeling. So try subtly and deftly (it's easy to go overboard and become an Eddy Haskell) to form a connection with the employer.

If you can discover what kind of person you're dealing with, what his or her passion is, it will be easier for you to become a bit of a chameleon for bonding purposes. Any connection you can discover with the person can help. Find a topic such as a shared alma mater or an outside interest upon which you can build a connection. Do what you can to size the person up. If they mention a hobby or a recent vacation, express real interest. If you can get them to like you as a person, in addition to making them feel you're the best candidate for the job, you'll have done yourself a tremendous favor.

Making an end run

Trying to use humor or other methods of endearment in an interview is risky, but so are most business ventures. Similarly, being completely straightforward in the interview holds risks, but telling the emperor he has no clothes might impress some interviewers.

We all know at least one person who has a knack for making immediate connections, one of those people who never meets a stranger. But the ability to establish an instant rapport with someone can be learned. Think about those people in your life who have a knack for meeting people. What are their secrets? How do they do it? Are they able to project a genuine enthusiasm, a guilelessness that disarms people? While it can be dangerous to try to take on someone else's personality for an interview, try to discover ways you can better connect with someone. The following is a list of things you might want to keep in mind by way of forging a bond with your interviewer.

• Listening. Remember your grade-school teachers. "Don't just listen. Show me you're listening." Let the interviewer see your interest and enthusiasm. Concentrate on what they're saying.

Visit Vault at **www.vault.com** for insider company profiles, expert advice, career message boards, expert resume reviews, the Vault Job Board and more.

V∆ULT CAREER LIBRARY   **27**

• Read 'em and weep. Or make 'em laugh. Try to discover what motivates your interviewers. What kind of person do they look like? How are their offices decorated? Do some research on your interviewer. Find out who they are and what they do outside of work. What are their hobbies and passions? It's amazing how much even the most reserved person will open up if you find the right subject.

• If they're trying to be funny, don't be too nervous to laugh.

Asking for the job

If you know you want the job, don't be afraid to let the interviewer know this, point blank. If an interviewer senses wishy-washiness, they'll offer the job to someone else. They want to hire someone who wants the job, not someone who will grudgingly accept it. Express interest in the position and the company.

Questions to Expect: The Quality Search

Interviewers, inevitably, seek the ideal candidate. To become this perfect hire, put yourself in the mind of the interviewer. Take a good look at yourself. What does this person look like? How does this person dress, and carry him or herself? Which qualities does this interviewee demonstrate in his or her answers?

Increasingly, interviewers will ask behavioral questions — questions that seek to understand you through the prism of your past behavior and accomplishments.

One cool customer

If you're the person who can step into the bloody heart of the fray with ice water in your veins when the office resembles Custer's camp on the Little Bighorn, then you'll be a valuable asset to the company. If, on the other hand, you get frazzled when someone asks for the company's address, you might be a dangerous liability when the bullets start to fly and scalps are being taken. So your interviewer is going to be watching you to see how you handle the stress of the interview and your ability to remain composed. The following are some questions you should know how to answer by the time you're sitting in the hot seat:

• You're in customer relations and an unsatisfied customer is complaining bitterly about the product or service. How do you handle the situation?
• You've been given multiple tasks. There is no way you can complete all of them on time. What do you do?
• Describe some situations that really bother you.
• You're right. You know you're right. And, yet, everyone is taking issue with what you say. How do you react?
• How well do you handle pressure in the workplace?

How bad do you want it and what will you do to get it?

During the interview, one quality for which your interviewer will undoubtedly be searching — in your answers, handshake, appearance, and voice — is enthusiasm about the industry, the company and the particular job opening. They're counting on you to bring in a jolt of fresh-faced exuberance. You can express your energy and aggressiveness in the interview, but true excitement is difficult to fake. Here are some questions designed to measure the true level of your enthusiasm.

- What do you feel are your best and worst qualities, and how will these relate to the position?
- What interests you about this position, industry, organization?
- What are your long-term career goals?
- What motivates you?
- How important is winning to you?
- What is the most difficult thing you've ever had to do. Why?
- Has anyone ever really pushed you? How did you respond?

Where you've been and what you've done

What you've done in the past serves as the clearest indication of what you'll be able to do in the future. If you can portray yourself in your interview as someone with a string of past successes by telling honest anecdotes in which you emerge as the hero, you're on your way to winning the job at hand.

Remember, however, that an experienced interviewer will be on to you like your first grade teacher if you try to snow him or her. Here are some questions you should know how to answer in the category of past performance:

- Describe your duties at [this particular position].
- Of which of your past accomplishments are you most proud?
- What, based on your experience, have you found to be your optimal work conditions?
- What are the most valuable lessons you've learned from past work experiences?
- Which of the skills you've picked up at the positions listed on your resume do you feel will best translate into this position and why?
- What are your long-term goals in this industry and at this company?
- Describe a problem you encountered at one of your jobs and how you handled it.

Writing and rapping

These two arts form the bedrock of civilization and important skills for any job. Any experienced interviewer will be searching for soundness, if not outright eloquence, in written and oral communication. Your oral communication abilities will be on display, from the moment you meet the interviewer to the time you bid them adieu.

Your writing skills will be evaluated in the resume and cover letter, and sometimes, in a formal writing sample. Those mistakes on your resume — the misspelling of your own name, the missing dot in your e-mail address — will imply a dangerous lack of attention to detail and may be viewed by a potential

Visit Vault at **www.vault.com** for insider company profiles, expert advice, career message boards, expert resume reviews, the Vault Job Board and more.

VAULT CAREER LIBRARY   29

employer as the tip of the iceberg. If this person can't manage these small details, he or she may think, then how will they be able to handle the larger requirements of this job?

It's a good idea to remember that communication extends beyond just words. Facial expressions, gestures, style and cleanliness of dress, tone of voice, posture, scent, and hairstyle send a message of one kind or another to your interviewer from the moment you stride confidently through the office door. So think about these questions.

- Compare and contrast your oral and written communication skills.
- What experience have you had with public speaking? In your view, what are the key attributes of a successful public speaker?
- Let's say someone refuses or is hesitant to embrace your ideas. How do you persuade that person you're right?
- What problems have you had with past employers and co-workers and how did you deal with these situations?
- Describe the optimal work relationship between a manager and his or her employees.
- What do you find most troubling about writing a research paper or giving a speech?

Sense of responsibility

Your interviewer is also going to be looking for a sense of accountability, a willingness to shoulder the burdens of the job. They will also be especially alert to any signs that you might not stay in the position long enough to make it worth hiring and training you.

A corollary to this sense of responsibility is whether or not you can be a self-starter. Employers are looking for self-sufficient workers — people who can produce for them from the word go. In the past, companies were interested in a worker for life. They welcomed people into the fold, trained them, nurtured them, and made lifelong projects out of them. In today's climate of short-term and shifting positions, employees at every level are expected to produce, to think creatively, and to make decisions about the organization's direction. Here's how your interviewer will try to determine if you have the right attitude.

- Describe some ways in which you've been a leader.
- What criteria do you use to make important personal decisions? Professional decisions?
- Under what circumstances have people depended on you?
- Describe the biggest setback you've dealt with. What was your response?
- What, so far in your life, has given you the greatest satisfaction?
- Do you prefer to have a lot of supervision or do you work well on your own?

Schmoozing/Networking

Schmoozing to Find a Job Through People

"I tell my clients that 15 percent of jobs are filled through the newspaper, five percent are filled through companies like mine, and 80 percent are filled through word-of-mouth," says Beth Anrig, the owner of Beth Anrig and Associates, a job placement service in Connecticut. Anrig places individuals in positions in a wide variety of industries, ranging from banking to publishing. "Do you know how most jobs are filled?" Anrig asks. "A manager asks a couple of people if they know anyone good."

We've moved past the point where we expect that jobs will be mainly filled through company recruiting and advertising. According to widely cited statistics, 75 to 80 percent of all job seekers find their new position through referrals; most openings never see the light of day (or newsprint). By schmoozing, you make word-of-mouth work in your favor. You can learn about a variety of industries and make friends and contacts whom you can call upon for career advice or assistance. Now how to do it?

Schmoozing to Find a Job When in School

If you're still in school, you have golden schmoozing opportunities all around you. Many students forget that there are numerous people at their university who already know them and are predisposed to want them to succeed – their professors. If you think your history professor only knows about the French Revolution, think again. He's probably pretty savvy about life in this century as well.

Make sure you are on a first-name basis with each and every one of your professors. Even if you're enrolled in huge lecture classes and can barely see the prof, figure out when his or her office hours are (hint: they'll be printed on the syllabus or posted on the office door) and go. Most professors only see students when they're begging for extensions on papers or explaining how they slept through the midterm. Your schmoozing should come as a welcome change.

Introduce yourself to your professor at the beginning of the semester. Tell them you're looking forward to taking the class, and if you're majoring (or thinking about it) in the subject, let them know that too. If you have any questions about something in lecture or are curious about something you've read, ask. But make sure to ask non-class-related questions as well. How did they get interested in sociology? What research are they doing now? Can they recommend any other good classes?

Because, after all, you ultimately want to get a job after you graduate, ask your professor for advice about that too. What have other students in his/her subject done after graduation? What does the professor recommend you do? You'd be surprised how many professors consult with companies part-time. If you're at a larger university, you might want to consider taking a class at your university's business or law school, as professors at professional schools often have an even wider variety of career contacts.

Visit Vault at **www.vault.com** for insider company profiles, expert advice, career message boards, expert resume reviews, the Vault Job Board and more.

VAULT CAREER LIBRARY   31

Tap alumni resources

Other woefully underused routes to schmoozing for a job in school are career counselors and alumni.

Career counselors want to help you get a job. That's their job. At the same time, they also have to find jobs for the other couple of thousand students at your university. But you, smart schmoozer that you are, have an advantage – not all those students are going to bother to schmooze their career counselors. As early as possible in your school career, go to your school career center, introduce yourself and discuss your career goals. Thank your counselor for any particularly good advice or leads he gives you. Most students neglect career counselors until the spring of their senior year. Don't make the same mistake.

Alumni already have a point of similarity with you. Ron Nelson points out, "Just having that little thing like a school connection takes you from 'Who the hell are you and why are you calling me?' to 'Oh, okay, you went to Vanderbilt too, what can I do for you?' It's not a big thing, but it's enough."

Tamara Totah, the former headhunter for The Oxbridge Group, also recommends using alumni contacts from your school, although she cautions that you should never directly ask them for a job. "The minute they hear that they get worried," she says. "Talk to them about what different opportunities may be available in the industry. People will spend 30 minutes with you. They know how tough it is."

Always intern

Internships are an essential component of the job hunting process. Part of the reason they are so valuable is that they give you work experience that later can be used to help you in a job search.

Once you get inside a company as an intern, you should not feel restrained by the department that you're working in – or even by your assigned supervisor. Figure out what you most want to do in the organization and schmooze the person who does it. A good way to do this is to ask this person to lunch. A good line is: "I'm trying to absorb as much information as I can in this internship, and what you do seems particularly interesting. I wonder if you are available for lunch anytime this week."

The person will almost always say "Yes." When he describes what he does at lunch, try to relate the skills that he employs to skills that you have. For example, if he tells you about the press release he is writing for company X, slip in how that's similar to your college newspaper writing experience. With any luck, your schmoozee will then offer you a chance to draft a press release. If not, try to give him another gentle nudge: "Oh, writing press releases seems like so much fun!"

When you are given menial errands to do, take it in good cheer. No one likes a whiner. If you feel like you must say something, couch it in humor. One State Department intern remembers telling his boss, "Although being a Deputy Assistant Secretary of Photocopying has its moments, I was wondering if I could do more substantive work here?" The question got his message across without rancor – and the intern received some interesting assignments. Remember: as long as you do a few things that look impressive, you won't have to put on your resume that you ran errands and photocopied stuff 99 percent of the time. So instead of complaining about your menial tasks – or even non-verbally grumbling by acting dour – express an interest in doing specific, substantive work.

Schmoozing for a Job Out of School

Once you're out of school, you'll have lost (sniff!) some of the support structure for which all your tuition dollars paid. What happens when you've found a job, and then found that you're not too happy with it? Don't be afraid – most people in this age of downsizing and corporate restructuring and increasing specialization change careers at least six times during their lives. With all the job hopping, people increasingly accept that job changing is a part of life. Your schmoozing talents will help you ease these transitions.

The informational interview

It's not a job interview – exactly. But it does get you face-to-face with someone in an industry that interests you. Informational interviews are an invaluable opportunity to learn about the inside scoop into the career field that interests you. Many people are prepared to spend 10 minutes to an hour of their time to talk to those looking for a job, assess their skills and background, and give them some pointers in breaking into their chosen field.

Says Beth Anrig, "I tell all my clients that the best thing to do is to set up informational interviews." One caveat – "never call them that," she says. Informational interviews sound too much like interviews, and that sounds like asking for a job. Everyone is over-networked, in the official sense. No one has the time anymore to do something that is just like a job.

So don't frame the "informational interview" as any kind of interview. Instead, say that you want to talk with them, or get coffee, or chat. Your goal is to have a conversation, not an interview. Ask semipersonal questions: What got you started in this industry? What other careers did you consider? Are you happy in your choice? At the same time, talk honestly and openly about your own career aspirations, and why the industry in question appeals to you. If you click, keep the person abreast of your career progress and decisions.

But never, says Totah, our erstwhile New York headhunter, ask for a job outright. "If they don't have one and you ask that, they're going to want to boot you out five minutes later." Totah says. "Believe me, if you're talking about careers, they know you want a job. If they like you and they can help you in some way they will." Schmoozing means you don't spell it out.

When calling someone for an informational interview, make it clear you are not asking for a job. The point is, if they like you, they will help you find a job. Appeal to your contact's expertise. "Everyone likes to give advice," says Anrig. "If you tell them that you are calling because a mutual acquaintance has suggested they are a real authority in their field or an inspiring example, they will be hard-pressed to turn you down."

Though the informational interview isn't a job interview (exactly), it's still important to do your research on the company and the industry. It's rude to waste someone's time during the workday, and it doesn't reflect well on you. "Most people are very generous about helping people make connections," says Wicke Chambers, our communications consultant from Atlanta. "I have a lot of business contacts and am will-

Visit Vault at **www.vault.com** for insider company profiles, expert advice, career message boards, expert resume reviews, the Vault Job Board and more.

V∧ULT CAREER LIBRARY   **33**

ing to call up and set up informational interviews for people coming out of college and recent grads. I myself am approached for interviews constantly."

However, Chambers says, "What I do mind is people asking to talk to me about my job and then having absolutely no idea what they want. I've interviewed with people who don't know whether they want to be a florist, an airline pilot or a public relations executive. I don't care a hill of beans if someone hasn't at least got an idea about what they want to do and how I can help."

YOURS ALWAYS FLEW FURTHER.

FURTHER. FASTER. SMARTER. SAFER. More effective. More efficient. More powerful. You've always been about

making things better. So has Boeing – better technology, a better world, and better careers. If you want your career

to fly further, let it take off at Boeing. The job categories listed below include some of the key skills we typically seek.

- Structural Analysis/Design
- Electrical Engineering
- Systems Engineering
- Embedded Software Engineering
- Business and Planning Analysis
- Programmer/Analyst
- Control Systems Engineering
- Ops Analysis
- Avionics

If you would like to view a comprehensive listing of all available positions, please visit: boeing.com/employment/college. Security clearance requirements are indicated in the position listings. U.S. Citizenship is necessary for all positions requiring a security clearance.

Boeing is an equal opportunity employer supporting diversity in the workplace.

Apply at: *boeing.com/employment/college*

Forever New Frontiers

WORKPLACE DIVERSITY

Overview

Every year, many new college and professional school grads get their first jobs as entry-level employees in Corporate America. The client service industries in particular – management consulting, investment banking, law and accounting – employ a new army of young worker bees every fall season. Lured by the opportunity to make a great deal of money and gain a broad education in the business world, recent grads often enter the corporate environment with no understanding of the written and unwritten rules of Corporate America to guide their behavior. They simply expect their new employers to train them completely.

This section of *The College Career Bible* is for the benefit of those with little practical experience with the inner workings of the corporate world. Women and minorities need to be particularly savvy in navigating the maze of office protocol and politics. The corporate world has historically been a heterosexual, white male playground. Women usually lack the prior experiences, role models and mentors to guide their climb up the corporate ladder. Minorities face those and additional obstacles. Often, new female and minority hires start their jobs ready to conquer the world, only to find their enthusiasm and confidence eroded as they face each additional pitfall. And no wonder. They see few successful survivors of their kind at the top of the ladder. In 2002, only 11 Fortune 1000 companies were led by women. Among *Fortune's* list of the "Best 50 Companies for Minorities," only 24 percent of officials and managers that the employers honored were actually minorities.

Mentors

A Crucial Advantage

What makes the difference between a career that thrives and one that stalls? For many women and minorities, the narrow gap between failure and success is bridged by mentorships. Mentors are people who share their general business knowledge, as well as their knowledge of a specific company, with lucky mentees (someone who is mentored). Here is some advice on how to make these valuable relationships work for you.

The importance of mentors for women and minorities

Decision-makers often consciously or unconsciously bond with and champion those who remind them of themselves. Minorities in particular need in-house mentors who champion them because they usually don't have natural role models and networks at their company. Mentors will educate you about your company's office politics and cultural norms, teach you valuable job skills and pass on industry knowledge.

You mentor does not need to share your minority status. In fact, a straight white male mentor can be a major asset in your rise up the corporate ladder. It takes time, patience and investment to develop a meaningful relationship with someone who seems to be very different from yourself – but it is worth it.

Mentors can keep you with an employer

After several years at the prestigious consulting firm Booz Allen & Hamilton, Cathy Mhatre had her first child. Mhatre credits her mentors at Boozo Allen with keeping her at the firm. "I've now been at Booz Allen for six years, which is unusual for any consultant. One of the main reasons I am still here is because there were people who wanted to keep me here." Mhatre estimates that she has "four to six" mentors at the firm, and advises, "Because women mentors are scarce in general, find enlightened men."

Identifying Potential Mentors

Find out if your employer assigns you a mentor – then keep looking

Increasingly, employers assign mentors to incoming employees – a practice that has been common at law firms for some time and is spreading rapidly to other industries as well. Some consulting firms have entire mentor family trees – with a "founder" mentor, his or her mentees, their mentees, and so on. Make sure to take advantage of these mentors, who have specifically volunteered to serve as resources.

At the same time, the most valuable mentors are normally the ones that evolve from everyday working relationships. If someone appears willing to share their experience and skills with you and takes an interest in your career, it is likely that they would like to mentor you in some way.

Visit Vault at **www.vault.com** for insider company profiles, expert advice, career message boards, expert resume reviews, the Vault Job Board and more.

V∧ULT CAREER LIBRARY 39

Mentors can be found inside or outside your company. Look around your department, your company and the professional business organizations to which you belong. Identify people you really admire with whom you cross paths. Don't limit yourself to obvious choices (e.g., the most popular/powerful executive, the person who had your job before you, the person of the same race or gender as you). Any impressive, intelligent and insightful person you meet can evolve into a future mentor.

Mentors within the company can help champion or cultivate you. In your company, mentors know all the players, politics and pitfalls. Ideally, they are well respected and secure in their positions. They may be a few rungs up the corporate ladder and can help you understand different managers' personalities and preferred working styles, office politics and the lessons they have learned.

Mentors outside of work provide objectivity. Choose mentors outside of your office who know your personality and have wisdom from a wide range of experiences. Develop relationships with at least one or two people who have no impact on your career to whom you can openly vent, turn to for perspective and ask for candid feedback. You will appreciate their distance when a work issue is too controversial to discuss with a fellow colleague, even in confidence.

In many cases, you may not even need a personal relationship with these people in order to learn from them. Observe their traits from a distance, and emulate them when you get in a position of power. For example, one director at Oracle recalls that he admired a manager who recognized hard work by comping subordinates on expensive dinners and hotel rooms. This director is now implementing this practice, which breeds loyalty.

Approaching potential mentors

Be patient and build connections through regular interactions, evolving conversations in the office, over lunch or outside of the office. Don't wait for a potential mentor to invite you to lunch or coffee – you make the offer. Tell them you would love to hear about their background (people love to talk about themselves). Be direct in seeking their counsel in dealing with your own professional situations. Try to get on projects with them so you can demonstrate your personality and performance. If you do a good job with them, hopefully they will be impressed (and even see themselves in you). Bond over nonprofessional common interests. An African-American woman discovered a shared love of cooking with a senior white male executive, who often sought her out to exchange recipes.

You can try approaching speakers at seminars or classes; they may be receptive because they like working with younger, ambitious people who remind them of their younger selves and who are receptive to their wisdom.

Establish a broad group of mentors

Cultivate different mentors for different areas of your professional life. You should not expect one person to provide all of the counsel and guidance you need to get ahead. Pick and choose different people you admire for different reasons and use them as a resource in areas where they shine. Quality matters too –

one or two superstar mentors may do you more good in the end than a dozen slackers. Company and independent organizations for women and minorities are a great way to expand your network of mentors.

Getting the most from a mentor

Once you have mentors, be open to their advice. Do not be defensive – they have nothing to gain in giving you this advice. Mentors will only value and continue your relationship if you're communicative and sincerely value their counsel. Make sure you report back to them on your successes and setbacks.

How to Get a Mentor

Mary Cranston, chair of law firm Pillsbury Winthrop LLP

Mary is the chairperson of one of the largest law firms in America. She has been practicing law since 1975, and has litigated over 300 class action cases in state and federal court, focusing on antitrust counseling and litigation, and securities litigation. She has been named to the National Law Journal's list of the 100 Most Influential Lawyers in America, and California Daily Journal's list of the 100 Most Influential Lawyers in California.

Her advice on how to get a mentor:

Be a good mentee. Approach individuals who have skills you want to acquire. If you just say, "Help me," they will be less likely to help. But if you say, "I had a great idea; can we work on it together?" your chances are much higher. Think about how you can contribute to the relationship, then you're more likely to get help from a mentor.

Tips for Building a Relationship with a Potential Mentor

Kristi Anderson, executive recruiter, TMP Worldwide

Show overwhelming interest in their kids! Pretend you like their kids, remember their names and ask about them often. Remembering to ask who won that high school football game will go a million miles in endearing yourself to a potential mentor.

Ask your mentor for advice often, even when you don't need it. People, especially successful people, like to hear themselves talk and to demonstrate their wisdom. Don't ask dumb or simple questions with a definitive answer, but ask your mentor open-ended questions regarding his style and experience in handling a particular business situation. Then just sit back and feign interest in the long-winded response. Even when I don't need the advice, I will pose such a question to a mentor. It makes a mentor feel like he is bringing you along in your professional development.

Visit Vault at **www.vault.com** for insider company profiles, expert advice, career message boards, expert resume reviews, the Vault Job Board and more.

V/ULT CAREER LIBRARY   41

Tips for Mentees

It's not enough to find a good mentor – it's just as important to use them correctly. Here are a few tips to make the most of your mentor relationship.

- Find mentors at all levels of the company. The classic mentor is someone a few levels above you in an organization – close enough to your experience to guide you upwards in the ranks, experienced enough to have some pull. But you can also gain experience from mentors at your level and at other companies as well. Your business school professors are another invaluable set of potential mentors.

- Don't approach someone and formally ask them to be your mentor. This kind of artificiality is akin to handing your business card to someone and asking them to be your contact – it's too artificial to take root. If someone wants to be your mentor, they will indicate that fact through the interest they take in you.

- Keep in touch with your mentors. Mentorship is a relationship, and relationships are built from frequent, informal contact. This is important even when your mentor is assigned to you by your company. If you move on from a company, stay in touch with your mentor there.

- Establish trust. Everything you discuss with your mentor is between the two of you.

- Have realistic expectations. Your mentor is an advisor and advocate – not someone to do your career networking for you, or someone to cover your errors.

- Don't pass up the opportunity to have a mentor. Having a mentor can make a major difference in your career path and your self-confidence.

Finding a Mentor During a Meltdown

Ashley Fieglein, director, General Atlantic Partners

During my investment banking career, I learned the importance of choosing a mentor even though I was the only woman in an all-male office. Four years into investment banking, with hundreds of hours of lost sleep under my belt, I reached a moment where I really needed to let go. A client had yelled at me. I had a stack of work on my desk guaranteeing another lost weekend. And I had gotten a call saying that two of the projects were "urgent" and needed yesterday. I felt panicked. I noticed the teardrops on my desk, even though I wasn't aware I was crying. I got up and closed the door to my office. And the hysteria set in. I sobbed. And then I suddenly realized that I really wasn't going to be OK.

I picked up the phone and called one of the senior bankers with whom I had worked very closely over the four years. He showed up in my office in a matter of minutes. In spite of my embarrassment, I let him rub my back while I sobbed. He closed the door, gave me a glass of water and waited until I caught my breath.

He offered to help manage the situation, to get me more support and to get me more time. And then he sent me home. No arguments allowed, though I protested that things had to get done, but he insisted that they would be OK I think he probably stayed extra hours that night to oversee the analysts working on my projects. I was sound asleep in my bed, catching up on some long overdue rest.

When I came back in the next morning, everything seemed manageable. The client who had reamed me the night before had called back to apologize. The work was no longer insurmountable. And the urgency had subsided.

My newly-found mentor never said a word to me about the incident afterwards. I ended up calling him crying at least once or twice more, and he always supported me kindly. He always took my tears seriously. He understood that this was my way of expressing anger. And I completely trusted his support of me.

Visit Vault at **www.vault.com** for insider company profiles, expert advice, career message boards, expert resume reviews, the Vault Job Board and more.

VAULT CAREER LIBRARY

43

Appearance

Take extra care in your appearance. It is the first impression you make in terms of your professional credibility, and it will be easy for others to be judgmental of your looks. As a new hire at the bottom of the food chain, you should not be making any personal statements with your clothes. Nothing should distract from the quality of your work. Strive to look well-groomed and polished, a look you can achieve on any budget.

Presentation Counts
Siobhan Green, project manager

At my performance evaluation for my first job, I was shocked to be rated poorly on my professional appearance. When I asked what that meant (I had a good wardrobe and thought I was more or less fitting in with the other staff), I was told that I should "dress more like Judy." So I watched her and noticed the difference. I didn't wear makeup and she did. Her hair, face and nails were always impeccable – and mine weren't.

The president of our company, whom I often accompanied to client meetings as a note taker, was the one who gave me the low review. He didn't really know what made Judy look more professional than me, but it bothered him enough to mention it to my supervisor and note it on my evaluation. I realized that if I wanted to continue working in that company, wearing nice suits would not be enough. I would have to make sure my nails were always clean and polished, get my hair trimmed regularly, and wear some eyeliner and lipstick, at least for meetings with clients and senior managers.

- **Dress appropriately for your industry and for your position.** Dressing outside your company norm suggests a lack of judgment and cultural fit.

- **Dress well to appear older.** Often, women and minorities can look much younger than their age. Remember that you will interact with senior executives and clients who are two to three times your age. One easy way to appear older, and more professionally credible, is to dress in a more subdued, conservative style. If you are wearing a suit, you are less likely to be mistaken for the summer intern or bike messenger.

- **Women should avoid inappropriately sexy clothes.** There is no quicker way to hurt your professional credibility. If you want to be taken seriously, observe limits: don't bare your midriff, wear low-cut necklines, see-through blouses or Ally McBeal-length miniskirts. Save it for the weekend (unless you are coming into the office). Use the 50 percent rule for judgment calls: if at least half the women go without pantyhose, wear open-toed shoes or moderately short skirts, then you can.

- **Minorities can display ethnic style – in moderation.** Wearing a kente-cloth pocket square with your suit is fine, but coming to work in a full-on dashiki is not. If you wear a piece of clothing for religious reasons (a yarmulke or a headscarf, for example), select pieces in subdued colors and make sure the rest of your clothing fits company standards.

Visit Vault at **www.vault.com** for insider company profiles, expert advice, career message boards, expert resume reviews, the Vault Job Board and more.

VAULT CAREER LIBRARY   45

- **Geeky isn't chic in the workplace.** Does your wardrobe consist of square glasses and faded T-shirts with funny slogans? Then you'll need to invest a little bit of time and money in upgrading your look. Overhauling your image will boost your self-esteem and the respect you command from others. Unfortunately, the bottom line is that co-workers in corporate America can be even more superficial than bullies in the schoolyard.

    – No clue what to wear? Buy some fashion magazines, ask your stylish colleagues some questions about where they shop, or talk to a sales clerk in the men's department in a classy department store or chain like Brooks Brothers.

    – Replace your glasses with simple wire frames.

    – If you work in a formal dress environment, aim to have three or four tailored suits, twice as many shirts and ties, two pairs of dress shoes (one brown and one black) and four casual outfits for Fridays. If you work in a business casual environment, aim to have at least four or five nice slacks (e.g., black, gray, khaki, navy blue, olive), twice as many shirts to mix and match and two pairs of casual shoes (one brown and one black). Women should buy simple suits in neutral colors (black, brown, gray). Your mint green pantsuit may look smashing on you, but it's so memorable that you won't be able to wear it more than once a month. A simple black skirt suit, on the other hand, can be worn at least once a week. In addition, you can split up the skirt and the jacket and wear them with other items to create more work-ready looks.

    – Remember that sock color needs to match shoe or pant color. And never wear athletic socks with a suit! Women, if you're wearing a skirt, wear non-shiny nude or black hose only.

Dressing Right Brings Respect
Former management consultant

When I started working, I brought with me all my clothes and shoes from college and summer jobs. I learned very quickly that while chunky heels and open-toed shoes, fitted tops and above-the-knee skirts weren't necessarily prohibited, I felt much better about myself and the respect I got from senior management by dressing more conservatively. And so my career wardrobe began with new French blue button-down shirts and conservative black pants.

- **Get your hair cut once a month** by someone other than your mother. Men, part your hair on the side instead of the middle.

- **In America, follow American standards.** Overseas, it can be quite common for corporate employees to wear the same outfit several times a week and not shower every day. Be forewarned that Americans who work in a corporate environment are typically extremely superficial about wardrobes and downright fanatical about personal hygiene. If you want to fit in as much as possible, shower and use deodorant every day, and try to have at least five fresh outfits in your wardrobe, one for every day of the week.

Dealing with Stereotyping

People stereotype others out of ignorance and convenience, not malice. As a minority in the corporate world, you may find yourself subtly or blatantly treated differently than your peers because of your assumed strengths, weaknesses and traits. This special treatment may not necessarily be unpleasant or negative. But you need to identify who is making what assumptions, and how these erroneous assumptions impact your work life. If there is any negative impact on your image at the company, and hence your long-term professional development, it is important to address the situation gracefully and request the same treatment your peers receive.

Stereotyping is often unconscious on the part of your colleagues. For example, there's an old stereotype that all Asians are good at math. And maybe you are Asian and really are quite good at math. So on, say, your first management consulting project, it seems to make sense for you to do the back office analysis while someone else interviews the client executives. But the more you do the back office number-crunching, the better you become at it, and the more it makes sense for you to do it again next time. Eventually, if you keep holding up with your calculator, you will fall behind in developing communication skills, professional presence and client relationships. Break the cycle and make sure you are learning an appropriately broad set of skills before you become pigeonholed as the "expert" of one task.

In the next section, we will outline common stereotypes of women, minorities and gay men. Specific ethnicities, age groups and sexual orientation will trigger specific stereotypes. These examples are meant to give you some idea of direct and indirect discrimination you may face based on commonly-held stereotypes. Generally, stereotypes stunt your professional development by skewing the mix of work you get, while your peers receive a more balanced training.

If you decide you are fine with the situation because it is an anomaly, is short-term or has upsides, that's fine. If you want to change the situation, you have to speak up early before the precedent is repeated too often. Whether or not you want to address the stereotype directly, at least you can inform your manager that you would like to broaden your skill set and get a good mix of challenging and diverse work. Don't approach your boss complaining. Tell him your reasoning and your proposed solutions, so that you steer the conversation toward getting his support for one option and the transition itself is assumed. The sooner you demonstrate consistent, undeniable interest and accomplishment in the areas outside of the stereotype, the sooner people will see you as a unique individual. It is not fair that it takes extra work, but the investment is worth it.

Visit Vault at **www.vault.com** for insider company profiles, expert advice, career message boards, expert resume reviews, the Vault Job Board and more.

VAULT CAREER LIBRARY 47

Common Stereotypes: Women

Assumption	Situation	Solution
You are bad at math but good at writing.	Whenever project tasks are distributed amongst the team, you always get the qualitative, not quantitative, tasks. You don't become better at math. If you are put on a quantitative task and have trouble with it, you are removed from the task instead of trained to do it better.	Make it a priority to learn new things, especially when you first start your job. Do not let yourself be removed from quantitative projects.
You are suited to detailed administrative work.	You are assigned administrative duties no one else wants: taking notes at the meetings, booking travel for the team, making copies, ordering lunch, getting coffee for clients, setting up or cleaning up a meeting.	Volunteer someone else for the task and try to get your manager's backing.
You are eye candy and probably not that bright, because you're attractive.	You are excluded from important meetings, but trotted out on fun business development outings so older male clients can flirt with you. People gossip about you.	Make sure your work stands on its own. Do not dress in a revealing or sexy manner.
You are too sensitive and emotional.	You don't get direct feedback about your performance so you don't advance. People are afraid you will cry, so they treat you gently. When you do cry, people assume you cannot handle stressful work.	Seek out truthful feedback. Remove yourself from stressful situations and control your temper and emotions.
You are timid.	People forget to ask you for your opinion because they assume you won't have one. You stop having opinions because you are never asked about them, stunting your critical thinking and communication skills.	Practice expressing yourself. Build alliances. Emulate strong speakers.
You are a pushover.	You are asked to do work that no one else wants to do, like staying late in the office for a last minute assignment, cleaning up other's unfinished work, and delivering bad news for other people.	Learn your boundaries. Embrace the word "No," especially if these requests do not come from a manager or senior executive.
You are a token hire.	Especially in a macho environment like investment banking or sales, your peers don't believe you made it here on merit, and do not give your work and opinions equal respect.	Work twice as hard to prove yourself. Try not to be too sensitive about routine male-bonding behaviors.
Work is not as important to you as it is to your male co-workers. Your family comes first.	Co-workers will not ask you for help on tough assignments. Your manager may be reluctant to invite you on business trips or to late-night client dinners.	Meet every deadline. Do not discuss family visits or shopping excursions, especially if you take time off for these activities. Clearly state you interest in attending a client event.

The de facto secretary

Women are often unconsciously slotted into an administrative role and given routine, detail-oriented work. While these projects may be important, and it's vital to be able to pitch in during a time crunch, it's difficult to shine by doing these routine tasks. The requests may seem benign at first. Can you take the notes during the meeting? Can you prepare FedEx packages? Can you coordinate the next meeting or the next business trip? If you are the most junior person on the team, assume that status is the reason for getting these chores. In the corporate world, the guy at the bottom of the food chain takes care of all the scrub work. The more machismo-laced an environment you work in, the more pronounced the hierarchy will probably be. Check with the second-most junior person to see if he had all the same "chores" before you arrived. Make sure you pass those duties on right away when a more junior person joins the team.

If you are not the most junior teammate, you may have been designated as a secretary for the team because of your gender. How should you handle the request? If the need is legitimate and you are the most appropriate person to perform the task (e.g., because you have the time or because your piece of the work is not as time-sensitive), go ahead and do it, and don't take it personally. If the need is not legitimate, or you are not the most appropriate person for the job, do not accept the role! Ask your manager to pass the chore to a secretary or another member of your department. Or tell your manager you would like to rotate the responsibility around the team because you took the duty last time. You could simply say, "I'm sorry. I don't have time to do that and meet my other deadlines. Can someone else pitch in?"

If a client asks you to do something administrative, go ahead and do it … once. Make sure you raise the issue with your manager and get his backing before you tell the client you cannot the second time. If you are asked to do something really demeaning, like making coffee, smile sweetly or make a little joke and say you don't know how to.

If you are the only woman on the team and you are constantly performing the admin duties, you will diminish your professional credibility and stunt your professional development compared to your male peers. Address the situation politely but directly with your manager and/or other perpetrators. Here are two common scenarios women in the corporate world face and how to address them.

The note-taker

You are always asked to take notes "because you have the best handwriting." This statement could be absolutely true – some guys really have atrocious handwriting!

But when you take notes, you are busy looking down at the paper and writing down what everyone else says. As a result, you don't get to participate in the discussion as much. At review time, your manager won't recall hearing you speak in meetings, forgetting that he asked you to take notes. He'll have the impression that you are timid (playing right into another common stereotype of women). Furthermore, if you are writing madly in a future meeting that includes a client or a senior executive, you lose the opportunity to interact with and impress an important person. You may even be mistaken for a secretary yourself.

Visit Vault at **www.vault.com** for insider company profiles, expert advice, career message boards, expert resume reviews, the Vault Job Board and more.

V/\ULT CAREER LIBRARY   **49**

If you are the most junior person on the team, you may have to take notes until someone new is hired. If you are not the most junior person, get a reality check from a trusted peer or manager in the office who is removed from the situation at hand. "I want to ask your opinion because I'm not sure if I am being too sensitive. Who takes notes in your meetings?"

The cyclical nature of stereotyping comes from the fact that the more you do something, the better you become at it than everyone else, so then everyone wants you to continue doing it. After several meetings of being the note-taker, you learn to outline exactly how your boss likes it, type everything up with graphs and charts inserted, and distribute to the group quickly. Of course everyone will want you to keep doing it because no one else does it as well. But continuing the role compromises your professional development, self-respect and the respect of your peers, even if it is gradual and unintentional.

Talk to your manager directly, but avoid any suggestion that the offense was intentional (even if you suspect it was). Address the professional rationale behind your request and your proposed solutions. "I don't want to always be the note taker because it prevents me from participating in the discussion in a meaningful way. The issues are so interesting I'd like to share my thoughts next time. Let's rotate the responsibility, or bring a secretary into the meeting to take the notes."

Be prepared to be brushed off as being hypersensitive. "Uh oh, you're not a militant feminist are you? You are way too sensitive!" Don't back down when faced with such resistance. Stand your ground, and calmly respond. "I know it's easy for you to jump to that conclusion, but humor me, and let's rotate the responsibility. I really would like to join in the conversation next time, and I think I have proposed fair solutions." Just make sure you don't clam up in the next meeting!

The teacher

Maybe you're repeatedly asked to train new hires. Why are you singled out every time? Is it because you are friendly, patient and verbal compared to your other colleagues? Is the responsibility of training only assigned to top performers who uphold the highest standards of work quality? Is training a total pain in the neck, and your boss knows you'll be a pushover? Ask your boss or the person who trained you how the responsibility is assigned. Then you can evaluate how you want to deal with the situation.

Perhaps you don't mind this assignment because you enjoy getting to know the new hires right away, you get a break from your normal workload and you get to expense more meals on the company. Or the training assignments reflect the fact that you're a star at the company. Maybe you actually hate sitting alone in your office all day crunching numbers and you really want to be a teacher at heart, so the opportunity to train new employees is a dream niche for you.

Now for the downsides. Because training is administrative, you may be expected to carry your full load of "real" work on top, meaning that you are working much later nights than everyone else to get everything done. Is training worth compromising your personal time? On the other hand, if your manager does reduce your workload to accommodate your training assignments, over time you might fall behind your colleagues in terms of advancement because you spend your days teaching and mentoring new hires instead of getting more challenging projects and interacting with senior colleagues and clients. Is training worth compromising your professional development?

Want to get out of doing training? Tell your boss you have already conducted the training twice as many times as the last person who did it. Or point out that you have missed client meetings because of training, which is detrimental to both your development and your relationship with your client. Suggest setting up a random system to rotate the responsibility amongst your peers by drawing numbers or assigning it alphabetically by last name. Or suggest that people pair up in teams to conduct training, so it's not as time-consuming for each person.

Address and Retrain Your Manager Immediately If You Feel Singled Out

Sonja Beals Iribarren, former director at Disney

As the most junior member of the team, I accepted the fact that I drew the duty of making copies during meetings, should the need arise. That I was often the only woman in the room seemed only a coincidence until a new, younger – and male – analyst joined the team. I think we were both shocked when my boss again asked me to step out and make a few copies at the next meeting. I did so without complaint, in the name of team spirit, but did speak to my boss privately immediately afterward and told him that I wanted that duty to fall to the new junior member of the team. I tried to keep the focus on the seniority issue and away from any discussion about gender, which I felt might be interpreted as militant feminism and would not ultimately serve my purpose. I was concerned that people's perception of me would be negatively affected if I continued to accept this duty without comment. It's not about making the copies – it's that people expect you to stand up for yourself. Honestly, I wouldn't be surprised if scenarios like these aren't a test to see how you handle yourself in these situations.

Common Stereotypes: Minorities

Assumption	Situation	Solution
You are good at math but bad at communicating.	You are always given back office analyses, but never put in front of senior executives or clients to present your findings.	Don't just hand over analyses to your manager with no explanation or interpretation. If you do a good job articulating your work to your boss, you can make the next step of presenting to others.
You have a chip on your shoulder.	People assume you are difficult to work with, keep their distance and minimize interaction. You leave the job without any significant relationships, mentors or networks to help you later on.	Be careful how you express your views. Show your casual, humorous side often.
You share the same traits as everyone else of your demographic.	You are compared to the other minority of the same race as you in the department. You are called the wrong name, as if people can't tell you apart. You compete with each other for the token slot.	Establish your identity and distinguish yourself.
You do not speak English well.	You are not given time to speak in meetings or written assignments.	Work to perfect your writing and speaking skills. Ask for and excel at, writing and speaking assignments.

Visit Vault at **www.vault.com** for insider company profiles, expert advice, career message boards, expert resume reviews, the Vault Job Board and more.

V/\ULT CAREER LIBRARY 51

People naturally categorize things into convenient buckets and make assumptions about those categories. Establish your own identity, and avoid "competing" with the one other person in the office of your race. For example, let's say that you are one of two Asian-American analysts in your starting class of twelve new hires. People you don't work closely with may mix you up and call you the wrong name. As a more serious pitfall, you may be compared to each other all the time, and there may also be an assumption that only one of you will be promoted.

Don't take it personally if the other person of your ethnicity is not quick to establish a close friendship with you. She may want to establish her own identity. It is an immature reaction on her part, but an explainable one. If a friendship is meant to be, over time it will develop as you both settle in to your new jobs.

Ways of establishing your personal identity include:

- Socialize with a variety of your peers.

- Befriend the perpetrators. People will not mistake you for someone else if they get to know you. Talk about things you have in common. Let them get to know you as a person with distinct interests, rather than a token minority.

- Correct people if they call you by another name. You can do this nicely, but don't let them persist in thinking you are someone else. Correct the person on the spot, introduce yourself and laugh it off to help the perpetrator save face. "It's a big office, so I often forget names of people I've only met once or twice, too."

- Establish natural friendships with peers of your ethnicity. There is no advantage to discriminating against people who look like you, and you come off like a jerk. And you might be sacrificing a friendship with someone with whom you would otherwise really connect because of shared experiences and insights.

Don't Assume You Will Bond Over Race

Former strategic planning analyst

During my interviews for a competitive position at a Fortune 100 company, I continually asked about the obvious lack of African-American employees in the department. To dispel my concerns, the recruiting manager arranged for me to meet a very senior African-American officer in the company, even though I would not actually be working with him in my prospective job.

Without thinking twice, I openly asked him about the dearth of African-Americans at the company. He replied, "If you are one of those black people who needs to be around other black people, you won't find them here!"

Shocked and disappointed, I quickly learned that not all people of color view themselves as leaders or mentors of junior employees of their same race. On the contrary, many prefer to ignore ethnicity and maintain distance from other colleagues of color in order to avoid labeling.

Geography Matters

Victor Hwang, former corporate lawyer, current COO LARTA (a nonprofit think tank)

If you're a minority, geography matters. I love Austin, Texas. I spent my formative years there. I love country music, barbecue, Longhorn football and big hair. I never encountered any overt prejudice in my professional life in Austin, but one does start to feel worn down after the third time someone has confused you with your minority co-worker, every lunch at a sushi restaurant starts a talk about "other Chinese food," and people think that your parents are Thai because they're from Taiwan. It may or may not be prejudice, really it's just ignorance, but it does take a toll on your self-esteem.

So I moved to Los Angeles and never looked back. There has been such a difference in my sense of professional opportunity since I've moved to Los Angeles. Climbing the professional ladder is hard enough already; one should eliminate as many controllable obstacles as possible.

Common Stereotypes: Gay Men

Assumption	Situation	Solution
You are creative.	People come to you with more questions and projects that involve visual aesthetic, creative design, or marketing, whether or not that is part of your job function.	Make it a point to shine in other areas. Make sure those areas are visible to management.
You don't have traditional masculine interests.	You are not invited to sports or bar outings. You miss out on the opportunity to network and bond out of the office.	Bring up your participation in sports, your home teams or your favorite non-gay bars and clubs. Invite yourself along.
You are checking out all the straight men in the office at all times.	Guys keep their distance. You are made to feel self-conscious.	Don't make any sexual references or jokes. Never flirt with or date co-workers.
You are flamboyant.	You are not put in front of the most conservative, stodgiest clients or senior executives.	Be mindful of corporate culture, behave conservatively and give people time to know you.
You are the token gay friend everyone wants.	Female colleagues want to be your best friend, talk to you about boys and fashion. Colleagues don't respect the same professional vs. personal boundaries with you. You're called "Will" from the popular show *Wiill and Grace*.	Be mindful of your interactions with others. Act professionally and conservatively, focus on work. Give people time to get to know the real you.

Visit Vault at **www.vault.com** for insider company profiles, expert advice, career message boards, expert resume reviews, the Vault Job Board and more.

VAULT CAREER LIBRARY 53

Diversity Employer Directory

Agilent Technologies

 Agilent Technologies

Corporate Headquarters
395 Page Mill Road
Palo Alto, CA 94306
Phone: (877) 424-4536
http://www.agilent.com/diversity/English/index.html

At Agilent, we believe that our global competitiveness will be accomplished not only by designing, manufacturing, marketing and selling superior products, but also by leveraging the diversity of our customers, stakeholders, employees and partners all around the world.

Our success is achieved through:·
- An environment that enables all to develop and contribute to their full potential
- Leaders that engage, focus, mobilize and leverage all cultures
- Strategies that direct our diverse, collective intelligence to solve urgent business challenges ·
  Excellent resources and tools that enable our people to excel
- Systems and Processes that align and support our vision for success Diversity and inclusion are key business mperatives that influence all aspects of our business in a positive way. They impact our ability to relate to and solve our customers' global concerns; our ability to hire, promote and retain outstanding people; and our reputation with the communities we serve around the world. Diversity of perspective is a catalyst for breakthroughs, creativity and innovation. An inclusive culture that fully harnesses all the resources, talents and skills of its employees, business partners and customers is essential. An inclusive workplace that leverages on the diversity of its people and optimizes their contributions will have the advantage in competing and winning in the global environment.

The Boeing Company

The Boeing Company
Boeing World Headquarters
100 North Riverside
Chicago, Illinois 60606
www.boeing.com/employment/college

With a heritage that mirrors the first 100 years of flight, The Boeing Company provides products and services to customers in 145 countries. Boeing is a premier manufacturer of commercial jetliners and a global market leader in military aircraft, satellites, missile defense, human space flight, and launch systems and services. Total company revenues for 2003 were $50.5 billion.

Boeing employs more than 156,000 people in 70 countries and 48 states within the United States, with major operations in the Puget Sound area of Washington state, Southern California, Wichita and St. Louis.

EOE statement: Boeing is an equal opportunity employer supporting diversity in the workplace.

Credit Suisse First Boston

11 Madison Avenue
New York, New York
10010
E-mail:
Diversity.recruiting@csfb.com
www.csfb.com/standout

CREDIT SUISSE | FIRST BOSTON

To attract outstanding young talent from among the nation's high schools, colleges and graduate programs, CSFB has developed a broad range of initiatives – some in partnership with external organizations – to increase the pipeline of students who are interested in careers in finance. For example, CSFB works with a number of external organizations, including the Robert A. Toigo Foundation, the Sponsorship for Educational Opportunity and the United Negro College Fund, which provide financial assistance to students of color and their families.

Schools CSFB recruits from
Columbia; Cornell; Duke; Howard; Georgetown; Harvard; MIT; Morehouse; NYU; University of Pennsylvania; Princeton; Spelman; Stanford; University of Michigan; Yale

Visit Vault at **www.vault.com** for insider company profiles, expert advice, career message boards, expert resume reviews, the Vault Job Board and more.

VAULT CAREER LIBRARY   55

Fitch Ratings

FitchRatings

One State Street Plaza
New York, NY 10004
Phone: 212-908-0500

Fitch Ratings is a leading global rating agency committed to providing the world's credit markets with accurate, timely and prospective credit opinions. Fitch Ratings is dual-headquartered in New York and London, operating offices and joint ventures in more than 40 locations and covering entities in more than 75 countries. Fitch Ratings complies with federal, state, and local laws governing employment, and provides equal opportunity to all applicants and employees. All applications will be considered without regard to race, color, religion, gender, national origin, age, disability, marital or veteran status, sexual orientation, and other status protected by applicable laws.

Schools Fitch Ratings recruits from
NYU; Cornell; Brown; Columbia

JC Penney Company Inc

JCPenney
PO Box 10001
Dallas, TX 75301-8115
Phone: (972) 431-1000
www.JCPenney.com

it'sallinside:

JCPenney

*Communication   Subcommittee
Mission Statement:*
Improve communications by enhancing the sensitivity level surrounding diversity & work-life impacting customer service and associate satisfaction/productivity.
Personnel Relations Subcommittee Mission Statement:
To foster the upward mobility of women and minorities into all levels of management, including senior management positions, by enhancing our current recruitment programs and implementing career development plans that allow the Company to retain, train and promote qualified women and minority associates.
Work-Life Issues Subcommittee Mission Statement
Identify Work-Life Issues that affect each associate's ability to perform to full potential. Encourage a supportive work environment that allows associates to maximize their contributions towards company objectives.

Schools JC Penney recruits from
Open to all accredited colleges and universities

Naval Financial Management Career (NAVY)

Financial Management
Intern Program
153 Ellyson Avenue, Suite A
Pensacola, FL 32508-5245
Phone: (850) 452-3783
E-mail: fmip@nfmc.navy.mil
www.navyfmip.com

The Financial Management Intern Program (FMIP) recruits high quality, prospective civilian financial managers for Department of the Navy Activities. The FMIP is a two year program of professional development through academic and on-the-job training. Entry level positions as Analysts, Accountants, and Auditors are available. Applicants may have any academic major; but those applying for Accounting and Auditor positions require 24 semester hours of accounting (6 hours may be in business law). A minimum cumulative GPA of 2.95 in an undergraduate degree from a nationally accredited university/college is required.

Schools Navy recruits from
Nationally accredited colleges and universities

Sodexho

200 Continental Drive,
Suite 400
Newark, DE 19713
Phone: (302) 738-9500 ext
5209
E-mail: John.lee@sodexhousa.com
www.sodexhousa.com

Sodexho

Sodexho is the leading provider of food and facilities management in the U.S. and Canada, with $4.9 billion in annual sales. Sodexho offers innovative outsourcing solutions in food service, housekeeping, grounds keeping, plant operations and maintenance, asset and materials management and laundry services to corporations, health care and long term care facilities, retirements centers, schools, college campuses, military and remote sites. Headquarters in Gaithersburg, MD, the company has more than 100,000 employees in 50 states and Canada.

Standard & Poor's

55 Water Street/
New York, NY 10041
Phone: 212-438-2000

1221 Avenue of the Americas
New York, NY 10020
Phone: 212-512-1000
www.standardandpoors.com/careers

Schools Standard & Poor's recruits from
Columbia; Boston College; NYU; USC; UCLA; Berkeley; Stanford; U Texas-Austin, U. of Chicago; U. Michigan; LSU; Indiana; U Wisconsin-Madison; U. of Illinois; Lehigh; Cornell; Harvbard; MIT; Wharton; CUNY-Baruch; Villanova; Emory; Penn St.; UNC-Chapel Hill; Florida; St. Josephs; U. of South Carolina; UVA; Howard; Spelman; Morehouse; Hampton

Symbol Technologies

Symbol Technologies, Inc.
One Symbol Plaza
Holtsville, NY 11742-1300
Phone: 631.738.2400
http://careers.symbol.com

Symbol takes pride in its focus and commitment to diversity college recruiting. Through continued efforts of support, involvement and outreach with targeted diversity-based university programs and professional student organizations, Symbol encourages a workplace of growing diversity where constant innovation and excellence are evident of our success. Talented individuals who join Symbol have the opportunity to participate in programs developed by our Diversity Team. Such programs include affinity groups and diversity skill-building. Respectively, these programs facilitate networking and professional development as well as the capability to capitalize from differences that exist within the workplace.

Schools Symbol Technologies recruits from
Stony Brook University; RIT; U. Rochester; Cornell; Columbia; Carnegie Mellon University; San Jose State University; U. Buffalo; Polytechnic; The Cooper Union; Binghamton University; MIT; CalPoly SLO; U. Louisville; Santa Clara; Stanford

Visit Vault at **www.vault.com** for insider company profiles, expert advice, career message boards, expert resume reviews, the Vault Job Board and more.

VAULT CAREER LIBRARY

57

GRADUATE
EDUCATION

AdmissionsConsultants®

We have admissions committee experience from the top graduate schools and we will maximize your admission chances!

Collectively, we have made over 100,000 accept/reject/waitlist decisions. We really do know what makes a good catchy introductory paragraph and we know exactly what the admissions committees want to see from different applicants. Our comprehensive services, which encompass far more than simple essay edits, will provide you with the competitive advantage you need in the application process.

We have consultants with admissions committee experience from top law schools and business schools as well as MDs with medical school admissions committee experience. We also have consultants with admissions committee experience from other graduate programs as well. As the world's largest pure admissions consultancy, the chances are good we have a consultant just right for your needs!

Professionally-run corporation
Large collective knowledge base
Exceptional qualifications
Honest and competent advice
Comprehensive service
One-on-one customized attention
Choice of consultants
Flexible hours
Quick turnarounds
Caring professionals
High success rate

CONTACT US TODAY
www.admissionsconsultants.com
703.242.5885
info@admissionsconsultants.com

BBB Better Business Bureau

Considering Graduate School

Graduate School: To Go or Not To Go

When it comes to graduate school, there are two main schools of thought. The first, (led by anxious parents everywhere) says, "Go right away! Otherwise, you'll forget what it's like to be in school, and you won't be able to study! And you'll never get a decent job in the real world anyway!" If this voice is the one currently pounding in your brain, tell it to be quiet and go take a nap. Then, listen to the more rational side of the debate, often specified in small print on graduate school applications: most graduate students are in their late twenties, as schools like it if you have both life and professional experience before pursuing a higher degree.

Of course, not all graduate degrees are created equal. First there are professional degrees (law, teaching, medicine) versus academic degrees (literature, art history). Some programs take only a year, others seem to take the rest of your life. Also, certain professions essentially require you to have more than a B.A. before even considering them (particularly in academia). Other fields are more willing to take a chance on a brash young thing, such as yourself.

Ultimately, the best thing to do is to ask people who are experienced in your chosen field. Ask them if they think you would be best off going to grad school right away, or if they feel you should wait awhile. Ask them about the best schools, and the best degrees for what you want to do. Don't forget to ask them if their companies ever pay for employees to get more education. Frequently, a company will chip in and give an employee flexible hours, in return for a guarantee of work for a certain period of time after he or she has graduated.

One thing graduate school should not be is a last resort. It is too expensive and time consuming to do without really knowing that it's what you want to be doing – at least for the time being.

Graduate School Options: Certification vs. a Degree

There are a multitude of factors you need to take into consideration when deciding whether to pursue an advanced degree, attend local classes towards a certificate, or study for and take your certification exam. The following factors will aid in your decision-making:

- *Stage in life.* Don't let an arbitrary and subjective detail like your age get in the way of your education or professional advancement. If you really want to do it, it doesn't matter whether you're 25 or 125.

- **Stage in career.** Will the degree help you in your career progression? If you have already broken into a field and have amassed experience in it, probably not. If you're looking to change jobs to another company, you may want to consider it. If you're an independent consultant and want to ensure that new clients find you credible, you may want to go back to school.

Visit Vault at **www.vault.com** for insider company profiles, expert advice, career message boards, expert resume reviews, the Vault Job Board and more.

VAULT CAREER LIBRARY   61

- **Impact on income.** Can you afford to go to school full-time? Can you find a good part-time program while you continue to work? Is it worthwhile to take out a loan? Will your employer help you out with a tuition assistance program?

- **Impact on relationships.** How will your time away from your friends and family impact your relationships? What's more important to you right now and in the future?

- **Volatility of field.** Is this field going to be around in the future – or are there tell-tale signs that it will be replaced by technological advancements or radically altered so that your specialty won't be needed? Check out trends and professional forecasts on web sites like Vault.com and SHRM.org for more insight.

- **Return on investment.** What are the benefits of each option?

- **Time and money.** Do you need this education by a certain deadline, for a certain reason, and on a certain budget? If so, certification will be much quicker and cheaper to attain than a degree. If time and money are of no concern, do both.

- *True motive.* Are you looking to make more money? Then, depending on your current employer's compensation system, you may have to change jobs to a company that rewards its employees based on education rather than tenure. Also, if you are over 40, it probably won't make a difference if you have another degree if you already have over 15 years of career-relevant experience.

- **Theoretical education.** If you want this, school is often a better option.

- **Practical application.** Certification might make more sense here.

It's no secret that having an advanced degree will make you more marketable in the job market, should you need to change employers. If you're just starting out or trying to break into a field, you should definitely pursue a relevant degree; it will open up doors for you and get you more money from the get-go. If you're already established in the field and have a wide array of experience, you'll probably be OK without a degree for future internal advancement – although getting a degree certainly wouldn't hurt you for credibility and possible job changes. Furthermore, achieving a professional certification (e.g., PHR/SPHR) is a boon for degreed professionals and seasoned ones alike.

Attending local college-run certificate programs can give you some added, high-level insight into areas of interest, but won't substitute for a degree or certification. And as far as which school to attend, research all the possibilities and select the one that's right for you. The right program may not be at a "big name" university, but at a smaller institution that offers you the perfect education and training. Be sure to check out the alumni association and career placement office to find out where the school's graduates have landed jobs and which companies actively recruit from the school. The decision to pursue either an advanced degree or certification all comes down to what you feel more comfortable with and your personal career goals.

Considering Graduate School?

Applying to graduate school can sometimes be a daunting task. Even after completing thorough research, selecting the college or university, and submitting the application, applicants are frequently left with unanswered questions and legitimate concerns about the evaluation process.

Some of the commonly-asked questions students have at this stage of the process are: "How much emphasis is placed on my undergraduate grades?" "Are my standardized test scores strong enough?" "How important are my written essay and work experience to my application?" and "Who makes the final admission decision?"

International students, required in almost all cases to submit a test score or documentation indicative of their ability to study in English, are faced with additional criteria by which their application will be judged, and may therefore find the evaluation process that much more intimidating. It should help to know that the application and evaluation process is relatively straightforward.

Regardless of the program, the evaluations are based on two main criteria:

- Academic background

- Personal background

In order to determine if one's academic background is admissible, the applicant is asked to submit the following items: official undergraduate and or graduate transcripts indicating one's coursework, showing credits and grades in these courses; a standardized test score (such as the GRE or GMAT) specifically requested by the program; and a TOEFL or TOESL test score report, if applicable.

To determine if one's personal or professional background is admissible, an applicant is asked to submit two or more letters of recommendation, preferable from academic or professional references; a written essay(s), which may pertain to a specific topic or reflect the applicant's objective in pursuing the degree program; and a resume or curriculum vitae summarizing the applicant's work experience to date.

In addition, some programs may request a portfolio or sample of one's work. Many schools will request a personal interview after evaluating the application. This may be done in person or over the telephone.

Academic background

The admission committee will begin by reviewing the main indicators of how well one will do in a graduate degree program: undergraduate grades, standardized test scores, and TOEFL or TOESL score.

When reviewing the undergraduate or graduate grades, the committee will look closely at the overall grade point average, as well as grades in the major or concentration. The standardized test score is examined, and depending on the type of program, special consideration may be given to a particular section of the test.

Visit Vault at **www.vault.com** for insider company profiles, expert advice, career message boards, expert resume reviews, the Vault Job Board and more.

VAULT CAREER LIBRARY   63

Personal background

While the grades and test scores are the most objective measire of the applicant's ability, the personal and professional criteria can do much to enhance an applicant's profile. The written essay, which for some schools may take the place of a personal interview, provides evidence of an applicant's writing ability and his or her motivation to pursue the program.

Letters of recommendation describe an applicant's skills and abilities in the workplace or the classroom. The resume informs of areas outside the classroom in which a student may demonstrate competence or knowledge. The combination will provide a clear picture of an applicant's admissibility and subsequent selection for the program.

Application tips

There are a few things you can do to ensure the smooth processing and evaluation of the application. The overall appearance of your application indicates your professionalism and organizational abilities, so be sure to write neatly or type your application, essay and resume (checking for any spelling or grammatical errors). International students should keep in mind any cultural differences such as the order of first and last names. Also, make sure to complete and send in your application in a timely manner – try not to leave it all for the last minute – especially if you're hoping for financial aid. Give ample notice to the people writing your recommendations, and leave yourself time to correct mistakes or find any additional information that might be required. You might even consider making a schedule for yourself so you don't cram all of your preparation into the week or two before the deadline.

Answer all questions on the application completely and, if necessary, attach any additional information on separate sheets of paper. Make every effort to have official transcripts and translations sent directly from your previous university.

Lastly, try to have standardized test scores sent to the university in advance, so they arrive at about the same time as your application.

The most important piece of advice that a prospective graduate student could receive is this: do not hesitate to ask questions.

There are many ways to obtain answers to specific questions about admissions policies: you can search the web, attend university information sessions, and e-mail, write, fax or telephone the admissions office.

Knowing the answers to your questions will help you discover whether your academic and personal profiles match your school of choice and allow you to go through the admission process with greater confidence. Good luck.

Law School

Choosing a Law School

Which law school should you attend? In some ways, this question seems simplistic: you want to go to the best law school that will admit you. But what defines a good law school? There are many books about law schools and surveys that rank them, notably the annual issue published by *U.S. News & World Report*, and it is a good idea to review these publications. Even to the uninitiated, some names pop up immediately: Harvard, Yale, Stanford, Columbia. By reputation and stringent academic requirements, schools like these claim to take only the cream of the crop. And a prestigious law school, with its higher profile, might lead to better employment opportunities after graduation than a less well-known school. But there are considerations other than reputation.

Admittedly, it's hard to wade through the volumes of press materials each law school will send you. Review the course catalogs, certainly, but also look for statistics about the percentage of graduates who go on to litigation, corporate law, or other areas of the law and the kinds of practices they join to get an idea of the kind of training the school focuses on. It's also a good idea to visit the school in person and, if possible, sit in on some classes. "I think it's important to meet with the students at the school," says one recent graduate, "because you get the real facts about what the school is like. Go to whatever mixers they set up for their applicants, if you can."

Another element you should consider is location. Not all of the best law schools are in big cities, but being in an urban setting has a number of advantages. You will have direct contact with many law firms, city agencies and government offices with the resources to hire interns and law students. "Going to a law school in a big city meant that I could have a variety of internships and summer jobs without worrying about housing or moving," says one junior corporate litigator. Many firms also prefer to hire summer associates from local schools. If you have your eye on practicing in New York, for example, it's often a good idea to go to a New York school. You'll be in closer proximity to interview at local firms and some classes (such as criminal law or professional responsibility) may focus on New York state law.

And then there are more practical considerations. Will the school provide housing? If you live off campus, what will your daily commute be like? Are you ready to pick and move alone or to take your family to a new city or state? Can you afford the tuition? Do you share the school's philosophy and emphasis? Is there a particular professor with whom you want to work?

Ultimately, the decision of which law school to go to is as personal as it is practical. Even if it's important to know school statistics and rankings, your choice needs to be a school that will teach the skills you want to learn, in a location where you can live comfortably. This is especially true if you are embarking on a second career and hesitate to uproot your whole life.

Visit Vault at **www.vault.com** for insider company profiles, expert advice, career message boards, expert resume reviews, the Vault Job Board and more.

VAULT CAREER LIBRARY 65

Law School Reputation

Reputation is a subjective quality, usually based on other subjective qualities and usually measured in national rankings and local prestige.

Every year, the magazine *U.S. News & World Report* publishes an issue devoted to ranking the colleges and universities of the United States. This is the ranking that people talk about for law schools. The magazine looks at subjective factors like ratings by academics, lawyers and judges, as well as statistical data like LSAT (Law School Aptitude Test) scores, bar passage rates, and acceptance and rejection rates. It conducts opinion polls and gathers statistics on average LSAT scores and undergraduate grade point averages (GPAs). Employers often use the rankings to determine which schools merit an on-campus interviewing visit. And, in a chicken and egg way, the fact that the law firms are paying more attention to those law schools leads to better applicants at those schools, since that's where law students see good career prospects. If you've missed the latest print issue, you can review the rankings online at http://www.usnews.com.

National ranking systems like those published by *U.S. News* have been criticized for subjectivity and an overdependence on reputation without consideration of issues like who gets jobs, what graduates think of their law school, and so on. Some critics, including a coalition of law school deans, have come up with alternative rankings. For more information about alternative rankings and criticism of subjective national rankings, refer to "Judging the Law Schools," an "unauthorized ranking" of law schools by Thomas E. Brennan, a former Chief Justice of the Michigan Supreme Court (www.ilrg.com/rankings/), and *The Ranking Game*, from Indiana University School of Law-Bloomington (http://monoborg.law.indiana.edu/LawRank/index.html). However, most lawyers and clients still use the *U.S. News* rankings as a yardstick of prestige

A school that ranks in the top of the *U.S. News list*, a "national" law school, offers advantages in the form of portability of degree. Students who attend national schools typically have an easier time finding jobs in different geographical regions than do those coming from lower-ranked schools. A national school may also have highly regarded faculty. "I went to the best law school I got into and would encourage everyone to do the same," says a Harvard alum working in a large Boston firm. "Law school is about getting a credential and access to the career, not an experience onto itself. It's called a professional school for a reason."

Of course, many successful corporate lawyers haven't gone to Harvard or Yale. A local school can be an excellent strategic and financially sound decision, especially for someone who knows the geographic area in which he wants to practice. And all firms hire from the top of their local school class. "I have realized that if you don't get into a top-10 national school, it is sometimes better to go to a local school with many local connections to firms than to go to a second-tier national school in a state in which you won't practice," says a Boston associate. "For example, people in Boston who went to Boston College Law School have good luck landing jobs in firms even though there are a lot of second-tier national schools ranked above them."

If you're lucky enough to get into several schools with good programs in areas of law which interest you, then you just need to think about personal comfort. This is where money and location come into play.

Ask Anna: Time Off Before Taking the Plunge

Anna Ivey is a private admissions counselor who works with people applying to the top business schools and law schools. Formerly the Dean of Admissions at the University of Chicago Law School, she has also practiced corporate and entertainment law in Los Angeles. She received her B.A. from Columbia and her J.D. from the University of Chicago Law School, where she served as an editor of The University of Chicago Law Review. To learn more about her admissions counseling, visit www.annaivey.com. To read more of her columns about law school, go to www.vault.com.

Question: I have a question regarding law school. I am confused about whether to take a year off between college and law school or whether to go straight through without taking time off. Part of me wants to spend a year traveling, but I am afraid that spending a year criss-crossing the globe (or at least Europe) will turn off law schools. The other option is to take a year off before law school but to get a job instead of traveling. What are your thoughts about this confusing topic?

Anna's Answer: Let me start by saying that I jump up and down with excitement when I hear that someone wants to wait before applying to law school. So many college students apply to law school because they don't know what else to do with themselves after they graduate. What a great problem you have – too many options!

With some exceptions, most law schools will tell you that they don't care in terms of admissions policy if you apply straight out of college or not, but if you have a chance to talk to admissions officers face-to-face, most of them will recommend that you wait before applying if you want to explore something else first. There are a couple of reasons for that.

First, if you really need to get something out of your system (say, you really want to see the Andes before you die), now's your best chance. Once you're on the lawyer track, it becomes very hard to hit pause to do something wild and crazy like hanging out in the Andes for a year.

Second, you'll be a much more interesting applicant if you apply after you've acquired some life experience in the real world. As an applicant, there's no downside to pursuing something interesting and productive after you graduate. You'll still have the benefit of your accomplishments through college, but you'll also have the benefit of all the interesting experiences that follow. From an admissions perspective, it doesn't really matter so much whether you spend that time traveling or working, as long as you're pushing your boundaries, acquiring new skills and learning something about the real world. When you're ready to apply, you'll have that much more to show off. Your résumé will be more interesting, you'll have a wider range of experiences to draw on for your personal statement and overall you'll make a more polished and mature impression. You will also make a much better lawyer down the road. (For those of you so inclined, take note that sitting on your butt for a year becoming the Halo champion on your Xbox won't cut it.)

You'll also fit right in if you take some time off: At Harvard Law School, 64 percent of the Class of 2005 took a year or more off before starting. At Northwestern Law School, over 80 percent of the Class of 2005 has at least one year of work experience and over 60 percent has at least two years' worth. (In fact, Northwestern, one of the more innovative law schools around, has broken from the pack and now states an express preference for work experience: "Long-term, our goal is that all entering students will have at least two years of postcollege work experience, another factor that helps us determine their motivation and ability to thrive in law school and beyond.")

Visit Vault at **www.vault.com** for insider company profiles, expert advice, career message boards, expert resume reviews, the Vault Job Board and more.

VΛULT CAREER LIBRARY 67

Something else to ponder: In my experience, many of the applicants who apply while they're still in school would love to explore other opportunities before applying to law school but feel pressured by their well-intended but poorly informed parents to apply right away. If you need some ammunition in defending your post-graduation plans, send them this article along with your hugs and kisses.

LSAT 101

For many students, few things are more dreaded than standardized testing, and the LSAT is among the most fearsome tests of all. The Law School Admissions Test is used to evaluate a candidate's verbal and math skills as well as her analytical thinking. The exam can be arduous and exhausting, but it is a necessary element of applying to law school. The LSAT is administered by the Law School Admissions Council four times a year and most schools require that you have taken the LSAT before you apply to law school. The test is roughly three and a half hours long and similar to the SAT – only harder. The test breaks down into the following sections:

- **Logical reasoning** (Two sections, 35 minutes each, 48 to 52 questions total). This section tests your ability to dissect an argument. The questions each consist of an argumentative passage of three or four sentences. There is usually a flaw with the argument, and your job is to find out what it is. Occasionally the argument is valid, and your job is to determine the conclusion. This section is pretty dense, so be prepared to do some thorough reading.

- **Analytical reasoning/games** (One section, 35 minutes, approximately 24 questions). This is traditionally one of the hardest sections of the LSAT. The best description of these "games" is that they involve logical reasoning of a system of relationships. You'll usually have to draw a diagram to figure out the relationships based on the rules given to you. There are four games and there are five to eight questions for each game.

- **Reading comprehension** (One section, 35 minutes, approximately 24 questions) As a lawyer, you're going to read through hundreds of cases, statutes, documents and memoranda. Reading comprehension is extremely important. This section includes four passages, each roughly 400 to 500 words long and followed by five to eight questions. Your must read each section and be able to answer each set of questions correctly.

- **Mystery section** (One of the above sections, possibly a little different in format)

- **Writing sample** (30 minutes) The writing sample will be on a topic chosen by the test committee. The essay is forwarded to all the schools to which you are applying, but, according to an admissions official at an accredited law school, their office relies more on the applicant's personal statement than the LSAT essay to evaluate a candidate's writing abilities. The essay is not factored into the total LSAT score. Rather than count on your work being ignored, however, you should be prepared to formulate an argument and present it clearly under pressure.

The LSAT is graded on a matrix that converts the raw score (0-100) to a 120-180 scale. There is no passing score, but it becomes increasingly harder to move up in the matrix. You don't need to get all the questions right in order to get a perfect score, but your score can drop based on the answer to a single question.

There are many courses designed help you to "beat" the LSAT, including Kaplan, the Princeton Review and the LSAT Center Course. These courses teach specific strategies for tackling each section. The LSAT doesn't change that much from year to year, so if you study older tests and practice a lot, you'll improve your chances of doing well on the real thing.

Visit Vault at **www.vault.com** for insider company profiles, expert advice, career message boards, expert resume reviews, the Vault Job Board and more.

VAULT CAREER LIBRARY   69

Business School

Why the MBA?

Is it a quant boot camp where students find themselves chained to their laptops and their spreadsheets? Is it a country club where students mix and mingle, discussing future business plans over cocktails? Or is it a mandatory two years that would-be CEOs must serve in order to get that bump in salary and that chance to rise into upper management?

The school part

Business school is definitely school. Particularly in the first year, when students in many programs take "core" classes in fields like accounting and corporate finance, the workload at business school is often described as "overwhelming." In class, students learn marketing strategies and management theories, negotiation tactics, the heavy quantitative lifting of valuing a company and other useful business concepts. Many business schools utilize "business cases" to illustrate concepts the students learn. Through these cases, students study the way these concepts have played out in real-world situations.

The business part

But business school is often as much about careers as it is than books and learning. While at school, future MBAs often have one foot in the classroom and one foot in the working world. For starters, unlike their graduate, law, or medical school counterparts, very few business school students enroll in the programs without having first gained experience in the working world. (Most programs require some work experience and will reject candidates.) The program itself is also shorter – the traditional full-time MBA program is two years, which serves as less of a hiatus from working life than other graduate programs. In fact, some students in full-time MBA programs continue to consult or work part-time with their former employers throughout their time at business school.

For some students, business school is a necessary step in their career path. In the investment banking and consulting industries, many large employers will not promote employees past the analyst level until they have received their MBA. It is common practice for these budding bankers and consultants to attend business school after a two- to three-year stint as an analyst following college; some of them return to their firms as associates.

Many other students earn their MBA degrees through evening classes while working full-time. For many of these evening and executive MBA students, getting an MBA is especially attractive because their employers are footing the bill for their degrees.

Career-minded

More so than students at other graduate programs, students at business school enroll to accomplish specific objectives related to their careers. According to a survey published by the Graduate Management

Visit Vault at **www.vault.com** for insider company profiles, expert advice, career message boards, expert resume reviews, the Vault Job Board and more.

VAULT CAREER LIBRARY   71

Admission Council (GMAC – the organization that administers the GMAT business schools admissions test), about half (51 percent) of business school students use the MBA degree to enhance their opportunities in their current occupation or industry; the other half (49 percent) seek to switch careers. Often, career switchers are experienced professionals who have worked in the corporate world in a non-business function (engineering, for example), who wish to transition to a business-oriented management track.

And on the whole, MBAs are satisfied with their degrees. According to a survey of the MBA graduates of the class of 2003 conducted by GMAC, more than two-thirds of graduates from business school feel the value of their MBA is outstanding or excellent (22 percent indicated the value to be good, while 9 percent indicated it was fair and 3 percent described it as poor).

What you'll gain

Most business school students expect to make more money once they graduate. This opportunity certainly exists. Any business school student who lands at a top investment bank or consulting firm (the two largest industry employers of MBAs) will find themselves immediately making $100,000+ a year. And in general, having an MBA on your resume puts you in a better position to negotiate and command a higher salary (even if you return to the same industry or even same company that you worked at previous to business school).

However, landing a six-figure job is no guarantee. During tough economic times, MBA hiring takes a larger hit than undergraduate hiring or direct-from-industry hiring – in part because of the cost of hiring MBAs. Many graduates of the class of 2001 and 2002 found themselves jobless for up to a year or more after graduation.

But there are other reasons to get the degree other than a bump in salary. Many recruiters and managers find MBAs to be more polished professionals in certain respects. According to the Corporate Recruiters Survey published by GMAC, recruiters find the following skills both highly attractive and well developed in MBA graduates:

- Ability to think analytically
- Quantitative skills
- Ability to integrate information from a wide variety of sources
- Information-gathering skills

GMAT 101

The following article is provided by Vault's partner, Manhattan GMAT. Learn more about the GMAT exam and about ways to prepare at www.manhattangmat.com. Sign up for the official test by calling 1-800-GMAT-NOW, or by going to the official GMAT website at www.mba.com.

The GMAT is the Graduate Management Admission Test, a standardized test used by business schools as a measure of an applicant's academic ability. Schools require applicants to take the GMAT and submit their scores in order to be considered for admission to M.B.A. and other business-oriented degree programs. The GMAT is a computerized test; administered six days a week, 52 weeks a year (except holidays), it can be taken virtually anytime. However, it can only be taken once per month and 5 times per year. The cost to take the exam is $225.

The Computerized GMAT CAT

The GMAT is offered ONLY on computer, which means that you do not use a pencil and paper to answer test questions. Instead, you will sit in front of a computer screen at an official testing center and take the GMAT in its CAT (Computer Adaptive Test) form. The basic features of the CAT format are as follows:

- You will see only one question on the screen at a time. Therefore, you may not skip around in a section and answer questions in the order that you please. Once you answer a question, you are not allowed to return to it, but you must answer one question in order to move to the next.

- The test is designed to adapt to your personal ability by giving you questions that reflect how well you have answered previous questions. Test questions are not pre-set in advance. Instead, as you take the test, new questions are generated for you based on how well you are doing. The test begins with a question of average difficulty. If you answer it correctly, you will receive a slightly harder second question. If you do not, you will receive a slightly easier second question. Your third question, in turn, will be based on your response to the second question and its difficulty level. In this way, the computer zeros in on your ability level and assigns you a corresponding score.

- Due to the GMAT's computer adaptive format, scores are not determined solely by the number of correct answers. Correct responses to difficult questions are worth more than correct responses to easy questions. Therefore, in order to score well you must be able to answer the more difficult questions correctly.

- No matter your ability level, the CAT presents you with a fair mix of questions for the content areas within a given section. For example, in the math section, all test-takers receive roughly the same mix of arithmetic, algebra, and geometry questions.

- Prior to the exam, there will be a computer tutorial designed to help you become familiar with computerized testing. You will be allowed as much time as you need to review the computerized format and practice entering in answers.

GMAT Format

- *Section 1:* You will be asked to compose two 30-minute essays. The first essay will ask you to analyze a given argument. The second essay will ask you to analyze a given issue. This section is called the Analytical Writing Assessment (the AWA).

- *Section 2:* You will be given 75 minutes to answer 37 multiple-choice quantitative questions. These questions come in two forms: (a) Problem Solving questions which ask you to solve a variety of arithmetic, algebraic, and geometric math problems and (b) Data Sufficiency questions which ask you to decide whether or not you are given sufficient information to solve a given math problem.

Visit Vault at **www.vault.com** for insider company profiles, expert advice, career message boards, expert resume reviews, the Vault Job Board and more.

VAULT CAREER LIBRARY   73

- *Section 3:* You will be given 75 minutes to answer 41 multiple-choice verbal questions. These questions come in three forms: (a) Sentence Correction questions which ask you to choose the most grammatically accurate way of expressing a given sentence, (b) Critical Reasoning questions which ask you to assess the logic of short arguments, and (c) Reading Comprehension questions which ask you to read short passages (up to 350 words each) and answer content, inference, and application questions based on the information presented.

The timed-portion of the GMAT lasts 3.5 hours. You are allowed a 5-minute break between each section. Note: the GMAT does not include any questions that test your business knowledge. It is designed solely to measure your writing, quantitative, and verbal ability.

GMAT Scoring

- After taking the GMAT, you will receive both quantitative (Section 2) and verbal (Section 3) subscores. Each subscore ranges from 0 to 60. These subscores are then combined into an overall score, which ranges from 200 to 800this is what is typically considered your GMAT score. You will also receive a separate score, ranging from 0 to 6, on the AWA essay portion of the exam (Section 1). Your scores are accompanied by a percentile ranking that tells you how you did in relation to everyone else who took the test. If you score in the 85th percentile, this means that 85 percent of all GMAT test-takers scored at or below your level.

- The median overall GMAT score is approximately 520. However, to be considered for top business schools, you will generally need a score of at least 600. In fact, according to the 2004 U.S. News business school rankings, 10 of the 15 business schools report that their average GMAT scores are in the 700+ range.

- Scores are reported to you immediately. After completing the GMAT, you are given the option of either viewing or canceling your scores. If you think that you did not do very well, you may cancel your scores (without seeing them!) and they will not be reported to any business schools, although the business schools will be notified of the cancellation on future score reports. Keep in mind, however, that once you cancel your scores, you will not be able to view them. Also, you will not be refunded your test registration fee. Your AWA essay-writing score is determined separately (graded by ETS writing professionals and a software program called Robo-reader) and mailed to you approximately two weeks after the test. The test fee covers reporting of these scores to five schools, and additional score reports can be purchased for $28.

Graduate Education Directory

Admission Consultants

1108 Hillcrest Drive
Virginia, VA 22180
Phone: 703.242.5885
Fax: 703.242.0654
www.admissionsconsultants.com

Recruiting Contact
David Petersam, President
Phone: 703.242.5885
E-mail: info@admissionsconsultants.com

We are the world's largest pure admissions consultancy. Our consultants have admissions committee experience from top graduate schools (including law, medical, and business) and they have made accept/reject/waitlist decisions on, collectively, over 100,000 applications. We offer expert and customized advice, very quick turn-around times, and honest assessments. Our success rate, which is fueled by our comprehensive approach and admissions committee experience, and over 8 years in business are unrivaled.Our large selection of specialized consultants begins to dwindle once the 'busy season' arrives, so contact us today and we will help pair you with the optimal consultant for your background!

Manhattan GMAT

g ManhattanGMAT

138 W. 25th St.
9th Floor
New York, NY 10001
800-576-GMAT
http://www.manhattangmat.com

Recruiting Contact
Kim Watkins, Director of Student Services
Phone: 212-721-7400
E-mail: kim@manhattangmat.com

As the name implies, we teach only one test: the GMAT. Developed by a team of Ivy League professionals, our unique and sophisticated curriculum teaches real GMAT content (not just short cuts and tricks) and material reflecting the exam's most current trends. Our staff is a handpicked group of real teachers with extensive classroom and tutoring experience and a track record of proven success. How high are our standards? Teachers must have a 99th percentile GMAT score just to land an interview. With 9-week prep classes, private tutoring, 1-day workshops, and online instruction, Manhattan GMAT has a program to suit your special needs.

Northcentral University MBA Online

505 W. Whipple St
Prescott, AZ 86301
Phone: 888-327-2877
Fax: 928-541-7817
http://www.ncu.edu

Admissions
888-327-2877
information@ncu.edu

Northcentral University is a fully accredited 100% distance learning university offering MBA degrees with a choice of 12 specializations. Our flexible enrollment policy allows Learners to begin courses on the first of each month, and complete them anytime within a 16-week term. Learners may begin their next course ahead of schedule upon completion of the previous course in order to move quickly through their degree program.

Specializations: Accounting, Applied Computer Science; E- Commerce; Health Care Administration; Criminal Justice Administration; Financial Management; Human Resources Management; International Business; Management; Public Administration; Management of Engineering and Technology; and Management Information Systems.

Visit Vault at **www.vault.com** for insider company profiles, expert advice, career message boards, expert resume reviews, the Vault Job Board and more.

VAULT CAREER LIBRARY   75

INDUSTRY OVERVIEWS

Does it matter who you are?

Or does it matter what you can do?

At Deloitte, our firm's success is measured by the quality of our team's insights and solutions. So, the more diverse our people's backgrounds and expertise, the better. With more than 120,000 professionals worldwide, sharing their unique perspectives across our functions, service lines and offices, we are uniquely positioned in the global marketplace to understand our clients' complex needs and exceed their expectations. Are you ready to be yourself and make a difference in everything you do?

Deloitte.

Audit.Tax.Consulting.Financial Advisory.

www.deloitte.com/us

Accounting

Why Accounting?

What exactly is accounting, and why do we need it? Accounting is a system by which economic information is identified, recorded, summarized and reported for the use of decision makers.

So what does that mean?

Put simply, accounting is the language of business. An accounting system essentially tracks all of the activities of an organization, showing when and where money has been spent and commitments have been made. This aids decision making by allowing managers to evaluate organizational performance, by indicating the financial implications of choosing one strategy over another and by highlighting current weaknesses and opportunities. It allows managers to take a step back, look at the organization, and assess how it is doing and determine where it should be going.

Accounting, however, is not the exclusive domain of Big Business. In all likelihood, you have been managing your own personal accounting system for years – it's called your checking account. Every time you record an entry in your check ledger, you are acting like an accountant. Your check ledger is an accounting log of all of your deposit and withdrawal activities, helping you identify your cash inflows and outflows and letting you know how much money you have left in the bank. It lets you know where your money went and helps you make decisions on how to plan your future purchases and expenses. If this log is not regularly balanced for accuracy, you would have an inaccurate picture of your cash position and might spend more than you have (a common situation, given the popularity of overdraft protection features offered by banks).

You get the picture. Now, imagine these functions performed on more complicated items and on a much larger scale. While you might have 500 checkbook transactions in a year, many organizations might have that many transactions every minute. This is what an accountant does. And, just as you would eventually be lost without a relatively accurate checkbook, organizations would not be able to make useful decisions without an accurate accounting system. Anyone who has pulled out his or her hair trying to balance their checkbook should have an appreciation for both the importance and challenges of accounting.

Why accounting?

So why would anyone choose a career in accounting as opposed to another business profession, like investment banking or management consulting? Isn't accounting boring and tedious?

As we discussed earlier, accounting has always had an image problem, stuck in the public consciousness as a profession populated by math geeks who love crunching numbers but little else. While this stereotype may have been accurate at one point in history, it no longer presents an accurate picture of what the career is like. While the basic mechanics of accounting can certainly become tedious, such functions are increasingly becoming automated, with accountants focusing more on analysis, interpretation and business strategy.

Visit Vault at **www.vault.com** for insider company profiles, expert advice, career message boards, expert resume reviews, the Vault Job Board and more.

VAULT CAREER LIBRARY   79

In fact, accounting has been rated one of the most desirable professions available. According to The 2002 Jobs Rated Almanac, "accountant" was the fifth best job in terms of low stress, high compensation, lots of autonomy and tremendous hiring demand. Furthermore, the National Association of Colleges and Employers' Winter 2002 Salary Survey ranked the accounting services industry first among the top five employers with job offers for graduating college students.

Accounting Uppers and Downers

Uppers

- **Collegial work environment.** Public accounting firms, particularly the Big Four firms (Deloitte & Touche, Ernst & Young, KPMG and PricewaterhouseCoopers; see sidebar on p. 10), tend to hire large classes of newly graduated accountants. Being surrounded by so many people with similar interests and concerns makes acclimation to the firm and the job much more agreeable. It also provides fertile ground for networking opportunities. According to one public accountant, "I started with a class of almost 100 other college graduates, and we bonded quickly through all of the training and client work. While most of these people have since left the firm, I still keep in touch with most of them, which is great since they've all fanned out to dozens of interesting companies. I've already turned some of them into clients and am working on many others. The networking opportunity is tremendous."

- **Applicability to many functions.** A strong knowledge of accounting is applicable across all management functions, including purchasing, manufacturing, wholesaling, retailing, marketing and finance. It provides a base from which to build broad knowledge about virtually all business functions and industries. As the collectors and interpreters of financial information, accountants develop comprehensive knowledge about what is occurring and close relationships with key decision makers, and are increasingly being called upon to offer strategic advice. Senior accountants or controllers are often selected as production or marketing executives because they have acquired in-depth general management skills.

- **Exposure to different companies.** Public accounting offers rapid exposure to a number of different clients and activities, accelerating the attainment of skills and experience. According to one Big Four audit senior who specializes in entertainment industry clients, "I've been with the firm for less than three years, but I've become intimately involved in work for large industry players like Sony, Viacom and Disney, as well as for a good number of smaller entertainment and media companies. Being able to learn about the business of entertainment from the industry's benchmark companies has really sped up my professional development. Few professions would have offered me such a great learning opportunity."

- **Better hours and less stress than investment banking and management consulting.** The hours and travel required by the accounting profession are much less stressful and more predictable than that found in investment banking and consulting. In public accounting, you generally know you'll be very busy for a few months out of the year and then settle in to a manageable 40- to 45-hour workweek, whereas I-bankers and consultants are notorious for regularly pulling 60-80 hour weeks (at least) and hopping on planes at a moment's notice. "As hard as I worked as an accountant, my life has truly been swallowed by my I-banking job," says one former auditor who, after attaining an MBA, is now an investment banker. "I pretty much work six days a week, with at least part of my Sunday spent on some work item or another. I actually had a life when I was an auditor – not anymore."

- **Great for women.** The profession has taken great strides to implement flexible work arrangements and other initiatives to provide lifestyle choices for women. According to the Bureau of Labor Statistics, women now account for approximately 60 percent of the accounting profession, with the outlook for women accountants looking bright. According to a CFO survey by Robert Half International, 58 percent of CFOs believe that the number of women accountants in management-level positions (such as vice president or chief financial officer) will increase in the next five years. According to one partner who has worked for several large firms, "At the risk of sounding politically incorrect, my 17 years of experience have shown me that women tend to make better accountants than men. In my observation, men often tend to be focused on the big picture, while women are more acutely aware of intricate detail. Well, accounting demands a detail-oriented approach more than any other skill, so you do the math."

Downers

- **Lower pay than investment banking and consulting.** The more manageable lifestyle has its tradeoff: lower pay. On average, starting base salaries in accounting are 15 to 20 percent lower than investment banking or consulting, not including the bonus incentives that can significantly increase a banker's or consultant's overall pay package. According to the same former auditor/current investment banker from above, "I do make a lot more money as an I-banker – I mean a LOT – which does make up somewhat for losing my personal life, but it doesn't feel that way all the time. Sometimes it seems that, if you divided my I-banking compensation by the number of hours I spend working, I would be making about minimum wage." Bonus incentives are much smaller in public accounting, if they exist at all. "You'll never become 'stinkin' rich' on an accountant's wage," adds one Big Four tax partner, "but I like to think that, since we are supposed to be conservative and intelligent in matters pertaining to money, we know best how to take care of our money and make it work for us. You will definitely lead a comfortable life."

- **Many bosses with different priorities.** Accountants, particularly public accountants, are usually assigned to multiple projects at any given time and must prioritize and, when needed, learn to say "no." This is particularly true in public accounting, where multiple, simultaneous projects for different clients are commonplace. According to one auditor, juggling projects "has honestly been the hardest part of my job. Forget the clients, they're relatively easy to deal with – it's the partners on those clients that get you. They all want you to focus on their projects first. On more than one occasion, a partner has screamed my head off, really got down and cursed, because of a perceived 'lack of focus' on my part. You just have to try to explain your situation, try to demonstrate that you have everything covered, and move on." However, this premium on time management is also present in investment banking and consulting.

- **Relatively conservative, conformist cultures.** Accountants are generally looking to see if reported numbers conform to one set of regulations or another (Generally Accepted Accounting Principles, the Internal Revenue Code, SEC regulations, etc.). This emphasis on regulations (in fact, one might say that

Visit Vault at **www.vault.com** for insider company profiles, expert advice, career message boards, expert resume reviews, the Vault Job Board and more.

V∧ULT CAREER LIBRARY

81

the entire accounting industry exists because of regulations) translates into a generally risk-averse culture and ethos that emphasizes conformity

- **Pressure to stay "chargeable."** This is one of the subtler, yet highly sensitive parts of being an accountant. Like attorneys, public accountants generally work under billable hour arrangements (they are paid by clients for each hour billed). This means that they must account for every single hour they work and accurately allocate them to each project they work on, whether client-related or otherwise. Being "chargeable" means billing a high percentage of your hours to work performed for paying clients as opposed to non-billable projects. This tracking of billable hours, while often tedious, is absolutely crucial to the profession – it is the basis for how public accounting firms determine revenues, expenses, profitability, efficiency, performance and a host of other metrics. With such vital items at stake, timesheets and chargeability often are the subject of much stress and consternation.

"Yeah, we can work 60 hours in a week," says one audit senior, "but not all of those hours are chargeable to a client. Some days, you can spend time on a proposal for new business, some time on developing a new product or service, and some time on performing general research on a specific issue. All of these activities are important to continued success, but they hurt you because none of them are chargeable to a specific client. In other words, the firm isn't getting paid for this work. While the firm values this non-chargeable work, it doesn't want you doing too much of it – it wants you out there making money for the firm. So when you find yourself doing this stuff, your chargeability goes down and your performance numbers suffer, which can hurt your reviews, your paycheck and ultimately your future at the firm. However, you can't err on the other side either – you bill too many hours to your clients and you run the risk of going over budget and having the client give you the third degree on why the job is taking you so long. It can be pretty stressful."

Public vs. Private Accounting

While there are many ways to classify accountants, the most common division is between public and private accountants.

Public accountants mainly deal with financial accounting (the preparation of financial statements for external parties such as investors). Private accountants deal with both financial and management accounting.

Public accountants

Public accountants receive a fee for services provided to individuals, businesses and governments. Public accounting firms vary greatly in size and the type of services provided. Most public accounting firms provide some combination of auditing, tax and management consulting services. Small firms mainly provide tax or bookkeeping services for smaller companies and organizations that do not have internal accounting departments. Larger firms usually provide these services to firms that have internal accounting departments. Because all public companies are required to have yearly audits, the large public accounting firms are extremely important for fulfilling this requirement.

The four largest accounting firms are known as the "Big Four," and are among the most well-known organizations throughout the world. (Previously, it was the Big Eight, which became the Big Six and then the Big Five when PriceWaterhouse and Coopers & Lybrand merged to form PricewaterhouseCoopers. Because of the collapse of Arthur Andersen, we're now down to the Big Four. See p. 10 for basic information on the Big Four.) The Big Four is made up of:

- Deloitte & Touche
- Ernst & Young
- KPMG
- PricewaterhouseCoopers

Many students pursuing accounting careers aim to start their careers at one of the Big Four firms. The Big Four have offices throughout the United States, as well as in many other countries. These firms recruit at a majority of the top schools throughout the world.

In addition to the Big Four, there are thousands of other accounting firms ranging from small proprietorships to large international partnerships. The difference between these firms and the Big Four is size, often measured in terms of billings. The Big Four have billings in excess of $1 billion a year. A large majority (97 percent) of companies listed on the New York Stock Exchange are clients of the Big Four.

Regional accounting firms represent clients that do most of their business within the U.S., although they may also have a few international clients. The largest regional firms can be thought of as somewhat smaller versions of the Big Four. And as the category name suggests, these practices tend to be stronger in certain regions. If you're considering working for a regional public accounting firm, be sure to research the quality of the firm's practice in your area. The large regional players include Grant Thornton, BDO Seidman, and Jackson Hewitt.

Local accounting firms operate in a small number of cities and tend to focus on small businesses and individuals. These organizations conduct more tax and tax planning engagements and traditionally handle more of the bookkeeping responsibilities for their clients.

While most people start their careers at a public accounting firm, many gain valuable experience in public accounting and switch to the private sector after two years (or however long it takes them to get certified as a CPA). Accountants with public accounting experience are well positioned to take financial officer positions at corporations, government agencies or non-profits.

Private accountants

Private accountants work for businesses, the government or non-profit agencies.

Corporations – Most corporations have an internal accounting group that prepares the financial information (both tax and audit) for the public accountants, tracks company performance for internal evaluation and works with management on issues related to acquisitions, international transactions and any other operational issues that arise in the running of the company. Within corporations, there are several roles that an accountant can take on. These include, but are not limited to the following:

Visit Vault at **www.vault.com** for insider company profiles, expert advice, career message boards, expert resume reviews, the Vault Job Board and more.

V/\ULT CAREER LIBRARY   **83**

• **Internal auditors perform financial accounting tasks within an organization.** Typically, these employees will perform audits of specific divisions or operational units of a company.

• **Management accountants can work in several different areas of a corporation.** On the finance side, accountants can work in the financial planning and analysis or treasurer's group, analyzing potential acquisitions and making funding decisions for the company. On the accounting side, there are opportunities within the accounting group to handle tax issues and to work with external auditors to prepare financial statements such as SEC filings. Additionally, on the accounting side, opportunities exist to work within specific divisions to track costs and analyze operational performance.

Government agencies – Government accountants can work at the federal, state or local level. Many government organizations have large accounting departments to analyze the performance and allocation of their funds. The Department of Defense (DOD), the General Accounting Office (GAO), the Internal Revenue Service (IRS) and the Securities and Exchange Commission (SEC) typically hire large numbers of accountants for services and evaluations within the organization. Accountants at the IRS typically review individual and corporate tax returns. The SEC hires experienced accountants to evaluate filings made by public companies. These accountants ensure that firms are complying with SEC regulations.

Non-profit organizations – Accounting for non-profits is very similar to for-profit accounting; they both follow Generally Accepted Accounting Principles (GAAP). In addition to understanding GAAP, non-profit accountants must also understand the FASB standards written specifically for these organizations as well as the tax regulations specific to those organizations. (For example, non-profit organizations are typically exempt from federal taxation.)

The accounting groups in these organizations are typically smaller than those in for-profit companies, so an employee may be responsible for more than one area of accounting (e.g., both financial statements and tax issues).

Public or private?

According to many college professors and career services counselors, most college students interested in accounting should try to start their careers in public accounting. This route carries a number of benefits, including higher salaries, more interesting and diverse work, exposure to many different industries and the ability to fulfill a requirement for certification.

One senior manager at a Big Four firm captures the general opinion of the majority of people we spoke with: "For someone just out of college, public accounting is really the only way to go," he says. "You gain experience and get up the learning curve much more quickly. A public accountant will perform three or four audits of entire companies in a year, whereas a private accountant could be stuck monitoring cash ledgers – one account – for a year. Even in the long term, there are benefits. You have more control over your career progression. In private, you'll often see highly productive and talented individuals mired in their jobs or limited to lateral career moves because they have to wait for the people above them to retire or otherwise leave the company. Public accounting is much more of a meritocracy – you'll advance as fast and as high as you want to."

However, public accounting life is not for everyone. Private accountants generally don't travel nearly as much as public accountants, and their work schedules are much more stable – they rarely have to pack a briefcase and go to a client at a moment's notice. Private accountants also do not have to deal with the chargeability issue (the pressure on public accountants to work on billable projects as much of the time as possible). Finally, they are not required to get their CPA and thus do not have to deal with the rigors of fulfilling the grueling certification requirements.

The CPA

Becoming a CPA is no easy task. It demands a higher education commitment than most other career paths. To qualify for certification, you must meet the requirements of the state or jurisdiction where you wish to practice. The state requirements are established by the state board of accountancy and vary from state to state. Because of these variations, first determine where you are planning to practice accounting and then review that state's certification requirements on the web site for the state's CPA society or board of accountancy.

Becoming a certified public accountant entails the successful completion of the following: (a) 150 credit hours of college-level education, which translates to five years of college and graduate level work; (b) achievement of passing grades on all four parts of the Uniform Certified Public Accountants Exam (the CPA exam); and (c) the requisite amount of accounting work experience as mandated by each state, often two years or so.

What you can do without becoming a CPA

You most certainly can perform accounting functions without being certified, and there are many successful people in the profession who have taken this route. Non-certified accountants are not required to fulfill the five-year requirement; they aren't even required to have a degree in accounting (although, obviously, it helps). A traditional four-year degree is all that is necessary to be a non-certified accountant. The actual functions of an accountant are not, as the saying goes, rocket science, and complicated mathematics is rarely needed; thus, advanced certification might not seem necessary. Internal auditors, management accountants and tax personnel may all practice their professions without the CPA or any other professional designation,

Furthermore, many accounting professionals (CPAs and otherwise) contend that the CPA exam is nothing more than a rite of passage, an intense exercise in memorization that adds little actual value to your technical development as an accountant. These people generally feel that all of the information you crammed into your brain disappears once the exam is over. Many of them even said that this "brain drain" should happen since much of this information will never be seen in your actual practice; if you ever do need it, you can quickly look it up.

Visit Vault at **www.vault.com** for insider company profiles, expert advice, career message boards, expert resume reviews, the Vault Job Board and more.

V∆ULT CAREER LIBRARY **85**

What you can't do

However, not being certified has a few significant drawbacks. Foremost among these is that it can be career limiting – most public accounting firms will not promote an auditor above a certain level (senior associate; these levels are discussed later in this guide) without at least passing the exam.

There are a couple of important reasons for this. First, only a CPA may sign an audit opinion. This signature is crucial, as it signifies that the auditor believes that the financial statements reasonably represent the company's actual financial position, giving the users of these statements more confidence that they can rely on them to make their decisions. Thus, an auditor without a CPA can not perform one of the most important activities of the profession.

Furthermore, a failure to pursue certification is often interpreted by public accounting firms as a lack of commitment to the profession, and few firms are willing to invest resources in someone who might leave the profession altogether (especially when there are so many others out there who are willing to pursue certification).

Another downside of not having a CPA is that you would miss out on the credibility that the certification carries. As with other advanced professional certifications, the CPA tends to give the stamp of "expert" in the eyes of the public and thus more perceived confidence in the accountant's abilities. Such credibility could mean the difference to a recruiter who's deciding between two otherwise comparable job candidates.

One final, ever-so-important downside of not having a CPA: you'll make less money. According to the staffing agency Robert Half International, the CPA can, on average, increase a candidate's base salary by 10 percent, with specialized fields (such as forensic accounting) commanding even higher salaries.

Now, this is not meant to scare you into pursuing the CPA, nor is it meant to suggest that you are a slacker if you don't pursue the CPA. You can still have a successful career in accounting without it. For example, public tax accountants generally do not sign off on audit opinions, and tax returns generally do not require the signature of a CPA. However, pursuing the CPA opens you up to many more opportunities and can only help a career in accounting. Thus, plans for certification should be seriously considered by anyone looking to break into the accounting field.

Employer Directory

Deloitte

Deloitte.

1633 Broadway
New York, New York 10013-6754

All candidate are to submit to opportunities via our career website located at www.deloitte.com/careers

Deloitte, one of the nation's leading professional services firms, provides audit, tax, consulting, and financial advisory services through nearly 30,000 people in more than 80 U.S. cities. Known as an employer of choice for innovative human resources programs, the firm is dedicated to helping its clients and its people excel. "Deloitte" refers to the associated partnerships of Deloitte & Touche USA LLP (Deloitte & Touche LLP and Deloitte Consulting LLP) and subsidiaries. Deloitte is the U.S. member firm of Deloitte Touche Tohmatsu.

BDO Seidman LLP

180 N. Stetson., Ste. 4300
Chicago, IL 60601
Phone: (312) 240-1236
Fax: (312) 240-3329
www.bdo.com

BKD LLP

Hammons Tower
901 E. St. Louis Street, Suite 1800
P.O. Box 1900
Springfield, MO 65801-1900
Phone: (417) 831-7283
Fax: (417) 831-4763
www.bkd.com

Clifton Gunderson LLP

301 SW Adams Street
Suite 600
Phone: (309) 671-4560
Fax: (309) 671-4576
www.cliftoncpa.com

Crowe Chizek and Company LLC

330 East Jefferson Boulevard
South Bend, IN 46624-0007
Phone: (574) 232-3992
Fax: (574) 236-8692
www.crowechizek.com

Deloitte & Touche LLP

1633 Broadway
New York, NY 10019
Phone: (212) 492-4000
Fax: (212) 492-4154
www.deloitte.com

Ernst & Young LLP

5 Times Square
New York, NY 10036
Phone: (212) 773-3000
Fax: (212) 773-6350
www.ey.com

Visit Vault at **www.vault.com** for insider company profiles, expert advice, career message boards, expert resume reviews, the Vault Job Board and more.

VAULT CAREER LIBRARY

87

Grant Thornton LLP
175 West Jackson Boulevard
20th Floor
Chicago, IL 60604
Phone: (312) 856-0001
Fax: (312) 565-4719
www.grantthornton.com

KPMG LLP
345 Park Avenue
New York, NY 10154
Phone: (212) 758-9700
Fax: (212) 758-9819
www.kpmg.com

McGladrey & Pullen LLP
3600 American Blvd. West
Third Floor
Bloomington, MN 55431-1082
Phone: (952) 835-9930
Fax: (952) 921-7702
www.mcgladrey.com

Moss Adams LLP
1001 Fourth Avenue
31st Floor
Seattle, WA 98154-1199
Phone: (206) 223-1820
Fax: (206) 652-2098
www.mossadams.com

Plante & Moran PLLC
27400 Northwestern Highway
Southfield, MI 48034
Phone: (248) 352-2500
Fax: (248) 352-0018
www.plantemoran.com

PricewaterhouseCoopers LLP
1301 Avenue of the Americas
New York, NY 10019-6022
Phone: (646) 471-4000
Fax: (646) 471-3188
www.pwcglobal.com/us

Advertising

An Introduction to Advertising

The concept of advertising existed long before we had a term for it. In 981A.D. the great Viking explorer Eric the Red left Norway to survey an island west of Iceland. Except for the southern coast this new land was little more than a gigantic iceberg. But Eric was a natural at advertising. To persuade immigrants to leave Norway and settle the island, he painted a picture of temperate climate, rolling meadows and lush farmland. To top it all off, he named it Greenland. Eric created a brand. Hundreds of land-starved Vikings boarded longships and headed west for this so-called "greenland."

Advertising is defined as the art of positioning and creating brands and persuading consumers to buy them through messages in mass media. The clothes you wear, the cars you drive, the food you eat and the soft drinks you consume are all brands.

Advertising is a creative and inclusive field unique in the business world. "Advertising agencies are idea stores, and just about everyone gets in on the act," says Chuck Bachrach, media director of the Los Angeles-based full-service advertising agency Rubin Postaer and Associates. "If you have a fire in your belly and want to work with smart, creative, fun people in a business that's virtually blind to race and gender, there's no business quite as satisfying."

Branding

David Ogilvy, founder of Ogilvy & Mather, knew something about brands, having created icons like The American Express Card and Rolls Royce. He defined a brand as: "The intangible sum of a product's attributes: its name, packaging, and price, its history, its reputation and the way it's advertised." The best way to understand a brand is to think of it as a friend. We choose brands in exactly the same way we choose friends. Brands are friends; products are strangers. Branding is an emotional process of involvement.

At its most basic level advertising, like friendship, is a three-stage process – awareness, trial and repeat. In the first stage, awareness, you hear about a brand. In the second stage, trial, you're persuaded to buy it and try it. If you like it, you buy it again and again. You're a repeat customer. Along the way, you find that you and the brand share the same values. You wouldn't think about using anything else.

A brand is an image, a conception in consumers' minds. Implicit within the image is a unique promise of value and trust that distinguishes it from its competitors. The job of an advertising agency is to use every tool at its disposal to clothe the brand with substance and endow it with personality – to make it a trusted friend.

Visit Vault at www.vault.com for insider company profiles, expert advice, career message boards, expert resume reviews, the Vault Job Board and more.

VAULT CAREER LIBRARY 89

Media Options

Once an advertising campaign is constructed, it needs to be, well, advertised. Here are the primary conduits for advertising.

Television

Network television: A network is any group of local television stations electronically joined to broadcast the same program at the same time. Network TV is essential for advertising national brands and reaches an audience of 99 percent of U.S. TV households. It offers advertisers a large choice of programs, each with their own demographics, ranging from Saturday morning children's shows to news and sports, to soap operas and prime time shows.

Spot television: Spot television is the purchase of advertising time on a market-by-market basis. Perhaps a brand has only recently entered a new geographic market and needs an advertising branding push only in that location. Or maybe the brand is only available or distributed in a select number of markets (e.g, In-n-out Burgers, a fast-food chain, is only located in California, Nevada and Arizona). In such cases, spot television makes sense. Additionally, buys can incorporate specific market characteristics. For example, viewing levels increase in cold weather markets during the winter, as Northerners cuddle in front of the cozy electronic hearth that is the television set.

Cable television: Introduced in 1960 to improve reception in remote areas, cable television now rivals the networks for audience. According to a lead researcher at Viacom, almost 84 percent of all television homes receive cable – that's 91 million homes! Cable TV provides advertisers with fairly precise demographic, psychographic and geographic targeting, and a more affluent audience than broadcast television because it only exists in households that can afford it. (Demographics are a basic, objective descriptive classification of consumers, such as their age, sex, income, education, size of household, ownership of home and so on.) Most cable TV channels are programmed for narrowcasting – attracting a specific demographic or interest. ESPN is all sports all the time. Animal Planet is designed for animal lovers. AMC aims for aficionados of old movies. If there's an interest with a sufficient audience, you can bet there is or will be a cable channel devoted to it, and advertisers wanting to reach that audience. Cable programs don't attract as many viewers, but wasted audience – those who fall outside of the demographic or interest group – is minimal.

Print advertising

There are three types of print advertising media – consumer magazines, trade magazines and national and local newspapers.

Magazines have a great deal to offer advertisers, with ads that have a long shelf life. Unlike with TV, readers take their time with a magazine. They refer back to it from time to time, increasing ad exposure opportunities, and they can, and often do, pass magazines on to friends and relatives.

Consumer magazines: In these publications, the editorial content appeals to the general public or a specific segment of the public. Educated and affluent consumers tend to be heavy magazine readers and light TV viewers. Consumer magazines offer audience selectivity. They can deliver a defined segment with a minimum of "wasted" (nontargeted) delivery. There are entire magazines devoted to particular subjects (e.g., *Road & Track*, *Golf Digest*, and so on). Magazines also sometimes offer regular features devoted to particular subjects that interest advertisers. For example, *The New Yorker* may offer an issue with a special travel section. Airlines, car rental companies and hotel advertisers in the featured area use the issue to target consumers.

There is an adage in the advertising industry: "The more you tell, the more you sell." Magazines offer room for long, detailed copy and are the perfect environments for products, like drugs or electronic devices, that require extended explanations.

Trade magazines: Aimed at professionals in a particular industry, these magazines are typically not carried on mainstream newsstands, though there are exceptions, such as *Variety* (for media industry insiders).

Newspapers: People get involved with what affects them personally – in their neighborhoods, at their workplace – and newspapers give them that local information more than any other media vehicle. Smart media buyers leverage these opportunities. Sections like these are replete with ads. Typical newspaper readers are college-educated, in their mid-forties, and a very attractive audience to automotive, electronics and travel advertisers. National newspapers like *The Wall Street Journal* and *USA Today*, and local papers like the *San Francisco Chronicle* or the *Washington Post*, offer a variety of advantages to advertisers. Newspapers are a perfect medium for limited time offers and new product announcements. They underscore the axiom that all advertising is local. Research shows that an ad in the *Charlotte Observer* that mentions Charlotte in the headline will attract more attention than an otherwise identical ad that omits the name of the city in the headline. And, just as in magazines, there is plenty of room for long, detailed copy required for technically oriented brands, like high performance automobiles.

Radio

Radio can be a useful part of a media plan. Like television, radio (AM & FM) is divided into network and spot (local). And like cable TV, it's narrowcasted – it offers stations that play music in virtually every flavor, talk shows, sports programs and news channels. But unlike its broadcast sibling, radio only offers sound, so you can't see the product. In addition, consumers often listen to the radio when they are driving or away from their homes, so they may not absorb the information as readily.

But radio also is much less expensive than TV. Its single dimension – sound – forces copywriters to stimulate the listener's imagination. The average radio station plays up to twenty radio commercials in an hour. In order to break through the "wallpaper" of background noise, intrusive delivery is everything. Music, pacing, humor, audio mnemonic devices – the Green Giant's "Ho, ho, ho,"0 for example – are employed to capture the listeners attention. Some advertisers even use the weather to their advantage. Coca-Cola and other soft drink marketers have issued standing orders for commercials to be played when the temperature reaches 90 degrees. In a media plan, radio ads can target audiences at a relatively low

Visit Vault at **www.vault.com** for insider company profiles, expert advice, career message boards, expert resume reviews, the Vault Job Board and more.

V∧ULT CAREER LIBRARY   **91**

cost. It's also a good way to "surround" consumers with a brand; not as effective by itself, but useful as a way to increase brand recognition and affection.

Out-of-Home

Out-of-home advertising ranges from billboards to bus signs to kiosks to spectacular signs in Times Square. It's used not to build but to reinforce an ad campaign. Only one copy point, or benefit, can be registered.

Major Career Paths in Advertising

Account services

Account services professionals manage the relationship between the agency and the client. They are the first line of contact with the client – and the first line of defense. Essentially, they are the project managers for advertising client accounts.

The account services hierarchy ranges from account coordinator at the entry level, to account directors (also called management supervisors) who oversee one or more client relationships in their entirety. Account services people are marketing and communications consultants; they must know as much about the brand as the client, and more about how to advertise it.

Successful account services pros must be all of the following.

- **Integrators**. Account people craft the communications marketing plan and insure that all of the agency's resources are working together to make the plan a reality.

- **Organized**. Account services professionals are detail-oriented, and masters of multi-tasking and following up. They are keepers of the overall timetable for ad production, placement and communication.

- **Generalists**. They must have a working knowledge of every agency discipline ranging from evaluating copy and art to media and production.

- **Advocates**. They are the client's advocate within the agency, and the agency's advocate to the client. Diplomacy and eloquence are key.

- **Students and lovers of advertising**. They must immerse themselves in advertising and marketing and learn the lessons of past and current successes and failures.

- **Cheerleaders**. As leaders of the team, account people must be superb "people" people, exhibiting grace under pressure. "When everyone's walking around moping because the client hates the new campaign, or there's been a screw up somewhere, it's my job to get everyone back on track. In account services, the glass is always half full," an account supervisor at a large agency notes (cheerfully).

Media services

Broadly, media services is responsible for the planning and buying of print, broadcast, out-of-home (billboards) and interactive media in the most effective and efficient way possible. Media planners are the strategists – they determine when and where it's most advantageous to buy advertising space for any given campaign. Buyers actually negotiate for, and purchase, the media space.

But that's hardly the whole story. These media specialists are also key members of the advertising branding team. They must find environments that extend and reinforce the brand image of their clients – and buy space for advertising those brands. Armed with consumer research, both proprietary and purchased, media professionals not only know the target audience's media habits – the programs they watch and listen to, the magazines and newspapers they read – they also know what influences consumers to make purchasing decisions. Purchase decision influencers are people who have a lot of influence over the purchase but aren't the "target market." For example, while men may purchase suits, women have significant influence over which suits their male partners and companions buy.

The result of their research and work is the media plan for the advertising campaign. Major media outlets will then compete to get on the plan (that is, to secure a portion of the client's ad budget for their magazine or television network or newspaper). The plan itself contains recommendations on where the client should spend their media budget to achieve the campaign's goals in the most efficient way. The plan outlines how many people the media recommendation reaches, how many times the commercial or print ad will run, and the total audience impressions the plan will attract.

Once the plan is approved, media vehicles like television stations, newspapers and magazines that weren't included in the plan fight to get included. So, in the midst of a buy, buyers not only have to contend with the job of purchasing media, they also have to entertain presentations from disappointed media sales reps. Media buyers, especially, frequently socialize with sales representatives from media organizations on a regular basis.

Creative services

Many people outside of the industry view creative as the "romantic" part of the business. Romantic and exciting though it may seem, copywriting and art direction is hard work. Creative services jobs are indeed exciting, but failure is easy to come by.

Once the creative strategy is set (by the account services folks) and approved by the client, and once the consumer research has been transformed into a media plan, it's time for the Big Idea – a creative translation of the strategy into a compelling and persuasive ad. And there is nothing more difficult than facing a hard deadline and sitting at a desk, well into the night, staring at a blank sheet of paper, in an office littered with balled up sheets of paper, while thinking, "Lord, send me an idea!"

Copywriters, who write the copy (words, script, whatever) and art directors, who visually design the ads, work as a team. Together, they create ads, not only for the current campaigns but for "back up" – campaigns that are continually tested in the event that the current advertising loses its effectiveness, or "wears out" – campaigns as well.

Visit Vault at **www.vault.com** for insider company profiles, expert advice, career message boards, expert resume reviews, the Vault Job Board and more.

VAULT CAREER LIBRARY   93

The creative process, for new ads, is initiated by the client.   Let's say the client calls the account executive and requests a four-color ad for Modern Maturity magazine. The account executive writes a creative strategy statement for the ad (obviously aimed at an older audience) and takes it to the creative supervisor.   The creative supervisor assigns the ad to a copywriter and art director team with a due date.   Once the ad is completed and approved internally, the copy and layout are presented to the client.

Account planning/research

Account planning, an import from British advertising agencies, is a relatively new discipline in the United States.   Most of the larger agencies and many of the smaller ones have embraced it.   Account planning uses qualitative research to determine why consumers behave the way they do.   Planners function as the voice of the consumer within the agency, and their main goal is to gain a deeper understanding of the way consumers react to their clients' product or service.   Planners burrow into the consumer's mind, plumbing for insights about the product, its position and competition, and research is their tool.   They live with the brand and its consumers. The insights they gain are considered the target market's psychographics – their attitudes, opinions and values.   These consumer psychographics help copywriters and art directors create more effective advertising.

Traffic

Traffic managers are the keepers of the creative process – schedules and approvals reside in their domain. If account services professionals are like the generals, setting and managing the overall strategy, traffickers are the foot soldiers and work with creative, media and the account group to insure that all deadlines are met.   Print publications and broadcast stations have unchangeable closing dates.   In addition, it's traffic's responsibility to see that the ads are approved at every stage of their development and forwarded to the media on time.   Successful traffic managers are organized, detail-oriented and able to work under pressure.   It is a difficult, highly stressful job.

Production

There are two types of production specialists at advertising agencies – print and broadcast.   Print production specialists are schooled in every aspect of the print production process and are experts at making ads look great in magazines, newspapers and out-of-home venues.   Most print production advertising professionals are hired from printing companies and other graphic design outlets.

Broadcast producers are in charge of the actual production of TV and radio commercials.   They work closely with the creative department to select directors, production facilities, talent, music and just about every other aspect of broadcast production.   Like their sisters and brothers in print production, broadcast producers are well-organized, able to work well under pressure, and experts at their craft.

Employer Directory

Arnold Worldwide

101 Huntington Ave.

Boston, MA 02199

Phone: (617) 587-8000

Fax: (617) 587-8070

www.arnoldworldwidepartners.com

BBDO Worldwide

1285 Avenue of the Americas

New York, NY 10019

Phone: (212) 459-5000

Fax: (212) 459-6645

www.bbdo.com

Cliff Freeman and Partners

375 Hudson St.

New York, NY 10014

Phone: (212) 463-3200

Fax: (212) 463-3225

www.clifffreeman.com

DDB Worldwide

437 Madison Ave.

New York, NY 10022

Phone: (212) 415-2000

Fax: (212) 415-3414

www.ddb.com

Dentsu

1-11-10 Tsukji

Chuo-ku

Tokyo, 104-8426

Phone: +81-3-5551-5111

Fax: +81-3-5551-2013

www.dentsu.co.jp

FCB Worldwide

150 E. 42nd St.

New York, NY 10017

Phone: (212) 885-3000

Fax: (212) 885-3918

www.fcb.com

Grey Worldwide

777 Third Ave.

New York, NY 10017

Phone: (212) 537-3700

Fax: (212) 537-3533

www.greydirect.com

J. Walter Thompson Co.

466 Lexington Ave.

New York, NY 10017

Phone: (212) 210-7000

Fax: (212) 210-7770

www.jwt.com

Leo Burnett Co.

35 West Wacker Drive

Chicago, IL 60601

Phone: (312) 220-5959

Fax: (312) 220-3299

www.leoburnett.com

Mad Dogs & Englishmen

126 Fifth Avenue

New York, NY 10011

Phone: (212) 675-6116

Fax: (212) 675-0340

www.maddogsandenglishmen.com

McCann World Group

622 3rd Ave.

New York, NY 10017

Phone: (646) 865-2000

Fax: (646) 487-9610

Ogilvy & Mather

Worldwide Plaza, 309 W. 49th St.

New York, NY 10019-7399

Phone: (212) 237-4000

Fax: (212) 237-5123

www.ogilvy.com

Visit Vault at **www.vault.com** for insider company profiles, expert advice, career message boards, expert resume reviews, the Vault Job Board and more.

VAULT CAREER LIBRARY   95

Saatchi & Saatchi
375 Hudson Street
New York, NY 10014
Phone: (212) 463-2000
Fax: (212) 463-9855
www.saatchi-saatchi.com

Young & Rubicam (Y&R Advertising)
285 Madison Ave.
New York, NY 10017
Phone: (212) 210-3000
Fax: (212) 210-4680
www.youngandrubicam.com

Aerospace & Defense

Industry Outlook

The aerospace and defense industry immediately felt the impact of the attacks of September 11 and the war on terrorism that followed. The severe economic blow to the commercial airlines led to a sharp decline in orders for new planes after 2001. And in 2002, the top 10 commercial airlines – which place the orders for these aircraft when business is good – lost more than $12 billion, with key players like United Airlines' parent company UAL and US Airways filing for bankruptcy. All of this has resulted in an anticipated 18 percent decrease in overall employment for aerospace products and parts manufacturing between 2002 and 2012 (compared to a projected 16 percent growth for all industries combined), according to the Bureau of Labor Statistics (BLS). Though there are signs that business is at least stabilizing, in 2004, total sales for civilian and military planes were expected to grow by less than one percent, to $148 billion – down $7 billion from 2002, according to the Aerospace Industries Association.

Drumming up defense

At the same time, since 2001, military action in Afghanistan and Iraq, as well as an increased need for U.S. defense, has led to stepped-up demand for military aircraft, missiles and defense contractors. In fiscal year 2004, for example, the Pentagon boosted its budget for procurement and research and development by 8 percent. While this trend is predicted to slow in coming years, defense budgets overall should continue to grow between 4 percent and 6 percent through the end of the decade, according to an analysis from *BusinessWeek Online*. As military equipment continues to age, manufacturers are calling for increased attention to R&D and procurement.

Bidding for planes

Traditionally, the federal government has been the aerospace industry's largest customer. There were about 2,800 establishments in the aerospace industry as of 2002, according to BLS. Of these firms, a handful fly above the crowd, reaping contracts from the Department of Defense after submitting to a competitive bidding process. The amount of time elapsing from the DOD's initial call for military aircraft or missile systems – through the bidding system and on into production of a prototype, approval, production of the equipment and delivery – can be several years. This time span has been trimmed in recent years, however, owing to new computer-aided design (CAD) technologies which bring the design of equipment into the virtual realm.

The bulk of the industry is taken up by firms producing civil (non-military) aircraft, including planes for commercial airlines and cargo transportation, as well as those for general aviation, like leisure planes and corporate jets. The sector also includes the production of military aircraft and helicopters, along with guided missiles and missile propulsion units. But not all of this equipment is used to serve defense purposes – it also covers space vehicles and the rockets that launch them. This industry also spans the seas, with shipbuilding added to the mix – in fact, analysts anticipate strong growth in this area as ships with average life spans of 30 years are phased out and replaced.

Visit Vault at **www.vault.com** for insider company profiles, expert advice, career message boards, expert resume reviews, the Vault Job Board and more.

VAULT CAREER LIBRARY 97

The commercial sector

In the private sector, commercial airlines and private businesses specify their requirements and then invite manufacturers to submit bids. Usually, a new aircraft won't go into production until a large contract is secured. For example, in April 2004, Boeing finally got the OK to start cranking out its new 7E7 Dreamliner commercial planes after sealing a deal worth approximately $6 billion with Japanese carrier Al Nippon Airways, which placed an order for 50 of the fuel-efficient flyers – the largest launch order ever for a new Boeing jet. Reportedly, the Dreamliner fleet could enter service by 2008. The efficiency of the Dreamliner – said to offer 20 percent more fuel efficiency over Boeing's 767 jet – could draw new airlines like JetBlue to the table to increase their competitiveness in the cutthroat low-cost carrier arena, observers say.

High flyers

Traditionally, Boeing has run neck-and-neck with rival Airbus for dominance of the aircraft manufacturing sector. Both giants have stumbled since 2001, with Boeing's aircraft orders plummeting by 45 percent and Airbus' by 28 percent during that year alone. The shaky situation led Boeing to slash 30,000 jobs, or about 30 percent of its commercial aircraft workforce, in 2002.

But both are bouncing back, albeit slowly – Airbus, based in Europe, is in the development process for the world's biggest jetliner, the 555-seat A380, expected to soar in 2006. So far, the company has around 130 orders for the jet. A historic market shift for the two industry giants began in 2003, when Airbus for the first time delivered more airplanes than Boeing for the year – 300, compared to 280 from Boeing, according to *BusinessWeek*.

Still, Boeing, with its wealth of (sometimes controversial) defense contracts in addition to its commercial airplane business, dominates the aerospace and defense industry as a whole, followed, in order of sales, by European Aeronautic Defence and Space Company, Lockheed Martin Corporation, Airbus, and Northrop Grumman Corporation. Other major players in the sector include Raytheon Corporation and the National Aeronautics and Space Corporation (more familiarly known as NASA).

In the industry's regional aircraft market (defined as planes with less than 100 seats), Bombardier, Gulfstream, and Textron's Cessna unit dominate. GE Aircraft Engines, Pratt & Whitney, and Rolls Royce are tops among manufacturers of jet engines.

Dominating defense

In the area of defense contractors specifically, Lockheed Martin and Northrop Grumman lead the pack, followed by Boeing, Raytheon, and BAE Systems. Lockheed maintains a healthy dominance in the sector thanks in part to its score of one of the richest defense deals in history, when in 2001 it beat out Boeing for a fighter jet contract worth $200 billion. More recently, though, Boeing was the winner over Lockheed for a contract to build a new submarine-hunting airplane for the Navy in a June 2004 contract estimated at up to $15 billion over 10 years. Boeing will subcontract with fellow defense heavies Northrop Grumman and Raytheon on the project. Controversy dogged Boeing in 2003 following an Air Force tanker deal that drew intense Congressional scrutiny.

The defense portion of the industry has been affected not only by the call to arms following the U.S. terror attacks, but also mega mergers and a shift in the way warfare is practiced. In 2002, the aerospace and defense industry spent about $30 billion on M&A. Northrop Grumman has been the most aggressive player, according to Hoover's, acquiring both Litton Industries and Newport News Shipbuilding in 2001 and TRW in 2002.

Since the Cold War, priorities among Pentagon types have shifted, from a philosophy of overwhelming force to a focus on equipment that's smarter, leaner, and more mobile. For instance, the firm General Atomics saw success in Afghanistan with the use of its unmanned Predator drones. Unmanned jets and other computer-guided equipment are seen as preferable to the traditional manned craft, being less costly to operate and posing less risk to military personnel in combat. Other buzz on the war front of the industry concerns "network-centric warfare," an area the top defense contractors have shifted resources toward in recent years. In this approach, computers, satellites, and sensors are all integrated so that soldiers and their planes, tanks and other equipment get a constant stream of precise, real-time information about what's happening on the front lines. One example is General Dynamics Corp., traditionally known as a manufacturer of ships and tanks, which told *BusinessWeek* its IT systems and technology operations alone would make up a third of total revenues in 2004.

A new world for defense

Another major shift in the defense industry since 2001 is the growth of companies focusing on homeland security. This sector includes everything from audio and video surveillance equipment, to disease and bioterror identification, to secure communications equipment. In addition, the Pentagon is increasingly – and controversially – relying on manpower from private military contractors (PMCs) to bolster its missions in Iraq, Afghanistan, and elsewhere. These projects might include rebuilding power and sanitation systems and other logistical support, or (more notoriously) conducting interrogations and security operations. While the military outsourced just one percent of its work, mainly for airfield maintenance, during the first Gulf War in the 1990s, contractors are handling as much as 30 percent of the military's services, including reconstruction, during the ongoing activities in Iraq today, according to Brookings Institution fellow P.W. Singer. These contractors include well-known giants like Kellogg Brown & Root (Halliburton), with a $3.97 billion contract for oil field reconstruction and maintenance in Iraq, and smaller PMCs. These latter companies are catching the eye of traditional aerospace and defense giants like Northrop Grumman, which recently acquired smaller PMC Vinnell. But all PMCs are catching the eye of Congress, the media and the public, who question the oversight of these companies and wonder if the military should be outsourcing so much of its operations to people who, in some cases, are seen as "mercenaries."

The final frontier

In the space sector, made up of manufacturers of satellites and rocket manufacturing and launch services, familiar names lead the pack, including Boeing, Lockheed Martin, and Northrop Grumman. In fact, according to Hoover's, major aerospace and defense companies continue to build space activities into their long-term investment plans – even though shooting for the stars isn't very profitable in the near-term. Other, more specialized leaders include Alcatel Space, Astrium, Orbital Sciences, and Arianespace.

These star players are keeping an eye on a pack of upstarts in the space race, private companies that rely on individual investors rather than federal dollars. If successful, these private liftoff firms promise to radically alter the space exploration game by stripping it of the costs, bureaucracy, and other padding that often accrue to federally funded projects. June 2004 saw the historic liftoff of SpaceShipOne, the first privately funded rocket. Later in 2004, an

Visit Vault at **www.vault.com** for insider company profiles, expert advice, career message boards, expert resume reviews, the Vault Job Board and more.

VAULT CAREER LIBRARY   99

unmanned rocket built by a small California company was set to carry an experimental satellite into orbit for the Defense Department in a project involving no federal dollars. The Bush Administration has come out in favor of increased involvement by such private companies in missions to send people to the moon and, one day, to Mars. In addition to these types of missions, many space visionaries – some of whom formerly headed the dot-com pack back in the Internet boom days – see all sorts of opportunities up beyond the clouds, ranging from tourism to mining for precious metals.

The employment outlook

Professionals who work in the aerospace product and parts manufacturing sector, the BLS reports, enjoy earnings that are substantially higher, on average, than those of their counterparts in other manufacturing sectors. Most jobs in the sector are in the areas of skilled production and management. The BLS reports that in 2002, 64 percent of jobs in aerospace manufacturing were in large establishments employing 1,000 or more workers.

Employer Directory

The Boeing Company

Boeing World Headquarters
100 N. Riverside
Chicago, IL 60606
www.boeing.com/employment/college

With a heritage that mirrors the first 100 years of flight, The Boeing Company provides products and services to customers in 145 countries. Boeing is a premier manufacturer of commercial jetliners and a global market leader in military aircraft, satellites, missile defense, human space flight, and launch systems and services. Total company revenues for 2003 were $50.5 billion.

Boeing employs more than 156,000 people in 70 countries and 48 states within the United States, with major operations in the Puget Sound area of Washington state, Southern California, Wichita and St. Louis.

EOE statement: Boeing is an equal opportunity employer supporting diversity in the workplace.

BAE Systems

Warwick House, PO Box 87, Farnborough Aerospace Center
Farnborough
Hampshire GU14 6YU, United Kingdom
Phone: +44-1252 373232
Fax: +44-1252 383000
www.baesystems.com

General Dynamics Corporation

3190 Fairview Park Dr.
Falls Church, VA 22042-4523
Phone: (703) 876-3000
Fax: (703) 876-3125
www.gendyn.com

General Electric Company

3135 Easton Tpke.
Fairfield, CT 06828-0001
Phone: (203) 373-2211
Fax: (203) 373 3131
www.ge.com

Honeywell International Inc.

101 Columbia Rd.
Morristown, NJ 07962-1219
Phone: (973) 455-2000
Fax: (973) 455-4807
www.honeywell.com

L-3 Communications Holdings

600 3rd Ave.
New York, NY 10016
Phone: (212) 697-1111
Fax: (212) 867-5249
www.L-3Com.com

Lockheed Martin

6801 Rockledge Dr.
Bethesda, MD 20817-1877
Phone: (301) 897-6000
Fax: (301) 897-6704
www.lockheedmartin.com

Northrop Grumman Corporation

1840 Century Park East
Los Angeles, CA 90067-2199
Phone: (310) 553-6262
Fax: (310) 553-2076
www.northgrum.com

Parker Hannifin Corporation

6035 Parkland Blvd.
Cleveland, OH 44124-4141
Phone: (216) 896-3000
Fax: (216) 896-4000
www.parker.com

Visit Vault at **www.vault.com** for insider company profiles, expert advice, career message boards, expert resume reviews, the Vault Job Board and more.

VAULT CAREER LIBRARY **101**

Raytheon Company

870 Winter St.

Waltham, MA 02451-1449

Phone: (781) 522-3000

Fax: (781) 522-3001

www.raytheon.com

Textron Inc.

40 Westminster St.

Providence, RI 02903-2596

Phone: (401) 421-2800

Fax: (401) 421-2878

www.textron.com

United Technologies Corporation

One Financial Plaza

Hartford, CT 06103

Phone: (860) 728-7000

Fax: (860) 728-7979

www.utc.com

Visit Vault at **www.vault.com** for insider company profiles, expert advice, career message boards, expert resume reviews, the Vault Job Board and more.

VAULT CAREER LIBRARY 103

Where do the best ideas come from?

From people who value originality, hard thinking, hard work and common sense. If we've built a reputation as the one firm for ingenious solutions to complex problems — it's because our people don't stop till they find them.

A great deal depends on working with the right people.^{sm}

bearstearns.com

EQUITIES   FIXED INCOME   GLOBAL CLEARING   INVESTMENT BANKING   WEALTH MANAGEMENT

Banking

Investment Banking

Investment banking is the business of raising money for companies. Companies need capital in order to grow their business; they turn to investment banks to sell securities to investors – either public or private – to raise this capital. These securities come in the form of stocks or bonds.

Generally, an investment bank is comprised of the following areas:

Corporate finance

The bread and butter of a traditional investment bank, corporate finance generally performs two different functions: 1) mergers and acquisitions advisory and 2) underwriting. On the mergers and acquisitions (M&A) advising side of corporate finance, bankers assist in negotiating and structuring a merger between two companies. If, for example, a company wants to buy another firm, then an investment bank will help finalize the purchase price, structure the deal and generally ensure a smooth transaction. The underwriting function within corporate finance involves raising capital for a client. In the investment-banking world, capital can be raised by selling either stocks or bonds to investors.

Sales

Sales is another core component of the investment bank. Salespeople take the form of: 1) the classic retail broker, 2) the institutional salesperson or 3) the private client service representative. Brokers develop relationships with individual investors and sell stocks and stock advice to the average Joe. Institutional salespeople develop business relationships with large institutional investors. Institutional investors are those who manage large groups of assets, like pension funds or mutual funds. Private Client Service (PCS) representatives lie somewhere between retail brokers and institutional salespeople, providing brokerage and money management services for extremely wealthy individuals. Salespeople make money through commissions on trades made through their firms.

Trading

Traders also provide a vital role for the investment bank. Traders facilitate the buying and selling of stock, bonds or other securities, either by carrying an inventory of securities for sale or by executing a given trade for a client. Traders deal with transactions large and small and provide liquidity (the ability to buy and sell securities) for the market. (This is often called making a market.) Traders make money by purchasing securities and selling them at a slightly higher price. This price differential is called the "bid-ask spread."

Visit Vault at **www.vault.com** for insider company profiles, expert advice, career message boards, expert resume reviews, the Vault Job Board and more.

VAULT CAREER LIBRARY   105

Research

Research analysts follow stocks and bonds and make recommendations on whether to buy, sell or hold those securities. Stock analysts (known as equity analysts) typically focus on one industry and will cover up to 20 companies' stocks at any given time. Some research analysts work on the fixed-income side and will cover a particular segment, such as high-yield bonds or U.S. Treasury bonds. Salespeople within the I-bank utilize research published by analysts to convince their clients to buy or sell securities through their firm. Corporate finance bankers rely on research analysts to be experts in the industry in which they are working. Reputable research analysts can generate substantial corporate finance business and substantial trading activity and thus are an integral part of any investment bank.

Syndicate

The hub of the investment-banking wheel, syndicate provides a vital link between salespeople and corporate finance. Syndicate exists to facilitate the placing of securities in a public offering, a knock-down, drag-out affair between and among buyers of offerings and the investment banks managing the process. In a corporate or municipal debt deal, syndicate also determines the allocation of bonds.

Commercial Banking

"Neither a borrower nor a lender be," Polonius advises Laertes in Hamlet. Good thing commercial banks haven't taken Shakespearean bromides to heart. (It didn't get Polonius anywhere, either.) Commercial banks, unlike investment banks, generally act as lenders, putting forth their own money to support businesses as opposed to investment advisors who rely on other folks – buyers of stocks and bonds – to pony up cash. This distinction, enshrined by fundamental banking laws in place since the 1930s, has led to noticeable cultural differences (exaggerated by stereotype) between commercial and investment bankers.

Commercial bankers (deservedly or not) have a reputation for being less aggressive, more risk-averse and simply not as mean as investment bankers. Commercial bankers also don't command the eye-popping salaries and elite prestige that I-bankers receive.

There is a basis for the stereotype. Commercial banks carefully screen borrowers because the banks are investing huge sums of their own money in companies that must remain healthy enough to make regular loan payments for decades. Investment bankers, on the other hand, can make their fortunes in one day by skimming off some of the money raised in a stock offering or invested into an acquisition. While a borrower's subsequent business decline can damage a commercial bank's bottom line, a stock that plummets after an offering has no effect on the investment bank that managed its IPO.

We'll take your money

Commercial bankers make money by their legal charter to take deposits from businesses and consumers. To gain the confidence of these depositors, commercial banks offer government-sponsored guarantees on these deposits on amounts up to $100,000. But to get FDIC guarantees, commercial banks must follow a myriad of regulations (and hire regulators to manage them). Many of these guidelines were set up in the Glass-Steagall Act of 1933, which was meant to separate the activities of commercial and investment banks. Glass-Steagall included a restriction on the sale of stocks and bonds (investment banks, which could not take deposits, were exempt from banking laws and free to offer more speculative securities offerings). Deregulation – especially the Financial Services Modernization Act of 1999 – and consolidation in the banking industry over the past decade have weakened these traditional barriers.

The lending train

The typical commercial banking process is fairly straightforward. The lending cycle starts with consumers depositing savings or businesses depositing sales proceeds at the bank. The bank, in turn, puts aside a relatively small portion of the money for withdrawals and to pay for possible loan defaults. The bank then loans the rest of the money to companies in need of capital to pay for, say, a new factory or an overseas venture. A commercial bank's customers can range from the dry cleaner on the corner to a multinational conglomerate. For very large clients, several commercial banks may band together to issue "syndicated loans" of truly staggering size.

Commercial banks lend money at interest rates that are largely determined by the Federal Reserve Board (currently governed by the bespectacled Alan Greenspan). Along with lending money that they have on deposit from clients, commercial banks lend out money that they have received from the Fed. The Fed loans out money to commercial banks, that in turn lend it to bank customers in a variety of forms – standard loans, mortgages, and so on. Besides its ability to set a baseline interest rate for all loans, the Fed also uses its lending power to equalize the economy. To prevent inflation, the Fed raises the interest rate it charges for the money it loans to banks, slowing down the circulation of money and the growth of the economy. To encourage economic growth, the Fed will lower the interest rate it charges banks.

Making money by moving money

Take a moment to consider how a bank makes its money. Commercial banks in the U.S. earn 5 to 14 percent interest on most of their loans. As commercial banks typically only pay depositors 1 percent – if anything – on checking accounts and 2 to 3 percent on savings accounts, they make a tremendous amount of money in the difference between the cost of their funds (1 percent for checking account deposits) and the return on the funds they loan (5 to 14 percent).

Corporate Finance

Stuffy bankers?

The stereotype of the corporate finance department is stuffy, arrogant (white and male) MBAs who frequent golf courses and talk on cell-phones nonstop. While this is increasingly less true, corporate finance remains the most white-shoe department in the typical investment bank. The atmosphere in corporate

Visit Vault at **www.vault.com** for insider company profiles, expert advice, career message boards, expert resume reviews, the Vault Job Board and more.

V∧ULT CAREER LIBRARY   **107**

finance is, unlike that in sales and trading, often quiet and reserved. Junior bankers sit separated by cubicles, quietly crunching numbers.

Depending on the firm, corporate finance can also be a tough place to work, with unforgiving bankers and expectations through the roof. Although decreasing, stories of analyst abuse abound, and some bankers come down hard on new analysts to scare and intimidate them. The lifestyle for corporate finance professionals can be a killer. In fact, many corporate finance workers find that they literally dedicate their lives to the job. Social life suffers, free time disappears, and stress multiplies. It is not uncommon to find analysts and associates wearing rumpled pants and wrinkled shirts, exhibiting the wear and tear of all-nighters. Fortunately, these long hours pay remarkable dividends in the form of six-figure salaries and huge year-end bonuses.

Personality-wise, bankers tend to be highly intelligent, motivated, and not lacking in confidence. Money is important to the bankers, and many anticipate working for just a few years to earn as much as possible, before finding less demanding work. Analysts and associates tend also to be ambitious, intelligent and pedigreed. If you happen to be going into an analyst or associate position, make sure to check your ego at the door but don't be afraid to ask penetrating questions about deals and what is required of you.

The deal team

Investment bankers generally work in deal teams which, depending on the size of a deal, vary somewhat in makeup. In this chapter we will provide an overview of the roles and lifestyles of the positions in corporate finance, from analyst to managing director. (Often, a person in corporate finance is generally called an I-banker.) Because the titles and roles really do not differ significantly between underwriting to M&A, we have included both in this explanation. In fact, at most smaller firms, underwriting and transaction advisory are not separated, and bankers typically pitch whatever business they can scout out within their industry sector.

Analysts

Analysts are the grunts of the corporate finance world. They often toil endlessly with little thanks, little pay (when figured on an hourly basis), and barely enough free time to sleep four hours a night. Typically hired directly out of top undergraduate universities, this crop of bright, highly motivated kids does the financial modeling and basic entry-level duties associated with any corporate finance deal.

Modeling every night until 2 a.m. and not having much of a social life proves to be unbearable for many an analyst and after two years many analysts leave the industry. Unfortunately, many bankers recognize the transient nature of analysts, and work them hard to get the most out of them they can. The unfortunate analyst that screws up or talks back too much may never get quality work, spending his days bored until 11 p.m. waiting for work to come, stressing even more than the busy analyst. These are the analysts that do not get called to work on live transactions, and do menial work or just put together pitchbooks all the time.

When it comes to analyst pay, much depends on whether the analyst is in New York or not. In the City, salary often begins for first-year analysts at $45,000 to $55,000 per year, with an annual bonus of approximately $30,000. While this seems to be a lot for a 22-year-old with just an undergrad degree, it's not a great deal if you consider per-hour compensation. At most firms, analysts also get dinner every night for free if they work late, and have little time to spend their income, often meaning fat checking and savings accounts and ample fodder to fund business school or law school down the road. At regional firms, pay typically is 20 percent less than that of their New York counterparts. Worth noting, though, is the fact that at regional firms 1) hours are often less, and 2) the cost of living is much lower. Be wary, however, of the small regional firm or branch office of a Wall Street firm that pays at the low end of the scale and still shackles analysts to their cubicles. While the salary generally does not improve much for second-year analysts, the bonus can double for those second-years who demonstrate high performance. At this level, bonuses depend mostly on an analyst's contribution, attitude, and work ethic, as opposed to the volume of business generated by the bankers with whom he or she works.

Institutional Sales and Trading (S&T)

The war zone

If you've ever been to an investment banking trading floor, you've witnessed the chaos. It's usually a lot of swearing, yelling and flashing computer screens: a pressure cooker of stress. Sometimes the floor is a quiet rumble of activity, but when the market takes a nosedive, panic ensues and the volume kicks up a notch. Traders must rely on their market instincts, and salespeople yell for bids when the market tumbles. Deciding what to buy or sell, and at what price to buy and sell, is difficult when millions of dollars at stake.

However, salespeople and traders work much more reasonable hours than research analysts or corporate finance bankers. Rarely does a salesperson or trader venture into the office on a Saturday or Sunday; the trading floor is completely devoid of life on weekends. Any corporate finance analyst who has crossed a trading floor on a Saturday will tell you that the only noise to be heard on the floor is the clocks ticking every minute and the whir of the air conditioner.

Visit Vault at **www.vault.com** for insider company profiles, expert advice, career message boards, expert resume reviews, the Vault Job Board and more.

VAULT CAREER LIBRARY 109

Shop Talk

Here's a quick example of how a salesperson and a trader interact on an emerging market bond trade.

SALESPERSON: Receives a call from a buy-side firm (say, a large mutual fund). The buy-side firm wishes to sell $10 million of a particular Mexican Par government-issued bond (denominated in U.S. dollars). The emerging markets bond salesperson, seated next to the emerging markets traders, stands up in his chair and yells to the relevant trader, "Give me a bid on $10 million Mex Par, six and a quarter, nineteens."

TRADER: "I got 'em at 73 and an eighth."

Translation: I am willing to buy them at a price of $73.125 per $100 of face value. As mentioned, the $10 million represents amount of par value the client wanted to sell, meaning the trader will buy the bonds, paying 73.125 percent of $10 million plus accrued interest (to factor in interest earned between interest payments).

SALESPERSON: "Can't you do any better than that?"

Translation: Please buy at a higher price, as I will get a higher commission.

TRADER: "That's the best I can do. The market is falling right now. You want to sell?"

SALESPERSON: "Done. $10 million."

S&T: A symbiotic relationship?

Institutional sales and trading are highly dependent on one another. The propaganda that you read in glossy firm brochures portrays those in sales and trading as a shiny, happy integrated team environment of professionals working for the client's interests. While often that is true, salespeople and traders frequently clash, disagree, and bicker.

Simply put, salespeople provide the clients for traders, and traders provide the products for sales. Traders would have nobody to trade for without sales, but sales would have nothing to sell without traders. Understanding how a trader makes money and how a salesperson makes money should explain how conflicts can arise.

Traders make money by selling high and buying low (this difference is called the spread). They are buying stocks or bonds for clients, and these clients filter in through sales. A trader faced with a buy order for a buy-side firm could care less about the performance of the securities once they are sold. He or she just cares about making the spread. In a sell trade, this means selling at the highest price possible. In a buy trade, this means buying at the lowest price possible.

The salesperson, however, has a different incentive. The total return on the trade often determines the money a salesperson makes, so he wants the trader to sell at a low price. The salesperson also wants to be able to offer the client a better price than competing firms in order to get the trade and earn a commission. This of course leads to many interesting situations, and at the extreme, salespeople and traders who eye one another suspiciously.

The personalities

Salespeople possess remarkable communication skills, including outgoing personalities and a smoothness not often seen in traders. Traders sometimes call them bullshit artists while salespeople counter by calling traders quant guys with no personality. Traders are tough, quick, and often consider themselves smarter than salespeople. The salespeople probably know better how to have fun, but the traders win the prize for mental sharpness and the ability to handle stress.

Research

If you have a brokerage account, you have likely been given access to research on stocks that you asked about. This research was probably written by an investment banks' research department.

To the outsider, it seems that research analysts spend their time in a quiet room poring over numbers, calling companies, and writing research reports. The truth is an entirely different story, involving quite a bit of selling on the phone and on the road. Analysts produce research ideas, hand them to associates and assistants, and then man the phone talking to buy-side stock/bond pickers, company managers, and internal salespeople. They become the managers of research reports and the experts on their industries to the outside world. Thus, while the lifestyle of the research analyst would initially appear to resemble that of a statistician, it often comes closer to that of a diplomat or salesperson.

The Players

Research assistants

The bottom-level number crunchers in research, research assistants generally begin with no industry or market expertise. They come from solid undergraduate schools and performed well in school, but initially perform mundane research tasks, such as digging up information and editing/formatting reports. Research assistants also take over the spreadsheet modeling functions required by the analyst. Travel is limited for the budding research assistant, as it usually does not make sense financially to send more than the research analyst to meetings with company officials or money managers.

Research associates

Burdened with numbers and deadlines, the research associate often feels like a cross between a statistician and a corporate finance analyst. Long hours, weekends in the office and number-crunching sum up the routine of the associate. However, compared to analyst and associate analogues in corporate finance, the research associate works fewer hours, often makes it home at a reasonable time, and works less on the weekend. Unfortunately, the associate is required to be present and accounted for at 7:30 a.m., when most morning meetings take place.

Mirroring the corporate finance analyst and associate positions, research associates can be bright, motivated kids directly out of top undergraduate universities, or at firms dedicated to hiring MBAs in research, the research associate role is the entry-level position once the MBA has been earned.

Visit Vault at **www.vault.com** for insider company profiles, expert advice, career message boards, expert resume reviews, the Vault Job Board and more.

VAULT CAREER LIBRARY   111

A talented research associate can earn much in the way of responsibility. For example, the research associate may field phone calls from smaller "B" accounts (i.e., smaller money managers) and companies less important to the analyst. (The analyst handles the relationships with the biggest buy-siders, best clients and top salespeople.) When it comes to writing reports, some analysts give free reign to associates in writing. Also, research associates focus on one industry and typically work for only one full-fledged research analyst. This structure helps research associates delve deeper into the aspects of one industry group and enable them to work closely with a senior-level research analyst.

To start, research assistants/associates out of undergraduate typically get paid similarly to the corporate finance analyst right out of college. After one or two years, the compensation varies dramatically, depending on performance and the success of the analysts in the industry group as well as the associate's contribution. For the MBA research associate, the compensation is similar to I-banking associates: as of this writing, $80,000 salaries with $30,000 signing bonuses, plus a $30,000 year-end bonus, are typical.

It All Depends on the Analyst

Insiders stress that the research associate's contribution entirely depends on the particular analyst. Good analysts (from the perspective of the associate) encourage responsibility and hand-off a significant amount of work. Others communicate poorly, maintain rigid control and don't trust their assistants and associates to do much more than the most mundane tasks.

Being stuck with a mediocre analyst can make your job miserable. If you are considering an entry-level position in research, you should carefully evaluate the research analyst you will work with, as this person will have a huge impact on your job experience.

Note that in research, the job titles for analyst and associate have switched. In corporate finance, one begins as an analyst, and is promoted to associate post-MBA. In research, one begins as a research associate, and ultimately is promoted to the research analyst title.

Research analysts

The research analyst, especially in equity, is truly a guru. Analysts follow particular industries, recommend stocks to buy and sell, and convince salespeople and buy-siders why they or their clients should or should not invest in Company XYZ. The road to becoming an analyst is either paved with solid industry experience, or through the research assistant/associate path.

Full-fledged analyst positions are difficult to come by. The skills required to succeed as an analyst include a firm grasp of: 1) the industry and dynamics of stock picking, and 2) the sales skills required to convince investors and insiders alike why a stock is such an excellent buy. An analyst lacking in either area will simply not become the next II-rated star (that is, an analyst highly rated by the annual *Institutional Investor* poll).

Research analysts spend considerable time talking on the phone to investors, salespeople and traders, pitching buy and sell ideas or simply discussing industry or company trends. Everyone tries to get the research analyst's ear, to ask for advice or (as we will discuss in-depth later) to pressure him or her to change a rating or initiate coverage of a particular stock. Analysts also travel regularly, visiting buy-siders or big money managers and companies in their field. Indirectly, they are trying to generate trading business with money managers, research ideas from companies or trying to build a reputation in the industry. All in all, analysts must be able to convincingly and quickly pitch an idea, and defend it thoroughly when the time comes.

In this atmosphere, research analysts must scrutinize every company that they maintain under coverage. Any news or company announcements will spur a deluge of phone calls to the analyst, with questions ranging from the big picture to the tiniest of details. They also must maintain a handle on an extremely important aspect of any company — the numbers. Inaccurate earnings estimates, especially when they are far from the mark, reflect poorly on the analyst. Why didn't an analyst know the company stock was going to come out with such low earnings? Or, why didn't the research analyst know that industry growth was slowing down? The analyst is responsible for staying on top of these things.

Compensation packages for research analysts run the gamut. Some II-rated star analysts in hot industries command multimillion dollar annual packages, especially during bull markets. Most banks figure their compensation for analysts with formulas that are usually incomprehensible to even the research analysts. The factors that go into analyst compensation typically includes a mix of the following:

• The performance of stocks under coverage (meaning that if their stocks perform like the analyst predicts, they get paid well)

• Trading activity within the firm of stocks under coverage

• Corporate finance business revenues of companies in their industry

• Performance evaluations of the research analyst by superiors

• *Institutional Investor* rankings (Once a research analyst finds himself listed as an II-ranked analyst, the first stop is into his boss's office to renegotiate his annual package.)

Note: As they progress in their careers, research analysts receive titles similar to investment bankers, namely VP, SVP and ultimately MD. However, the tasks of a research analyst tend to remain somewhat consistent once the analyst level is reached, with perhaps more selling of research and traveling involved at the most senior levels, and more oversight of a group of more junior analysts.

Visit Vault at **www.vault.com** for insider company profiles, expert advice, career message boards, expert resume reviews, the Vault Job Board and more.

VAULT CAREER LIBRARY   113

The Institutional Investor (II) Ratings Scorecard

Institutional Investor is a monthly magazine publication that, among other things, rates research analysts. The importance of the II ratings to investment banks and even many institutional investors cannot be overstated. Most industry watchers believe and follow the ratings as if they were gospel.

How do the ratings work? Essentially, II utilizes a formula to determine the best research analysts on Wall Street, surveys industry professionals, and publishes their rankings annually. Note the bias, however, toward research analysts at bulge bracket firms in these ratings. II's formula essentially involves surveys of "directors of research, chief investment officers, portfolio managers, and buy-side analysts at the major money management institutions around the world." Major money managers deal primarily with large investment banks for their trading needs and a portion of their research needs.

In 2000 Merrill Lynch and Morgan Stanley split the top spot in the II rankings. Both firms had 55 analysts rated including 22 and 12 first-teamers, respectively. Merrill Lynch had held the top spot alone for the two previous years while Morgan Stanley shot up from No. 3. Salomon Smith Barney came in third with 46 All-Americans, followed by Credit Suisse First Boston (38). Donaldson Lufkin & Jenrette (now a part of Credit Suisse First Boston) and Goldman Sachs were tied for fifth with 35 All-Americans.

The Product

Industry research reports

To establish oneself as a knowledgeable analyst, many researchers begin by writing and issuing an industry piece. For example, an industry research report on the oil and gas sector might discuss issues such as commodity prices, the general outlook for the sector and valuations of companies in the industry.

The time required to generate an industry piece depends on the length of the report, the complexity of the industry, and how important it is to show expertise to investors and management teams in the industry. For completely new industries for new analysts, a full six months or more is given to enable the analyst to fully understand the industry and develop a thorough report. Once it is printed, salespeople will use an industry research report to get up to speed and learn about a particular segment.

Touted as industry gospel, industry research reports take substantial time to produce and earn the firm nothing except awareness that the investment bank follows an industry and has expertise in that industry. However, the brand equity built by an industry piece can be substantial and make corporate finance banker cold-calling a much easier process.

Company specific research reports

Once an analyst's industry piece has been written and digested by the investment community, the analyst focuses on publishing research reports on specific companies. To create a well-rounded research universe, research analysts will typically write on the top industry players, as well as several smaller players in the industry. One of the most critical roles of an equity research analyst is to make future earnings estimates for the companies he or she covers. (The average earnings estimate of all analysts covering a company is called the "consensus" estimate.) Company-specific reports fall into three categories: initiation of coverage, updates and rating changes.

Initiation of coverage: This is exactly what it sounds like. These reports indicate that an analyst has not previously written research or covered the particular company. Usually an initiation of coverage report includes substantial information about the business, a detailed forecast model and risk factors inherent in the business.

Update: When a stock moves, news/earnings are released, or the analyst meets with management, an update report is put out. Often one-pagers, updates provide quick information important to current movements in the stock or will raise or lower earnings estimates.

Change of rating: Whenever an I-bank alters its rating on a stock (we will discuss these ratings later), a report is issued. These reports vary in length from one to five pages. Reasons for a downgrade include: lower than expected earnings, forecasts for diminished industry or firm growth, management departures, problems integrating a merger, or even overpriced stocks. Reasons for an upgrade include: better than expected earnings, new management, stock repurchases, or beneficial industry trends.

Conflict of Interest

It is crucial to note whether an investment bank has provided corporate finance services to the company under coverage. Usually at the end of a research piece, a footnote will indicate whether this is the case. If so, investors should be careful to understand the inherent conflict of interest and bias that the research report contains. Often covering a company's stock (and covering it with optimistic ratings) will ensure corporate finance business, such as a manager role in equity offerings, M&A advisory services, and so on.

Market commentary

Analysts usually cover a particular (small) universe of stocks, but some analysts, called market strategists, survey and report on market conditions as a whole. Most large banks publish market commentary reports on a daily basis (sometimes even several within a day), augmented with weekly, monthly and quarterly reviews. Included in such reports is information on the performance of stocks in major market indices in the U.S., major markets worldwide, and in various sectors — such as transportation, technology and energy — in the U.S. Some of these commentaries offer forecasts for the markets or for particular sectors. Naturally, economic data is paramount to stock market performance overall and thus pervades market commentaries.

Economic commentary

Similar to a market commentary, economic reports are also published periodically and cover economic indicators and trends. These reports are often stuffed with graphs of macroeconomic factors such as GDP, inflation, interest rates, consumer spending, new home sales, import/export data, etc. They provide useful information regarding government fiscal and monetary policy, and often link to fixed income reports. Often the same market strategist writes both the economic commentaries and the market commentaries for a firm.

Visit Vault at **www.vault.com** for insider company profiles, expert advice, career message boards, expert resume reviews, the Vault Job Board and more.

VAULT CAREER LIBRARY   **115**

Fixed income commentary

Analysts covering the fixed income markets publish periodic reports on the debt markets. Often tied to the economic commentaries, fixed income market reports comment on the performance of various fixed income instruments including U.S. government securities, mortgages, corporate bonds, commodity prices and other specialized fixed income securities. The five-point scale for rating stocks is ubiquitous in banking, but the definitions that banks refer to do not accurately measure what the analyst believes. The following scale reflects the general consensus on stock ratings, but keep in mind that these vary by firm.

Rating	Published Definition	Actual Meaning
Buy 1	STRONG BUY. The company's stock is a strong buy, and will outperform the market over the next 18 months.	The stock is a worthy buy. Or, if the investment bank writing the research just completed a transaction for the company, the analyst may simply believe it is a decent company that will perform as well as the market in the next 18 months.
Buy 2	MARKET PERFORM. The stock will perform approximately as well as the market over the next 18 months.	Be wary about buying this stock. It is either richly valued or has potential problems which will inhibit the firm's growth over the next 18 months.
Hold 3	HOLD. The stock will likely perform at or below the market over the next 18 months.	Sell. A hold rating by an analyst usually means that the stock should be sold, but that the analyst does not want to ostracize himself from the company by rating the stock a sell.
Sell 4	SELL. The stock will perform below the market over the next 18 months	Dump this stock as soon as possible. A Sell 4 rating issued by an analyst means the company is going to tank, and soon.
Sell 5	SELL IMMEDIATELY.	Rarely if ever seen. A Sell 4 tells clients to dump the stock, that it is heading into the toilet. A Sell 5 might only be issued after the firm is in bankruptcy.

AT LEHMAN BROTHERS,
WE DO GROUND-BREAKING DEALS.
RECRUITING YOU, FOR INSTANCE.

AT LEHMAN BROTHERS, OUR GREATEST INVESTMENT IS IN OUR HUMAN CAPITAL.
WE HIRE SMARTER — AND HAVE EARNED A REPUTATION FOR TARGETING
HIGH-POTENTIAL MEN AND WOMEN.
WE TRAIN SMARTER, TOO — OFFERING ONE OF THE MOST INTENSIVE
TRAINING AND DEVELOPMENT PROGRAMS IN THE INDUSTRY.

TO LEARN MORE, VISIT US ONLINE AT WWW.LEHMAN.COM/CAREERS

LEHMAN BROTHERS
Where vision gets built.®

Employer Directory

Bear Stearns & Co. Inc.

383 Madison Avenue
New York, NY 10179
www.bearstearns.com

Founded in 1923, Bear, Stearns & Co. Inc. is a leading investment banking and securities trading and brokerage firm, and the major subsidiary of The Bear Stearns Companies Inc. (NYSE:BSC). With approximately $40.0 billion in total capital (as of February 29, 2004), Bear Stearns serves governments, corporations, institutions and individuals worldwide. The company's business includes corporate finance and mergers and acquisitions, institutional equities and fixed income sales and trading, securities research, private client services, derivatives, foreign exchange and futures sales and trading, asset management and custody services. Through Bear, Stearns Securities Corp., it offers financing, securities lending, clearing and technology solutions to hedge funds, broker-dealers and investment advisors. Headquartered in New York City, the company has approximately 10,500 employees worldwide.

Citigroup global corporate and investment bank

388 Greenwich Street
New York, New York 10013
Phone: 212-816-6000
www.oncampus.citigroup.com

Citigroup's global corporate and investment bank provides Global Banking, Capital Markets and Transaction Services for corporations, institutional investors and governments in more than 100 countries. In both equities and fixed income we offer a dominant sales and trading platform, industry-leading research, top-tier institutional distribution, as well as strategic and financial advisory services on a wide range of M&A transactions and capital-raising activities. These include acquisitions, mergers, divestitures, restructurings, underwriting and distributing equity, debt and derivative securities. Citigroup Global Markets Inc. Member SIPC.

Schools Citigroup recruits from

Barnard; Baruch; Berkeley; Boston College; Brown; Bucknell; Cal Poly San Luis Obispo; Carnegie Mellon; Chicago; Claremont College; Columbia; Cornell; Dartmouth; Duke; Georgetown; Harvard; Holy Cross; Howard; Illinois; Johns Hopkins; Lehigh; Michigan; MIT; Morehouse; Notre Dame; NYU; Pace; Penn; Princeton; Rutgers; Stanford; Spelman; Stevens; Stony Brook; SUNY Albany; Texas A&M; UCLA; U of Florida; U of N. Carolina; U Texas; UVA; UWO; Vanderbilt; Villanova; Yale

Goldman Sachs

85 Broad Street
New York, NY 10004
www.gs.com/careers

Goldman Sachs is a leading global investment banking, securities and investment management firm that provides a wide range of services worldwide to a substantial and diversified client base that includes corporations, financial institutions, governments and high net worth individuals. Goldman Sachs provides a team-based, collegial environment where people take the time to properly train, mentor and support you, helping you find the best place for your talents. We offer our team members a chance to build a broad-based skill set that in turn provides them with a breadth of opportunities across all levels, regions and business areas.

Schools Goldman recruits from

We actively recruit at schools across the United States and welcome applications for both full-time positions and summer internships. Please view our calendar of events to see when we might be on your campus.

Lehman Brothers

LEHMAN BROTHERS

745 Seventh Avenue
New York, NY 10019
Phone: 212-526-7000
www.lehman.com/careers

Lehman Brothers serves the financial needs of corporations, governments and municipalities, institutional clients and high net-worth individuals worldwide. Founded in 1850, Lehman Brothers has the financial strength and support required to maintain leadership positions in all of its businesses. We are a leading underwriter of global equity and fixed-income securities. We are also a prominent adviser to corporations and governments around the globe, and our research analysts are considered among the best in the world. Lehman Brothers has the people, resources and knowledge necessary to serve institutional investors whenever and wherever the need for financing or investment opportunities arise. The Firm is headquartered in New York, London, and Tokyo and operates in a network of offices around the world.

Visit Vault at **www.vault.com** for insider company profiles, expert advice, career message boards, expert resume reviews, the Vault Job Board and more.

VAULT CAREER LIBRARY   119

Merrill Lynch

250 Vesey Street
New York, New York 10080
www.ml.com/careers

Merrill Lynch is a leading global financial management and advisory company with a presence in 35 countries across six continents, serving the needs of both individual and institutional clients with a diverse range of financial services. We have three principle businesses (Global Markets & Investment Banking, Global Private Client, and Merrill Lynch Investment Managers) that are supported by Corporate Resources groups.

We offer the following opportunities for undergraduates:
Global Markets
Investment Banking
Private Client
Credit
Investment Management
Operations
Technology
Accounting & Finance
Human Resources

We offer the following opportunities for MBA students:
Global Markets
Investment Banking
Private Client
Private Wealth
Research
Business Finance

SG Cowen & Co., LLC

1221 Avenue of the Americas
New York, NY 10020
Phone: (212) 278-4000
analyst.us-ib@sgcowen.com
www.sgcowen.com

SG Cowen & Co., LLC is a full-service investment banking firm and securities brokerage with a global commitment to the technology, health care, Consumer, Media and Communications and related high-growth sectors. SG Cowen & Co. provides innovative financing solutions to clients and investors worldwide. It is a part of SG Corporate & Investment Banking, and a subsidiary of Societe Generale, a diversified, global financial services institution. SG Cowen & Co. is a registered broker dealer and a member of SIPC.

Schools SGCowen recruits from:

Georgetown; Columbia; Brown; Harvard; Trinity; Richmond; UT Austin

Banc of America Securities LLC

9 West 57th Street

New York, New York 10019

Phone: (888) 583-8900

www.bofasecurities.com

Bank of America

100 North Tryon Street

Charlotte, NC 28255

Phone: (704) 388 2547

www.bofa.com

Bank One

1 Bank One Plaza

Chicago, IL 60670

Phone: (312) 732-4000

Fax: (312) 732-3366

www.bankone.com

Barclays Capital

200 Park Avenue

New York, NY 10166

Phone: (212) 412-4000

www.barcap.com

Bear, Stearns & Co., Inc.

383 Madison Avenue

New York, NY 10179

Phone: (212) 272-2000

Fax: (212) 272-4785

www.bearstearns.com

The Blackstone Group

345 Park Avenue

New York, NY 10154

Phone: (212) 583-5000

Fax: (212) 583-5712

www.blackstone.com

CIBC World Markets

425 Lexington Ave.

New York, NY 10017

Phone: (212) 856-4000

www.cibcwm.com

Credit Suisse First Boston

11 Madison Avenue

New York, NY 10010-3629

Phone: (212) 325-2000

Fax: (212) 325-6665

www.csfb.com

Deutsche Bank

60 Wall Street

New York, NY 10003

Phone: (212) 250-2500

www.db.com

Dresdner Kleinwort Wasswerstein

1301 Avenue of the Americas

New York, NY 10019

Phone: (212) 969-2700

www.drkw.com

FleetBoston Financial

100 Federal Street

Boston, MA 02110

Phone: (617) 434-2200

Fax: (617) 434-6943

www.fleet.com

Houlihan Lokey Howard & Zukin

1930 Century Park West

Los Angeles, CA 90067

Phone: (310) 553-8871

Fax: (310) 553-2173

www.hlhz.com

HSBC Bank USA

452 5th Ave.

New York, NY 10018

Phone: (212) 525-5000

www.us.hsbc.com

ING Group

Strawinskylaan 2631

1077 ZZ Amsterdam, The Netherlands

Phone: +31-20-541-54-11

Fax: +31-20-541-54-51

www.ing.com

Visit Vault at **www.vault.com** for insider company profiles, expert advice, career message boards, expert resume reviews, the Vault Job Board and more.

VAULT CAREER LIBRARY

121

Jefferies & Co.

520 Madison Avenue

12th Floor

New York, NY 10022

Phone: (212) 284-2550

www.jefco.com

J.P. Morgan Chase

270 Park Avenue

New York, NY 10017

Phone: (212) 270-6000

Fax: (212) 270-2613

www.jpmorganchase.com

Lazard

30 Rockefeller Plaza

New York, NY 10020

Phone: (212) 632-6000

www.lazard.com

Lehman Brothers

745 Seventh Avenue

New York, NY 10019-6801

Phone: (212) 526-7000

www.lehman.com

Morgan Stanley

1585 Broadway

New York, NY 10036

Phone: (212) 761-4000

www.morganstanley.com

Piper Jaffray & Co.

800 Nicollet Mall, Suite 800

Minneapolis, MN 55402-7020

Phone: (800) 333-6000

www.piperjaffray.com

Rothschild North America

1251 Avenue of the Americas

51st Floor

New York, NY 10020

Phone: (212) 403-3500

Fax: (212) 403-3501

www.rothschild.com

Thomas Weisel Partners

1 Montgomery St.

San Francisco, CA 94104

Phone: (415) 364-2500

Fax: (415) 364-2695

www.tweisel.com

UBS Investment Bank

299 Park Avenue

New York, NY 10171

Phone: (212) 821-3000

www.ibb.ubs.com

Wachovia

301 S. College Street

Suite 4000

Charlotte, NC 28288

Phone: (704) 374-6161

Fax: (704) 383-0996

www.wachovia.com

Wells Fargo & Company

420 Montgomery Street

San Francisco, CA 94163

Phone: (800) 411-4932

Fax: (415) 677-9075

www.wellsfargo.com

The information in this section was excerpted from the *Vault Career Guide to Investment Banking*. Get the inside scoop on banking careers with Vault:

- **Vault Guides:** *Vault Career Guide to Investment Banking, Vault Guide to Finance Interviews, Vault Guide to the Top 50 Banking Employers*

- **Employer Research:** Online Banking Employer Profiles, Employee Surveys and more

- **Message Boards:** Vault Investment Banking Career Advice Message Board

- **Career Services:** One-on-One Finance Interview Prep

Go to www.vault.com
or ask your bookstore or librarian for other Vault titles.

Visit Vault at **www.vault.com** for insider company profiles, expert advice, career message boards, expert resume reviews, the Vault Job Board and more.

VAULT CAREER LIBRARY   123

Discover the satisfaction of working for an organization that improves the quality of life for people everywhere by joining our talented team. Roche Diagnostics is the number one *in vitro* diagnostics company in the world! With our North American headquarters based in Indianapolis, we have some of the most talented and dedicated individuals in the industry. Our work is exciting, challenging and highly rewarding. Our success comes from having a clear focus on the needs of our customers.

Roche is one of the world's leading research-oriented healthcare groups in the fields of pharmaceuticals and diagnostics. Our innovative products and services address needs for the prevention, diagnosis and treatment of disease, thus enhancing people's well-being and quality of life.

We are always looking for people who want to become part of our winning team, whose daily work involves finding solutions that help people live better lives. Roche values our employees and recognizes their achievements through advancement opportunities and personal rewards.

We offer an excellent compensation and benefit program including 401(k). For information on our current openings, please visit our career site: **http://careers.ind.roche.com**. Roche is committed to providing equal opportunity to a diverse workforce.

We're People
Helping People
Enjoy Life

Biotech and Pharmaceuticals

The Global Pharmaceutical Industry

The pharmaceutical industry is a global powerhouse, worth an estimated $593 billion in 2003 with year-over-year growth averaging 8 percent, according to research by the Business Communications Company. A host of factors have led to the industry's healthy profits in recent years, including an aging population, increased awareness and use of drugs, and innovative new cures and preventive treatments for ailments ranging from asthma to toenail fungus.

The industry derives nearly half of its profits from the U.S. market, which lacks price controls on prescription drugs. This, of course, has been a hot topic on Capitol Hill – a Medicare reform package in 2003 attempted to address the issue, but advocates for the elderly and other groups are increasingly vocal about what they see as an unfair system.

Coming together

Mergers and acquisitions, along with other deals like co-development and co-marketing, have driven a rash of consolidation during the past decade. According to Business Communications Company research, the market share of the industry's top 10 companies rose to 46 percent in 2002, from 28 percent in 1990. In April 2003, Pfizer – already the world's largest drug company – acquired Pharmacia, the eighth-largest drug company. The $60 billion deal was the largest ever in the pharmaceutical industry. Other corporate marriages in recent years include the merger of Britain's Zeneca Group and Sweden's Astra in 1999 (now called AstraZeneca), Pfizer's purchase of Warner Lambert in 2000, and GlaxoWellcome's acquisition of SmithKline Beecham in 2000 (now called GlaxoSmithKline).

Patently challenging

Pharmaceutical companies are constantly challenged to stay one step ahead of expiring patents. Drugs receive 20-year patents – but the clock starts ticking the day the compound is discovered, so this time period includes the development process, clinical trials and an FDA review process, all of which together can take between eight and 12 years. When the patent expires, the company's market share for that drug plunges as other companies swoop in to offer cheaper generics. In recent years, blockbuster drugs like AstraZeneca's Prilosec and GlaxoSmithKline's Paxil lost their "exclusivity" and fell off the top 10 charts after 2002, to be replaced by similar-acting products Nexium and Zoloft, according to research by IMS Health.

Sometimes, these drugs are replaced by generic equivalents, offered at a much cheaper rate than their brand-name counterparts. Business Communications Company research indicates an average annual growth rate of more than 11 percent for the generic market alone through 2008, with sales in this sector reaching $64 billion by that year.

Meanwhile, drug companies continue their quest for the next Viagra – another blockbuster drug that will boost their bottom line. When Pfizer launched its "little blue pill" in 1998, it caused a veritable uproar

Visit Vault at www.vault.com for insider company profiles, expert phdvice, career message boards, expert resume reviews, the Vault Job Board and more.

VAULT CAREER LIBRARY   125

around the world and doubled the company's stock price. In its first month on the market, the anti-impotence pill generated over $100 million in sales to become the fastest-selling new drug in history. Even in the face of new competition from similar drugs, Viagra will likely remain a cash cow for Pfizer for some time since its patent doesn't expire until 2011. In 2003, the top therapy categories for prescription drugs were cholesterol and triglyceride reducers, anti-ulcerants, antidepressants, and antirheumatic nonsteroidals (NSAIDS).

Busy in the labs

Constant innovation is the key to survival and profit in the industry. In 2003, pharmaceutical companies poured an estimated $33.2 billion into discovering and developing new treatments (Pfizer leads the R&D pack with a budget of $7.9 billion for 2004). But the research can be a slow and costly process: only one out of every 5,000 to 10,000 compounds that are tested ever reaches the pharmacy shelf. In addition, the technology used in the development process is very expensive and constantly changing.

The world's most popular drugs are often up to four times as pricey in the U.S. as in other industrialized nations. That's because the U.S. is the only industrialized country that does not institute price controls on pharmaceuticals. The industry says the high prices help offset the costs of research and development, and provide an incentive for further development. According to AARP, prices charged by manufacturers to wholesalers for widely used brand name drugs increased by an average of three times the rate of inflation in 2003. Over the four-year period beginning in 1999, AARP tracked an average cumulative price increase of more than 25 percent for major prescription drugs.

Even with the benefits contained in the reform package of 2003 – which allows Medicare beneficiaries to buy a card for about $30 that may save them 10 to 15 percent off drug prices – many Americans are asking for relief from the rising prices. Several members of Congress have introduced proposals that aim to lower prescription drug prices, increase access to generic drugs and expand prescription coverage to Medicare recipients.

Other legislation seeks to allow the re-importation of U.S.-made drugs from other countries where the drugs cost less. But some Americans aren't waiting around for the legislation to be passed. They're getting their prescriptions filled in neighboring Canada and Mexico, where the prices are almost always cheaper. In fact, even some municipalities have gotten into the so-called "re-importation" game. In July 2003, the mayor of Springfield, Mass. announced that the city would begin buying drugs from Canada through a voluntary program for city workers and retirees. The initiative was expected to save the cash-strapped city up to $4 million.

Even the nation's most conservative lawmakers are putting pressure on the industry, with Sen. Trent Lott (R-MS) declaring in early 2004 that he would no longer vote against measures allowing Americans to purchase their prescriptions overseas.

The rumblings have the industry worried – in January 2004, Pfizer sent a warning to Canada, with a letter to all licensed Canadian pharmacies indicating that those caught breaching the company's ban on exporting its products from up north would result in Pfizer cutting off further supplies of its products. GlaxoSmithKline, AstraZeneca and Eli Lilly also have attempted to curtail re-importation of their drugs.

One lawmaker, Sen. Chuck Grassley (D-IA), came up with a compromise in April 2004, suggesting legislation that would reward drug makers that don't actively prevent the cross-border sales of their drugs, and penalize those that do.

Of primary concern to detractors of re-importation is safety – the Food and Drug Administration doesn't have jurisdiction over products coming from overseas. Consumer advocacy groups have conducted tests, however, finding no difference in the active ingredients of drugs purchased in the U.S. and those sold with Canadian labels. Still, the FDA, worried about counterfeiting and contamination of prescription medications, maintains a loose definition of "unapproved" drugs. In 2003, the agency intercepted two packages of prescription drugs from overseas, deeming nearly 90 percent "unapproved," though it never tested the drugs for their chemical contents.

Pharmaceutical companies still wield plenty of power in Washington – according to research by consumer advocacy group Public Citizen, the industry employed 675 lobbyists in 2002, spending a record $91.4 million on lobbying activities that year. Industry trade group the Pharmaceutical Research & Manufacturers of America (PhRMA), representing more than 100 brand-name drug companies, is reported to have shelled out $14.3 million in 2002. And they have friends in high places – Public Citizen says 26 lobbyists representing the industry's interests are themselves former members of Congress.

Departments in a Biotech Company

Biotech companies focused on healthcare applications contain all the major departments of conventional pharmaceutical companies – R&D, operations, quality control, clinical research, business development and finance and administration. In fact, the top 10 biotech companies are essentially mid-cap pharmaceutical companies. Each department houses several functional groups, or specific, logically related areas of activity. The three charts below illustrate how departments and functional groups are organized in different size companies.

As you think about a career in the biotech industry, it is useful to identify the general area(s) where your primary interests and aptitudes lie. The organization charts below provide a general map of the terrain. Note that the charts build on one another, with more groups evolving as a company grows from a small organization (fewer than 50 people) to a medium-size organization (51-300 people) to a large organization (over 300 people). Before discussing the basic career paths, let's take a closer look at how functional groups are organized in different departments.

Research and development

The research and development (R&D) department is responsible for discovering promising drug candidates. The three major functions include discovery research, bioinformatics, and animal sciences. The discovery research function is responsible for performing experiments that identify either targets on the cell or potential drug candidates. The animal sciences function provides cell cultures, grows microorganisms, and manages the care of animals used in discovery research. The extensive data generated from

Visit Vault at **www.vault.com** for insider company profiles, expert advice, career message boards, expert resume reviews, the Vault Job Board and more.

VAULT CAREER LIBRARY 127

experiments is analyzed with the assistance of the bioinformatics function, which assists discovery research in identifying the most biologically active compounds.

Operations

The operations department is responsible for making commercial quantities of a candidate drug available. Once a promising drug candidate has been identified, the process/product development function determines how to "scale up" quantities of a product to make enough available for clinical trials, since laboratory-size quantities are usually very small. When a product emerges from clinical trials successfully, the manufacturing and production function creates the final product – complete with packaging and labeling – that we see on pharmacist and drugstore shelves. Also housed under the operations umbrella is the environmental health and safety function, which assesses the environmental impact of a potential product.

Clinical research

Once a drug candidate emerges from R&D, the clinical research department takes over and becomes responsible for shepherding the drug through the FDA approval process. The clinical research function sets up and manages the clinical trials needed to determine a drug's safety and effectiveness or "efficacy." The regulatory affairs function ensures that all FDA reporting requirements are completed and submitted in a timely manner. Finally, the medical affairs/drug information function is responsible for overseeing all the information related to a drug candidate.

Quality

The quality department has groups focusing on quality control, quality assurance, and validation. These groups ensure that products are manufactured along rigorous, consistent standards of quality. This usually entails that well-defined and documented procedures are followed when producing a product either for clinical trials or as an end product.

Finance and administration

The finance and administration department contains these two functional areas as well as information systems and legal. All activities relating to the financial management of the company, its legal relationships to investors, creditors, and employees are housed in this department. The company-wide computer systems – separate from computing specifically directed at analyzing research data – are also managed here.

Business development

The business development group is typically responsible for identifying prospective new alliance partners and managing existing alliances. The marketing function studies markets, identifies target customer bases, and sets pricing and promotion strategy. The sales function actually meets with potential customers in the field – usually specialist physicians in targeted areas of specialization (e.g., cardiologists, endocrinologists, urologists, etc.)

Project management

Finally, many biotech companies also have a separate project management department, which is responsible for ensuring that work requiring the collaboration of several internal departments is discharged smoothly and efficiently. This department oversees special projects that don't naturally fit into any of the traditional formal functions but that require cross-functional collaboration.

To Lab or Not To Lab?

Given the breadth of choices, you might well wonder how to focus your own career aspirations. You may be turned on by science while in college enough to earn a major in a scientific discipline but not be sure you want to make research your life-long career. That's fine, as long as you have a sense of how to manage the critical early years of professional experience. To help you get a wide-angle view of the major career paths available, we have found it helpful to think in terms of two fundamental paths: laboratory research oriented and non-laboratory research oriented. Within each path are several different career tracks, discussed later.

Laboratory research-oriented career paths are found in the research and development (R&D) department. This area is also called "discovery research" because the work involves discovering new processes, drugs and technologies. These careers involve "bench work," referring to a laboratory bench, where scientists set up experiments to generate data. In biotech research, two other areas – bioinformatics and animal sciences – are especially tightly integrated.

Non-research oriented career paths include everything else. Several functions – operations, manufacturing, and quality – have an engineering bent and are primarily focused on the applications of science. Others, like clinical research, include all the jobs needed to set up and manage clinical trials and oversee submissions to regulatory agencies. Note that the "clinical research" function includes all the jobs needed to set up and manage clinical trials. They are put here rather than in the research-oriented path since they require knowledge of medicine and occur in clinical settings – such as hospitals or clinics. Still others are business-oriented and include support functions, such as finance, administration, legal, IT, business development, and sales/marketing. Finally many companies have a project management function that helps coordinate projects that overlap among several internal functions.

The common denominator is that careers in most of these functions require at least an undergraduate foundation in a life science. This includes the more generic business functions. Many careers require advanced training in science in addition to education in a functional area. For example, attorneys specializing in intellectual property often also have a Ph.D. in a life science. Business development people typically have either a Bachelor's or a Master's in a scientific area in addition to an MBA. The industry sets these educational prerequisites for employment outside the lab because a thorough grounding in the vocabulary of genetics, an orientation to the basic concepts behind the products, and a familiarity with the issues and challenges facing the industry are necessary to get people effectively on the same page. The bottom line is this: If you are up and coming in the educational system, you are joining a limited pool of

Visit Vault at **www.vault.com** for insider company profiles, expert advice, career message boards, expert resume reviews, the Vault Job Board and more.

VAULT CAREER LIBRARY   129

qualified talent competing for the available jobs. That's good news if most of your career is still ahead of you.

Laboratory Research Careers

Within a lab context, you can choose from three career paths: discovery research, bioinformatics, and animal sciences.

Discovery research

Since biotech is still in its infancy, most jobs in biotech companies, especially the smaller ones, are in discovery research. Discovery researchers can range from protein chemists to geneticists to biochemists to many other disciplines in the life sciences. There are jobs at all levels. With a Bachelor's, you can get an entry-level job as a research associate and work for several years, though you will need an advanced degree for more senior jobs. Most responsible positions, however, require a Ph.D. You can definitely break into the industry after undergraduate studies. Entry-level research positions will get your feet wet and give you a chance to experience the culture of research first-hand before committing yourself to advanced studies.

Animal science specialists

Instead of using chemicals the way traditional pharmaceutical chemists do, discovery research scientists use cells, which have to be obtained from animals, cultivated, separated, and utilized in special facilities. Discovery researchers rely on veterinarians and other animal science specialists. They grow cultures, make and purify DNA, and help conduct the earliest phases of testing, when a drug's safety is determined via animal testing.

Bioinformatics

Since nearly all experimental setups are computerized and reams of data are generated with each experiment, the results of biotech experiments are analyzed by specialists who straddle the fence between the biological sciences and information technology. These data analysts are called bioinformatics professionals and comprise some of the most sought-after employees in the industry. They help discovery researchers identify those molecular structures that have the most favorable response profile, and thus the most promising drug candidates.

Bioinformatics has three realms of activity: you can create databases to store and manage large biological data sets, you can develop algorithms and statistics to determine the relationships among the components of these datasets, or you can use these tools to either analyze or interpret biological data – e.g., DNA, RNA or protein sequences, protein structures, gene expression profiles, or biochemical pathways.

Non-Laboratory Research Careers

As discussed previously, non-laboratory research careers in biotech encompass a large range of functions, including engineering, careers in medical and clinical settings, administrative/support functions, and sales and marketing.

Engineering careers

Engineering careers have a strong practical application. Where discovery research scientists identify potential drug candidates, engineers are more concerned with figuring out first, how to ensure that enough material is available for clinical testing, and second, how to manufacture an approved drug. Engineering careers require a great capacity for precision, order, defined processes, and a need to see tangible results after a day's work. If you like your work to be exact and practical, engineering-related careers may be just the thing.

Four career paths exist in engineering: process/product development, manufacturing, environmental health and safety, and quality. The first three functions are usually grouped together under the operations department. Although engineering-related, the quality department is usually found as a separate function in the organization, regardless of its size, probably because its mandate requires independent judgment.

Process/product development

Process/product development engineers ensure that the first goal is achieved. They need to understand how a product's input ingredients behave when relatively larger quantities of the product are needed. It turns out that problems come up when scaling up quantities. Think of it as having to take your Grandma's favorite recipe for chocolate cake that comfortably serves eight and increasing it by an order of magnitude – now you need to make cake for 80. Chances are the mixer, pans and ovens used to make the eight-serving cake will not be able to handle the new cake. For that, you'll need industrial size equipment; you may have to adjust the oven temperature and time for baking; you may even need to substitute some ingredients that don't behave quite the same way. These are the types of adjustments process engineers need to explore to make larger batches of materials available for testing. Most entry-level positions require a Bachelor's degree and at least some industry exposure, which you can achieve with a well-placed internship or co-op program while still in college.

Manufacturing

Where process development careers have an investigative component, manufacturing careers are plant-based and focused on producing FDA-approved products for end consumers. Plant managers oversee this task through very strict standards of consistency and quality that have been codified and adopted industry-wide. Among the many different types of tasks and procedures performed are fermentation, protein purification, solvent extraction, tissue culture, preparation of bulk solutions, non-critical aseptic fills of buffers, filling and labeling of vials under sterile and non-sterile conditions, large-scale bioreactor operations, critical small- or large-volume sterile fills and aseptic manipulation of cell cultures.

Visit Vault at **www.vault.com** for insider company profiles, expert advice, career message boards, expert resume reviews, the Vault Job Board and more.

VAULT CAREER LIBRARY   131

To qualify for jobs, even at the entry level, employers expect some familiarity with terms such as GMP, GLP, and cGMP (see Glossary). Manufacturing of biotech products requires expensive facilities because the end products are often proteins, which are bigger and harder to produce than the small molecules that make up conventional drugs. You must be able to run complex equipment and ensure that procedures are followed and standards are maintained throughout the manufacturing process.

Environmental health and safety

Fully developed companies also maintain an environmental health and safety group to assess the impact of a product on the environment and ensure that any toxic by-products of research or manufacturing are properly disposed. Environmental engineers test and monitor air and water quality, investigate the health effects of potential toxins, dispose of regular as well as hazardous wastes, develop procedures to control pollution and give input on how to manage the land around a facility. This task becomes especially important in industrial applications of biotechnology, where chemical spills can have devastating effects on the environment if they are not contained quickly. Keeping up and complying with environmental regulations also falls under this group. Environmental engineers prepare permit applications, perform regulatory reviews, inspect the operations at the company's facilities and participate in environmental audits.

Quality

Careers in the quality function focus on developing and implementing standards, methods, and procedures to inspect, test, and evaluate the precision, accuracy, efficacy and reliability of a company's products. These support tasks ensure that the company's submissions to the FDA as well as the products bought by consumers adhere to industry standards. In a tightly regulated industry with a significant potential for liability if a product is defective, careers in the quality function help ensure the safety of the consuming public.

Medical and clinical setting careers

When a product has been demonstrated to be safe in animals – that is, it's passed Phase 1 testing – it is ready to be tested on a small sample of humans and be submitted as a candidate for a new drug to the FDA. These activities occur in clinical settings, involve interpretation of massive amounts of clinical data, and require extensive documentation to the regulatory body. Two basic paths exist: clinical research and regulatory affairs. Jobs in these functions are usually grouped together in most companies.

Clinical research

First, let's clarify the term "research" in clinical research. Clinical researchers are physicians, nurses, and data management professionals who administer and interpret the reactions of patients who have been enrolled in clinical trials. Often, these patients suffer from the disease condition targeted and need to pass a set of qualification criteria set by physician specialists, who must ensure that their overall health status is sufficiently stable to participate in testing the drug candidate. Once a drug is administered to an enrolled patient, the latter is carefully monitored for reactions to the drug. These include desired effects and other "adverse" or undesired effects. Both sets of data are captured both manually and electronically. Sometimes, manual data has to be transferred to electronic form. All data eventually becomes housed in databases, where physicians and database managers interpret the overall effects of the drug on the total population of patients enrolled in the study. These activities thus constitute research in a clinical setting using clinical data.

Medical knowledge at all levels is required for careers in clinical research – physicians identify prospective patients and interpret clinical data; nurses administer drug candidates and help monitor patient reactions; even database specialists need to have some understanding of the type of data the medical professionals generate in order to collaborate with physicians in interpreting it. With the hundreds of biotech drug candidates in the pipeline, clinical research jobs are expected to continue to be plentiful.

Regulatory affairs

Regulatory affairs is the other clinically oriented track. Jobs in this function involve dealing with all aspects of the regulatory environment surrounding drug approval, including submitting New Drug Applications (NDAs), preparing submissions to the FDA summarizing clinical trial results, keeping up with legislation affecting regulatory policy, ensuring the drug company meets new regulations, and working with the marketing function to make sure the message sent to consumers is consistent with federal compliance requirements. Careers in this function often require extensive reading and writing skills, as well as enthusiasm toward activities that protect both the company and the consuming public.

Administrative and support function careers

Biotech companies have a myriad of other careers that support the R&D and clinical testing functions. Typically, the finance and administration department houses these career paths: finance, administration, information systems, legal, and facilities management. Although most companies have a separate project management function, the essence of this group is administrative and that's why we are including it here.

Finance

Although entry-level jobs in the finance function often don't require industry-specific experience, the more senior positions usually ask for exposure to the biopharmaceutical environment. Accounting positions fall into this function. Jobs are available at all levels, including analysts, managers, directors, and vice presidents. Increasingly, understanding how licensing deals work and how to initiate and implement mergers and acquisitions is essential for finance jobs in the biotech industry. Furthermore, leaders in finance play key roles in obtaining the financing needed to run the many small research-oriented biotech companies. To fulfill this mission, they need to have understanding of the company's core technology and be able to communicate its potential value to private equity investors and venture capital firms.

Administration

Administrative support includes administrative assistants, human resource professionals, safety managers, librarians, and external relations officers. In the larger firms, the latter comprise of public relations specialists, who deal with the media; investor relations specialists, who deal with Wall Street investment houses and the financial press, and government relations specialists, who represent the company to government committees and stay abreast of important legislation. Since some aspects of biotech research

Visit Vault at **www.vault.com** for insider company profiles, expert advice, career message boards, expert resume reviews, the Vault Job Board and more.

VAULT CAREER LIBRARY   **133**

remain controversial, the specialists in this last function play the special role of advocate for their companies.

Information systems

The information systems function is responsible for the company's computing and networking equipment, as opposed to the specialized equipment used by the bioinformatics group in discovery research. There are jobs for programmers, analysts, network specialists, cyber-security experts and web site developers and site maintenance personnel. As a company grows, it needs more sophisticated software to maintain its human resource function, in order to keep up with employee benefits, compensation, and training data. Working collaboratively with the HR manager, the IS department determines what hardware and software to acquire, installs it and ensures it is properly maintained.

Legal

You probably understand that biotech companies need lawyers to keep the company on the right side of the law. But if you think there's one generic biotech lawyer, think again. With alliances, partnerships, regulations (U.S. and international), patents, trademarks, labor laws, benefits plans, and mergers and acquisitions to keep up with, lawyers come in several varieties: patent/intellectual property (IP) attorneys, labor/employment law attorneys, and contract attorneys. Patent/intellectual property attorneys are entrusted with protecting the innovations generated by discovery researchers. The most important ingredient here is that the IP attorney "speak the same language" as researchers; thus, many companies require advanced science as well as legal education. Labor/employment law attorneys look after the company's human resources policies and ensure that hiring practices adhere to federal labor law. Contract attorneys help draft agreements that business development people enter into with alliance partners, participate in negotiations, and review terms of contracts involving the selling of the company or the acquisition of other companies.

Facilities management

In discussing facilities management jobs, first we should define what this means in biotech. In this context, they refer to the facility that houses the company – as opposed to the facilities housing animals used in experimentation. This career track requires some understanding of real estate, leases, zoning requirements, etc. as well as the specific needs of the company. Many companies need clean rooms and other areas in which to house special equipment. Nearly all need facilities that are wired to support powerful computing, networking, and other data transfer equipment.

Project management

While project management is more a function than a career path, it is possible to manage projects as a career. The key here is to be able to work with lots of different types of people, be very organized, and be able to push back to meet deadlines when necessary. Project managers make significant contributions when members of different functional groups need to come together around a task, usually geting a drug candidate into clinical trials or launching a product. It's not so much that functional specialists (scientists, marketers, regulators) are not cooperative; rather, each function has its own mandate and its own criteria for reward. A project manager can make a unique contribution by ensuring that each function has its say without tilting the company's resources (time, money, etc.) too much in any single direction.

Sales and marketing careers

Career paths in this function include sales, marketing, new business development, and alliance management.

Sales and marketing careers in biotech are going through enormous changes, as a result of several factors: Differences in drug pricing across different geographical areas are becoming increasingly important political issues; biotech drugs typically have smaller sales forces which have very high levels of product knowledge; marketing, at least in the U.S., is increasingly directed toward the consumer, as opposed to the physician; and consumers are clamoring for the government and insurers to pick up at least part of the cost of prescription drug costs. Beyond this complex web of economic forces, lies the business development function, which is itself composed of finding new business partners and managing existing alliances. Finding your way through this terrain is largely a matter of your skills set and preferences – where you experience satisfaction and where you get frustrated.

How it Comes Together

Developing and marketing a drug requires extensive collaboration between and among company functions, between corporate functions and external groups (i.e., government agencies), and increasingly, between corporate entities themselves (i.e., smaller research-oriented biotech companies and larger Big Pharma firms with manufacturing and marketing capability). For you to thrive in this industry, it is useful to become familiar with how people in different functions work together and where collaborative effort will be required.

Discovery researchers are primarily engaged in the focus of their research. As such, they tend to work together in groups, which are often organized hierarchically, with the most senior scientists also acquiring managerial responsibilities within the group. Except for the smallest startups, most companies have several groups of scientists, each pursuing different research objectives. Larger companies may also have several sets of groups dedicated to different therapeutic and diagnostic areas. Mid-level and senior scientists like to communicate with colleagues in other types of institutions, such as government-run laboratories (i.e., National Institutes of Health) and research centers in large universities. Thus, they attend symposia focused on their specialty areas to stay abreast of results obtained by colleagues outside the corporate world as well as to share their own results. Scientists also regularly share results in-house through company-sponsored meetings. Such forums, which permit the free and open exchange of ideas, have helped make the U.S. the leading center of global scientific research and development.

Visit Vault at **www.vault.com** for insider company profiles, expert advice, career message boards, expert resume reviews, the Vault Job Board and more.

V\ULT CAREER LIBRARY 135

Employer Directory

Roche Diagnostics

9115 Hague Road
Indianapolism, Indiana 462520
http://careers.ind.roche.com
www.roche.com

Roche Diagnostics is the world's leading provider of diagnostic systems and decision-oriented health information. We are dedicated to the discovery, development, manufacturing, marketing and servicing of products and solutions for medical laboratories, physicians and patients, as well as for research and industry. Roche Diagnostics is a diverse, inclusive company that seeks, celebrates and leverages diversity to maximize the competitive advantage of people. We offer a variety of opportunities at our U.S. diagnostics marketing and sales headquarters in Indiana and at our global molecular business area headquarters in California.

Abbott Laboratories

100 Abbott Park Rd.
Abbott Park, IL 60064-6400
Phone: (847) 937-6100
Fax: (847) 937-1511
www.abbott.com

Amgen Inc.

One Amgen Center Dr.
Thousand Oaks, CA 91320-1799
Phone: (805) 447-1000
Fax: (805) 447-1010
www.amgen.com

AstraZeneca plc

15 Stanhope Gate
London, W1Y 6LN
Phone: +44-20-7304-5000
Fax: +44-20-7304-5183
www.astrazeneca.com

Aventis

Espace Europeen de el Enterprise, 16
Avenue de l'Europe F-67917
Strasbourg, 67300
Phone: +33-3-88-99-11-00
Fax: +33-3-88-99-11-01
www.aventis.com

Bayer Corporation

100 Bayer Road
Pittsburgh, PA 15205-9741
Phone: (412) 777-2000
Fax: (412) 777-2034
www.bayerus.com

Becton, Dickinson and Company

1 Becton Drive
Franklin Lakes, NJ 07417-1880
Phone: (800) 284-6845
Fax: (201) 847-6475
www.bd.com

Eli Lilly and Company
Lilly Corporate Center
Indianapolis, IN 46285
Phone: (317) 276-2000
Fax: (317) 277-6579
www.lilly.com

Genentech, Inc.
One DNA Way
South San Francisco, CA 94080-4990
Phone: (650) 225-1000
Fax: (650) 225-6000
www.gene.com

Genzyme Corporation
500 Kendall St.
Cambridge, MA 02142
Phone: (617) 252-7500
Fax: (617) 252-7600
www.genzyme.com

GlaxoSmithKline plc
980 Great West Road
Brentford, Middlesex,
Phone: +44-20-8047-5000
Fax: +44-20-8047-7807
www.gsk.com

Johnson & Johnson
One Johnson & Johnson Plaza
New Brunswick, NJ 08933
Phone: (732) 524-0400
Fax: (732) 524-3300
www.jnj.com

McKesson
1 Post Street
San Francisco, CA 94104
Phone: (415) 983-8300
Fax: (415) 983-7160
www.mckesson.com

Merck & Co., Inc.
One Merck Drive
Whitehouse Station, NJ 08889-0100
Phone: (908) 423-1000
Fax: (908) 735-1253
www.merck.com

Novartis AG
Lichtstrasse 35
Basel, CH-4002
Phone: +41-61-324-1111
Fax: +41-61-324-8001
www.novartis.com

Pfizer Inc.
235 E. 42nd St.
New York, NY 10017-5755
Phone: (212) 573-2323
Fax: (212) 573-7851
www.pfizer.com

Schering-Plough Corporation
2000 Galloping Hill Road
Kenilworth, NJ 07033-0530
Phone: (908) 298-4000
Fax: (908) 298-7653
www.sch-plough.com

Wyeth Pharmaceuticals
2000 Galloping Hill Road
Kenilworth, NJ 07033-0530
Phone: (908) 298-4000
Fax: (908) 298-7653
www.sch-plough.com

Visit Vault at **www.vault.com** for insider company profiles, expert advice,
career message boards, expert resume reviews, the Vault Job Board and more.

VAULT CAREER LIBRARY   **137**

The information in this section was excerpted from the Vault Career Guide to Biotech and Vault Guide to Top Pharmaceuticals and Biotech Employers. Get the inside scoop on biotech/pharma careers with Vault:

- **Vault Guides:** *Vault Career Guide to Biotech, Vault Guide to Top Pharmaceuticals and Biotech Employers*

- **Employer Research:** Online Pharma/Biotech Employer Profiles, Employee Surveys and more

- **Message Boards:** Vault Biotech and Pharmaceuticals Career Advice Message Boards

- **Career Services:** Vault Resume and Cover Letter Reviews, rated the "Top Choice" by *The Wall Street Journal* for resume makeovers

Go to www.vault.com

or ask your bookstore or librarian for other Vault titles.

Consumer Products/Marketing

Consumer Products/Marketing Industry Overview

The consumer products industry

Encompassing everything from dish soap to automobiles, the consumer products industry is a vast empire made up of the multitude of material products available to customers, stretching across dozens of related industries. To get a handle on the market, analysts often divide it into two categories, "durable goods" and "non-durable goods." As the names imply, the former comprises items with (relative) staying power, like cars, home furnishings, jewelry and electronics. The latter category includes more ephemeral merchandise, with a life expectancy of less than three years, like clothing, personal care items, and office and cleaning supplies. Others break the industry down into products that are "staples" and those that are "discretionary" – the difference between what consumers need and what they'd like to have.

Consuming billions

Even in the midst of a weak economy, the numbers are staggering: In March 2004 alone, retail sales in the U.S. topped $300 billion. Yearly spending by U.S. consumers on items sold by retailers hovers around $10 trillion. And that doesn't count the increased presence of U.S.-made consumer products in the farthest reaches of the globe – as American and European markets become increasingly saturated, retailers are turning toward new markets, especially in hot spots opened to the West in the past decade, like China and Russia.

Confidence game

Economists measure how well the economy is doing by looking at consumer confidence – a measure of how American consumers feel about factors like job stability and business conditions (and by extension, how willing they are to part with their hard-earned pennies). During early 2003, which saw the beginnings of military actions in Iraq, along with mounting unemployment, consumer confidence plummeted, according to figures released by New York research firm The Conference Board. By early 2004, however, the numbers had begun to rebound, suggesting a renewed optimism.

Marketing steps in

With consumer confidence shaky in recent years, the consumer products industry has had to get creative about marketing – making discretionary products seem necessary, and distinguishing brands from the wealth of competitors in the field. In fact, research conducted by consulting firm McKinsey & Co. suggests that public companies that offer strong, well-leveraged brands contribute to higher stock prices – and happier shareholders.

Getting a grip on target audiences is the key to successful marketing – with baby boomers, the 81 million Americans born after the second World War and before the mid-1960s, making up the largest group of con-

Visit Vault at **www.vault.com** for insider company profiles, expert advice, career message boards, expert resume reviews, the Vault Job Board and more.

VAULT CAREER LIBRARY 139

sumers, spending nearly a trillion dollars per year, consumer goods manufacturers have gotten savvy about selling to them. And with an estimated 34 percent of the U.S. population expected to be over age 50 by 2015, manufacturers are setting their sights on the burgeoning market for senior-oriented products, as well. But another hot demographic is the "Generation Y" group, made up of a so-called "new baby boom" of people born in 1977 or later. Kids and teens, with budgets often solely comprised of discretionary income, are coming increasingly into focus as targets for marketers, particularly of non-durable goods like clothing and personal care products. Dividing up prospective consumers by demographics like age, race and location is only one way by which marketers drum up business for consumer goods. Another method, known as psychographics, instead looks at lifestyle choices, beliefs, attitudes and activities to form a brand that responds to the desires of consumers.

Surfing for goods

As Internet access for personal use becomes the norm in the U.S., consumer products manufacturers are finding it imperative to maintain a presence online. Even if they're not selling their products to consumers directly over the web, manufacturers are expected to provide at least some information about their products on their sites. In fact, while Internet sales only comprise about 5 percent of all retail transactions, many consumers use the web to hunt for information and comparison-shop before heading out to buy a product.

The age of technology

Other technologies that promise to revolutionize the way consumer products are produced and delivered are customer relationship management (CRM) and radio frequency identification (RFID). With CRM, retailers use software and other applications to maintain databases recording their transactions with customers, establishing profiles to better serve consumers and keep them coming back. A retailer who knows that Bob likes a certain type of golf club, for instance, can use the Internet or other media to inform him when similar or complementary items go on sale. Multiply this by a thousand Bobs, and it becomes clear that CRM has an effect on the entire life-cycle of consumer products, allowing retailers to get a better handle on demand for their inventory and to fine-tune their orders from manufacturers. RFID gives manufacturers and retailers another way to track and control inventory. By inserting a tiny microchip into or onto an item or its packaging, everyone from the producer to the stock clerk to the cashier can gather data about a product as it makes its way through the supply chain. With retail giant Wal-Mart demanding that its top suppliers be RFID-ready by 2005, major consumer goods manufacturers are preparing for a big investment in the new technology.

Marketing and Brand Managers

What is a marketer? The allure of brand management

Marketing encompasses a wide variety of meanings and activities. Some marketing positions are very close to sales, while others set overarching marketing strategy. What marketing positions have in common is the sense of ownership over the product or service, as well as the need to understand customer needs and desires and translate those needs into some kind of marketing communication, advertising campaign or sales effort. The manager of product or service marketing is called the brand manager – he or she is the ruler of that marketing universe.

Careers within the marketing/branding arena are high-profile. The business world is now realizing that strong brands and solid marketing programs drive shareholder value, and that companies can no longer make fundamental strategy decisions without truly understanding how to market a product. Today's business challenges – the quest for company growth, industry consolidation and deregulation, economic webs, and the emergency of new channels and technologies – make marketers even more valuable.

The titles of brand manager, product manager, and to a lesser extent, marketing manager are often used to describe the same function – some companies use one title, others use another. Marketing manager tends to be used in industries other than consumer packaged goods; product manager is often used in tech industries. "Brand management" implies more complete supervision of a product. The typical brand management framework gives a brand "group" or "team" – generally comprised of several assistant brand or assistant marketing managers and one supervising brand manager – responsibility for all matters relevant to their product or products. Whether this responsibility is in fact complete depends somewhat on the size of the company relative to the number of brands it has, the location of the brand group, and most importantly, on the company's attitude toward marketing.

How important is the individual brand manager?

Consider the company to determine the level of brand manager responsibility. The first factor: the size of the company relative to its number of brands. For a company with hundreds of different brands – Nabisco, for example – brand managers, or even assistant brand managers, may have a great deal of power over a specific brand. At companies with a few core products, brand managers will focus on narrower aspects of a brand. As one recently hired assistant brand manager at Coca-Cola comments: "They're not going to take an MBA and say, 'Okay, you're in charge of Sprite.'" Brand managers at such companies will instead be focused on marketing to a particular demographic or geographic group, or perhaps handling one aspect of the product's consumption (plastic bottles, cases of aluminum cans, and so forth).

International brand managers have historically held more sway than managers in the company's home market, but keep in mind that the daily tasks of international brand managers often lean more toward questions of operations, rather than questions of strategy or marketing. ('How much should we produce?' or 'How is our distribution network affecting sales?' rather than 'What do we want our brand identity to be?') International brand management is sometimes split into two positions. Global brand managers are more

Visit Vault at **www.vault.com** for insider company profiles, expert advice, career message boards, expert resume reviews, the Vault Job Board and more.

VAULT CAREER LIBRARY   **141**

strategic, concentrating on issues such as protecting brand equity and developing product offerings that can be rolled out into subsidiaries. Local brand managers are more tactical. Local managers focus on executing global plans that are delivered to them, and tweak them for local consumers. Also know that with the increasing trend toward globalization and the truly global presence of certain brands, companies have sought to impose more centralization and tighter controls on the marketing of those brands from country to country. In the past, individual country managers have had more discretion and leeway to make decisions about a brand's packaging, advertising, etc. Now, companies have established tighter guidelines on what can be done with regard to a brand around the world, with the goal of protecting and enhancing the value of the brand and ensuring a consistent product and message worldwide.

Finally, consumer products companies place varying levels of importance on their brand or marketing departments. Some companies, such as the Ford Motor Company, are driven as much by financial analyses of production costs or operations considerations as by marketing. The level of emphasis on finance or operations matters at a firm will influence not only the independence and authority of marketing managers, but also potential marketing career paths. At some companies, marketing is the training ground for general management. At General Mills, marketing is considered so important that employees in other functions who show promise are plucked from their positions and put into the department.

Careers in Marketing

Taking charge of a brand involves tackling many diverse job functions – and different subspecialties. Decide where you'd like your main concentration to lie.

Brand management

In a typical brand management organizational structure, positions are developed around responsibility for a particular product rather than a specific functional expertise (i.e., you're an assistant brand manager for Cheerios). This structure enables you to be the "master of all trades," acquiring an expertise in areas such as manufacturing, sales, research and development, and communications. In brand management, the marketing function is responsible for key general management decisions such as long-term business strategy, pricing, product development direction and, in some cases, profit and loss responsibility. Brand management offers a terrific way to learn intensively about a particular product category (you could be a recognized expert on tampons!) and to manage the responsibility of running a business and influencing its performance.

The core of brand work is brand strategy. Brand managers must decide how to increase market share, which markets and demographic groups to target, and what types of advertising and special promotions to use. And at the very heart of brand strategy is identifying a product's "brand identity." Brand groups then figure out how to exploit brand strategy, or, in some cases, how to change it. PepsiCo's Mountain Dew has built the drink's popularity among youth as a high-caffeine beverage into a "brand identity" of cutting-edge bravado that has boosted market share, while the Banana Republic chain underwent a transformation from an outdoor adventure store that sold actual army-navy surplus to an upscale, chic clothing store. In both cases, the brands have benefited from a shift in brand identity, and consequently, a shift in their market. Brand identity is normally created and confirmed through traditional print, radio, and TV advertising. Advertising is usually produced by outside agencies, although brand insiders determine the emphasis and target of the advertising.

Some liken a brand manager to a hub at the center of a hub and spoke system, with the spokes going out to departments like finance, sales, manufacturing, R&D, etc. It is the job of the brand manager to influence the performance of those groups – over whom he or she has no direct authority – in order to optimize the performance of his or her brand or product line.

Advertising

If you enjoy watching commercials more than television programs, then consider the advertising side of marketing. As an account executive, your role is to serve as a liaison between your brand management client and the departments within your agency. Account executives manage the creative production process from beginning to end, from researching what benefits a product offers, to writing the strategy for a typical commercial. Account executives must also handle matters such as briefing the creative department on how to execute the advertising strategies, working with the media department to buy ad time or space, and determining how to spend the marketing budget for advertising. (Will potential consumers be best reached via TV, outdoor billboards, print or radio – or through a general saturation campaign?) Along with managing the creative process, account executives at ad agencies are increasingly becoming strategic experts in utilizing traditional media, digital media, direct marketing and other services.

Direct marketing

Ever wonder who is responsible for making those coupons you receive in the mail? Or the Saab videotape you've received every two years since you bought your car in 1993? You can thank direct marketers. Direct marketers are masters in one-to-one marketing. Direct marketers assemble databases of individual consumers who fit within their target market, go after them with a personal approach, and manage the production process from strategy inception to out-the-door distribution.

Direct marketers have two main objectives: to stay in touch with their current consumer base and to try and generate more business by finding individuals who fit a target set of criteria but are not currently using their particular product. For instance, if you've ever checked out of the supermarket and got a coupon for Advil after buying a bottle of Tylenol, chances are a direct marketer is trying to convince you to switch brands by offering you a monetary incentive.

It's important to note that direct marketing isn't just through snail mail. It operates in multiple media such as the Web, telemarketing, and in-store promotions. Direct marketers have a powerful new tool in their arsenal – the Internet. Marketers are able to track the online habits and behavior of customers. They can then serve up customized banner advertisements that are much more likely to be relevant to them. Many consumers have agreed to receive promotional offers on certain subjects – marketers can then send them targeted e-mail messages that allow for much easier access to purchase or action (a click on a link, for example) than a conventional mail direct marketing programs.

Visit Vault at **www.vault.com** for insider company profiles, expert advice, career message boards, expert resume reviews, the Vault Job Board and more.

V∧ULT CAREER LIBRARY **143**

Affiliate/property marketing

If you're working with a major brand company like Nike, Disney, Pepsi, or L'Oreal, chances are you'll do a lot of cross-promotion, or "affiliate marketing." For instance, Nike has marketing relationships with the NBA, NFL, and a variety of individual athletes and athletic teams. Disney has a strong relationship with McDonalds; cute toys from the entertainment company's latest flick are often packaged with McDonalds Happy Meals upon the release of each new movie. L'Oreal works with celebrities like Heather Locklear and sponsors events such as the annual Academy Awards.

Marketers must manage the relationship between any two entities. If Disney wants to promote the cartoon du jour with McDonalds, or Pepsi wants to make sure that all Six Flags theme parks have a Pepsi Ride, then marketers ensure both parties are getting what they need out of the deal and staying true to their own brand image.

Price marketing/sales forecasting

Pricing is largely driven by market pressure. Most people, for example, won't pay more than $2.00 for a hamburger in a fast food restaurant. On the other hand, brand managers always have some pricing leeway that can greatly affect market share and profitability. An increase of a nickel in the price of a product sold by the millions can make huge differences in revenue – assuming the price rise doesn't cause equivalent millions less of the products to be sold. Brand managers need to figure out the optimal pricing strategy for their product, though it's not always a case of making the most money. Sometimes it makes more sense to win market share while taking lower profits. How do brand managers justify their prices? Through extensive research. Paper towels, for example, may be much more price-sensitive than a luxury item like engagement rings or smoked salmon.

Brand and marketing managers don't always have free reign over pricing. At some companies, such as those that sell largely through mail order, or those with complex pricing systems, pricing and promotional offers may be limited to what the operational sales system can handle. Explains one marketing manager at a long-distance phone company (an industry with notoriously tangled pricing plans): "It's very easy to offer something to the customer. It's very difficult to implement that in the computer system."

Another large part of the general management duties of brand managers is forecasting product sales. This means not only keeping track of sales trends of one's product, but anticipating responses to marketing campaigns and product launches or changes. The forecasts are used to determine production levels. Once a year, brand groups draw up budgets for their production, advertising and promotion costs, try to convince the finance folks that they absolutely need that amount, get less than they ask for, and then rework their budgets to fit the given budget. As one international brand manager at one of the world's biggest consumer goods companies puts it: "You don't determine the production and then get that budget; you get the budget, and then determine the production."

High-tech marketing

Not everyone markets applesauce for a living. Many people choose to enter the world of high-tech marketing because they want to work with products and technologies that reshape and improve the word around us. These marketers feel that they would rather change the way a person interacts with the world in a sophisticated way, rather than spend time understanding what hair color teenagers find most appealing. High tech marketers spend much of their time understanding research and development issues and working on new product launches.

Technology companies like Intel, Dell, and Microsoft have recognized the power of branding and are utilizing traditional marketing tactics more and more. Amazon's extensive marketing campaign in 1998 helped brand that company in the mind of consumers still new to e-commerce as the company to purchase books (and other products) online. Intel became perhaps the first semiconductor company readily identifiable to the public through its heavily branded "bunny people." Marketing in the high tech world will continue to grow in importance over the next decade, as technology companies become more consumer-oriented (see Microsoft's X-Box). Marketing a service or software product versus a more tangible product is a bit different. It may be a bit more challenging to understand how consumers relate to the product. Inventory and distribution issues may be tracked differently.

Market research

If you are an analytical person who enjoys numbers and analysis, and enjoys tracking consumer behavior, then market research may be the field for you. A product is much more effective when a company understands the consumer it is targeting. That's where market researchers come in. Market researchers employ a variety of different qualitative and quantitative research techniques to understand consumers. Surveys, tracking systems, focus groups, satisfaction monitors, psychographic and demographic models, and trial/repurchase estimations are all methods researchers use to understand how consumers relate to their products. Researchers who find that consumers associate lemon scents with cleanliness, for example, may suggest that cleansers could drive up sales by adding a lemon aroma.

Public relations

Public relations professionals manage company communications and relations with the outside world. You can work for an internal PR firm (large companies have their own departments that manage the public relations of all of their brands) or you can work for a PR agency and be placed on a brand account. Public relations executives write public releases to local and national publications and develop ideas that will increase the "buzz" surrounding their brand. Some PR firms have excellent reputations for pulling off "stunts" that get their products in the news and increase their brand recognition. Public relations executives may also be forced to defend a brand in the face of public scrutiny – such as the Tylenol brand during the rash of poisonings in the 1980s. While event-driven functions like press releases and stunts are important, perhaps the most important function of a PR professional is to establish strong relationships with media representatives and to persuade them to cover an interesting story about the company they represent.

Visit Vault at **www.vault.com** for insider company profiles, expert advice, career message boards, expert resume reviews, the Vault Job Board and more.

VAULT CAREER LIBRARY   145

Marketing consulting

Although most well-known consulting firms are known for their expertise in general strategy, many consulting firms now hire industry or functional experts that focus on marketing issues. These firms need people with expertise in the areas of branding, market research, continuous relationship marketing, pricing strategy, and business-to-business marketing – they tend to hire people with previous marketing experience and value consultants who have been successful marketing managers and have lived through the full range of business issues from the inside. McKinsey and Monitor are two general strategy firms that have begun to hire marketing specialists. Other boutique marketing consulting firms, such as Kurt Salmon, focus on certain product categories like beverages, healthcare, and retail. All major ad agencies are also attempting to reinvent themselves as marketing partners focused on marketing strategy beyond simple advertising.

What is a Brand?

Marketing analysis is primarily concerned with identifying a market, understanding it, and developing a product to fill a need in the market. (There are of course, other logistical details, such as understanding what is required to make the product profitable.)

But a product is just a physical object or service. A brand, on the other hand, is a product that has consistent emotional and function benefits attached to it. Products are interchangeable – a brand builds value. Brands engage the consumer, inspire an emotional reaction, and are consistent in their appearance. What attributes create brands?

Consistent strategy

Products that are constantly changing their strategies/market positions will never hold a consistent place in the consumer's mind. Owning a piece of the consumer's mind makes a brand a brand. When you think of a coffee shop, you now think of Starbucks – that's because Starbucks is a successful brand.

Consistent appearance

What do people think of visually when they think of your brand? Everyone knows Nike's logo – an elegant, high-speed swoosh.

Positioning

Good brands must stand for different things than their category competitors. Volvo cars, for example, are associated with safety, while Corvettes stand for sporty speed, and Saturns for value and good customer service.

Connection with target audience

A brand must build an emotional connection with the consumers who use it. The consumer must feel that there are no substitutes in the marketplace. Consumers may choose Pepsi or Coke in a blind taste test – but that "preference" has little to do with the drink they actually buy in the supermarket.

Top 12 Ways to Revitalize a Brand

Despite the fact that product categories are becoming more complex every day and marketing budgets are down, brand managers are constantly feeling pressure to increase sales, profits, and market share. This list is adapted from an article in Brandweek and provides excellent examples of how companies improved the marketing of brand name products.

1. **Create new usage occasions.** (Wednesday is Prince Spaghetti Day; Orange juice is not just for breakfast anymore)

2. **Find customers outside your existing target group.** (The Bank for Kids; Gillette for Her product line; and Pert for Kids shampoo)

3. **Discover a new way of using the product.** (Lipton Recipe Soup Mix; Baking Soda can be used as toothpaste; Jell-O pudding can be used as cake filling; Comet Disinfecting Powder not only cleans surfaces in your house, but also is great to use on old garden tools and old sneakers)

4. **Position your product as the one used by professionals and experts.** (Chapstick and Picabo Street; Tide and its "professional launderettes")

5. **Tell a compelling story about your product's origins.** (Jack Daniels; Nantucket Nectars; Ben & Jerry's)

6. **Create a jingle that relates to your product's unique feature.** (Heinz ketchup's "Anticipation"; Wisk's "Ring around the Collar"; Alka Seltzer's "Plop, Plop, Fizz, Fizz")

7. **Develop a new delivery vehicle or packaging convenience.** (Lysol Toilet Bowl Cleaner's "Angle Neck"; the Colgate "Pump")

8. **Create a character to personify your product, ingredient, or attribute.** (Post's California Raisins; Kraft's Cheesasaurus; Dow's Scrubbing Bubbles)

9. **Use media vehicles in a new way.** (P&G created the "soap opera" to advertise their brands; the "Got Milk" campaign effectively uses mouth-watering billboards; newspapers as a means of distributing product samples)

10. **Look for effective tie-ins/partnerships.** (United Airlines serving Starbucks Coffee; McDonald's distributing Disney toys; Gillette distributing razors at Boston Red Sox baseball games)

11. **Promote your product as benign addiction.** (Lay's "Bet You Can't Eat Just One"; Snackwell's "Won't be able to say no")

12. **Become a reason for family and friends togetherness.** (M&M's Make Friends; Kodak Golden Moments; McDonald's after the big baseball game; "Celebrate the Moments of Your Life" with Folgers)

Visit Vault at **www.vault.com** for insider company profiles, expert advice,
career message boards, expert resume reviews, the Vault Job Board and more.

VAULT CAREER LIBRARY **147**

Employer Directory

Procter & Gamble

PO Box 599

Cincinnati, OH 45201

Phone: 1-888-486-7691

http://www.usjobs.pg.com

careers.im@pg.com

Two billion times a day, P&G brands touch the lives of people around the world. We have one of the largest and strongest portfolios of trusted, quality brands, including Pampers, Tide, Ariel, Always, Whisper, Pantene, Bounty, Pringles, Folgers, Charmin, Downy, Lenor, Iams, Crest, Clairol Nice'n Easy, Actonel, Dawn and Olay. Nearly 98,000 P&G people working in almost 80 countries worldwide make sure P&G brands live up to their promise to make everyday life just a little better.

Schools Procter & Gamble recruit from:

Because we do web-based recruiting, students from any US undergraduate school can apply for US jobs at Procter & Gamble. See our website for a listing of schools where we have "in person" campus presence.

Avon Products

1345 Avenue of the Americas

New York, NY 10105-0196

Phone: (212) 282-5000

Fax: (212) 282-6049

www.avon.com

The Black & Decker Corporation

701 E. Joppa Rd.

Towson, MD 21286

Phone: (410) 716-3900

Fax: (410) 716-2933

www.bdk.com

Campbell Soup Company

Campbell Place

Camden, NJ 08103-1799

Phone: (856) 342-4800

Fax: (856) 342-3878

www.campbellsoup.com

The Coca-Cola Company

One Coca-Cola Plaza

Atlanta, GA 30301

Phone: (404) 676-2121

Fax: (404) 676-6792

www.cocacola.com

The Clorox Company

1221 Broadway

Oakland, CA 94612-1888

Phone: (510) 271-7000

Fax: (510) 832-1463

www.clorox.com

Colgate-Palmolive Company

300 Park Avenue

New York, NY 10022

Phone: (212) 310-2000

Fax: (212) 310-3405

www.colgate.com

 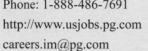

The Dial Corporation
15501 N. Dial Blvd.
Scottsdale, AZ 85260-1619
Phone: (480) 754-3425
Fax: (480) 754-1098
www.dialcorp.com

Eastman Kodak Company
343 State St.
Rochester, NY 14650
Phone: (585)-724-4000
Fax: (585) 724-1089
www.kodak.com

General Mills, Inc.
One General Mills Blvd.
Minneapolis, MN 55426
Phone: (952) 764-2311
Fax: (952) 764-2445
www.generalmills.com

The Gillette Company
Prudential Tower
Boston, MA 02199-8004
Phone: (617) 421.7000
www.gillette.com

Hallmark Cards, Inc.
2501 McGee St.
Kansas City, MO 64108
Phone: (816) 274-5111
Fax: (816) 274-5061
www.hallmark.com

Hasbro, Inc.
1027 Newport Ave.
Pawtucket, RI 02862
Phone: (401) 431-8697
Phone: (401) 431-8535
www.hasbro.com

Hershey Foods Corporation
100 Crystal A Dr.
Hershey, PA 17033-0810
Phone: (717) 534-6799
www.hersheys.com

H.J. Heinz Corporation
600 Grant St.
Pittsburgh, PA 15219
Phone: (412) 456-5700
www.heinz.com

Johnson & Johnson
One Johnson & Johnson Plaza
New Brunswick, NJ 08933
Phone: (732) 524-0400
Fax: (732) 524-3300
www.jnj.com

Kimberly-Clark Corporation
351 Phelps Dr.
Irving, TX 75038
Phone: (972) 281-1200
Fax: (972) 281-1490
www.kimberly-clark.com

Kraft Foods Inc.
Three Lakes Drive
Northfield, IL 60093-2753
Phone: (847) 646-2000
Fax: (847) 646-6005
www.kraft.com

Liz Claiborne, Inc.
1441 Broadway
New York, NY 10018
Phone: (212) 354-4900
www.lizclaiborne.com

Mattel, Inc.
333 Continental Blvd.
El Segundo, CA 90245-5012
Phone: (310) 252-2000
www.mattel.com

Nestle USA, Inc.
800 N. Brand Blvd
Glendale, CA 91203
Phone: (818) 549-6000
Fax: (818) 549-6952
www.nestleusa.com

Newell Rubbermaid, Inc.
10 B Glenlake Pkwy., Ste. 600
Atlanta, GA 30328
Phone: (770) 407-3800
www.newellrubbermaid.com

Nike, Inc.
One Bowerman Drive
Beaverton, OR 97005-6453
Phone: (503) 671-6453
Fax: (503) 671-6300
www.nikebiz.com

PepsiCo, Inc.
700 Anderson Hill Road
Purchase, NY 10577-1444
Phone: (914) 253-2000
Fax: (914) 253-2070
www.pepsico.com

Sara Lee Corporation
3 First National Plaza
Chicago, IL 60602-4260
Phone:(312) 726-2600
Fax: (312) 726-3712
www.saralee.com

Unilever
Unilever House
Blackfriars
London, EC4P 4BQ
Phone: +44(0)20-7-822-5252
Fax: +44(0)20-7-822-5951
www.unilever.com

Energy/Oil and Gas

Today's energy industry is almost unrecognizable from the relatively staid business of only 10 years ago. The changes have brought both unexpected opportunities and devastating uncertainties, and this is by no means the first time the industry has faced such upheavals. Throughout its history, energy has been an industry that welcomes innovation and fresh perspectives. With the array of careers available in energy – and the certainty that people need to buy what they sell – makes it worth a close look by job seekers.

Energy Industry History

The beginnings

The modern electricity industry in America was born with the work of Thomas Edison in 1878. People had known about electricity for generations before him – think Benjamin Franklin and his kite – and the practical applications of harnessed electric power were clear to everyone. By the time Edison turned his considerable imagination to the problem he already had a reputation as an innovative thinker and clever businessman. It is a bit of an exaggeration to say he 'invented' the lightbulb; rather he fine-tuned the filaments inside the bulb to create the first commercially viable, safe, and efficient means of indoor lighting.

In September 1878 Edison announced his breakthrough design to the world, and in a matter of days potential investors flooded his workshop in Menlo Park, New Jersey, with bids to market the new technology. A month after his discovery, he incorporated the Edison Electric Light Company, and a month after that he devised the first electric meter. A few years later his first power plant opened in lower Manhattan, and an industry was born.

Throughout the 1880s companies sprang up across the country and the globe to provide service. A number of these companies were franchises Edison set up himself, and many of their descendant operations still bear his name. Early power companies were limited to only a few city blocks because of primitive generation and transmission technology. But slowly, new technology emerged, and more and more companies jumped into the growing market in a pell-mell fashion. By the early 20th century, most major cities had a number of utilities, serving the approximately 8 percent of American homes that had electricity. These early days were the wild adolescence of the industry, and business could be cutthroat. There are stories about companies hiring gangs of thugs to chop down competitor's power lines. Overtime, the industry began to understand the value of economies of scale in providing service by using bigger turbine generators. Waves of consolidation began to create industry giants.

Yet the early power system remained inefficient, redundant, and expensive. It was still considered a luxury item, and the emergence of "natural monopolies" where one utility would dominate the market began to worry some reformers. Some states began to experiment with tighter regulation, but the industry changed dramatically in the 1930s, when two major initiatives from President Franklin D. Roosevelt's New Deal recast electricity as an essential service.

Visit Vault at **www.vault.com** for insider company profiles, expert advice, career message boards, expert resume reviews, the Vault Job Board and more.

VAULT CAREER LIBRARY   151

Transforming the industry

The first initiative culminated in the enactment of the Public Utility Holding Company Act of 1935, better known as PUHCA. This sweeping law had the practical consequence of identifying electricity as a vital service fundamentally different from regular good and services, and subjected the industry to a host of conditions and requirements it needed to meet. Each utility was allowed to operate as a full, vertical monopoly over a specific geographic space, or service area. Companies would be allowed to generate power in their plants, transmit it over their wires, and sell it to consumers who would have no choice about who to buy their power from. In exchange , every aspect of their business – from where they could built what, to what they could charge customers – would be subject to approval by state regulators.

The second initiative was to ensure every American had access to electricity through rural electrification programs. In the old system, there was absolutely no incentive for a company to string out a power line to one single farmhouse miles and miles away from the rest of the power grid. As a result, in 1930 only 10 percent of American farms had service, making life much harder for them than need be. Part of the New Deal was a package of laws that set up federal agencies to ensure power got to them, and to work out means to pay for it. One continuing legacy of this initiative are the large public power authorities that still provide service in many parts of the country.

The regulated system remained in place for decades, and with everything micromanaged, energy became the sleepiest major industry in America. Consumers began to take cheap and reliable electricity for granted. Investors eagerly entrusted long-term investments with these companies whose dividends came back like clockwork. Researchers continued to slowly develop new technologies, and the business side stagnated. Executives were thought to have the easiest jobs in corporate America, while lawyers and policy specialists remained mired in the trench warfare of rate hike petitions and siting permission cases with regulators which could take years to settle.

Trends moved at glacial speeds, with a few exceptions. One trend was the emergence of nuclear power, which many enthusiastically predicted would usher in the era of electricity that was "too cheap to meter." Through the 1960s and 1970s many utilities sank piles of money building nuclear plants, taking on huge amounts of closely managed debt along the way. But the optimism disappeared overnight with the Three Mile Island incident in 1979. Nuclear plants, once the wave of the future, became white elephants for their owners, who were saddled with huge insurance, maintenance, and security costs.

Another major development was the move toward opening the power grid to new technologies and renewable power sources in the 1970s. Most of the time, there was very little incentive for utilities to invest in unproven, emerging technologies. They were too expensive to build, and produced too little power, compared with a big, dirty coal-fired power plant. But public demand began to turn with the early environmental movement, leading to passage of the Clean Air Act, which had serious implications for the power industry. Meanwhile, the general energy crisis of the decade made people rethink electricity as well, and President Jimmy Carter included it in his push for a new energy policy.

The trends culminated in the Public Utility Regulatory Policies Act of 1978, better known as PURPA. The law included a number of provisions revising, and in some cases loosening, the strict regulatory protocol. Among them, it allowed private companies to build power plants – known under the law as "qualifying facilities," or QFs – and required utilities to purchase the power they produced. The provision was designed to encourage investment in renewable technologies like wind and solar power, and it worked to an extent. But it also provided a critical opening for early natural gas power plants. Today the vast majority of planned power to be built in coming decades is fueled by natural gas, which is relatively cheap and clean and better adaptable to hourly demand conditions. Today, PURPA is seen as one of the first moves of the deregulation of the energy industry.

Deregulation

The tidy and highly regulated energy world underwent massive transformation starting in the 1980s, when proponents of deregulation turned their attention to electricity. They were encouraged by the success of other industries that were deregulated in the 1970s, like airlines, trucking, and telecommunications. A major proof of their argument was the successful deregulation of the natural gas industry, which shared many key aspects with electricity. Both were essential commodities that required contiguous systems and a high-degree of coordination. After many years of debate and tinkering, free market principles applied to natural gas markets brought down prices, and encouraged new investment.

According to proponents, such principles must work for electricity as well. Without government controls, more companies would join the market to compete, bringing prices down. Companies would be encouraged to invest in new technologies, which would create more efficient and environmentally friendly systems. Providers would be beholden to their customers, who would be able to pick and choose among them for the best deal.

Deregulation had its opponents. Many cited the same reasons that had propelled the debate in the 1930s. They warned that electricity was an essential service, and that consumers must be protected from raw market forces. After all, companies would be serving their shareholders foremost, not their customers, and the urge to cut costs could lead to disaster. They also pointed out that electricity is a different type of commodity than airline routes and gas pipelines: electrons move instantaneously, and rely on incredibly complex systems. Without the right balance, the system would crash and everyone would be in the dark.

In many states, the proponents won by appealing to many different sides of the debate. Utility companies were excited because they would no longer have to maintain big, expensive power plants – and many salivated at the prospect of unloading their costly nuclear plants. They eagerly looked forward to a new market in which they could become light, nimble, modern companies with the glamour and profit-margins of dot.com start-ups. A host of other companies – mostly trading and gas companies – eagerly eyed the chance to get a piece of a multibillion dollar market that had been largely closed to them for so long. Customers were fascinated by the promise of lower monthly utility bills, and politicians were eager to be the ones to proclaim in the next election that they helped lower voters' power bills.

State by state, legislatures began to craft laws to deregulate and bring competition to their states. Regulators rewrote market rules, and a whole new crop of retailers, traders, and investors joined the market. Energy companies suddenly began to recruit top-notch MBA candidates and the most promising young scientists and engineers, none of whom would have thought twice about the boring energy sector of just ten years earlier.

Visit Vault at **www.vault.com** for insider company profiles, expert advice, career message boards, expert resume reviews, the Vault Job Board and more.

VAULT CAREER LIBRARY   **153**

Not everyone jumped on the bandwagon though. States that already had low electricity rates – like some Rocky Mountain states and some in the deep South – saw no reason to fuss with their system and took a pass. Efforts to deregulate at the federal level never picked up enough steam, and only some slight changes were passed.

Deregulation gone haywire

The hesitant ones appeared visionary after 2000, when things suddenly began to go wrong. The California energy crisis that began that year was a glaring cautionary example for the entire industry, and it almost single-handedly brought the deregulation movement to a screeching halt. States suddenly began to reconsider their deregulation plans, or sought to scale back the ones they had already passed.

This blow was quickly followed in late 2001 by the spectacular collapse of Enron, which horrified the industry. In a matter of months, the eighth largest company in America was exposed as a gigantic fraud as it dissolved into bankruptcy and infamy. Along the way, it tarred the reputation of the whole corps of new energy services company that had emerged to compete in the new markets. They were branded "energy pirates," and saw their high-flying hopes vanish along with their market cap. All this drama played out against a recession and capital crunch that hurt the energy industry as badly as any other.

Despite all this, the genie of competition shows no sign of going back in the bottle. The current political climate in Washington and most state capitals remains committed to the idea of competition and restructured energy markets, though they are pursuing their goals in a less hard-charging and more deliberate attitude. The industry has responded to the current challenges by maturing and rethinking the irrational exuberance of its youth.

And hopes that the industry will bounce back are underpinned by one salient fact everyone agrees upon: as long as people are attached to their computers, televisions, and lightbulbs, there will always be demand for the industry's goods and services.

Understanding the New Energy Industry

Today's industry is a mosaic of businesses and sectors, some old some new, operating in many different environments and frameworks. This is a basic look at how things stand today around the nation. Individual corporations can have operations in many different sectors, depending on their regulatory restrictions and corporate strategies, so they are by no means exclusive.

Generation

These are the operations that create the power. The basic production facilities – known as "base-load plants" – burn fossil fuels, and create hundreds of megawatts per hour. The workhorse of American power generation remains coal, which is cheap and abundant in the United States, and fuels roughly half of the nation's electricity load. The problem is that it is also the dirtiest fuel source available, and many plants today operate under "grandfather" exemptions to the Clean Air Act or with a host of expensive filtering equipment to keep it compliant with Environmental Protection Agency rules.

The other major base load fuel – accounting for about 20 percent of the nation's load – is nuclear power. These plants produce very large amounts of electricity from very little fuel, with no air pollution. But ever since Three Mile Island and Chernobyl, the drawbacks have been obvious. Though unlikely, an accident would be unthinkably catastrophic. The plants produce considerable amounts of thermal pollution – usually in the form of hot water that cannot be simply dumped into a river or reservoir. And in recent years, the problem of what to do with spent fuel rods has become critical. In 2001, over vociferous opposition, Congress allowed the U.S. Department of Energy to begin work on a permanent nuclear fuel dump at Yucca Mountain in Nevada. Until then, spent nuclear fuel will continue to be stored where it always has been: in closely monitored pools near the reactor where they were used.

The remaining 30 percent of the nation's electric load is accounted for by natural gas and renewable power sources. Gas in particular has been a favorite fuel source, and is forecast to be the major fuel for the 21st century. These plants are called "peaker plants" because they are easy to turn on and off to adapt to specific conditions in the service area. The turbines themselves are essentially jet engines rigged to produce power, and are very efficient, cheap to run, and produce much less pollution than other sources. The drawbacks are that they rely on natural gas markets for their supplies, and in general do not produce the huge amounts of megawatts needed to keep the grid up and running.

Despite the hopes and promises of supporters, renewable fuel technologies for generation remain relatively marginal in most parts of the country. The preeminent renewable fuel remains hydropower, particularly in the West. Hydropower has the advantage of producing no pollution and is easy to manipulate when reservoirs are at ideal conditions. Its primary drawback is that it is subject to the weather, and drought conditions can cause serious troubles. Hydropower dams also usually face opposition from environmentalists, who worry about the effects they have on fish and other wildlife.

Among other renewables, wind power has only recently begun to come into its own. Early wind turbines were inefficient, produced little power, and were even known for chopping up birds who strayed too close. All that has changed as more research has produced efficient turbines that can harness even mild winds, and that spin slow enough that birds don't get in their way. Already, a number of major wind power projects have been announced in the Pacific Northwest, the Dakotas, and Pennsylvania. The drawback is that most places do not have enough wind to make turbines worthwhile, and even the windiest spots need dozens of turbines spread out over many acres to produce a sufficient amount of power. Even then, wind is too inconsistent to be relied on to provide a major portion of the grid's power at any given time. Yet wind power is still far ahead of other renewable sources, like solar, geothermal, and biomass, which are still years away from being deployed in an commercially significant way.

Retail

These are the companies that actually sell the power to consumers. Power markets have a wholesale, or "bulk," side and a retail side. In the first, power is measured in megawatts per hour, while the later is usually in kilowatts per hour. As you would expect, companies in a competitive market will try to buy bulk

Visit Vault at **www.vault.com** for insider company profiles, expert advice, career message boards, expert resume reviews, the Vault Job Board and more.

V∧ULT CAREER LIBRARY   **155**

power as cheaply as possible, and sell it to individual homes and businesses for as much as they can get. More and more, retailers buy power from suppliers through "forward" contracts, which essentially guarantee they will receive x amount of power for y hours at z dollars per megawatt/hour. Contracts can be for as long as several months, or as little as a few hours. Another option are so-called "spot" markets, in which power was bought and sold for the coming hours. These markets proved to be far too dangerous though, as seen in California and other parts of the country, and are now usually used solely to shore up supplies not covered by forward contracts.

On the sales end, retailers in competitive markets have to woo customers to subscribe with them. Many simply offer the lowest price possible, or offer innovative or flexible payments schemes. Some position themselves as "green" providers, promising that a set portion of their power load will come from renewable sources.

Transmission

Generators and retailers, wholesale and retail markets, are connected by a vast transmission grid that is both essential for a functional market, yet one of the salient problems preventing full-blown competition from steaming ahead. Much of the grid is made up of the high-tension power lines you see running into the distance beside highways (the wires that lead to your home are technically part of the retail world; in deregulated markets, they are usually still owned by the local utility, which is required to provide "open-access" to other providers). The problem with the system is simply a matter of physics: electrons travel instantaneously, and the system requires carefully managed, redundant systems to ensure it doesn't short-circuit itself. This requires central control, and weather trouble, over-scheduling, or any number of variable can cause major problems.

For years, industry participants and government officials have argued about how to adapt this system to a competitive market. They have made some steps, most importantly through a federal regulatory order issued in the late 1990s that mandated the grid should be managed by several "regional transmission organizations" (RTOs), who could serve as the disinterested air traffic controllers of the grid. The most controversial part of the order required utilities to cede ownership, or at least operational control, of their transmission assets to these RTOs. But exactly what form RTOs should take remains an open question. The old utilities want a separate, for-profit entity to run the grid, with the contributors of the grid staying on as co-owners. Other parties envision RTOs as non-profit agencies, or what they call "independent system operators." So far, both models, as well as a few hybrids, are in place across the nation or are still in the planning stages.

Regulation and policy

Deregulation does not mean no regulation, and there are still enough market watchers to make it a substantial part of the industry. The federal government and each state still employ a small army of analysts, lawyers, economists, accountants, and technicians to keep watch over the system. Meanwhile, companies that do business in a given state employ a number of lawyers and lobbyists to represent their interests in the ongoing battles that take place at regulatory agencies. These cases include rate cases, environmental approvals for new plants and facilities, and fielding complaints from consumers and competitors.

Types of Energy Companies

Energy companies work in many ways within this framework. The foundation of the energy industry remains the "investor-owned utilities," or IOUs. These are the big names to whom most people write a check every month – companies like ConEdison in New York, PECO in Pennsylvania, Commonwealth Edison in Chicago. They were the original players protected by PUHCA for so many decades, and remain the biggest players in the industry, with valuable structural assets, capital reserves, and skilled manpower.

In competitive environments, many of these companies have set up subsidiaries to operate in other markets. Some have created "merchant" generation companies, which own power plants and sell the power in wholesale markets. Some have set up their own energy trading operations to trade in open markets. There are still enough rules and regulation in place that keep these operations separate and distinct, but they demonstrate how these companies remain the biggest and best able to adapt to the new energy industry.

Other major players from the regulated era include public power authorities. These are quasi-governmental agencies that own power plants and power lines, and sell it to consumers. They were created to serve areas under-served by the IOUs, and are charged with serving their consumers first and foremost. They are usually funded through charges collected and government-backed bond issues. Some were formed by the federal government to market power from the massive New Deal era power projects, notably the giant hydropower dams that power the Tennessee Valley Authority and the Bonneville Power Authority in the Pacific Northwest. Others were formed by states or municipal entities, including Santee Cooper in South Carolina and the Los Angeles Department of Water and Power in Los Angeles. A similar sector are rural electric cooperatives, which are member-owned and operated systems in rural areas and usually serve agricultural communities.

Public power plays a key role in the new energy industry. In the policy debates surrounding deregulation they were notable for representing their "customer first" guiding ethic, and were very aggressive in shaping the debate and speaking for consumers. In addition, they remain major employers, as they run plants and have operations similar to regular utilities. Many exist within deregulated markets and have had to adapt to competitive wholesale and retail markets.

The industry is rounded out by companies that fill niches within the new framework. These include merchant generators who own plants, some with a specialty in certain types of plants. For example, Exelon owns many nuclear plants around the country. Others specialize in bringing to market renewable sources. Other companies specialize in trading, and retailers that sell directly to customers.

Visit Vault at **www.vault.com** for insider company profiles, expert advice, career message boards, expert resume reviews, the Vault Job Board and more.

VAULT CAREER LIBRARY   **157**

The Oil and Gas Industry

The price of oil sends a ripple effect throughout the world's economy, affecting not only how much drivers have to shell out at the pump, but other forms of transportation, the cost of all goods and services, and the availability of basics like food and shelter. Nearly half of petroleum production in the U.S. goes toward gas, according to the NPRA (gasoline is a mixture of hydrocarbons for use in a spark-fueled internal combustion engine, like a car). Other products include asphalt, solvents, and even the wax used in things like chewing gum and crayons. Leading companies, ranked according to sales, are Royal Dutch/Shell, Exxon Mobil, BP, TOTAL S.A., ChevronTexaco, Petroleos de Venezuela, Petroleos Mexicanos, Eni S.p.A., Repsol YPF, S.A., and PetroChina Company Limited, according to Hoover's.

Rockefeller's riches

The modern oil industry in the U.S. was born in the late 19th century, when, after investing in a Cleveland oil refinery during the Civil War, John D. Rockefeller founded Standard Oil in 1870. As of 1880, Standard refined 95 percent of all oil in the U.S. Branded an illegal monopoly in 1911, Standard was divided into 34 companies, including many still around today, like Mobil, Chevron, Shell, and Esso (later renamed Exxon).

As Americans took to the road, demand for oil gushed ever higher. In the 1930s, the oil giants turned to Texas to seek their fortunes. Soon thereafter, Chevron, Texaco, Exxon and Mobil went overseas to expand their reserves, buying up rights to oil fields in Saudi Arabia (a bargain at $50,000).

Oil gets organized

In 1960, top oil-producing countries Iran, Iraq, Kuwait, Saudi Arabia and Venezuela met in Baghdad to form the intergovernmental organization OPEC, which stands for Organization of the Petroleum Exporting Countries. Today's list of 11 members, which collectively supply about 40 percent of the world's oil output and control more than three-fourths of total crude oil reserves in the world, are Algeria, Indonesia, Iran, Iraq, Kuwait, Libya, Nigeria, Qatar, Saudi Arabia, the United Arab Emirates and Venezuela. The members meet twice a year to decide on their total output level of oil, considering actions to adjust it if necessary in response to oil market developments. Basically, it's all about supply and demand --if oil production rises faster than demand, prices fall, which OPEC claims hurts both producers and, eventually, consumers (in the form of inflation).

Membership in OPEC is open to any oil-exporting nation that shares the organization's ideals. OPEC countries seek to ensure that oil producers get a good rate of return on their investments and (according to OPEC) that consumers continue to be able to access steady supplies of oil.

Oil stateside

Oil is certainly a slippery subject in the U.S., where high prices at the gas pump and the environmental issues associated with extraction and production always garner plenty of attention. The issue of drilling in the Arctic National Wildlife Refuge, for instance, was a huge topic in the election of 2000, and promises to resurface in 2004. Many of these decisions rest on politics and power: While the Clinton administration had proposed selling some 6 million acres in the Gulf of Mexico, off the coast of Florida, this amount was gutted at the behest of Florida Gov. Jeb Bush in 2001. But at other times, true environmental concerns hold sway. For example, the last oil refinery built in the U.S. was completed in 1976; though a handful more could contribute to lower gas prices, the risks and controversy surrounding their construction (refineries need to be built near water, and disasters like the Exxon Valdez oil spill have contributed to what the industry sees as a NIMBY– "not in my back yard" – attitude among the public) have all but scuttled the possibility of any new refineries any time soon.

In the U.S., according to the National Petrochemicals and Refiners Association (NPRA), there are 149 refineries, owned by 57 companies, with aggregate crude oil processing capacity of 17 million barrels per day (a barrel is 42 gallons). Back in 1981, there were 325 refineries, capable of producing 18.6 million barrels per day. Total U.S. demand for oil in 2002 was 17.5 million barrels per day. OPEC puts the world demand for oil at 76 million barrels per day, predicted to rise to more than 90 million barrels per day by 2020. Meanwhile, at the end of 2001, the latest year for which OPEC figures are available, world proven crude oil reserves stood at 1.075 million barrels. Saudi Arabia dominates these holdings, with crude oil reserves of 262,697 million barrels. Iraq comes in a distant second at 112,500 million barrels; these countries are followed by Iran, the UAE and Kuwait.

For a variety of reasons, including price and the obvious fact that U.S. demand outstrips supply, the U.S. imports a portion of its oil from other nations. In fact, according to the NPRA, while 96 percent of refined petroleum product demand is produced domestically, the U.S. imports 60 percent of the crude oil it refines from other countries.

Troubled times

The 1970s saw two crises in oil pricing – an Arab oil embargo in 1973 and the outbreak of the Iranian revolution in 1979. In both cases, oil prices rose sharply. After a peak in prices in the early part of the 80s, the market saw a sharp decline followed by a collapse in 1986. By the 1990s, prices had recovered, though they never regained the high levels of the previous decade. Another collapse occurred in 1998 following economic instability in Asia – prices sank to $10 a barrel. By 2000, they had climbed back up to over $30 a barrel.

Oil alliances

At the end of the 1990s, following the Asian crisis, the industry witnessed several mega-mergers among major international oil companies, including the well-known Exxon-Mobil and Chevron-Texaco marriages (British Petroleum also merged with Amoco and Arco to form BP, and Conoco joined with Phillips Petroleum to become ConocoPhillips). Many small independent companies weren't so lucky, and went into bankruptcy.

Though the industry has recovered recently as oil prices rose sky high during the Iraq war (hitting $40 a barrel in the first quarter of 2004), the industry began to see pressure as environmental concerns became

Visit Vault at **www.vault.com** for insider company profiles, expert advice, career message boards, expert resume reviews, the Vault Job Board and more.

VAULT CAREER LIBRARY **159**

more pronounced, leading producers to worry about an impending drop-off in demand. Supply may also become an issue as continued unrest in Iraq has prevented the exporting of crude oil from that country.

Russia rising

With oil resources naturally limited, the industry constantly has to search for new supplies. Since the collapse of the Soviet Union, Russia has been taking steps to modernize its oil infrastructure. With proven oil reserves of 60 billion barrels (mostly situated in Western Siberia), Russia also holds the world's largest natural gas reserves. International oil services companies like Halliburton and Baker Hughes have begun working with the major Russian oil companies in recent years, and the country's economy is becoming increasingly reliant on oil exports – in 2002, energy accounted for nearly 20 percent of Russia's GDP. In February 2003, BP invested $6.75 billion in Russia, creating a new joint venture company with Russia's fourth-largest oil company, TNK. In August of that year, Russia approved a $13 billion merger between two of its oil superpowers, Yukos and Sibneft, creating one of the largest publicly traded oil companies in the world, but the deal was suspended a few months later due to "technical difficulties."

Analysts say the country has great potential, and could eventually produce 10 million barrels of oil per day by 2010 – President Putin has made the energy sector the centerpiece of Russia's growth strategy in the coming decades. But this promise is dampened by an inefficient infrastructure, including government corruption and the legacy of the Soviet collapse. Russia poses a geographical challenge, as well – exports are limited by the capacity of the pipeline system intersecting the vast region. New pipeline systems, such as the Baltic Pipeline System, have been developed in recent years, and negotiations are underway for others (as well as for "reversal projects" that re-route the direction of oil pipelines to maximize transport of oil out of Russia). Similar measures are underway involving natural gas. Two mega-projects, Sakhalin I and Sakhalin II, are taking place on Sakhalin Island, located off of the east coast, site of a former penal colony. The area is rich in oil and natural gas reserves, and oil giants including Exxon and Shell are backing the projects, with oil exports anticipated for 2005 and natural gas exports expected in 2007 and 2008.

Africa is another source of oil reserves. In February 2004, Exxon Mobil began a $3 billion development project off the coast of Angola, and in July 2003, crude oil production began for the first time in the nation of Chad, the result of the World Bank's single largest investment in sub-Saharan Africa. But companies doing business in the continent are vulnerable to dramatic political unrest and violence in many countries. In March 2003, Chevron/Texaco, Royal Dutch/Shell, and TotalFinaElf shut down their operations in the Niger Delta region of Nigeria due to clashes between soldiers and militant groups in the area. Production began to resume a month later, but the region remains unstable.

Green concerns

So-called "greenhouse gases," produced through the burning of fossil fuels, are increasingly acknowledged to be a major factor behind a trend in global warming, a trend that threatens major environmental repercussions in coming decades. The Kyoto Protocol, developed by a group of nations over the last decade to limit greenhouse gas emissions, was a hot topic as the Bush administration came into power in 2000. The administration decided not to sign on to the protocol, which would have required the U.S. to reduce its 1990 levels of greenhouse gas emissions by 7 percent by the years 2008-2012. The administration's own solutions to the global warming problem have raised the ire of many environmentalists, who see U.S. energy policy as too friendly to the interests of corporations.

Meanwhile, corporations have taken their own baby steps to ease the environmental impact of their products. In January 2003, 14 U.S. oil corporations and subsidiaries launched the Chicago Climate Exchange, a trading program allowing participating members to earn redeemable credits for exceeding emissions reduction goals.

Today, the U.S. oil industry spends a lot of time lobbying Congress for a "comprehensive energy policy." According to the NPRA, such a policy would include tax incentives for new and existing refinery capacity, reasonable environmental regulations that balance the need for cleaner fuel with market demand, and a clearer policy toward individual states adopting requirements for fuel formulations (California, Connecticut, and New York, for instance, have tougher restrictions on what can go into fuel in order to reduce potentially harmful emissions – restrictions the industry says cost refineries millions).

But the bottom line is that oil is a non-renewable resource, and experts warn that there is an urgent need to develop a large-scale alternative energy infrastructure. In addition to alternatives already in use, such as solar, wind, and geothermal energy systems, new technologies are in development – but it's a race against time. According to the Alternative Energy Institute, the world's supply of oil will reach its maximum of production, and the midpoint of its depletion, around 2010. Already, about 65 percent of known oil n the U.S. has been burned. Soon, the AEI warns, more than half of the world's petroleum reserves will be owned and controlled by countries in the Middle East, a fact that highlights the problems wrought by political instability in the area.

The other gas

As a power source, natural gas has become a contender in recent years. Today, a third of energy used in the U.S. is fueled by natural gas. As demand for electricity boomed in the 1990s, the market revved up, and with it came the entry of "energy merchants" like the infamous Enron, which set out to purchase natural gas cheaply, convert it into electricity, and reap profits from the "spark spread" – the markup on the sale of power. These merchants eventually manufactured a "shortage" in electricity that sent prices soaring, which in turn affected the price per cubic foot of natural gas.

But the U.S. has limited domestic resources for natural gas production. As the supply is depleted, U.S. production falls by roughly 2 percent a year. Importing gas from other countries, including Russia, Qatar and Trinidad, and building pipelines in places like Alaska and Canada are touted as options, but they're expensive and unwieldy ones.

What does this mean for the oil industry? According to author Paul Roberts, a tight market for natural gas means less resources are available to devote toward new applications like synthetic gasoline, hydrogen for fuel cell-fired cars, or other energy alternatives. As a result, the oil economy doesn't have much to fear from the green-fueled car of the future for a while.

Visit Vault at **www.vault.com** for insider company profiles, expert advice, career message boards, expert resume reviews, the Vault Job Board and more.

VAULT CAREER LIBRARY   161

Employment prospects

The Bureau of Labor Statistics (BLS) classifies jobs in the industry as "oil and gas extraction," including both oil and natural gas. This category offers something for everyone: There are management and administrative jobs for white-collar types (20 percent of the industry in 2002); hardier souls might choose to work as derrick and rotary drill operators or roustabouts (11 percent). There are also plenty of opportunities for the scientifically-minded, with jobs in geology and engineering (23 percent). According to the BLS, most establishments in the industry employ fewer than 10 workers, with about 77 percent of the U.S. workforce concentrated in California, Louisiana, Oklahoma, and Texas.

Though earnings are relatively high in the industry, BLS predicts a drop-off in overall employment in coming years, with an anticipated wage and salary decline of 28 percent by 2012 (as compared to an overall drop in all industries of 16 percent). The industry is known for its fluctuations – as prices skyrocket, companies invest in new technologies and expand their explorations, while lower prices have the opposite effect. Still, new technologies for exploration, including 3-D and 4-D seismic exploration methods, new drilling techniques, and technologies for exploring deep under the sea, will continue to produce a demand for skilled workers.

Getting Hired

Energy companies are in many ways similar to other major American corporations. Most have financial structures that are recognizable to anyone with business experience, and they respond to similar cycles of supply and demand. Yet energy also features many unique quirks: it operates in a stringent regulatory environment, and it is responsible for the production and distribution of a vital service. It's ups and downs have ripple effects across the economic spectrum, as energy costs make up a substantial portion of the bottom line of almost every business in the nation, from interstate shipping to web hosting.

As you proceed in your job search, here are a few general principles that you should keep in mind – whether you are interested in power, oil, or gas.

Patience

Every industry has its ups and downs, and the energy industry is no exception. Every corner of the economy has been hurt by the recent recession. But unlike the economy at large, the power sector has had to deal with the twin blows of the Enron scandal and the California crisis. Enron managed to cast many energy companies in a negative light, causing investors to steer clear, and almost wiping out their access to capital markets. Meanwhile, California put the brakes on the deregulation movement and has dampened the prospects of what had been seen as one of the great growth opportunities in business.

Most power companies report that they are in the middle of serious "restructurings" after the flush years of the 1990s, preferring to wait and see how the economy recovers before investing in new ventures and hiring new staff. As a result, jobs will be hard to come by for awhile. Persistence and patience are essential. You should also keep in mind that while the sector may be in rough shape, it is likely to bounce back very quickly once things begin to turn around. The infrastructure for a vibrant industry is in place, and every expert agrees that demand for the industry's good and services will expand considerably in the coming years. It is, after all, a more than $218 billion a year industry.

It is important not to loose sight of the fact that traditionally, the power sector has been one of the most stable and recession-proof industries in business. Its products and services only grow in demand, and it has a firm infrastructure in place. Many industry watchers agree that the current slump is simply a correction of roughly 10 years of uncritical exuberance and recklessness, and that long-term prospects are very good.

A case in point can be found in the related oil and natural gas industries, which have survived the recession quite well. Ironically, the oil and gas sectors have even been relatively immune to recent political turmoil. For a long time, trouble in the Middle East usually resulted in supply disruptions and general uncertainty. This time around, supplies have remained stable, and rising prices have actually improved the bottom line of many oil companies. Part of this is the result of the industry's aggressive efforts to exploit new sources.

Opportunity

Throughout the 1990s the energy industry was one of remarkable evolution, and that is likely to continue despite the bad economy. Some parts of the power sector have certainly shriveled on the vine in recent years, but many predict that many of the changes have been simply put on hold, as policymakers and investors remain committed to the basic principles of greater competition.

At an energy conference in February 2003, FERC Chairman Pat Wood reiterated the value of the current approach. "There should be little disagreement today on whether we should continue to rely on markets for wholesale power supply," he said. "Markets have earned our support. Markets have performed well in wholesale power for all the same reasons they have served customers of other industries and made our economy and our nation so strong. Markets put investment risk where it belongs, with investors, not solely on the backs of captive customers. We should not loose sight of how market forces have already brought electric and natural gas customers billions in lower energy costs."

Throughout the 1990s, most power companies aggressively expanded in an effort to take better advantage of the emerging deregulated markets. Part of their push was to recruit talented business minds from completely different industries to improve their competitiveness. After all, these were issues the industry had never really had to deal with in the days of full regulation. That hiring trend has essentially dried up now, as the economy shrinks and the future of the markets remain uncertain. But many companies remain committed to diversity in principle, and the barrier to entry may be lower than you think if you present yourself the right way.

Energy remains in many ways a world of its own, with its own esoteric set of quirks and manners. For many positions, there is simply no shortcut around experience in energy. This is why many companies put an emphasis on their college recruitment programs. In a tight economy, companies frequently look for specific skills to fill niches. Your best bet is to honestly assess what you have to offer, and try to plug yourself into a specific niche. Once you are on the right track, careers can be diverse and flexible; the biographies of many energy employees usually features a few surprising sidetracks and experiences. But

Visit Vault at **www.vault.com** for insider company profiles, expert advice,
career message boards, expert resume reviews, the Vault Job Board and more.

V∆ULT CAREER LIBRARY   **163**

the bottom line, across the industry, is that nothing on your resume will impress recruiters more than energy experience in some form or another.

Geography

You will help your cause if you are geographically flexible. On the power side, the industry is decentralized. Consolidation has created more larger, regional entities than ever existed before, but not as many as in other industries. It is a unique aspect of the power industry that no matter where you are – whether in a big city or in rural farm country – there are a limited number operations within driving distance.

Because there is no central hub for the power sector, utility operations cover the entire nation. Though some players are much larger than others, the sector is characterized by a number of smaller public power agencies and co-operatives, who often pay competitive salaries, have a smaller pool of applicants, and can help you get the experience you need to advance in the industry. It will help you if you are ready to relocate to the right job.

Some aspects of the industry are relatively concentrated, however. The old energy trading companies – Enron, Dynegy, Reliant, and El Paso – were all famously headquartered along a single street in Houston that came to be known as "Power Alley." They are still there, if there once world-conquering ambitions have been drastically tempered. Still, many natural gas producers and pipeline operators can be found around there, with major operations often located across Texas and Louisiana.

The oil industry remains largely headquartered in Texas. But many of these companies maintain large operations in New York, near capital markets, and have extensive operations across the globe..

Keeping current

It is an understatement to say the goalposts in the energy industry are changing – in fact, the sidelines, referees, teams, and the very rules of the game are changing with stunning speed. As you search for a job, you cannot afford to overlook the details, and there is no way around spending an appropriate amount of time researching and reviewing the company, market, and regulatory system you are targeting. You will need to arrive at your interview with a formidable array of information at your fingertips, as every employer needs people that have a firm understanding of just what is happening in a constantly changing market.

In the power sector, you'll have to understand the market conditions in the state. When researching companies, you need to understand what lines of business the company runs. It is not always crystal clear: some utilities have separate trading and generating operations, and you will hurt your pitch if you are applying for a division that focuses solely on one line and mistakenly assume it works in others. More importantly, regulatory rules and market conditions change month by month and even day by day. There is no way around it – you'll need to know who the key regulatory bodies are in your region, what are the market rules, and who are the main competitors.

In oil and gas, market conditions change hour by hour. While the regulatory and legal frameworks are comparatively static, you need to understand just what is happening. You need to know the current average costs of a barrel of crude. You need to understand refining capacity and should have some understanding of drilling and exploration operations. If you are applying for a major multinational company you will have to understand the geopolitical conditions in regions where the company has operations. This web of variables add up to the very underpinnings of a company's entire operations.

Doing your homework is particularly important if you have little or no experience in energy. Nothing will turn off recruiters as much as approaching energy like it is any other business. You should know your way around the specific political, economic and market issues your target companies face both to show that you have a basic grounding in their business and that you have an aptitude to learn more on the job.

The information in this section was excerpted from the *Vault Guide Top Energy/Oil & Gas Employers*. Get the inside scoop on energy careers with Vault:

- **Vault Guides:** *Vault Guide Top Energy/Oil & Gas Employers*

- **Employer Research:** Online Energy/Oil & Gas Employer Profiles, Employee Surveys and more

- **Message Boards:** Vault Energy Career Advice Message Board

- **Career Services:** Vault Resume and Cover Letter Reviews, rated the "Top Choice" by *The Wall Street Journal* for resume makeovers

Go to www.vault.com

Visit Vault at **www.vault.com** for insider company profiles, expert advice, career message boards, expert resume reviews, the Vault Job Board and more.

V∧ULT CAREER LIBRARY   **165**

Employer Directory

ConocoPhillips

600 North Dairy Ashford
Houston, TX 77079
Phone: 281 293 3947
www.conocophillips.com/careers

ConocoPhillips is an international, integrated energy company. It is the third largest integrated energy company in the United States, based on market capitalization, oil and gas proved reserves and production; and the largest refiner in the United States. Worldwide, of non-government controlled companies, ConocoPhillips has the eighth largest total of proved reserves and is the fourth largest refiner in the world. ConocoPhillips is known worldwide for its technological expertise in deep-water exploration and production, reservoir management and exploitation, 3-D seismic technology, high-grade petroleum coke upgrading and sulfur removal. Headquartered in Houston, Texas, ConocoPhillips operates in more than 40 countries. The company has approximately 37,200 employees worldwide and assets of $84 billion. ConocoPhillips stock is listed on the New York Stock Exchange under the symbol "COP." ConocoPhillips actively recruits for undergraduate, masters and doctorate level students in a variety of disciplines for roles across the United States. To find out more about our opportunities for internships and graduate roles please contact your local career services or visit our website www.conocophillips.com/careers

Schools ConocoPhillips recruits from:
University of Texas at Austin; Texas A&M; Oklahoma State University; University of Oklahoma; Texas Tech; University of Tulsa; Colorado School of Mines; Kansas State University; University of Alaska; University of Arkansas; Baylor University; University of California-Davis; Cal Poly-Pamona; Cal Poly-San Luis Obisbo; LSU; McNeese; University of Missouri-Rolla; Mississippi State University; Morehouse College; Montana State University; Montana Tech University; New Mexico State University; Penn. State; Southern University; University of Houston; University of Wyoming; UCLA

Alliant Energy Corporation

4902 N. Biltmore Ln.
Madison, WI 53718
Phone: (608) 458-3311
Fax: (608) 458-4824
Toll free: 800-255-4268
www.alliant-energy.com

Amerada Hess Corporation

1185 Avenue of the Americas
New York, NY 10036
Phone: (212) 997-8500
Fax: (212) 536-8593
www.hess.com

American Electric Power Company, Inc.

1 Riverside Plaza
Columbus, OH 43215-2372
Phone: (614) 716-1000
Fax: (614) 716-1823
www.aep.com

Anadarko Petroleum Corporation

1201 Lake Robbins Dr.
The Woodlands, TX 77380-1046
Phone: (832) 636-1000
Fax: (832) 636-8220
www.anadarko.com

Baker Hughes Incorporated

3900 Essex Ln., Ste. 1200
Houston, TX 77027-5177
Phone: (713) 439-8600
Fax: (713) 439-8699
Toll free: (888)-408-4244
www.bakerhughes.com

BP plc

Britannic House

1 Finsbury Circus

London EC2M 7BA,

Phone: +44-171-496-4000

Fax: +44-171-496-4630

www.bp.com

ChevronTexaco

6001 Bollinger Canyon Road

San Ramon, CA 94583

Phone: (925) 842-1000

Fax: (925) 842-3530

www.chevrontexaco.com

Consolidated Edison, Inc.

4 Irving Place

New York, NY 10003

Phone: (212) 460-4600

Fax: (212) 982-7816

www.conedison.com

Duke Energy Corporation

526 S. Church St

Charlotte, NC 28202

Phone: (704) 594-6200

Fax: (704) 382-3814

www.duke-energy.com

Exelon Corporation

10 S. Dearborn St., 37th Fl.

Chicago, IL 60680-5379

Phone: (312) 394-7398

Fax: (312) 394-7945

www.exeloncorp.com

ExxonMobil Corporation

5959 Las Colinas Blvd.

Irving, TX 75039-2298

Phone: (972) 444-1000

Fax: (972) 444-1350

www.exxon.mobil.com

FirstEnergy Corporation

76 S. Main St.

Akron, OH 44308

Phone: (800) 646-0400

Fax: (330) 384-3866

www.firstenergycorp.com

GE Energy

4200 Wildwood Pkwy.

Atlanta, GA 30339

Phone: (678) 844-6000

Fax: (678) 844-6690

www.gepower.com

Halliburton Company

5 Houston Center, 1401 McKinney, Ste. 2400

Houston, TX 77020

Phone: (713) 759-2600

Fax: (713) 759-2635

www.halliburton.com

Marathon Oil Corporation

5555 San Felipe Rd.

Houston, TX 77056-2723

Phone: (713) 629-6600

Fax: (713) 296-2952

www.marathon.com

Occidental Petroleum Corporation

10889 Wilshire Blvd.

Los Angeles, CA 90024-4201

Phone: (310) 208-8800

Fax: (310) 443-6690

www.oxy.com

Visit Vault at **www.vault.com** for insider company profiles, expert advice,
career message boards, expert resume reviews, the Vault Job Board and more.

VAULT CAREER LIBRARY   **167**

Pacific Gas and Electric Company

1 Market St., Spear Tower, Ste. 2400

San Francisco, CA 94105

Phone: (415) 267-7000

Fax: (415) 267-7268

www.pgecorp.com

Schlumberger Limited

153 E. 53rd St., 57th Fl.

New York, NY 10022-4624

Phone: (212) 350-9400

Fax: (212) 350-9457

www.slb.com\

Shell Oil Company

One Shell Plaza

Houston, TX 77002

Phone: (713) 241-6161

Fax: (713) 241-4044

www.shelloil.com

Sunoco, Inc.

10 Penn Center, 1801 Market St.

Philadelphia, PA 19103-1699

Phone: (215) 977-3000

Fax: (215) 977-3409

Toll Free: 800-786-6261

www.sunocoinc.com

TXU Corp.

Energy Plaza, 1601 Bryan St., 33rd Fl.

Dallas, TX 75201-3411

Phone: (214) 812-4600

Fax: (214) 812-7077

www.txucorp.com

Unocal Corporation

2141 Rosecrans Ave., Ste. 4000

El Segundo, CA 90245

Phone: (310) 726-7600

Fax: (310) 726-7817

www.unocal.com

Valero Energy Corporation

1 Valero Place

San Antonio, TX 78212-3186

Phone: (210) 370-2000

Fax: (210) 370-2646

www.valero.com

The Williams Companies, Inc.

1 Williams Center

Tulsa, OK 74172

Phone: (918) 573-2000

Fax: (918) 573-6714

Toll Free: (800)-945-5426

www.williams.com

Fashion

Do you thrill to the thought that gray might – just might – be the new black? Do you tire of fashion trends before they even hit the stores? Then a career in fashion could be the right choice for you. Those who truly love the field say that the perks – fabulous clothes, exposure to famous people and brands, extraordinary diversity, awareness of upcoming trends and cool job status-are worth the struggle. Still, fashion is not all glitz and glamour. Even more than talent, an understanding of the industry is what lands the job.

Even though the fashion industry is difficult to break into, opportunities abound there – creative jobs in design and marketing; retail sales and buying positions; corporate careers in finance, planning, and distribution. This guide covers where to begin and what options are available in the industry.

Yet whether you are seeking a place on the catwalk or in the haute couture clubhouse, the fashion business is just that – a business. Insiders from all over the fashion world say that their jobs are high on stress and low on pay. Moreover, insiders conclude, people are often judged as much on looks as on performance. With its rigorous hours, capricious culture and wobbly corporate ladder, the fashion industry certainly isn't for everybody. Yet for a dedicated minority, there is no more exciting and inspiring place. Lecturing at a forum hosted by the Fashion Group Foundation, designer Isaac Mizrahi characterized fashion this way: "I hope you all adore what you're doing. It's really got to be this obsession. You have to love cloth. You have to love chalk. You have to love pins. You do it because you love to do it, and can't stop doing it."

Designers create and produce garments, textiles and accessories. Some have formal training and some do not. Almost all designers begin as assistant designers for a few years and eventually become designers. In a large company, a designer may move up the ladder to be a design director. A design director manages the designers from each group. For example, at a company like Bebe, there may be a designer for each group (such as dresses, suits, knits, and denim), but a design director will coordinate the efforts of all the designers so the brand presents a cohesive image. Product development usually refers to retailers that develop their own product in conjunction with manufacturers. Product development differs from design in that it usually doesn't require as many technical skills. In fact, product developers may work with designers from other companies to create products for their own brand.

Fashion Design Jobs

Assistant Designer: Helps the designer create new designs. May help with sketches and research.

Designer: Creates plans for clothes that fit the image, season and price point of the brand.

Assistant Technical Designer: Assists designer or technical designer in all aspects of quality and fit procedures. Must have strong computer skills.

Technical Designer: Follows design direction to develop garments through technical sketches, specific measurements for garments, receiving and reviewing samples and sketching and measuring garments for technical packages.

Visit Vault at **www.vault.com** for insider company profiles, expert advice, career message boards, expert resume reviews, the Vault Job Board and more.

VAULT CAREER LIBRARY   **169**

Sample Pattern Maker: Translates designers' sketches into wearable works of art by draping and making patterns to create sample garments. Almost all patternmakers draft patterns on computers.

Textile Designer: Creates textiles by using various fibers and knitting or weaving techniques for industries ranging from apparel to upholstery.

The Scoop on Design Careers

Most fashion experts would agree that design, one of fashion's most competitive and exciting fields, requires technical and art training, leadership, ingenuity, highly developed patternmaking skills and a keen understanding of the aesthetic as well as the practical and cost-effective. Design also calls for absolute dedication. Some of the most successful designers refer to their vocation as an "obsession" or a "way of life." Given the hardships, designers have to be crazy about what they do. How else would they be able to survive the grueling hours, low entry-level pay, and lack of guarantees of success?

The first step toward becoming a designer is reconsidering your decision. Our insiders say there is no shame in being a realist: "Fashion students often come in bright-eyed and idealistic. They think they are ready for the hard work and difficult hours so long as they can have the glamour too. What they don't realize is that very, very few designers hit it big." Aspiring designers also err when it comes to focus. "You have to think about what consumers really want," advises another source. "It's vital to know the realities of the job market. Pay attention to what people are going to buy rather than what you want to create." And it never hurts to look at your other options. "Students don't know that there are a hundred other jobs in fashion besides design," says an insider from a New York fashion school. "There are trim buyers, pattern makers, sample makers, quality control experts and fashion consultants. Often, these jobs are not only better-paying, they are 100 percent more secure."

For those who have listened to the naysayers and still want to be designers, the advice is – go for it. Insiders from such famous New York City fashion schools as Pratt, Parsons and FIT all concede that someone has to be the next Donna Karan or Calvin Klein. Why not you? If you think you have the guts, the talent and the backbone, "go global and go for the top," declares one enthusiastic source.

The climb may take some time, however. "It's very rare for a young fashion designer to set up his own label immediately after graduation," confesses a source. In reality, most graduates will spend five or more years working for a designer, gaining experience, earning a reputation and making contacts. Some fashion professionals will even start a design career outside of the industry in order to break into the field. Internships at major fashion houses or other jobs, like pattern work or retail, can sometimes launch you into design. The bottom line: don't be too hasty. Think about each job as a stepping stone in your career – so that you will always know what options you have.

Our Survey Says: Fashion Industry Culture

Image

In the fashion industry, your image is an important factor in your career. In some fields, such as modeling, a certain "type" is required. In other fields, such as public relations, good looks are preferred. Evidence of fashion's obsession with appearance is everywhere. Many retail employees must sport the clothing of their company. Designers serve as walking examples of their work. Even employees at fashion magazines "dress accordingly." Appearance is more important for fashion professionals who interact with the public and who work for high-end employers. (If you work in finance or planning, your dress matters less. And if you work at Kohl's versus Bloomingdale's, being "fashionable" is not as important.)

The "beauty prerequisite" is a source of pride, but also of contention. "You're often judged by what you wear and what you look like," says a designer who specializes in women's couture. Noverto Gonzalez, who worked as an assistant buyer at Saks Fifth Avenue says, "You have to represent whom you work for. The industry can be pretentious. They look at your shoes, bag and watch to check out the label." Certainly, appearance alone probably won't make or break a fashion career. Most fashion employers are looking for traditional skills and abilities. Nevertheless, in the fashion industry appearance may count more than it does in other industries.

Read the magazines and follow celebrities if you want to keep up with the latest trends. Check the publication section in this guide for trade papers, but also consider magazine staples like *Vogue, Harper's Bazaar* and *W*. You may also want to look at the French, English or Spanish editions of these magazines.

Do good and be beautiful

Fashion is home to glamour, beautiful people and of course, celebrities. Everyone knows the name of at least one supermodel; most people could name quite a few more. In fashion, namedropping and networking are the norm. But another common, if less known, aspect of the fashion world is philanthropy. "Philanthropy," designer Kenneth Cole said at a fashion charity event, "has been part of our corporate culture from the beginning."

This warm-and-fuzzy consciousness isn't simply motivated by the heart: the wallet has something to do with it. Specifically, mixing philanthropy with commerce is a sales tool called cause-related marketing. Since public service is an ideal conduit for sales, many famous designers embrace one cause or another. However, these causes are often as changeable as the industry itself. Points out one fashion insider: "Fashion may embrace fur-wearing one day and protest it the next. Its loyalties are superficial." There are drawbacks to here-today-gone-tomorrow activism. Nevertheless, public service organizations can benefit by the media attention given to "fashionable causes."

Visit Vault at **www.vault.com** for insider company profiles, expert advice,
career message boards, expert resume reviews, the Vault Job Board and more.

VAULT CAREER LIBRARY   171

Melting pot

The glass ceiling is not much of a problem in an industry where "women outnumber men." "Race is rarely, if ever, an issue" and "a large number of the men in design are gay," says an insider at an upscale department store. In fact, an insider at The Gap is happy to report, "Gender and ethnicity are just not an issue." In almost all aspects of the industry, the pervasion of different cultures, races, religious faiths and sexual orientations is common. "I expected to see a lot of white upper-class yuppies," remarks one J. Crew insider, "but this wasn't what I envisioned. The proverbial New York City melting pot boils over into the [J. Crew] corporate office."

L'Oreal is one brand that prides itself on its international flavor. In fact, it boasts that many of its employees are multilingual. Nike is also sound in the diversity department. At this company, different ethnic groups gather for "informal meetings." One member of the company's "Hispanic caucus" finds Nike "a fun place to meet other Latinos and network." Of course, not all employees are content with their company's heterogeneity. At companies like Lands End and L.L. Bean, some employees complain of a lack of diversity. But others argue that the predominately white demographics simply reflect the surrounding communities. "Maine and Wisconsin are not exactly known for large mixes of ethnic communities," says one. "It would follow that the minority headcount is proportional to the community and state." An Asian-American L.L. Bean insider agrees, "I have always felt that the employee makeup simply reflects the general population [in Maine]." As production continues to grow overseas, fashion industry employees are becoming more accustomed to a global marketplace. Companies may buy their fabric from Korea, cut and sew in Sri Lanka, pack and ship in Hong Kong, warehouse in the U.S. and sell in Canada and Mexico.

While the fashion industry is one of the most ethnically diverse around, insiders still complain of "a herd mentality." Complains one: "At my last job, everyone had a blonde bob. Fortunately, my new job is more diverse. It doesn't seem that race or sexuality is that important – it's all about how you look. Class and style are what are most important." Speaking of blondes, one celebrity dresser "can't wait to dress Gwyneth Paltrow." Why? "Because everyone wants to dress her!" He continues, "I enjoy meeting celebrities on a personal level, although not everything about my job is glamorous. It's not glamorous running around buying shoes at the last minute and sitting around a seating chart at 3 a.m., guessing who will be happy sitting next to each other." An assistant designer agrees that the industry is, at best, unpredictable. "I'm not doing what I thought I'd be doing," she says. "There are some people [in this industry] with high profile jobs, but most of us end up working for other famous people."

Networking

Ask around the fashion industry and you'll find people who dreamed of working there all their lives and people who stumbled into their positions by chance. One associate designer maintains, "To get into the creative end of the industry, you need a proper education. You need to study design. Technical people such as buyers and inventory planners, on the other hand, are more likely to have 'fallen' into their jobs." No matter how they got there, however, fashion professionals admit that having industry contacts is often more important than having talent. "To find a job," reveals an employee from Federated, "it's important to use the people you know. I found my first job through contacts, the next by sending an exploratory note and the third was luck – I got it out of a newspaper advertisement. I'd say my first job was the easiest to find."

While many people – and fashion students in particular – might feel dismayed by this need to know the "right people," one insider says worry is unnecessary. "Students often think they cannot make connections while confined within college walls," says a career counselor from a top New York fashion school. "This is a myth. Connections is just another word for relationships. You have relationships with other students, professors, career counselors, the school administration and many others. At fashion schools, most of the teachers have previous experience in the fashion industry." What does that mean? An acquaintance at your school or workplace might already have valuable job information!

It all comes down to networking. To find the right fashion job for you, it is necessary to discuss your job search with the people you know – and with the people they know. Ask questions, inquire about openings, and request informational interviews. Fashion students should attend as many college-sponsored events as possible and seek relevant internships. After a fashion internship has ended, they should keep in touch with their managers. A fashion career counselor confirms, "Those who serve as intern advisors often grow very fond of their interns. They want to know that you've graduated; they want to help and advise you."

Internships

Most fashion internships are in design, marketing, and production – and unpaid. Like the entertainment industry, actual education isn't as important as work experience. You will need some education to get in the door, but after that your resume or connections will get you farther. If you want to go into fashion or retail, get an internship or even a part-time job in sales or merchandising to get started. Each experience on your resume will help land a better internship or full-time job the next time. Although some internships are posted in the trade papers (check the Publications section), many internship searches are self-directed because many are never publicized. If the position is at a popular company or designer, the internship will never be posted since everyone will want it on his or her resume.

Make sure to express your desire to learn and help the company – even if you think your level of responsibility is not as high as you would like. Once you are in the company, you can find out about other positions before they may even be open. Build your resume, and you can get the interviews and introductions. Of course, your initial job in the fashion industry may not pay well. There are several options here – you work to get the experience or to learn enough to start your own business. If you are thinking of the latter, take any experience you can. It will pay off later.

Visit Vault at **www.vault.com** for insider company profiles, expert advice, career message boards, expert resume reviews, the Vault Job Board and more.

V∧ULT CAREER LIBRARY   **173**

Day in a Life: Assistant Product Manager, Federated Merchandising Group

Noverto Gonzales graduated from the University of North Texas with a BA in Merchandising in 1999. His first summer internship was at J.C Penney in Texas. It was a ten-week program: five weeks as assistant department manager on the retail floor and five weeks as an assistant buyer. He knew he wanted to live in New York City, so the summer before he graduated, Noverto landed another internship in the city. He was offered an internship at Barney's and Saks Fifth Avenue but chose the one at Saks since a salary came with it. The Barney's internship paid a small stipend at the end of the summer. His New York City job search was entirely self-directed.

After graduation, he was offered a position at J.C. Penney (in Texas) and Saks Fifth Avenue. J.C. Penney was very supportive and knew he wanted to go to New York. He began his career as an assistant buyer at Saks Fifth Avenue Catalog. He moved on to Federated as an assistant product manager. Federated operates Bloomingdale's, Macy's West and East, Goldsmith's, The Bon Marche, Burdines, Lazarus and Rich's department stores. At the Federated Merchandising Group, he worked with other product managers, buyers, the design team and the technical design team. Federated Merchandising Group, a division of Federated Department Stores, is responsible for the conceptualization, design, sourcing and marketing of private brands which are exclusive to Macy's, Rich's, Lazarus, Goldsmith's, The Bon Marche, Burdines and Bloomingdale's. These private labels include: INC, Style & Co., Alfani, Tools of the Trade, Charter Club, JM Collection, Tasso Elba, Club Room and Greendog.

Noverto Gonzalez's Day

9:00 a.m.: Get into office and check email. Our overseas office in Turkey has left me some notes. Update production time and action plans. The approvals for fit samples, lap dips and trims are managed by product development. For example, if our designer doesn't like a button on a sample, we have to find a replacement.

10:30 a.m.: Fit model comes in. We have fittings three times a week. I keep a "Fit" book and take notes of things that were changed. The designer and assistant designer are also in the meeting.

11:30 a.m.: I go back to my office to update the open purchase orders. If the parameters of the order change, I have to update it and make sure the legal documents are correct as well. Some of essential information is color, style number, vendor, country of origin, first cost and landed cost. I also deal with quota issues.

12:30 p.m.: Get back to the office and work on design samples. Go over current season sales and look through styles and colors. Look at different types of bodies or fabrication. Often, I have to address costing issues. If we want our cost of production to be something specific, like $5, we might have to negotiate with our vendors. Or we would look at the price of a set and then increase the price of the pant and decrease the shirt. Every year we are pressured to reduce cost from last year.

2:00 p.m.: Grab a quick and late lunch.

2:30 p.m.: Attend line development meeting. We're always working on three seasons at once. Develop fall, go into meeting for holiday, and check spring production calendar. The seasons Federated followed were Fall, Holiday, Spring and Summer.

4:00 p.m.: Check e-mail and update my calendar. Once a week, I track all shipments. I reconcile the shipping logs, purchase orders and sales. If the shipment does not have a corresponding receipt number, I ask someone in the D.C. (distribution center) or e-mail a vendor and ask for proof of shipment.

5:30 p.m.: Track advertising samples. These samples are used for our ads. The buyers request ad samples.

6:00 p.m.: Go home!

Noverto comments: "My favorite part of the industry is working with fashion forecasting offices. You know what's going on next year. The ironic thing is that there are so many trends but most things end up looking the same! Every company does similar things. The worst part of the industry is that it is pretentious. You always have to stay on top. If something doesn't sell then you're responsible for it."

Day in a Life: Dress Buyer, Victoria's Secret Catalog

Sylvia Dundon graduated from the Fashion Institute of Technology with a BA in Marketing (concentration Merchandising Management) and an AAS. Buying and Merchandising in December 1998. It took two years to obtain her AAS and another three years for her BA since she was working at the Gap and Victoria's Secret while she was attending school. She began her career as an Assistant Buyer at Victoria's Secret Catalog and later was promoted to Associate Buyer.

Sylvia Dundon's Day

9:00 a.m.: Check e-mail and voice mail. Prioritize who gets called back first based on what time zone they're in.

9:30 a.m.: Check sales on computer – especially dress sales for the items I bought most recently. If the catalog just dropped (that is, was sent out), wait a few days for the sales to hit. Work with the planner. ("At Victoria's Secret, the planner is the buyer's partner. The planner executes the actual purchase order, financial planning, stock models, and markdowns.")

10:30 a.m.: Decide how to allocate five pages of the catalog. For example, how many dresses should I feature per page? Do I think I'll sell more dresses with three per page or should I focus on one large picture of a single dress? I have to justify my decisions to management and work with merchandise manager. Some of my decisions are based on what sold in the catalog last year.

11:30 a.m.: Sample fitting. Go to the fit room and work with your technical specialist and fit model. The fit model tries on samples and we make sure the garment is the right specifications and fit. If the garment is not correct, we send our corrections to the vendor. A sample garment usually goes through one to three rounds of corrections.

Visit Vault at **www.vault.com** for insider company profiles, expert advice, career message boards, expert resume reviews, the Vault Job Board and more.

V∧ULT CAREER LIBRARY **175**

12:00 p.m.: Layout and film review. I go visit the Creative Department and look at a layout of our catalog. The point is to review the actual photography and layout (for colors). If the color of the garment is wrong, I cut a swatch from the garment as a sample so the Creative Dept. can fix the photo to match. If the skirt in the photo is too long, they can fix the length, too. If everything looks great, I just approve the layout.

12:45 p.m.: Run out to buy a sandwich so I can eat at my desk and check voice mail.

2:00 p.m.: Roll out my sample rack. Send out samples for a photo shoot. Work with in-house model for shoot samples to make sure they fit and look right according to Victoria's Secret standards.

3:00 p.m.: Meet a few vendors. I cut a few fabric swatches for product development. Sometimes I go out into the market or vendor showrooms to look at their lines. If I really like something, I will ask them to send samples for me the next day.

4:00 p.m.: Go to a fashion forecast meeting. This meeting includes both the fashion and design departments and is intended to make sure that we're all aware of the trends and direction that Victoria's Secret wants to take that season. Even though we're buying different categories (dresses, shirts, etc.), we all want to have the same mindset. I also see slide shows of samples bought in Europe. All the buyers get to see the main themes for the season – which include a color palette and the general trends.

6:00 p.m.: Address production issues. Approve a button or lab dip. The lap dip is the color intended for production. Quite often, the manufacturer hasn't produced the correct color, so I have to ask them to do another lab dip.

7:00 p.m.: Address the e-mails I didn't get to during the day. Go home!

Employer Directory

Abercrombie & Fitch Co.
6301 Fitch Path
New Albany, OH 43054
Phone: (614) 283-6500
Fax: (614) 283-6710
www.abercrombie.com

Ann Taylor Stores Corporation
100 Ann Taylor Drive
P.O. Box 571650
Taylorsville, UT 84157-1650
Phone: (212) 541-3300
Fax: (212) 541-3379
www.anntaylor.com

The Body Shop International PLC
Watersmead
Littlehampton
West Sussex BN17 6LS, United Kingdom
Phone: +44-1-903-731-500
www.the-body-shop.com

Chanel S.A.
135, Avenue Charles de Gaulle
92521 Neuilly-sur-Seine Cedex, France
Phone: +33-1-46-43-40-00
www.chanel.com

Dolce & Gabbana SPA
Via Santa Cecilia, 7
20122 Milan, Italy
Phone: +39-02-77-42-71
www.dolcegabbana.it

Donna Karan International Inc.
550 Seventh Avenue
New York, NY 10018
Phone: (212) 789-1500
Fax: (212) 921-3526
www.donnakaran.com

Eddie Bauer, Inc.
15010 NE 36th St.
Redmond, WA 98052
Phone: (425) 755-6100
Fax: (425) 755-7696
www.eddiebauer.com

Estee Lauder Companies Inc.
767 Fifth Ave.
New York, NY 10153-0023
Phone: (212) 572-4200
Fax: (212) 572-6633
www.elcompanies.com

Federated Department Stores
7 West Seventh Street
Cincinnati, OH 45202
Phone: (513) 579-7000
Fax: (513) 579-7555
www.federated-fds.com

Gap Inc.
One Harrison Street
San Francisco, CA 94105
Phone: (415) 427-2000
Fax: (650) 874-7828
www.gapinc.com

Guess?, Inc.
1444 S. Alameda St.
Los Angeles, CA 90021
Phone: (213) 765-3100
Phone: (213) 744-7838
www.guess.com

J. Crew Group Inc.
770 Broadway
New York, NY 10003
Phone: (212) 209-2500
Fax: (212) 209-2666
www.jcrew.com

Visit Vault at **www.vault.com** for insider company profiles, expert advice,
career message boards, expert resume reviews, the Vault Job Board and more.

VAULT CAREER LIBRARY   177

Tommy Hilfiger
25 West 39th St., 14th Floor
New York, NY 10018
www.tommy.com

Kenneth Cole Productions, Inc.
603 West 50th St.
New York, NY 10019
Phone: (212) 265-1500
Fax: (212) 830-7422
www.kennethcole.com

L'Oreal USA
575 5th Ave.
New York, NY 10017
Phone: (212) 818-1500
Fax: (212) 984-4999
www.lorealusa.com

Levi Strauss & Co.
1155 Battery St.
San Francisco, CA 94111
Phone: (415) 501-6000
Fax: (415) 501-7112
www.levistrauss.com

Limited Brands
3 Limited Parkway
Columbus, OH 43216
Phone: (614) 415-7000
Fax: (614) 415-7440
www.limited.com

Nike, Inc.
One Bowerman Drive
Beaverton, OR 97005-6453
Phone: (503) 671-6453
Fax: (503) 671-6300
www.nikebiz.com

Nordstrom, Inc.
1617 Sixth Ave.
Seattle, WA 98101-1742
Phone: (206) 628-2111
Fax: (206) 628-1795
www.nordstrom.com

Pacific Sunwear of California, Inc.
3450 E. Miraloma Ave.
Anaheim, CA 92806-2101
Phone: (714) 414-4000
Fax: (714) 414-4251
www.pacsun.com

OshKosh b'Gosh, Inc.
112 Otter Ave.
Oshkosh, WI 54901 (Map)
Phone: (920) 231-8800
Fax: (920) 231-8621
www.oshkoshbgosh.com

Polo Ralph Lauren Corporation
650 Madison Avenue
New York, NY 10022
Phone: (212) 318-7000
Fax: (212) 888-5780
www.polo.com

Reebok International Ltd.
1895 J. W. Foster Blvd.
Canton, MA 02021
Phone: (781) 401-5000
Fax: (781) 401-7402
www.reebok.com

Revlon, Inc.
237 Park Ave.
New York, NY 10017
Phone: (212) 527-4000
Fax: (212) 527-4995
www.revloninc.com

Use the Internet's
MOST TARGETED
job search tools.

Vault Job Board

Target your search by industry, function, and experience level, and find the job openings that you want.

VaultMatch Resume Database

Vault takes match-making to the next level: post your resume and customize your search by industry, function, experience and more. We'll match job listings with your interests and criteria and e-mail them directly to your in-box.

VAULT

> the most trusted name in career information™

Isn't it time for a Quiet Conversation™ about your future?

The result could be the opportunity to build your own financial services practice.
Visit www.nmfn.com for more information.

Northwestern Mutual
FINANCIAL NETWORK®

It's time for a Quiet Conversation.™

Financial Services and Insurance

Brokerage Services

Sales is a core area of most securities firms, comprising the vast majority of people and relationships and accounting for a substantial portion of revenues. Securities salespeople can take the form of a classic retail broker, an institutional salesperson, or a private client service representative. Retail, brokers develop relationships with individual investors and sell securities and advice to the average Joe. Institutional salespeople sell securities to and develop business relationships with large institutional investors – those that manage large groups of assets such as pension funds or mutual funds. Lying somewhere in between retail brokers and institutional salespeople are private client services (PCS) representative, who provide brokerage and money management services for extremely wealthy individuals. A firm's PCS unit is often referred to as its Wealth Management department. All salespeople, no matter who they're selling to, make money through commissions on trades made through their firms.

Retail brokers

Some firms call them account executives, others call them financial advisors, and still others give them the financial consultant moniker. Regardless of the official designator, firms are still referring to your classic retail broker. The broker's job involves managing the account portfolios for individual investors – usually called retail investors. Brokers charge a commission on any stock trade and also give advice to their clients regarding stocks to buy or sell and when to buy or sell them. To get into the business, retail brokers must have an undergraduate degree and demonstrated sales skills. The Series 7 and Series 63 examinations are also required before selling commences. Having connections to people with money offers a tremendous advantage for a starting broker.

Private client services

As a private client services (PCS) representative, your job is to bring in individual accounts with at least $2 million in assets. The PCS job can be exhilarating, exhausting and frustrating – all at once. It involves pounding the pavement to find clients, and then advising them on how to manage their wealth. PCS is a highly entrepreneurial environment. Building a roster of clients is all that matters, and managers typically don't care how PCS reps spend their time – whether it be on the road, in the office or at parties – as long as they're bringing in cash. Culture-wise, therefore, one typically finds a spirited entrepreneurial group of people in PCS, working their own hours and talking on the phone for the better part of the day.

Call it a comeback

Typically, where the equities markets go, the brokerage industry follows. Which means the brokerage industry was hit particularly hard in the past few years with the end of the long running bull market. However, most recent results indicate that equities are back on track. For the third quarter 2003, all the major stock indexes posted positive results. Thw NASDAQ Composite rose 10 percent, the S&P 500 went

Visit Vault at **www.vault.com** for insider company profiles, expert advice, career message boards, expert resume reviews, the Vault Job Board and more.

VAULT CAREER LIBRARY   181

up 2.7 percent and the Dow Jones Industrial Average increased by 3.8 percent respectively. And from a year earlier, all of these indices posted double-digit year-to-date gains.

As a result, some of the top retail brokerage firms have been cashing in. Merrill Lynch's global private client business reported its best results in 14 quarters. For the third quarter of 2003, the firm's brokerage division put up pre-tax earnings of $466 million, an increase of 47 percent over its 2002 third quarter. Another giant in the industry, Morgan Stanley also recently reported healthy quarterly earnings. For the three-month period ended November 30, 2003, the firm's individual-investor group netted earnings of $79 million, a sharp increase from the $11 million loss it reported for the same period a year earlier. While unveiling its earnings, Morgan Stanley also reported that it hopes to hire 1,800 new brokers during fiscal 2004, this after reducing broker headcount by 12 percent in fiscal 2003. Merrill also plans to increase its brokerage staff. The firm said it would increase the number of brokers on staff by 5 percent during each of the next three years, beginning with 2004.

A Day in the Life: Credit Analyst

Looking for a job with high visibility, lots of responsibility, variety, market impact, and access to the highest levels of company management? Consider working as a credit analyst for one of the major rating agencies such as Standard & Poor's, Moody's Investors Service, or Fitch Ratings. Rating agency analysts are responsible for issuing opinions incorporating letter grades regarding the creditworthiness of a variety of types of debt issuers. A company's credit rating determines the interest cost it pays on its debt. Clients, known as issuers, range from industrial companies, to municipalities and states, to sovereign governments, financial institutions, and mutual funds, the newest focus of ratings.

Analysts usually require an MBA or other graduate degree along with expertise in a particular industry. Alternatively, many ratings analysts begin their careers working as commercial bank lenders. Good writing, communication, and financial analysis skills are also important. Other key attributes for aspiring analysts are an ability to juggle multiple tasks, maintain composure under stress, and a keen interest in financial markets.

Analysts at major rating agencies interact with senior company management, sell-side and buy-side analysts, other members of the investor community, and the press. In corporate finance, analysts are responsible for surveying a list of companies within a specific industry sector. They monitor companies' operating performance in order to anticipate and/or respond to changes that effect their creditworthiness: which is defined as the ability and willingness to pay. Analysts issue press releases, meet with company management, interact with investment and commercial bankers, tour company facilities, attend analyst briefings, respond to investor and press calls, and publish industry and company-specific articles.

The work can be quite stressful because it involves managing the often optimistic expectations of issuers and their bankers, and at times delivering bad news in the form of "negative rating surprises." But overall, it can be extremely rewarding. It is interesting, challenging, and critically important to financial markets.

Wondering where people go from there? Given the high visibility of the position, particularly for analysts working in dynamic, growing industries, the skill set analysts develop is highly valued. Working as an analyst can be an entr?e into many exciting career paths: investment banker, buy-side or sell-side analyst, portfolio manager, or even a position in industry.

Given the nature of the work, an analyst's activities can vary considerably from day to day. However, there are certain aspects of the position that are fairly typical. Below is a brief description of what a day in the life of a ratings analyst can be like.

The Rating Game: A Day in the Life

8:45 a.m.: Arrive at the office. Scan the Wall Street Journal while waiting for computer to boot up. Breathe a sigh of relief that there are no major articles on any of my companies. Check voicemail. Good Brite Lite Leisure's treasurer finally got back to me on my question about their capital spending plans.

9:10 a.m.: Computer is up. Dial into news wire service. Run search on my list of 34 companies. Fortunately I subscribe to an alert service which allows me to run just one search to see what's happening with my companies. Make a mental note to put in calls to the chief financial officers of two of my companies to follow up on recent news releases.

10:10 a.m.: Dial into replay of earnings conference call for Acme Entertainment. I prefer to listen to the replays rather than the live calls, because then I can rewind in case I miss something. I will definitely need to put out a press release, as the company has just announced a major acquisition during the call. Wish again that management would give me advance warning about these things.

11:00 a.m.: Attend rating committee for casino operator. The vote is a close one with four of the analysts on the credit committee voting for a low investment grade rating of 'BBB-' and three voting for a high speculative grade rating of 'BB+'. It is always interesting to attend these committees, because I get to learn more about a different industry segment. Also since most of the companies I follow are speculative grade or "high yield" companies, sending in on other committees helps me understand the different analytical challenges investment grade issuers pose. This is one way the company ensures consistency in the rating process across groups.

12:00 p.m.: Draft press release announcing credit downgrade on Acme Entertainment. Review with boss. Make minor changes based on her comments. Hold quick committee with other members of industry group to make sure they are in agreement with rating action. I prefer to get the release ready to go before I call the company so that I can send it out as soon as possible after we talk. Preferably before I begin to get calls from investors based on news of the acquisition.

2:00 p.m.: Press release is finally done. I've spoken to the CFO to deliver the news. Luckily, he anticipated the move and was not argumentative about it. Our group editor has just sent the release out over the newswires and I have a copy of the final version. Grab a quick lunch and finish reading the Journal before calls begin to come in about the rating downgrade.

Visit Vault at **www.vault.com** for insider company profiles, expert advice, career message boards, expert resume reviews, the Vault Job Board and more.

VAULT CAREER LIBRARY **183**

3:30 p.m.: Check newswires again. Go through faxes. It's a slow news day. Update spreadsheets for three of my companies that announced quarterly earnings today. It looks like I may have to draft another release based on some of these numbers.

4:30 p.m.: Take a quick walk over to my friend Susan's cubicle to see how her day is going. Trade notes about what deals we're working on. Make plans to have lunch sometime later in the week.

5:00 p.m.: Finally a few minutes of quiet – until I remember I need to begin my industry article since I am behind on publishing goals for the year. I need to think of a good title for it; I want something that will grab the reader and focus my ideas.

5:15 p.m.: Call from investment banker regarding potential new issuer. Who says the market is cooling? This is my second new deal this month! Get him to give me a quick overview of the company. Then discuss timing-the company wants a fast turnaround since their roadshow starts in two weeks- and size of deal, explain rating process.

6:00 p.m.: Have a brief discussion with department manager about my ideas for potential articles. Also, update her on new deals that are coming in.

6:15 p.m.: Review my calendar for tomorrow. I need to be in a little early to go over materials for my 10:00 am management meeting.

6:30 p.m.: Get stuff ready to head to the gym. On second thought, maybe I'll take my friend up on her offer for dinner.

Integrity. Objectivity. Independence.

{If these values appeal to you, then speak to us.}

Standard & Poor's is the world's foremost provider of independent credit ratings, indices, risk evaluation, investment research, data and valuations. An essential part of the world's financial infrastructure, Standard & Poor's has played a leading role for more than 140 years in providing investors with the independent benchmarks they need to feel more confident about their investment and financial decisions.

Undergraduate opportunities are available in two of Standard & Poor's core businesses, Corporate Value Consulting (CVC) and Ratings.

Associate

Standard & Poor's Corporate Value Consulting (CVC) offers a collaborative approach to quantifying underlying tangible and intangible assets for clients involved in an acquisition, divestiture, restructuring, recapitalization, tax appeal, or shareholder buyout.

Research Assistant

Standard & Poor's Ratings business is comprised of: Corporate & Government Ratings (includes bank and insurance ratings) and Structured Finance Ratings, which pioneer the development of new analytical criteria for a broad spectrum of financial instruments.

Preferred candidate(s) will have a bachelor's degree in finance, accounting, economics, engineering or related discipline. Excellent analytical and oral/written communication skills are essential. The ability to work with financial models and data is required for the Research Assistant positions.

To learn more about these opportunities, please visit our website at **www.standardandpoors.com/careers**

YOUR CONFIDENCE IS SHOWING.
YOU'VE GOT STANDARD & POOR'S

STANDARD &POOR'S

www.standardandpoors.com

Credit Card Services

Credit card nation

Issuing credit cards is one of the most common ways in which financial services firms provide credit to individuals. Via the credit card, firms provide individuals with the funds required to purchase goods and services, and in return, individuals repay the full balance at a later date, or make payments on an installment basis. While you're most likely familiar with a how a credit card works, you might not be familiar with just how large the credit card industry is today. In the U.S. alone, the market for credit card issuance was worth $738 billion in 2002, a sharp 26 percent rise from the $586 billion the industry was worth in 1998. As of July 2003, Citigroup was the top card issuer ranked by owned and managed credit card receivables, with $113.3 billion in receivables, followed by MBNA with $98.5 billion and Bank One with $74.2 billion.

Heavy metal

The credit card traces its roots back to 1914 when Western Union began doling out metal cards, called "metal money," which gave preferred customers interest-free, deferred-payment privileges. Ten years later, General Petroleum Corporation issued the first metal money for gasoline and automotive services, and by the late 1930s, department stores, communication companies, travel and delivery companies had all began to introduce such cards. Then, companies issued the cards, processed the transactions and collected the debts from the customer. The popularity of these cards grew until the beginning of World War II, when "Regulation W" restricted the use of cards, and as a result, stalled their growth.

After the war, though, cards were back on track. Modes of travel were more advanced and more accessible, and more people were beginning to buy expensive modern conveniences such as kitchen appliances and washing machines. As a result, the credit card boomed in popularity, as consumers could pay for these things on credit that otherwise they couldn't afford to buy with cash.

Charge-it

In 1951, New York's Franklin National Bank created a credit system called Charge-It, which was very similar to the modern credit card. Charge-It allowed consumers to make purchases at local retail establishments, with the retailer obtaining authorization from the bank and then closing the sale. At a later date, the bank would reimburse the retailer and then collect the debt from the consumer. Acting upon the success of Franklin's Charge-It, other banks soon began introducing similar cards. Banks found that cardholders liked the convenience and credit line that cards offered, and retailers discovered that credit card customers usually spent more than if they had to pay with cash. Additionally, retailers found that handling bank-issued cards was less costly than maintaining its own credit card program.

Also in the 1950s, the Diner's Club charge card was created. This card, which gave users 60 days to make repayment, was the first to allow consumers to pay for goods and services from a variety of retailers. Another 1950s credit card milestone was the BankAmericard, created by California's Bank of America.

The BankAmericard was the first "revolving credit" card – it gave cardholders the option to pay their debts in whole, or in monthly minimum payments while the issuers charged interest on the remaining balances.

The association and the Master

Bank of America continued its credit card innovations in the 1960s with the introduction of the bank card association. In 1965, Bank of America began issuing licensing agreements that allowed other banks to issue BankAmericards. To compete with the BankAmericard, four banks from California formed the Western States Bankcard Association and introduced the MasterCharge. By 1969, most credit cards had been converted to either the MasterCharge (which changed its name to MasterCard in 1979) or the BankAmericard (which was renamed Visa in 1977).

Cutting the cost of transaction processing and decreasing credit card fraud were the next innovations introduced to the industry. Electronic authorizations, begun in the early 1970s, allowed merchants to approve transactions 24 hours a day. By the end of the decade, magnetic strips on the back of credit cards allowed retailers to swipe the customer's credit card through a dial up terminal, which accessed the issuing bank card holder's information. This process gave authorizations and processed settlement agreements in a mater of minutes.

The debut of the debit, the climb of the cobrand

The 1990s saw the debit card rise in popularity. The debit card grew from accounting for 274 million transactions in 1990 to 8.15 billion transactions in 2002. The 1990s also witnessed the surge of cobranded and affinity cards, which match up a credit card company with a retailer to offer discounts for using the card (think Citibank's AAdvantage cards and American Express' Mileage Rewards program). Although cobranded cards took a dip in the late 1990s – according to some industry experts, this was because issuers had exhausted the most lucrative partners – they've recently returned in full force. Consider some of the deals struck between some of the largest credit card companies and retailers in the past year: Bank One and Disney launched a card allowing holders to earn points at Disney theme parks and hotels and for Disney cruises and other products. Bank One also recently partnered with Starbucks to release a cobranded card that offers holders rewards at the specialty coffee retailer.

The two that tower pay up

In September 2003, a federal court upheld a lower court ruling that cost credit card powerhouses Visa and MasterCard a combined $3 billion. The court found Visa and MasterCard rules preventing the companies' member banks from also issuing American Express and Morgan Stanley's Discover cards to be illegal and harmful to competition. MasterCard was forced to pay $2 billion in damages and Visa paid $1 billion. As a result of the ruling, Amex and Discover will be free to partner with the thousands of banks that issue Visa and MasterCard, which should allow Amex and Discover to gain ground on the two credit powerhouses. The two still, though, have a ways to go to catch up the two industry leaders. In 2002, Visa reported total credit volume of $609 billion, MasterCard posted a volume of $530 billion, Amex had $234 billion, and Discover had $97 billion.

Visit Vault at **www.vault.com** for insider company profiles, expert advice, career message boards, expert resume reviews, the Vault Job Board and more.

VAULT CAREER LIBRARY **187**

FitchRatings

Fitch Ratings Corporate Description

Fitch Ratings is committed to providing the most forward thinking and transparent research and ratings. In servicing the capital markets, Fitch has a presence in more than 75 countries with 40 offices worldwide. Growing rapidly, Fitch now rates more than 1,600 banks, 70 sovereigns, 1,100 corporates and maintains surveillance on 3,300 structured financings and 26,000 municipal bond ratings in the U.S. tax-exempt market. Fitch also rates over 800 insurance companies. With a combined analytic and professional staff of more than 1,200, many of whom possess over 10 years of specialized industry experience, Fitch exceeds expectations.

Our ratings are recognized by regulatory authorities in the U.S. (NRSRO), U.K., France, Japan and Hong Kong among others. Fitch Ratings is dual headquartered in New York and London and is wholly owned by FIMALAC, S.A., Paris.

ANALYTICAL POSITIONS

Entry level analysts are key contributors to all analytical departments: Structured Finance, Corporate Finance, Public Finance, Credit Products, Credit Policy and Fitch Risk Management. If you join Fitch, you will:

- Provide support to lead analyst on new issue ratings.
- Gather and analyze financial statements, as well as the latest industry, regulatory, and economic information.
- Develop an understanding of legal and accounting issues affecting a security.
- Run computer models and spreadsheet-based applications to evaluate credit risk and cash flow coverage. Present analysis at rating committee meetings.
- Develop an ability to differentiate among rating categories.
- Write research reports and press releases.
- Adopt Fitch style: high level of service to our clients and a team-oriented approach to ratings analysis.

CANDIDATES MUST POSSESS

- BA/BS or MBA degree.
- Ability to apply advanced mathematical concepts.
- Excellent verbal and written communication skills.
- Proficiency in Microsoft Word/Excel.

For more information about our career opportunities as a Financial Analyst in New York or Chicago, please log on to www.fitchratings.com and visit the "Careers at Fitch" section of our website.

Summer Internships available
Equal Opportunity Employer M/F/D/V

www.fitchratings.com

opportunity for advancement

dental insurance

life insurance

medical insurance

401(k)

annual salary increases

tuition reimbursement

Insurance

Risky business

The insurance industry combines to form a multi-trillion-dollar market dealing in risk. In exchange for a premium, insurers promise to compensate, monetarily or otherwise, individuals and businesses for future losses, thus taking on the risk of personal injury, death, damage to property, unexpected financial disaster, and just about any other misfortune you can name.

The industry often is divided into categories such as life/health and property/casualty. Life insurance dominates the mix, making up about 60 percent of all premiums. The bigger categories can be subdivided into smaller groups; property insurance, for instance, may cover homeowner's, renter's, auto, and boat policies, while health insurance is made up of subsets including disability and long-term care.

But these days, you can find insurance for just about anything – even policies for pets (a market that grew 342 percent from 1998 to 2002, with sales of up to $88 million, according to research firm Packaged Facts), weddings and bar mitzvahs, and the chance of weather ruining a vacation. Even insurance companies themselves can be insured against extraordinary losses – by companies specializing in reinsurance. Celebrity policies always get a lot of press – while rumors that Jennifer Lopez had insured her famous asset (sorry) for $1 billion proved to be unfounded, other such policies do indeed exist. In fact, the phrase "million dollar legs" comes from Betty Grable's policy for that amount (a similar policy is held by TV's Mary Hart); other notable contemporary policies include Bruce Springsteen's voice, reportedly covered at around $6 million.

The world's top five

Though the U.S. is well ahead of the rest of the world in terms of insurance coverage, with nearly 40 percent of the world's premiums in 2002, insurance is a truly global industry. Ranked by sales, the top five insurance companies are Germany's Allianz, the Netherlands' ING, New York-based American International Group, Inc. (AIG), France's AXA, and Nippon Life Insurance Company, of Japan. Other leading U.S. insurers include State Farm, MetLife, Allstate, Prudential, Aetna and Travelers.

Consolidation is the name of the game – Hoovers reports that the top ten property/casualty insurers account for nearly half of all premiums written. Perhaps the most notable example of the mergers and acquisitions mania in the industry was the $82 billion merger in 1998 between Citicorp and the Travelers Group, which created Citigroup. Some insurance companies have also begun to reconfigure themselves from mutual insurers, or those owned by policyholders (e.g., State Farm), to stock insurers, or those held by shareholders (e.g., Allstate). This process, known as "demutualization," promises to raise even more capital for insurance companies to indulge in more acquisitions.

The last 25 years have seen a shift in the industry away from life insurance toward annuity products, focusing on managing investment risk rather than the (inevitable) risk of mortality. With increasing deregulation in the U.S. and Japan, these insurers are moving ever closer to competition with financial services firms. Indeed,

Visit Vault at **www.vault.com** for insider company profiles, expert advice, career message boards, expert resume reviews, the Vault Job Board and more.

VAULT CAREER LIBRARY   189

the business of the insurance industry doesn't end with insurance. The world's top insurance companies have broadened their array of financial services to include investment management, annuities, securities, mutual funds, health care management, employee benefits and administration, real estate brokerage, and even consumer banking. The move towards financial services follows the 1999 repeal of the Glass-Steagall Act, which barred insurance companies, banks and brokerages from entering each other's industries, and the Gramm Leach-Bliley Act of 1999, which further defined permissible acts for financial holding companies. Now insurance companies are free to partner with commercial banks, securities firms, and other financial entities.

At the speed of the Internet

Like many other industries, the insurance market has been transformed in recent years by the Internet. Traditionally, insurance products have been distributed by independent agents (businesspeople paid on commission) or by exclusive agents (paid employees). But insurers who sell over the Web reap the benefits of lower sales costs and customer service expenses, along with a more expedient way of getting information to consumers. is transforming those traditional methods by cutting costs and increasing the amount of information available to consumers. By 2005, Celent Communications estimates that the online insurance market will top $200 billion, or 37 percent of personal insurance premiums, up from 19 percent in 2003. Of course, an automated approach to doing business means fewer salespeople are needed – Celent reports that insurance giant Cigna, for instance, eliminated 2,000 jobs in 2002 because of increased efficiencies.

With more IT comes a greater need for IT security – Celent estimates that U.S. insurers will spend around $618 million on security alone in 2004, and more than $770 million by 2006. Aside from the threat of viruses, hackers, and the like, regulations have made security a top priority – the Health Information Portability and Accountability Act (HIPAA), for instance, which went into effect in 2003, sets strict standards for the privacy and security of the patient information transferred between health insurers and providers.

Recovering from September 11

The September 11 terrorist attacks sent shockwaves through the industry. Not only did they constitute perhaps the largest insured loss in U.S. history – with estimates ranging between $40 billion and $50 billion in claims for loss of life and property, injuries and workers' compensation – they also caused insurers and re-insurers to take a hard look at how they would handle the risks associated with possible future terrorist acts. The Terrorism Risk Insurance Act, signed into law by President Bush in November 2002, aimed to deal with the nearly incalculable risk posed by this threat. Among other things, the law defines a terrorism-related event as one with a minimum of $5 million in damages. It provides for the sharing of risk between private insurers and the federal government over a three-year period, with each participating company responsible for paying a deductible before federal assistance is available. If losses are incurred above the insurer's deductible, the government is obliged to pay 90 percent. While the measure met with a considerable amount of grumbling from all parties involved, for the most part the industry acknowledged that the plan at least allows for the potential risk to insurers from terrorism-related disasters to be quantified.

Fraud: The $100 billion challenge

Another trend in the industry is the problem of fraud, which costs an estimated $85 billion to $120 billion per year, according to the Insurance Information Institute. Fraud comes in two flavors, "hard" and "soft," with hard fraud being a deliberate invention or staging of an accident, fire, or other type of insured loss to reap the coverage. Soft fraud covers policyholders' and claimants' exaggeration of legitimate claims, such as when victims of burglaries overstate the value and amount of lost property, or when car accident claimants pad damage claims to cover their deductibles.

Unhealthy healthcare

Medical malpractice is another hot topic. Health insurers generally get a bad rap from the public, with a 2003 Harris Poll indicating that just 40 percent of health insurance companies do a good job of taking care of their customers (in fact, only the tobacco industry ranked lower in the poll). The media and politicians give plenty of air time to horror stories about managed care companies slighting critically ill patients, and insurers refusing to cover necessary treatments or technologies. Is this reputation deserved? Depends on who you ask, but the industry has its own battles in health care – for example, it sees medical malpractice claims, which have skyrocketed in recent years, as a true crisis. Indeed, according to the Insurance Information Institute, some insurers have quit writing malpractice policies entirely rather than shoulder the risk (the median malpractice award in 2001, the latest year for which this figure is available, was $1 million). Insurance company Farmers, which racked up more than $100 million in malpractice-related losses in 2003, announced it would get out of malpractice overage in September of that year.

Working in insurance

According to the U.S. Bureau of Labor Statistics, the industry employed 2.2 million people in 2002. Of these jobs, three out of five were with insurance carriers, while the remainder were with insurance agencies, brokerages, and providers of other insurance-related services 2 out of 5 jobs. Another 141,000 workers in the industry were self-employed in 2002, mostly as insurance sales agents. Most insurance agents specialize in life and health insurance, or property and casualty insurance. But a growing number of "multi-line" agents sell all lines of insurance. An increasing number of agents also work for banking institutions, non-depository institutions, or security and commodity brokers.

Visit Vault at **www.vault.com** for insider company profiles, expert advice,
career message boards, expert resume reviews, the Vault Job Board and more.

VAULT CAREER LIBRARY **191**

A close friend of mine from school *recommended* Nationwide as a place where I could reach my career goals.

Recommended...

Nationwide®

I wanted an employer who would respect my skills and knowledge, challenge me to do great work, and reward me for results.

Nationwide can be that place. They're one of the largest financial services companies in the country. And, they need talented employees from diverse backgrounds with all sorts of job skills, from finance and accounting to information systems and almost everything in-between. They offer great benefits, a casual work environment, and lots of extras not found in other companies.

I'm glad my friend recommended Nationwide.

Maybe she'll come work here, too!

Looking for a great place to begin your career? Visit our Web site at **www.nationwide.com** and tell us about yourself. EEO, M/F/D/V

Nationwide Is On Your Side.®

Insurance Agent

Most people would rather not think about insurance at all. But when the time comes to buy into a plan, an insurance agent can be a big help. Insurance agents sell one or more types of insurance, such as life, property, casualty, health, disability and long-term care. Insurance policies provide protection to individuals and businesses against loss or catastrophe.

We'll help you plan

Insurance agents don't just hawk the same insurance plans to everyone they meet. They consider the financial status and life situation of their clients and assist them in selecting their optimal insurance policy. Some policies can be designed to provide retirement income, funds for the education of children, or other benefits. Increasingly, insurance agents and brokers offer comprehensive financial planning services to their clients, such as retirement planning counseling. Because of this, many insurance agents and brokers are licensed to sell mutual funds and other securities.

Insurance professionals prepare reports, maintain records, and help policyholders settle insurance claims. Specialists in group policies may help employers provide their employees the opportunity to buy insurance through payroll deductions. Agents may work for one company or independently for several companies. Brokers do not sell for a particular company, but direct their clients to companies that offers the best rate and coverage.

The insurance industry is broadly split into two main categories: property and casualty and health and life. Property and casualty insurance agents and brokers sell policies that protect individuals and businesses from financial loss as a result of automobile accidents, fire or theft, tornadoes and storms, and other events that can damage property. Health and life agents sell insurance that covers medical bills and provides compensation to a family in the event of a death.

People, people, people

An insurance agent's success is contingent upon his or her ability to seek out and retain clients and on the agent's reputation among colleagues. Difficulty in developing a client base drives many insurance agents from the field early. However, those who are able to withstand such adversity can look forward to high salaries and career autonomy.

Actuary

Actuaries are vicarious risk-takers. They calculate risk by analyzing statistics and, based on their analysis, make decisions regarding pricing and investment strategies. Some actuaries work in the financial services industry, but seven out of 10 are employed in the insurance industry. Whatever the industry, actuaries decide whether a venture is financially sound.

Visit Vault at **www.vault.com** for insider company profiles, expert advice, career message boards, expert resume reviews, the Vault Job Board and more.

VAULT CAREER LIBRARY   **193**

Actuaries in the insurance industry calculate the probability that there will be a return on their investment; to do this, they consider probabilities of death, dismemberment, disability, or property loss. Actuaries are the reason teenagers driving sports cars pay such prohibitively high premiums. Actuaries ensure that insurance prices will enable the company to pay all claims and expenses and that the price yields a profit. Their keen mathematical skills and analytical abilities are a boon in investing, classifying risk, planning pensions, managing credit, and pricing corporate offerings. Once they reach upper-level management positions, actuaries are often called upon to determine and implement complex company policies. Actuaries also often testify in court to verify the loss incurred by a policyholder who has been disabled or killed and in divorce cases as to the current value of pension benefits. Actuaries may also appear before public agencies to contest legislation that affects their businesses. These professionals also work as independent consultants who are hired by insurance companies, corporations, hospitals, labor unions, and health care providers for their advice. Due to the breadth of topics they may work on, it is important for the actuary to keep current with many different industries and fields.

Actuaries earn competitive salaries from the time they start and are paid for every hour of credit that they earn from "actuarial exams." Actuaries spend up to eight months a year studying for these exams, which test everything from specific knowledge (casualty insurance, life insurance, pension services) to linear algebra, probability, calculus, statistics, risk theory and actuarial mathematics. Actuaries are pressured to complete the entire series of examinations as soon as possible in order to advance in the field. The first set of exams brings the actuary to the associate level and takes four to six years to complete. Preparation for the exam requires hours of study outside of work, dramatically impacting the personal and social lives of potential actuaries. Actuaries can spend up to 10 years or more taking exams and studying to reach the title of Fellowship, particularly if they stop along the way to get married and have families. The long hours required to gain titles and prestige in the actuarial field do not go unrewarded – starting salaries are very high and continue to climb for more experienced actuaries.

Employer Directory

Nationwide Insurance

One Nationwide Plaza

Columbus, OH 43215

www.nationwide.com/jobs/colrecruiting/undergrad.htm

If you're seeking an organization that would value the unique skills and abilities you bring to the workplace, consider Nationwide. Nationwide is one of the largest insurance and financial services companies in the world, with more than $148 billion in assets. We are an industry leader in property and casualty insurance, life insurance and retirement savings, and asset management. Our leadership and continued growth provides a variety of employment opportunities for qualified individuals to begin or advance their careers. We do business in all 50 states, the District of Columbia, and the Virgin Islands, Asia, Europe, and Latin America.

Naval Financial Management Career (NAVY)

153 Ellyson Avenue, Suite A

Pensacola, FL 32508-5245

Phone: 850-452-3783

E-mail: fmip@nfmc.navy.mil

www.navyfmip.com

The Financial Management Intern Program (FMIP) recruits high quality, prospective civilian financial managers for Department of the Navy Activities. The FMIP is a two year program of professional development through academic and on-the-job training. Entry level positions as Analysts, Accountants, and Auditors are available. Applicants may have any academic major; but those applying for Accounting and Auditor positions require 24 semester hours of accounting (6 hours may be in business law). A minimum cumulative GPA of 2.95 in an undergraduate degree from a nationally accredited university/college is required.

Schools FMIP recruits from

Nationally accredited colleges and universities

Visit Vault at **www.vault.com** for insider company profiles, expert advice, career message boards, expert resume reviews, the Vault Job Board and more.

VAULT CAREER LIBRARY   195

Northwestern Mutual Financial Network

720 E Wisconsin Ave

Milwaukee, WI 53202-4797

Phone: 414 271 1444

www.nmfn.com

tammybrudnicki@northwesternmutual.com

NORTHWESTERN MUTUAL FINANCIAL NETWORK... has been named a "Top 10 Internship" in America's Top Internships by the Princeton Review eight consecutive times since 1996 and named America's 2000 Top Sales Force co-winner (with Cisco Systems) by Sales & Marketing Management Magazine. The Internship Program provides career opportunity to college students who want to "test drive" a career in sales. Financial Representative positions are also available. Reps provide guidance and innovative solutions to clients to develop a customized plan that meets long-term financial goals. The position is an opportunity to build your own business while providing financial security for your clients.

Schools Northwestern Mutual recruits from

Nationwide

Standard & Poor's

55 Water Street

New York, NY 10041/10020

Phone: 212-438-2000

1221 Avenue of the Americas

New York, NY 10020

Phone: 212-512-1000

www.standardandpoors.com/careers

Schools Standard & Poor's recruits from

Columbia; Boston College; NYU; USC; UCLA; Berkeley; Stanford; U Texas-Austin, U. of Chicago; U. Michigan; LSU; Indiana; U Wisconsin-Madison; U. of Illinois; Lehigh; Cornell; Harvbard; MIT; Wharton; CUNY-Baruch; Villanova; Emory; Penn St.; UNC-Chapel Hill; Florida; St. Josephs; U. of South Carolina; UVA; Howard; Spelman; Morehouse; Hampton

The Advest Group, Inc.
90 State House Sq.
Hartford, CT 06103
Phone: (860) 509-1000
Fax: (860) 509-3849
www.advest.com

AFLAC Incorporated
1932 Wynnton Rd.
Columbus, GA 31999
Phone: (706) 323-3431
Fax: (706) 324 6330
www.aflac.com

A.G. Edwards, Inc.
One North Jefferson Avenue
St. Louis, MO 63103
Phone: (314) 955-3000
Fax: (314) 955-5547
www.agedwards.com

The Allstate Corporation
2775 Sanders Rd.
Northbrook, IL 60062
Phone: (847) 402-5000
Fax: (847) 836-3998
www.allstate.com

American Express Company
World Financial Center
200 Vesey St.
New York, NY 10285
Phone: (212) 640-2000
www.americanexpress.com

American International Group, Inc. (AIG)
70 Pine St.
New York, NY 10270
Phone: (212) 770-7000
Fax: (212) 509-9705
www.aig.com

Bank of America Corporation
100 North Tryon Street
Charlotte, NC 28255
Phone: (704) 388 2547
www.bofa.com

Bank One
1 Bank One Plaza
Chicago, IL 60670
Phone: (312) 732-4000
Fax: (312) 732-3366
www.bankone.com

Berkshire Hathaway, Inc.
1440 Kiewit Plaza
Omaha, NE 68131
Phone: (402) 346-1400
Fax: (402) 346-3375
www.berkshirehathaway.com

Capital One Financial Corporation
1680 Capital One Dr.
McLean, VA 22102
Phone: (703) 720-1000
www.capitalone.com

The Chubb Corporation
15 Mountain View Rd.
Warren, NJ 07061-1615
Phone: (908) 903-2000
Fax: (908) 903-3402
www.chubb.com

Discover Financial Services
2500 Lake Cook Road
Riverwoods, IL 60015
Phone: (224) 405-0900
Phone: (224) 405-4993
www.discoverfinancial.com

Visit Vault at **www.vault.com** for insider company profiles, expert advice,
career message boards, expert resume reviews, the Vault Job Board and more.

V∧ULT CAREER LIBRARY   **197**

Edward Jones & Co.
12555 Manchester Road
Des Peres, MO 63131
Phone: (314) 515-2000
Fax: (314) 515-2820
www.edwardjones.com

Fitch Ratings
1 State Street Plaza
New York, NY 10004
Phone: (212) 908-0500
Fax: (212) 480-4435
www.fitchratings.com

GE Consumer Finance
1600 Summer St.
Stamford, CT 06927
Phone: (203) 357-4000
www.geconsumerfinance.com

Guardian Life Insurance Company of America
7 Hanover Sq.
New York, NY 10004-2616
Phone: (212) 598-8000
Fax: (212) 919-2170
www.guardianlife.com

Hartford Financial Services Group, Inc.
Hartford Plaza, 690 Asylum Ave.
Hartford, CT 06115-1900
Phone: (860) 547-5000
Fax: (860) 547-2680
www.thehartford.com

HSBC Bank USA
452 5th Ave.
New York, NY 10018
Phone: (212) 525-5000
www.us.hsbc.com

MasterCard International
2000 Purchase St.
Purchase, NY 10577
Phone: (914) 249-2000
Fax: (914) 249-4206
www.mastercard.com

MBNA Corporation
1100 North King Street
Wilmington, DE 19884
Phone: (302) 453-9930
Fax: (302) 432-3614
www.mbna.com

MetLife, Inc.
1 Madison Ave.
New York, NY 10010-3690
Phone: (212) 578-2211
Fax: (212) 578-3320
www.metlife.com

Moody's Corporation
99 Church St.
New York, NY 10007
Phone: (224) 405-0900
Fax: (224) 405-4993
www.metlife.com

The Mutual of OmahaCompanies
Mutual of Omaha Plaza
Omaha, NE 68175
Phone: (402) 342-7600
Fax: (402) 351-2775
www.mutualofomaha.com

New York Life Insurance Company
51 Madison Ave.
New York, NY 10010
Phone: (212) 576-7000
Fax: (2120 576-8145
www.newyorklife.com

Principal Financial Group, Inc.

711 High St.

Des Moines, IA 50392

Phone: (515) 247-5111

Fax: (515) 246-5474

www.principal.com

Prudential Financial, Inc.

751 Broad Street

Newark, NJ 07102-3777

Phone: (973) 802-6000

Fax: (973) 367-6476

www.prudential.com

Standard & Poor's

55 Water Street

New York, NY 10041/10020

Phone: (212) 438-2000

Fax: (212) 438-7375

www.standardandpoors.com

State Farm Insurance Companies

1 State Farm Plaza

Bloomington, IL 61710-0001

Phone: (309) 766-2311

Fax: (309) 766-3621

www.statefarm.com

Visa International

900 Metro Center Blvd.

Foster City, CA 94404

Phone: (650) 432-3200

Fax: (650) 432-7436

www.visa.com

Visit Vault at **www.vault.com** for insider company profiles, expert advice, career message boards, expert resume reviews, the Vault Job Board and more.

VAULT CAREER LIBRARY   **199**

Department of the Navy
Financial Management Civilian Careers

153 Ellyson Avenue, Suite A
Pensacola, FL 32508-5245

fmip@nfmc.navy.mil

Telephone: 850-452-3783/85   Fax: 850-452-3821   Internet Address: www.navyfmip.com

Navy's Financial Management Civilian Careers is a two-year program of professional development through academic and on-the-job training. Emphasis is on practical work experience supplemented by academic training. Through a series of rotational work assignments within the organization's geographic area and one out-of-area assignment – each employee gains necessary professional competence.

Of more than 200,000 civilians employed at Navy and Marine Corps locations throughout the world, more than 7,600 work in financial management. To provide a continuous, well-trained, motivated, and mobile financial management work force, the Navy recruits, hires, and trains eligible civilians as analysts, accountants and auditors.

Employees are placed at Navy or Marine Corps locations called "home ports" and are managed throughout the two year training program by the Financial Management Intern Program Office.

Expertise/Education sought: All Majors; Business, Finance, Economics; Accounting

Entry-Level Positions Available: Analysts, Accountants, and Auditors

The Program

Home port financial managers guide employees through On-the-Job (OJT) training assignments that are outlined in the Individual Development Plan (IDP). The OJT consists of rotational training assignments in all areas of financial management and periodic academic training. Rotational assignments are typically at the home port and other local sites, with one out-of-town assignment during the second year of training.

Employees are promoted non-competitively with satisfactory performance. Most begin at the GS-7 pay grade and complete the program at the GS-11 pay grade - an increase of approximately $15,000 in two years!

Typical Financial Management Functions

❖ Formulating budget estimates in support of program objectives and priorities; presenting and justifying budget requests; developing plans for allocating resources; monitoring program execution; reviewing and analyzing funding documents; conducting comparative analyses to examine trends; reviewing budget policy and statutes to ensure compliance.

❖ Reviewing and interpreting accounting and financial management policy, procedures, standards and statutes to ensure compliance; monitoring and examining accounts, specific appropriations or financial records for account status and reporting requirements; and verifying accounts documentation.

❖ Planning and conducting performance and financial reviews of major programs and entities to evaluate the reliability, efficiency and effectiveness of the organization; making recommendations based on findings that identify cost savings through improved operations; and following up on recommendations to ensure implementation.

Benefits

Competitive Salary; Flexible Hours; Generous Leave Benefits for Family Care; Holidays, Vacation and Personal Illness leave; A portable Retirement Plan with Tax-Deferred Savings and government matching funds options; Choice of Health Care plans; Life Insurance; and Tuition Assistance.

U.S. Citizenship Required   *An Equal Opportunity Employer*

Government and Politics

Life on Capitol Hill

Behind the headlines on any given day in the nation's capital there are a thousand sub-plots taking form: the Member of Congress and her staff working at breakneck pace to prepare a bill to reform Federal education programs; a last minute compromise to pass a key piece of legislation; a House member positioning himself for a run for even higher office; a reporter about to break a big story about a new scandal. The environment is continually changing, and the confluence of national politics, local interests, ambitions, and personal agendas creates a sense of constant flux and excitement.

In any position on Capitol Hill, an employee's first responsibility is ultimately to serve the interests of his Member (and his or her constituents). And all of the 535 total Members of Congress have very distinct interests. Some love the national spotlight, and spend what seems to be a majority of the their time before a news camera (or in search of one). Others are masters of the legislative process and use their position to propose and advance legislation. Many style themselves as hometown heroes who keep a low profile and focus on directing Federal benefits to their districts.

Despite their style, certain elements mentioned above will be true of all Members of Congress: all will attempt to direct Federal resources to their districts and attend to their constituents needs; all will use the media to communicate their messages and build (or repair) their images; and all will be involved in the legislative process to some degree, either as legislative technicians, advocates, or simply as voters.

Each Member of Congress also has his or her own distinct management style. The organization of a Member's office greatly reflects the individual personality and goals of the Member. Some offices are very formal, requiring business attire at all times, while others are less traditional. Some Members are very hands-on in running their offices, while others delegate much of the decision-making to their senior staff. Some have track records of keeping loyal staff, while others turn over staff on a championship pace. All of these factors – and many more – contribute to the pace of life on Capitol Hill.

Why Capitol Hill?

If you ask Hill staffers why they choose to work on Capitol Hill, you will get a number of different answers. Most, however, will express some common themes: they want to work on issues that they believe in; they want the opportunity to serve their country; and they enjoy using the skills needed to succeed on the Hill and pace of life it requires.

"One of the most exciting aspects of working on the Hill is the opportunity to participate in the workings of our democracy," says one Senate staffer. "The prestige of the place is nice, but for me the real satisfaction comes from knowing that the work we do makes a difference in the lives of real people."

A former House staffer stresses the opportunity to work on a variety of issues as one of the prime benefits of working for Congress. "I can't think of anywhere else where you can work on so many different issues in the course of the day. It's perfect for people who are curious about a lot of things and enjoy the intel-

Visit Vault at **www.vault.com** for insider company profiles, expert advice, career message boards, expert resume reviews, the Vault Job Board and more.

VAULT CAREER LIBRARY 201

lectual challenge of understanding multiple issues and putting that knowledge to use on a day-to-day basis."

Another staffer, while acknowledging the benefits of working for Congress, says that the lifestyle will not be for everyone. "Things move very fast on the Hill. If you can't keep up, or you can't – for lack of a better term – multitask, you will probably not be happy here in the long run. This is a place for high energy people who get charged up from going into work every day not knowing exactly what to expect."

Working on the Hill can provide unique experiences that very few other positions afford, including international travel, the opportunity to work with national media, and the opportunity to be involved in shaping history.

"One of the greatest experiences was seeing a piece of legislation that my boss was active in passing signed into law," relates one staffer. "Looking back on that bill today, it is clear that it has helped small businesses to grow and provide good jobs for a lot of people in our district and across the country."

The opportunity for travel, both domestically and internationally, is also cited as a benefit of working on the Hill, particularly for higher-level staffers. "Many organizations sponsor fact finding trips both here in the United States and abroad," says one staffer. "These travel opportunities allowed me to gain a better understanding on a lot of key issues."

Considering Working on the Hill?

If your considering working on the Hill, you should make sure you know what you're getting into. Here, we give you a quick self-assessment test to see if a career on Capitol Hill seems like a good fit for you.

The Hill is probably for you if

- You like excitement and the idea that every day can bring something different.

- You enjoy following public affairs and reading the newspaper.

- You like talking about politics...a lot.

- You don't mind starting off paying your dues by answering the phone, writing letters, and taking calls from angry constituents.

- You don't care what your work space looks like, so long as you have a desk and a computer.

- You work well under pressure.

The Hill is probably not for you if

- You'd rather be doing anything other than talking about politics.

- You prefer stable, predictable environments.

- You don't like talking to random people during the course of your day.

- You want the security of a distinct career path.

- You don't like long, unpredictable hours.

Capitol Hill Internships

Some of the most powerful people in Washington have never run for office, yet they command as much power as many of Members of Congress. And many of them began their careers answering phones or writing letters as interns on Capitol Hill.

Traditionally seen as the starting point to a career in government and politics, Capitol Hill offices are flooded with resumes every year from undergraduates eager to gain experience and contacts to begin their ascent to Washington power broker. Internships are available in the personal offices of Members of Congress – both Senators and Representatives. Additionally, Committees on both the House and Senate side offer internships.

"Interning is the best way to get your foot in the door," said one former intern who used the experience to find a full time position. "The minute I walked in on the first day of my internship, I knew that I wanted to work on Capitol Hill. The office was buzzing with activity, the televisions were tuned to the House floor, and everyone in the office was young and dedicated. Interning allows you to experience the excitement of Capitol Hill and build the skills and contacts you will need to start a career."

There are two important considerations to make in applying for internships on Capitol Hill: where you want to work and what you want to do. Most of the internships offered by Congress will be with Members' personal offices. The Congressional committees and House and Senate leadership offices all offer internship opportunities as well. The following descriptions provide some of the differences and advantages of each type of internship. Please read the subsequent sections on Capitol Hill to gain more in-depth understanding of Congressional offices and the range of activities employees do in each on a day-to-day basis.

Personal offices

Personal offices of both Senators and Members of the U.S. House of Representatives reflect the individual personality and management style of the Members. Representatives' Washington, DC offices usually employ 8-10 employees. Senators' Washington offices are much larger in terms of employees and the staff sizes are based on the population of the state each Senator represents. (Please see the next section for information on typical DC offices).

In general, House offices will feel more intimate (some might say cramped) than the Senate offices. In the House, interns generally work on a variety of topics, depending where the staff feels their skills can be best utilized. Due to their larger staffs, Senate offices may be able to provide a greater degree of spe-

Visit Vault at **www.vault.com** for insider company profiles, expert advice, career message boards, expert resume reviews, the Vault Job Board and more.

V**A**ULT CAREER LIBRARY   **203**

cialization in an area of interest to the intern, such as the legislative process or media relations. Despite these differences, much of the experience will be the same regardless whether one chooses the House or Senate; answering the phone, responding to constituent inquiries, processing requests for flags flown over the U.S. Capitol, and helping visitors are all part and parcel of the intern experience.

In applying for internships, students should definitely consider the Members of Congress that represent their home towns and their college's or university's location. To find information on a Member of Congress, including an internship application, visit the Member's personal web site. Web sites for House Members can be accessed at www.house.gov and Senators sites can be found at www.senate.gov.

Committees

The Committees of the U.S. Congress offer internships. The Committees are where much of the legislative process takes place. Internships with a committee provide the opportunity to learn about specific areas of legislation (e.g. tax policy or the annual appropriations process) and to dig deeper into the legislative process than a similar internship in a Member's personal office. Since Committee staffs do not answer to constituents as Members' staffs do, interns will spend much less time writing letters. However, they most likely will not get the same level of interaction with a Member of Congress and the senior staff as interns do in a personal office.

Leadership offices

The Republican and Democrat members of the House and Senate elect leaders to organize their parties, set their agendas, count votes, and communicate their messages. The top elected leaders in each party are given separate offices and staffs to carry out their responsibilities. These leadership offices are another source of Capitol Hill internships for students. Since there are fewer leadership offices and staff members, and since members of the leadership enjoy high profile positions, internships with these offices will be very competitive.

Outside the Washington Beltway

While most students focus on internships inside the Beltway, there are opportunities where they live and study to build experience and make contacts. One of the best ways to become involved in the process is to volunteer for a political campaign. Closely contested Senate and House races require an army of unpaid labor to help achieve a victory on Election Day. Volunteers will often have the opportunity to work closely with the candidate and his or her top campaign staff. Moreover, a victory by their candidate provides a ready-made path to an internship or position on Capitol Hill. Contacting the appropriate local or national party committees can help turn up races that need assistance.

Additionally, many Members of Congress offer internships in their district offices. While the work focuses more on constituent aid than on the legislative process, the schedule may be more flexible to accommodate school hours and the experience could provide entry into the Washington, DC office after graduation.

When to intern

The busiest time in Washington for interns is during the summer. The streets of Washington literally seem to be teeming with undergraduates. Summer internships provide a good opportunity to network with other interns and enjoy a wide range of social activities. Furthermore, Congress tends to be very busy during the early summer months of June and July. Congress takes an August recess during Washington's hottest month, and the pace of life slows down greatly on the Hill and across the city. Internships at times other than the summer can be a very good option since there will be fewer interns and more work to go around. Often, they are combined with college programs for credit. However, students should work to ensure that Congress is in session while they are in Washington; interning during November and December of an election year will greatly reduce the value of the experience since Congress rarely has any official activities scheduled during this time.

Advocacy Organizations

For students more interested in a cause than a specific political agenda, or for those students who want to broaden their Washington, DC experience beyond Capitol Hill, nearly every organization and every cause is represented in some form or another within the nation's capital. Many of these are large organizations that provide internships for students. However, please be aware that internships will vary from organization to organization: some will be well structured, others less so; many will offer pay or stipends, but many more will not; some will be smaller organizations while others will be larger and more bureaucratic. It is imperative for students to do their research.

While the list of advocates within Washington is too numerous to cover in great detail, there are many organizations on the right, left, and even in the center that students may wish to explore.

For example, students interested in the issue of gun control could apply for internships on either side of the debate, depending on their philosophy, and still work with some of the most influential organizations in Washington. The National Rifle Association and the Brady Campaign to Prevent Gun Violence both offer legislative internships in their Washington area headquarters.

Students interested in environmental issues should consider the liberal-leaning World Wildlife Federation or Sierra Club, while those who favor a conservative philosophy on the environment could look into opportunities with a think tank or the Council of Environmental Republican Advocacy or a business organization.

There are many organizations that are also non-partisan, and that represent a professional group or other point of view. For example, the American Medical Association represents the interests of doctors before Congress and works closely with members of both parties.

Please note that it is very common for organizations with distinct agendas on both the left and the right to describe themselves as "non-partisan." While this is true in a legal sense, the fact is that many of these organizations do favor the left or the right in their activities. Students who aren't sure about an organiza-

Visit Vault at **www.vault.com** for insider company profiles, expert advice, career message boards, expert resume reviews, the Vault Job Board and more.

V/\ULT CAREER LIBRARY   **205**

tion's true nature should cast a critical eye on its issue advocacy efforts, board of directors, and web site to determine its true leanings.

For a comprehensive list of advocacy organizations in Washington, as well as White House and Congressional staff, corporate offices and trade associations, check out the Capitol Source, which is published by the National Journal Group. It is available in Washington area bookstores and can be ordered on-line at www.njdc.com/about/capitolsource.

Examples of advocacy organizations

While many advocacy organizations are legally non-partisan, their politics can be considered different shades of liberal, conservative, or middle of the road. Below are some examples of various types of advocacy organizations and their ideological leanings.

American Heart Association: While headquarters in Dallas, the American Heart Association, like many medical groups, maintains an advocacy office in Washington, DC to lobby for greater research funding and promote legislation that encourages healthy lifestyles, such as anti-tobacco measures. It is considered a moderate organization. www.americanheart.org

AARP: The nation's leading seniors organization is also one of the most influential advocates in the nation's capital, making its presence felt on a number of high profile issues, including Social Security, Medicare, and healthcare issues. It is generally considered a moderate organization. www.aarp.org

Brady Campaign to Prevent Gun Violence: The Brady Campaign, named after the former White House press secretary wounded during the attempted assassination of President Ronald Reagan, works to enact gun control laws and regulation through grassroots organization and campaign support to similar-minded candidates. It is considered a liberal organization. www.bradycampaign.org

Citizens for a Sound Economy: CSE fights for lower taxes, less government, and fewer regulations. It recruits and trains grass roots activists across the country to influence the economic agenda on the national, state and local levels. It is considered a conservative organization. www.cse.org

Christian Coalition: The Christian Coalition supports policies on the federal, state, and local levels that reflect its moral values. Examples include opposition to abortion and gambling and support for lower taxes, among many social and economic issues. It is considered a conservative organization. www.cc.org

Concord Coalition: The Concord Coalition advocates for fiscal responsibility while ensuring Social Security, Medicare, and Medicaid remain secure. It was founded by the late former Senator Paul Tsongas (D-MA) and former Senator Warren Rudman (R-NH) and is considered a moderate organization. www.concordcoaltion.org

National Resources Defense Council: The NRDC supports environmental protections and engages in advocacy on issues ranging from global warming to nuclear waste. It is considered a liberal organization. www.nrdc.org

National Rifle Association: The National Rifle Association provides an array of services to gun owners and is a well known legislative advocate in the nation's capital. The NRA opposes legislation that regulates gun ownership and supports candidates that agree with its positions on gun issues. It is considered a conservative organization. www.nra.org

Common Cause: Common Cause is a strong proponent of campaign finance reform and actively lobbies to reduce the amount of money in the political process. It is considered a liberal organization. www.commoncause.org

The Staff Assistant

If you are coming out of an undergraduate program, or are a recent graduate, and want to start your career on the Hill, your first position will most likely be as a staff assistant (or possibly as a legislative correspondent)

The staff assistant role is viewed as the traditional entry-level position for those with little to no Capitol Hill or legislative experience. It is not glamorous, and the pay is low, but it does provide the first important entrée to Capitol Hill.

The primary responsibilities of the staff assistant tend more toward administrative work. On the surface, a staff assistant is often seen as a glorified, college educated receptionist. As a staff assistant, you will usually be the first person a visitor sees upon entering the office. Your responsibilities include greeting guests, arranging tours of the Capitol, opening and sorting the mail, and answering the phone.

However, as a staff assistant, you will also have the opportunity to assist the more senior staff in a variety of areas and learn the ropes on Capitol Hill. As you learn the fundamentals of your position, you will have more time to put your education to use. Staff assistants often have the chance to work with Legislative Assistants to research legislation and other issues, take on special projects for the chief of staff, or help the Press Secretary by proofreading speeches and organizing media lists.

Moreover, the position of staff assistant reinforces one of the foremost truisms of work in Washington: proximity to power is key. As a staff assistant, you will perform many mundane tasks. You will be paid far less than you could command in an entry-level position elsewhere. You will also work directly for a Member of Congress and position yourself for far more interesting jobs in the future. Therefore, newcomers to Washington are hungry for an entry-level spot on Capitol Hill. It is the proximity that provides experience and opens doors to bigger opportunities.

"Getting started on the Hill means lots of time doing stuff they didn't teach you in college, like answering the phones and spending a lot of time dealing with constituents. But I wouldn't give up this job for anything. A lot of my friends off the Hill make more money, but in the long run my time on the Hill will open a lot more doors for me down the road," says one staff assistant.

"Working as a staff assistant is both frustrating and exciting," another explains. "Frustrating because some of the work can be tedious and some of the people you deal with can be quite rude. It's exciting because our office moves so fast. The Senator is very involved on many high profile issues and is always being asked to appear on television. I've been able to meet many high profile Washington dignitaries and leaders."

Visit Vault at **www.vault.com** for insider company profiles, expert advice, career message boards, expert resume reviews, the Vault Job Board and more.

VAULT CAREER LIBRARY 207

Day in the Life: Staff Assistant

8:30 a.m.: Come in to open up the office. Since you are the first person a visitor sees upon entering the office, it is your responsibility to ensure that the reception area is neatly kept and that there are plenty of brochures about things to do in Washington, DC.

8:40 a.m.: Catch up on the latest news by reading the *Washington Post*, *Roll Call* (the newspaper of Capitol Hill), and your home town papers on-line.

9:30 a.m.: Open and sort the mail. It is amazing how many people take the time to write to their Congressman. As you read each incoming letter, you must determine which Legislative Assistant or Legislative Correspondent is responsible for answering the correspondence. Reading the mail gives you a chance to learn about the issues Congress is considering.

10:30 a.m.: Welcome a family from the Member's district visiting Washington with their three children. You have already arranged a tour of the Capitol with one of the office staff.

11:30 a.m.: Answer yet another call from a constituent expressing his opposition to a bill pending before Congress. This is the tenth call you have received today on the same topic, all before lunch. One of the interests groups must be ginning up a strong grassroots operation to defeat this bill!

12:30 p.m.: Finally, time for lunch. Find one of the interns to cover the front desk so that you can slip away for 45 minutes. Head down to the Rayburn Cafeteria with two other office mates to grab a quick bite and gossip about the latest scandal stirring in Washington.

1:15 p.m.: The bells signal the first vote of the day. Activity in the office picks up as the Member prepares to go to the floor.

2:00 p.m.: Research an issue for one of the Legislative Assistants. Request several documents from the Congressional Research Service (CRS).

3:30 p.m.: The strange person who claims that the CIA implanted a chip in his brain and is monitoring his thoughts calls yet again asking to speak to the Congressman. You tell him that your boss is not available, but that you will be sure to pass along the message.

4:00 p.m.: Head down to the basement of the Capitol Building to pick up flags that have been flown over the U.S. Capitol to send to constituents that have requested them. The tunnels under the Capitol are mazelike – you are always surprised when you don't get lost.

5:00 p.m.: Time to call it a day, and head out to happy hour. Members' offices are required to pay overtime to all "non-exempt" employees, including staff assistants, so unless there's something pressing, you can only work an eight-hour day.

The Foreign Service

The Foreign Service is often the first thing that comes to mind when people think of a global career. And unlike many of the other opportunities covered in this book, a Foreign Service career is indeed that – a career. Joining the Foreign Service means accepting a professional (and personal) life spent overseas, with constant rotations every few years. It can be very rewarding, exciting and occasionally glamorous work.

While the salary generally does not match what you can make in the private sector, generous allowance perks and subsidies help make up the difference. For example, there is a hardship "bonus" for postings in difficult areas of the world, up to 25 percent above your base salary. One Foreign Service Officer commented on the pay: "There's a lot of internal grumbling about the salary, but it's really not that bad. When you look at the remuneration, you have to look at the whole package, including subsidized housing and unlimited access to American military exchanges and the American-priced foodstuffs."

Applicants enter the Foreign Service in one of five career tracks: Management Affairs, Consular Affairs, Economic Affairs, Political Affairs and Public Diplomacy. Which career track you enter as a beginning FSO (Foreign Service Officer) will influence the nature of your assignments and your career, and there is little crossover between the tracks once you have made your decision. FSOs often undergo intensive training before being posted to their first overseas assignment, including, in some cases, up to two years full-time language study. Check out www.state.gov for more information on the application procedure, and also www.afsa.org, the American Foreign Service Organization, for more information on what life is like in the Foreign Service.

Qualifications

While potential FSOs come from all backgrounds, being accepted is extremely competitive – roughly 40,000 applicants apply for the Foreign Service exam every year, only about 400 are eventually accepted. If you are serious about joining the Foreign Service, be prepared to do your homework!

The exam is offered once a year, and studying for it can be a grueling exercise. Successfully completing the exam (and then the subsequent oral interviews) requires extensive and intensive knowledge of U.S. and world history, international relations and major political issues. Says one foreign service officer who joined in the mid 1990s: "The applicants who do best on the test are those who have literally spent a lifetime preparing for it: They're naturally interested in foreign affairs and world events, have often done their degree in that area, and have followed the news their whole life. This type of background will be invaluable."

Check out www.state.gov for more information on the exam, study hints and guides.

Potential FSOs come from a wide variety of backgrounds, and knowledge of a foreign language is not required (though it will make you a more attractive candidate). In addition to deep knowledge of world affairs, the State Department looks for personal characteristics and traits that will best represent America overseas.

Uppers and downers

The Foreign Service is an excellent training ground and a superior way to see the world. With the world a constantly changing place and an increasingly wide array of international issues – think medical, environmental, social and religious, as well as economic and political – on the agenda, the Foreign Service can provide an exciting and stimulating career path.

Visit Vault at **www.vault.com** for insider company profiles, expert advice, career message boards, expert resume reviews, the Vault Job Board and more.

VAULT CAREER LIBRARY   **209**

The lifestyle and constant rotations have a downside, too, and that is the impact on your personal life. While picking up and exploring a new city and a new job every few years can be exciting in your twenties, the lack of stability can be more problematic as you get older. Having a spouse or partner who is willing to rotate with you is a plus. The State Department is gradually lengthening the time of each rotation, expanding the average to three or four years.

Employer Directory

Naval Financial Management Career (NAVY)

153 Ellyson Avenue, Suite A

Pensacola, FL 32508-5245

Phone: 850-452-3783

E-mail: fmip@nfmc.navy.mil

www.navyfmip.com

The Financial Management Intern Program (FMIP) recruits high quality, prospective civilian financial managers for Department of the Navy Activities. The FMIP is a two year program of professional development through academic and on-the-job training. Entry level positions as Analysts, Accountants, and Auditors are available. Applicants may have any academic major; but those applying for Accounting and Auditor positions require 24 semester hours of accounting (6 hours may be in business law). A minimum cumulative GPA of 2.95 in an undergraduate degree from a nationally accredited university/college is required.

Naval Financial Management Career recruits from:
Nationally accredited colleges and universities

U.S. Secret Service

950 H Street, Suite 3800

Washington, D.C. 20223

Phone: 202-406-5830

www.secretservice.gov

rhcc@usss.treas.gov

The United States Secret Service is one of the most elite law enforcement organizations in the world. It has earned this reputation throughout more than 139 years of unparalleled service to this nation. As one of the oldest Federal law enforcement agencies in the country, the United States Secret Service has dual missions that include investigations, as well as protection of the President and Vice President of the United States and others. These unique challenges distinguish the United States Secret Service from all other law enforcement organizations.

Central Intelligence Agency

P.O. Box 4090

Reston, VA 20195

Phone: (703) 482-0677

www.cia.gov

Democratic National Committee

430 S. Capitol Street, S.E.

Washington, DC 20003

Phone: (202) 863-8000

www.democrats.org

Democratic Senatorial Campaign Committee

120 Maryland Avenue, N.E.

Washington, DC 20002

Phone: (202) 224-2447

www.dscc.org

Federal Bureau of Investigation

J. Edgar Hoover FBI Building

935 Pennsylvania Avenue, NW

Washington, DC 20535

Phone: (202) 324-3000

www.fbi.gov

National Republican Senatorial Committee

425 Second Street, N.E.

Washington, DC 20002

Phone: (202) 675-6000

www.nrsc.org

National Republican Congressional Committee

320 First Street, S.E.

Washington, DC 20003

Phone: (202) 479-7000

www.nrcc.org

Office of Management and Budget

725 17th Street, NW

Washington, DC 20503

Phone: (202) 395-3080

Fax: (202) 395-3888

www.whitehouse.gov/omb

Republican National Committee

310 First Street, S.E.

Washington, DC 20003

Phone: (202) 863-8500

www.rnc.org

Small Business Administration

409 Third Street, SW

Washington, DC 20416

Phone: 1-800-U-ASK-SBA

www.sba.gov

U.S. Department of Commerce

1401 Constitution Avenue NW

Washington, DC 20230

(202) 482-2000

www.commerce.gov

U.S. Department of Education

400 Maryland Avenue, SW

Washington, DC 20202

Phone: (800)- USA-LEARN

www.ed.gov

U.S. Department of Health and Human Services

200 Independence Avenue, S.W.

Washington, DC 20201

Phone: (202) 619-0257

www.hhs.gov

U.S. Department of Justice

950 Pennsylvania Avenue, NW

Washington, DC 20530-0001

Phone: (202) 353-1555

www.justice.gov

U.S. Department of Labor

Frances Perkins Building

200 Constitution Avenue, NW

Washington, DC 20210

Phone: (866) 487-2365

www.dol.gov

U.S. Department of State

2201 C Street NW

Washington, DC 20520

Phone: (202)-647-6575

www.careers.state.gov

U.S. Environmental Protection Agency

1200 Pennsylvania Ave.,NW

Washington, D.C. 20460

Phone: (202) 272-0167

www.epa.gov

Visit Vault at **www.vault.com** for insider company profiles, expert advice, career message boards, expert resume reviews, the Vault Job Board and more.

VAULT CAREER LIBRARY

213

Cardinal Health

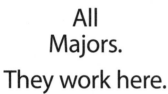

All Majors. They work here.

Product Development

Manufacturing

Packaging

Distribution

Automation

Consulting

For Health Care and Life Sciences

Cardinal Health is a dynamic, *Fortune* 17 company with a simple mission: to be a vital partner in the development, delivery and improvement of health care. With revenues exceeding $50 billion, Cardinal Health is a leading provider of products and services to the health care industry with a strong record of financial performance. We are driven by our desire for growth, our focus on customers, our commitment to operational excellence and our need to develop leaders. Our greatest strength lies in our 50,000+ employees on five continents working together to bring our customers the power of integration, innovation and partnership. *Working together. For life.*[SM]

Set your goals.

Let us guide you and help you achieve your goals through a wide-range of professional opportunities across a variety of disciplines. Gain real world business experience where you'll take on projects and responsibilities, draw on your knowledge, push your creativity and problem-solving skills to a higher level. Or you may flourish in a well-thought-out Development Program offering opportunities to gain experience in several areas of Cardinal Health or within a specific discipline. Whatever you choose, Cardinal Health can help you set your career along the right path... and be there with encouragement and opportunities throughout your career.

We offer full-time positions and internships in the following disciplines:

Engineering
Finance and Accounting
Human Resources
Manufacturing
Purchasing
Operations and Logistics
Sales and Marketing
Chemistry

Pharmaceutics
Biology
Project Management
Event Coordination
Medical Writing
Pharmacy
Quality

Experience it!

Learn the best practices of an industry leader.
Explore your interests.
Make your recommendations count.
Advance your career around the corner,
around the country, around the world.

To apply for one of these full-time positions or internships please visit www.cardinal.com/college. Successful candidates must pass a background check and drug screen. We are an Equal Opportunity Employer M/F/D/V - Diversity Works Here.
www.cardinal.com

CardinalHealth
Working together. For life.[SM]

Health Care

Health Care Industry Overview

The health care industry

You can't live with it, you can't live without it – this pretty much sums up the attitude many Americans have toward today's health care industry. The industry is made up of a variety of providers of patient care, including hospitals, nursing homes, and physicians' offices, as well as those who help coordinate, manage, and pay for that care, like HMOs and other health insurers. It's no secret that the sector is a volatile one. Despite making up nearly 15 percent of the nation's GDP, with U.S. health care spending at $1.6 trillion in 2002, the industry has had a tough time figuring out how to turn healthy profits in a way that benefits both providers and patients.

Having a senior moment

By the year 2050, seniors will outnumber children for the first time in world history, according to the AARP. With approximately one million people turning age 60 each month worldwide, the phenomenon known as "global aging" promises to have a deep impact on the demand for and delivery of health care services. In the U.S., the Baby Boom generation – those born shortly after the Second World War up to the mid-1960s – makes up a sizable portion of the total population. In fact, people aged 50 and older are the fastest-growing demographic group in the nation. This shift is already sparking interest in all issues affecting senior health – from preventive health care to ward off problems later in life, to programs promoting home care and assisted living as alternatives to the dreaded nursing home option for seniors who can't take care of themselves.

Creaky Medicare

With an aging population comes growing pressure on the nation's reimbursement system for seniors and low-income patients. In the U.S., the federal government looms large in health care – though not as large as some patient advocates would prefer (we'll get to health care reform later). In fact, ranked by sales, the government's own Centers for Medicare & Medicaid Services (CMS, formerly known as the Health Care Financing Administration) ranks number one in the industry, according to Hoover's data. Around 40 million people currently are eligible for Medicare coverage, more than twice as many as when the program was first established in 1966 under President Johnson. In 2002, Medicare spending made up about 17 percent of total health care expenditures, or $267 billion, roughly equal to the 16 percent coming from Medicaid (which is administered by the states and covers low-income patients as well as older people).

Medicare claims are submitted by health care providers through fiscal intermediaries or carriers, entities that have contracted through the government to serve as middlemen in the payment process. After navigating a tricky labyrinth of rules, these claims are reviewed and either accepted or denied by the contrac-

Visit Vault at **www.vault.com** for insider company profiles, expert advice, career message boards, expert resume reviews, the Vault Job Board and more.

V∧ULT CAREER LIBRARY 215

tors. Top Medicare contractors include BlueCross BlueShield organizations in a number of states, plus other companies such as Palmetto GBA and Empire Medicare Services.

The Medicare program, perennially the subject of reform packages in Congress, is a political hot potato. Under the Bush Administration, a heated battle was waged between patient advocates and lobbyists for insurers and pharmaceutical companies in an effort to get prescription drug costs under control. In 2003 the administration established a prescription drug discount card for Medicare beneficiaries, but critics argued that it wasn't the solid overhaul the program ultimately requires.

Flying without a net

The rest of the population – those who aren't eligible for Medicare or Medicaid coverage – either have to buy private insurance on their own, get it at discounted rates through an employer, or just go without and hope for the best. An alarming number of Americans, including many children, are in the latter category. In early 2004, almost 44 million Americans (about 15 percent of the population) were uninsured. Not only do these people risk financial meltdown when faced with unexpected medical emergencies, they're also less likely to maintain their good health and prevent more serious conditions later on through routine visits to doctors, dentists, and the like. In addition, reports indicate that health care is more expensive overall for the uninsured. For example, some hospitals bill uninsured clients a higher rate for the same procedures provided to those with health coverage, since big insurance companies are able to negotiate discounts with providers.

The situation isn't rosy for consumers fortunate enough to have coverage, either. Private health insurance companies paid for 35 percent of the total health expenditures in the U.S. in 2002, nearly $550 billion. But as the cost of providing health care coverage continues to rise, many employers are finding they can no longer afford this benefit, and are passing more of the costs onto employees in the form of higher premiums and stingier reimbursement plans.

Unmanageable care

Managed care, which came into prominence in the 1980s and 1990s as a response to rampant inflation in health care costs, has changed the face of the industry. Under these systems, insurers (also known as "payors") figured out that they could rein in costs by establishing networks of providers who participate in a network, or health maintenance organization (HMO), which in turn covers a host of covered patients' needs. But in order to be reimbursed profitably, health care providers have to curb their costs themselves. This includes keeping strict limits on the amount of time they spend with patients to maximize the number of appointments they can squeeze in during a day – leading to the hour-in-the-waiting-room, five-minutes-in-the-exam-room doctor visits many Americans experience today. Top managed care corporations include Anthem, HealthNet and UnitedHealth Group.

As illustrated by Hollywood dramas and prime time news programs, the public largely sees HMOs as stingy and heartless, willing to deny society's neediest members basic procedures that are deemed too costly or unnecessary through an impenetrable system of rules and limits. For their part, managed care organizations argue that without these limits, the cost of health care would rise for everyone in the network (and society at large), nullifying the benefits of such a system. Meanwhile, the government has gotten into the managed care game, allowing patients to participate in the "Medicare+Choice" program, which also operates under the provider network philosophy. As with much government-speak, the program actually controls costs by limiting patient choice, not adding it, skeptics contend.

The doctor will see you now

At the other end of the spectrum, consumers who can flash the cash increasingly are turning to "concierge" or "boutique" physician practices. These private practices offer the attentive, personal, and thorough care associated with pre-HMO days and Norman Rockwell paintings – for a price. Patients shell out an annual fee up front that can range from several hundred to tens of thousands of dollars to join an exclusive roster of clients seen by a participating internist. So rather than scrambling to see up to 30 patients a day as in a typical managed care practice, boutique physicians can limit their number of cases to a select handful. Some of these practices charge for appointments above and beyond the annual fee (which is just a sort of retainer for their services); some accommodate reimbursement by health plans for things like specialized tests. As health care costs skyrocket and patients grow frustrated with insurance plans and the quality of managed care, these practices are becoming more popular – and profitable – business options for those doctors who don't see exclusive care for the well-off as an ethical dilemma.

The quest for reform

Every time a campaign season rolls around, the health care coverage crisis gets a lot of buzz – but since the failed initiative led by Hilary Clinton early in her husband's tenure as president, few mainstream candidates have been willing to outline a specific, coherent strategy for reform. In fact, rejection of sweeping health care reform is somewhat of a tradition in the U.S., going back to the days when President Truman stumbled in the 1940s after introducing a universal coverage proposal. In addition, of those citizens who actually get out and vote each season, a large majority (92 percent in the 2000 election) have health insurance anyway, so officials aren't exactly running to fix the problem of the uninsured, according to an April 2004 *BusinessWeek* article. So while many reformers say a "single-payer plan" – one in which the government takes over the administration of all health care costs – is the only reasonable way to tame the coverage dragon, it may take a while to show up as a viable proposal.

Liability looms

Another type of reform that gets plenty of Congressional buzz is in the area of medical malpractice liability. In fact, the powerful American Medical Association has made the issue its top priority recently. The association has taken to identifying states that are in a "medical liability crisis" owing to exploding insurance premiums and their effect – providers limiting or halting certain services because of liability risks. As of June 2004, there were 20 such states on the AMA's list. One such state, Massachusetts, is a case in point – according to Massachusetts Medical Society research, 50 percent of the state's neurosurgeons, 41 percent of orthopedic surgeons, and 36 percent of general surgeons had been forced to limit their scopes of practice because of insurmountable medical liability costs. With multi-million-dollar judgments against providers making headlines regularly, a solid industry of trial lawyers is devoted to representing patients

Visit Vault at **www.vault.com** for insider company profiles, expert advice, career message boards, expert resume reviews, the Vault Job Board and more.

VAULT CAREER LIBRARY   **217**

who complain of poor care (and in some cases, abuse or the deaths or loved ones). At the same time, such judgments cause liability insurers to panic, and many are refusing to cover health care providers at all. The insurers who have stayed in the medical liability market can charge a premium that providers increasingly can't afford to pay. For lawmakers, the issue is a tough one – how do you set a cap on the amount a plaintiff can receive for the preventable death of a loved one? Patient advocates frame the issue as a David-versus-Goliath scenario, charging that the monolithic medical community wants to limit consumers' rights to sue providers for poor care. Meanwhile, as the industry waits for the federal government to come up with a solution, states have begun to tackle the issue themselves, setting their own limits on the amount of money a malpractice judgment can reap for the plaintiff.

Hot hospitals

In 2002, hospital spending increased by 9.5 percent from the year before, to $486.5 billion. Growing demand for hospital services, along with higher rates from private insurers, have led to the fourth straight year of growth in this sector. Among the approximately 6,100 hospitals in the U.S., a few tower over the rest. Each year, *U.S. News & World Report* publishes a ranking of the nation's top hospitals, surveying doctors around the country about hospitals' reputations in 17 medical specialties as well as other factors like staffing, morbidity rates and technology. In 2004, *U.S. News & World Report's* list named Baltimore's Johns Hopkins Hospital as number one overall – a position the institution has held for 14 years running. Second-ranked was the Mayo Clinic, followed by Massachusetts General, The Cleveland Clinic, and UCLA Medical Center.

Tenet Healthcare, the nation's second-largest hospital chain, provides a cautionary tale about the perils of doing business in health care. The company, with 98 acute care hospitals and numerous other facilities nationwide, has been the subject of federal investigations into the way it handled Medicare payments over the last few years. Charles Grassley, chair of the Senate Finance Committee, has said that Tenet "appears to be a corporation that is ethically and morally bankrupt." In May 2003, beleaguered CEO Jeffrey Barbakow stepped down after 10 years of heading the firm. The company paid a record settlement amount of $375 million in 1994 for alleged kickbacks and bribes to doctors as inducements to refer patients to its psychiatric hospitals. Tenet made headlines again as, 10 years later, in June 2004, it began talking to the feds about a possible $1 billion settlement to end an investigation into charges it performed unnecessary heart surgeries on patients – and muttering about a possible bankruptcy filing. Another headline-grabbing health care scandal recently involved HealthSouth, the nation's largest provider of physical rehab, outpatient surgery and diagnostic services. In 2003, the Securities and Exchange Commission hit HealthSouth with charges of cooking the books, accusing the company and its founder and CEO, Richard Scrushy, of overstating earnings by $1.4 billion since 1999. Scrushy was forced to leave his company in disgrace, though he still maintains his innocence. Who says health care isn't full of intrigue?

The dreaded "home"

The term "nursing home" strikes fear in the hearts of many American consumers, primarily due to media reports detailing abuse and foul conditions at many facilities – and often because of consumers' first-hand experiences with these institutions. But the nation's nursing homes – also sometimes called "skilled nursing facilities" (SNFs) or "long-term care facilities" – have traveled a rocky road in recent years. Indeed, their crisis helps illustrate larger trends in the health care industry as a whole, particularly among providers that, like nursing homes, rely heavily on federal and state dollars to reimburse them for the cost of patient care. By 2001, nine of the top nursing home corporations in the country, including top names like Genesis Health Ventures, Vencor, Sun Healthcare Systems, and Mariner Post-Acute Networks, had passed through the bankruptcy court system, saddled with hundreds of millions in debt.

What brought these billion-dollar companies to this low point, when they have such a steady stream of consumers desperate for their services? For one thing, many long-term care facilities overextended their debt burdens in the 1990s, investing in rehab facilities and other ancillary services that promised big (some would say "inflated") paybacks from Medicare. Then Medicare struck back, as Congress passed the Balanced Budget Act of 1997, which, among other things, sought to reduce federal health care spending by instituting entirely new payment systems for major health entities like nursing homes, home care agencies, hospitals, and doctors. Under the old system, providers were basically paid a fixed amount, or fee, for each service they provided to Medicare patients. Fair enough, but patient advocates and Congress began to worry that nursing home clients were receiving a bit too much care – excessive and unnecessary therapy services, for instance – simply because facilities could make more money by providing and charging the feds for it. In the BBA, Congress mandated a new "prospective payment system" (PPS) that set up strict guidelines for how long-term care facilities were to be reimbursed for care provided to Medicare and Medicaid patients. Under PPS, facilities are basically paid a fixed per-diem for a patient's care depending on the severity of her needs (or "acuity level"), classified under a host of intricate rules. The system also set certain limits, or "caps," on services such as rehab, under which Medicare would only pay a fixed amount per patient annually.

The combination of leftover debt and poor financial management, plummeting federal dollars, and sky-rocketing liability insurance due to high-profile malpractice judgments – plus a host of other factors like low staffing due to undesirable working conditions and a higher acuity level among the patient population – sent at least 10 percent of the nursing home industry into Chapter 11 by 2001, by some estimates. Most of the nursing home giants have recovered and are learning to adjust to the new payment system, but the situation provided a valuable lesson to other health care providers, like rehab hospitals, whose new Medicare PPS systems took effect after the long-term care revamp had done its damage. Congress, acknowledging that it may have been a bit enthusiastic with the red ink, also kicked in some million-dollar concessions to boost reimbursements after intense industry lobbying.

Others weren't so lucky – many providers of those once high-paying ancillary services, like physical therapy, were forced to close their doors in the aftermath of PPS. Home health care providers, also highly dependent on Medicare and Medicaid payments, weathered a similar crisis to that of long-term care under their own new payment system – and, like their counterparts, managed to eke out some financial givebacks from Congress during the last few years.

Virtual care

Despite fancier defibrillators and sleeker MRIs, many observers have argued that the health care industry actually is a dinosaur when it comes to technology. In fact, less than 5 percent of the total amount of health

Visit Vault at **www.vault.com** for insider company profiles, expert advice, career message boards, expert resume reviews, the Vault Job Board and more.

VAULT CAREER LIBRARY **219**

care spending in the U.S. will go toward information technology in 2004, CMS estimates. But both providers and payors have caught on to the benefits of doing business electronically in recent years. From the providers' side, patient advocates argue that care can be improved by standardizing practices using digital technology – for instance, using hand-held devices to transcribe, translate, and store doctors' near-illegible notes in patient records. These types of solutions may help cut down on the estimated 44,000 to 98,000 patient deaths per year said to be caused by provider errors (as outlined in a widely publicized 1999 Institutes of Medicine report).

One Chicago-area hospital profiled in a July 2004 *BusinessWeek* article has taken the plunge and gone entirely "paperless" over the past three years. Evanston Northwestern Healthcare's $60 million project has made nearly every point along the patient care continuum virtual, putting everything from surgical bay orders to medical records transcription online. The hospital predicts the overhaul will save $10 million per year. Patients benefit from such a system, too – at Evanston, doctors can access results of mammograms in just one day, as opposed to three weeks under the old system, and the hospital has slashed the late administration of meds to patients by 70 percent. Among the IT solutions health care systems will be investing in over the coming decade are information systems that can standardize the clinical treatment of diseases and bar-code systems for managing drugs and lab samples. Even the government has gotten onboard the IT bandwagon – the Bush Administration has said it wants all U.S. patient care records in an electronic format by 2014.

Going with the flow

Payors also have gone digital, requiring electronic filing of claims by providers and switching to online systems to provide essential information like updates on Medicare rules. As more and more patient health information flows through virtual data streams, however, systems needed to be put in place to help the disparate entities in the health care chain communicate with one another in a standardized way, and, most importantly, to protect the privacy of that free-flowing patient data. Thus was born the Health Insurance Portability and Accountability Act (HIPAA), signed by President Clinton, which covers both the privacy of medical records and the transmission of claims among payors and providers.

HIPAA, which promises hefty fines if providers violate a host of intricate stipulations, sent the health care world into a minor panic – and thus a multi-million-dollar software, education, and consulting industry was born. As the HIPAA rules began to be enforced, in 2003, visitors to doctors' offices may have noticed subtle changes, such as an extra "Notice of Privacy Practices" sheet in their clipboard upon check-in, one requirement of the law. Such requirements often are seen as busywork by harried health care providers, but some of the law's provisions respond to very real concerns – such as the fear that prospective employers or other decision-makers could hijack a patient's medical records off the Information Superhighway. Other, less extreme examples include the regulation of how much information hospitals and other providers can reveal regarding patients under their care, and the setting of limits on the amount of time patient records can be left to molder in basement file drawers. On the claims-processing side, HIPAA mandates an electronic transaction standard for Medicare claims sent between providers and Medicare contractors. The reward for compliance with the standard, in theory anyway, is more efficient and timely payment of these claims.

Where the jobs are

In spite of its daunting complexity, the health care industry has one big upside – it's a reliable producer of job opportunities. The health services industry, the largest of all industries categorized by the Bureau of Labor Statistics (BLS) as of 2002, provided nearly 13 million jobs that year. Of the 20 occupations the BLS projects to grow the fastest in coming years, half are in the health services sector. And of new wage and salary jobs that will be created by 2012, about 16 percent will be in health services – more than in any other industry.

While employment in the health care industry conjures visions of crushing med school debt and grueling internships, in fact the majority of jobs in the sector require less than four years of college education. Graduates of one- and two-year certification programs might work as medical records and health information technicians. Service occupations abound, including medical and dental assistant, nursing and home health aide, and facility cleaning jobs. The BLS predicts particularly strong growth in jobs outside the inpatient hospital sector, such as medical assistants and home health aides. In the industry, there's a constant clamor for more nurses, as facilities face growing regulatory pressure to meet mandatory staffing levels. A large and vocal organized labor presence exists in the industry, despite efforts at union-busting by facilities.

Visit Vault at **www.vault.com** for insider company profiles, expert advice, career message boards, expert resume reviews, the Vault Job Board and more.

VAULT CAREER LIBRARY   221

Employer Directory

Aetna, Inc.

151 Farmington Avenue
Hartford, CT 06156
Phone: 860-273-0123
E-mail: College@aetna.com
http://www.aetna.com/working/index.htm

Aetna is one of the nation's leading providers of health care, dental, pharmacy, group life, disability and long-term care products, serving approximately 13.7 million medical members, 11.8 million dental members and 11.7 million group insurance customers, as of December 31, 2002. The company has expansive nationwide networks of more than 552,000 health care services providers, including over 332,000 primary care and specialist physicians and 3,373 hospitals. Aetna provides these benefits to employer and plan sponsor customers in all 50 states, ranging from large multi-site national accounts to middle-market and small-employer groups.

Aetna offers competitive salaries and a full range of benefits to satisfy the needs of our diverse work force. These benefits include medical, dental, life insurance, and disability. In addition, we offer tuition reimbursement, a 401(k), paid time off, and bonus programs that reward excellent work.

To learn more about Aetna, please visit www.aetna.com.

Schools Aetna recruits from

University of Connecticut; University of Hartford; Central Connecticut State University; Howard University; Hampton University; University of Puerto Rico; Michigan State University; Eastern Connecticut State University; Western Connecticut State University; Southern Connecticut State University; Lincoln University

Oxford Health Plans

48 Monroe Turnpike
Trumbull, CT 06611
Phone: 800-889-7658

Schools Oxford recruits from

Fairfield; Sacred Heart; Quinnipiac; Rutgers; L.I.U. CW Post; Hofstra; Columbia; NYU; CUNY; Univ of Scranton; Seton Hall

Visit Vault at **www.vault.com** for insider company profiles, expert advice, career message boards, expert resume reviews, the Vault Job Board and more.

VAULT CAREER LIBRARY

223

AdvancePCS, Inc.
750 W. John Carpenter Frway., Ste 1200
Irving, TX 75039
Phone: (469) 524-4700
Fax: (469) 524-4702

Anthem, Inc.
120 Monument Circle
Indianapolis, IN 46204
Phone: (317) 488-6000
Fax: (317) 488-6028
www.anthem-inc.com

Baxter International Inc.
One Baxter Parkway
Deerfield, IL 60015
Phone: (847) 948-2000
Fax: (847) 948-3642
www.baxter.com

Becton, Dickinson and Company
1 Becton Drive
Franklin Lakes, NJ 07417-1880
Phone: (800) 284-6845
Fax: (201) 847-6475
www.bd.com

Boston Scientific Corporation
One Boston Scientific Place
Natick, MA 01760
Phone: (508) 650-8000
Fax: (508) 647-2200
www.bsci.com

Caremark Rx
211 CDommerce St., Suite 800
Nashville, TN 37201
Phone: (205) 733-8996
Fax: (205) 733-0704
www.caremark.com

CIGNA Corporation
1 Liberty Place
Philadelphia, PA 19192-1550
Phone: (215) 761-1000
Fax: (215) 761-5515
www.cigna.com

Express Scripts, Inc.
13900 Riverport Dr.
Maryland Heights, MO 63043
Phone: (314) 770-1666
Fax: (314) 702-7037
www.express-scripts.com

Guidant Corporation
111 Monument Circle, 29th Fl.
Indianapolis, IN 46204
Phone: (317) 971-2000
Fax: (317) 971-2040
www.guidant.com

HCA, Inc.
One Park Plaza
Nashville, TN 37203
Phone: (615) 344-9551
Fax: (615) 344-2266
www.hcahealthcare.com

Health Net Inc.
21650 Oxnard St.
Woodland Hills, CA 91367
Phone: (818) 676-6000
Fax: (818) 676-8591
www.health.net

Humana Inc.
The Humana Bldg.
500 West Main Street
Louisville, KY 40202
Fax: (502) 580-1000
Fax: (502) 580-4188
www.humana.com

Kaiser Foundation Health Plan, Inc.

1 Kaiser Plaza

Oakland, CA 94612

Phone: (510) 271-5800

Fax: (510) 271-6493

www.kaiserpermanente.org

MedTronic, Inc.

710 Medtronic Pkwy. NE

Minneapolis, MN 55432-3476

Phone: (763) 514-4000

Fax: (763) 574-4879

www.medtronic.com

PacifiCare Health Systems, Inc.

5995 Plaza Dr.

Cypress, CA 90630

Phone: (714) 825-5200

Fax: (714) 825-5045

www.pacificare.com

Quest Diagnostics Incorporated

One Malcolm Ave.

Teterboro, NJ 07608

Phone: (201) 393-5000

Fax: (201) 462-4715

www.questdiagnostics.com

Tenet Healthcare Corporation

3820 State St.

Santa Barbara, CA 93105

Phone: (805) 563-7000

Fax: (805) 563-7070

www.tenethealth.com

UnitedHealth Group Incorporated

UnitedHealth Group Center

9900 Bren Rd. East

Minnetonka, MN 55343

Phone: (612) 936-1300

Fax: (612) 936-7430

www.unitedhealthcare.com

WellChoice, Inc. (Empire Blue Cross/Blue Shield)

11 W. 42nd Street

New York, NY 10036

Phone (212) 476-1000

Fax: (212) 476-1281

www.empireblue.com

WellPoint Health Networks Inc.

1 WellPoint Way

Thousand Oaks, CA 91362

Phone: (805) 557-6655

Fax: (805) 557-6872

Visit Vault at **www.vault.com** for insider company profiles, expert advice, career message boards, expert resume reviews, the Vault Job Board and more.

VAULT CAREER LIBRARY 225

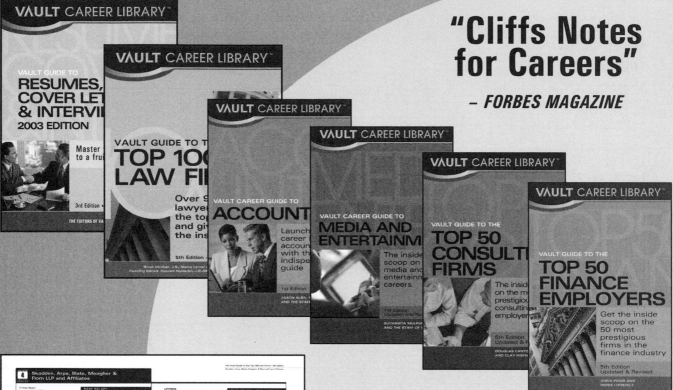

High Tech

The Scope of High Tech Careers

There are certainly many companies that can be considered "technology" companies because the products or services they produced involve computers, software or networking systems. Prominent examples include Microsoft, IBM, Cisco Systems and Dell Computer. But technology careers also extend beyond high tech industries. IT is integral in most businesses, and its definition is continually being redefined. Although most jobseekers know that IT involves widespread technologies, few trying to enter the field probably know just which technologies or which jobs it encompasses.

Authorities describing IT demonstrate how widespread yet "blurry" the field is. First of all, "There is not a government-wide definition of who is classified as an Information Technology worker," says Roger Moncarz, an economist for the U.S. Bureau of Labor Statistics. "There's a wide sampling of estimates out there, for exactly how to define an Information Technology worker."

Moncarz continues, "Based on our definition of information technology workers, and based on government occupational surveys, we come up with 3.3 million to 3.5 million IT workers in America. The Information Technology Association of America (ITAA), in their recently released study, says there are 10.4 million IT workers. So there's wide discrepancy."

Regardless of who may define it, one thing is certain: IT is everywhere. Offices large and small must maintain, utilize, and upgrade IT infrastructures to be effective in the marketplace. Because of the ubiquitous and demanding nature of the technology, IT jobs run the gamut from entry-level, low-tech positions to tech-savvy engineering managers.

Information Technology (IT) is a huge, ever-changing field. It encompasses the products and services necessary to store, convert, and deliver information electronically. This includes the entire computer infrastructure of an organization: computer hardware, packaged software, computer system architecture, documents outlining technical procedures, many other computer-related products, and lots and lots of people.

Computers and IT continue to have an explosive impact of on life and business. More than ever, companies must rapidly evolve, incorporating new technologies into their daily operations to remain competitive. From one-man sales companies to international medical labs, almost every type of business utilizes an IT infrastructure to run, to expand, and occasionally, to simply comply with the law.

IT is essential to business because it allows people to communicate faster, more efficiently, and with more capabilities than older technologies. A lone costume maker in Illinois can suddenly turn her enterprise into an international business by putting up a website. A corporate executive can instantaneously deliver vital information to associates in Japan, South Africa, and England through the power of a secure network. A student whose laptop gets stolen can immediately retrieve all of his lost information from a backup database server. A doctor can use a computer program that makes all of his patients' correspondences and information secure from prying eyes. There is power in IT.

Visit Vault at www.vault.com for insider company profiles, expert advice, career message boards, expert resume reviews, the Vault Job Board and more.

VAULT CAREER LIBRARY 227

Since technology issues are so critical to a company's health, a significant portion of business is involved with IT. In fact, one in every 14 jobs in America is an IT or IT-related position. IT careers cover a broad range of businesses, skill paths, office sizes, and backgrounds.

Categories of Tech Professionals

Let's take a look at three major categories of workers: hardware, software, and support personnel.

Hardware

Hardware-oriented workers create and maintain electronic communications infrastructures. They build computers, which both businesses and home users buy. They also build large computers called servers, which mostly businesses buy. When businesses buy computers and servers, company hardware employees set up the computers, connecting them to each other and the server. This way, all of the computers have a common set of resources available to them, and all of the computers can communicate with each other. Hardware employees are often the ones who decide the architecture of the computer clusters and the resources they contain.

Software

Software employees create programs that use and manipulate computer infrastructures. Through typing code and commands into the computers, they design the software interfaces between people and hardware. They also use those interfaces to create utilities and applications that perform specific tasks like tracking business records.

Nowadays, they build systems for the Internet and other networks. They make sure that information flows efficiently between computers within an organization, or to and from a website. At the same time, they keep the information safe, making sure that only authorized people can access sensitive information.

Support

The hardware and software infrastructures at most companies are so large and complex, that separate departments must plan them and support them. Support role employees include people in customer care, leadership and managerial roles, and testing departments. Analysts and managers decide the future of business IT infrastructures. Constantly examining new technology and how it can make business more effective, they weigh the costs and benefits to buying new hardware or modifying existing systems. Quality assurance testers make sure that the systems perform as they were designed and planned. Performing tests and discovering the limits of the systems make sure that the infrastructure investments are worth the cost and effort in the long run. Customer, sales, and user support people make sure that company employees know how to use the systems, and that the systems are in good working order. They also help customers use the software, information, or hardware that the company distributes.

Tech workers = nerds?

When people think of IT workers, especially programmers and engineers, they often think of the ultimate nerd. They may get images of the lone man with a five o'clock shadow, messy hair, and a pocket protector, sitting in a dark room and staring at a computer screen all day and night. Or, they may get an image of the espresso junkie who rides a Razor Scooter in the office, playing foosball and starting Nerf gun fights all day long. These stereotypes of IT are becoming less true.

The IT field has come to resemble traditional corporate culture more than it did during the dot-com heyday. IT employees must be able to communicate well and work sensitively with others, they must travel for some jobs, and they must deal with all sorts of environments to succeed.

Instead of wearing pocket protectors and bad hair, most successful tech workers know how to present themselves professionally to managers and non-tech departments. Increasingly, even programmers need to communicate constantly with analysts, business development offices, and other corporate departments.

Rather than work odd hours and obsess over minor code details, successful engineers know how to prioritize their tasks and follow project requirements efficiently. They need to be around during regular business hours in order to coordinate with business departments. They may work long hours, but that is usually to keep up with tight deadlines born from tighter budgets.

In a nutshell, many IT departments no longer have the time or money to accommodate the stereotypical nerd. While some tech offices still have foosball tables and video games in the office, the number of such offices has been dwindling for years. Companies have been downsizing, and employees have had to take on multiple roles. Workers simply cannot afford the time to fool around in the office, much less gain a reputation of doing so. Companies cannot afford to have departments full of antisocial geeks, since so much of business depends on smooth interdepartmental communication. Many companies have even engaged in efforts to make their tech employees more sociable and stronger communicators.

Contrary to the stereotypes, IT employees must often face a workplace higher in stress, higher in its demands, and lacking in diversity.

Common Positions for Recent College Grads

Entry-level network employees

Desktop support or customer service workers (more specific information on these positions below) do the most basic network maintenance. These workers sit at their desks, receiving phone calls or emails from people who need help using any of the company's software or hardware. Specifically in the network capacity, they provide end user support for network-based applications and perform routine network repairs. Desktop support workers who work exclusively with network matters may be referred to as LAN support workers, or network maintenance workers. These support workers only deal with client machines and cables; they do not touch the server.

If people phone in and report network problems, like if an employee's client computer can no longer communicate with the network, the desktop or LAN support worker recommends solutions to the problem over the phone, such as reconfiguring the client operating system to detect the network. If that does not help, the support worker schedules and performs repairs on the client hardware and software. Such repairs can

Visit Vault at **www.vault.com** for insider company profiles, expert advice, career message boards, expert resume reviews, the Vault Job Board and more.

VAULT CAREER LIBRARY   229

include tightening loose network cables attached to the client machines, installing more RAM on client machines, or reinstalling client application software. They also go all around the office configuring the individual client computers to communicate with the network.

Entry-level network employees make about $29,000 to $40,000 a year. They usually work regular 40-hour workweeks, although they must work after hours or weekends if the network requires maintenance or repairs at those times. These workers should know the common concepts and procedures of network repair and upkeep, but they usually rely on existing guidelines and instructions, reporting to a project leader or more senior LAN support worker.

In time, which can be as short as a year, the support worker can prove enough network competence and knowledge to become a junior network or systems administrator.

Junior administrators

Junior administrators are task-oriented employees who do basic server work. They do not research, gather data from managers, or make planning decisions. Instead, they perform specific tasks given to them by senior admins. However, although they are junior, these admins do not tool with end-user applications or client machine operating systems. Those duties still belong to desktop support personnel. At the junior level, a lot of network and systems duties overlap.

Junior network administrators do basic network configuration and basic network maintenance, such as opening or closing server ports as needed. They also do a lot of the network monitoring. The computer programs that monitor networks produce warning messages if network problems arise, so junior administrators must watch for these messages.

"The junior sys admin also does basic configuration and maintenance," says Greg Land, a junior systems administrator for HotJobs.com. "If there's some kind of network problem, they might replace server memory modules, or replace server CPU's." Also, if senior sys admins determine that a certain amount of server resources need to be allocated for something like company email, the junior sys admins configure the server software accordingly.

With experience and demonstrated competence here comes seniority. Within about two to four years, junior admins can attain senior ranks. Both salary and responsibilities increase substantially here. While junior admins are task-oriented, senior admins are project oriented.

Junior software engineers

A recent college graduate with little experience could get a job as a junior software engineer. Inexperienced software engineers usually start off supporting existing software. They review and analyze the results of software tests, and they help to implement software by installing the programs or applications. They also debug and modify programs according to the direction of senior engineers.

They sit at their desks, in cubicles or in rooms of several engineers, typing on computer screens that are full of text windows. They use various utilities to graphically map out program designs, and they use many purely text interfaces to install or modify their software projects. Rather than developing entire software packages, they create small dependency programs or functions that the main programs use. Beginner developers may make $55,000 to $87,750 per year.

Good analytical and problem-solving skills are necessary for success here. And, at this point, their biggest asset is programming know-how. There are a lot of parts to the job, all of which involve sitting in front of a computer screen: aiding with small portions of program design, debugging existing portions of software, installing programs or dependencies, documenting and mapping programs, etc. These engineers may look like the typical nerd, with bad hair and five o'clock shadows, spending most of their time at text screens and cavorting with other like-minded engineers. Deadlines can be insanely demanding, and software engineers often work over 40 hours a week and on weekends.

Support specialists

Computer support specialists, or technical support specialists/workers, or customer service representatives, or helpdesk workers/technicians provide technical assistance to users over the phone or via email. Using diagnostic programs, they help customers or fellow employees troubleshoot and repair their hardware or software. Support specialists also help users install hardware and software.

These workers sit at their desks taking calls and answering emails all day from people having problems using company hardware or software. More technically trained workers go around the office helping users install or repair their client computers. Other experienced ones may take more complicated technical calls from customers. "It's helpful for people entering IT to have experience in helpdesk, because it gives them exposure to a wide variety of issues on any level of an IT product," says Anthony Dickerson, a technical support worker from a proprietary banking software company.

Helpdesk positions also help technical people get used to dealing with customers and building professional relationships. In addition to that, helpdesk often teaches people to stay calm in bad situations. For example, Ingrid Johanns worked in technical support for a health care company. She relates, "The software guys were working on a system that would make automatic calls to patients, to remind them to do something (do an exercise, go to an appointment, etc). And they screwed up. The system accidentally called people at two in the morning, and it would not stop calling until the recipient had listened to the message fully. Very bad. And my job at the time, being in customer support... well, they had me call all the patients and apologize for the call. I wanted to kill those software guys. It was their fault – they should have made those TOTALLY AWKWARD calls. Anyway, you really learn how to call people and talk with them about anything. You get over that awkward feeling really fast by overdosing on awkwardness."

Support specialists must often help people who do not know much about computers, and they must typically answer questions that the product manuals often do not. Thus, specialists must communicate carefully with users to diagnose problems and to walk the users through solutions. Good communication skills are paramount to advancement here. Good analytical and problem solving skills are also essential.

Support specialists get different types of questions at different types of companies. Workers at a hardware sales company may get questions about how to manually configure computer components. Workers at an

Visit Vault at **www.vault.com** for insider company profiles, expert advice, career message boards, expert resume reviews, the Vault Job Board and more.

VAULT CAREER LIBRARY   **231**

e-commerce site may get questions about how to access personal information through the company's web-site.

Specialists also need to understand the various stresses that each business will offer. For instance, special-ists at a financial web site may get many frantic phone calls from customers worried about their money. "I've had a customer service job at a credit card company for clients, and I've done customer service at a medical insurance group, Blue Cross/Blue Shield" says Dara Sanderson, who now works at WebMD. "Both of them were different. The one at Blue Cross/Blue Shield was a little less frantic, but the ques-tions you got were more important because you're dealing with people's health. Both of them were the type of job that could be very tedious, and there are days when you would dread having to deal with peo-ple. But neither were mentally very difficult to handle though."

Usually, helpdesk workers only need to work 40 hours a week, although customer service offices must often operate 24 hours a day. Thus, they may work evenings or weekends if the company provides sup-port over extended hours. Also, overtime work may be necessary when unexpected technical problems arise.

Employer Directory

Agilent Technologies

 Agilent Technologies

Corporate Headquarters

395 Page Mill Road

Palo Alto, CA 94306

1 (877) 424-4536

www.jobs.agilent.com

Agilent delivers innovative technologies, solutions and services to a wide range of customers in communications, electronics, life sciences and chemical analysis. The breadth and depth of our expertise enable us to offer solutions across our customers' entire product life cycle from research and development to manufacturing to installation and management. With insight gained from this unique and comprehensive perspective, we can help our customers get the best products and services to market quickly and profitably. With customers in more than 110 countries, our global presence offers a distinct competitive advantage. Agilent's manufacturing, R&D, sales and support capabilities around the world give customers the flexibility they need in today's competitive environment.Agilent provides technologies, solutions and services to help our customers accelerate vital progress in their industries . . . to make dreams real.

Schools Agilent Technologies recruits from

Agilent focuses on identifying schools that are aligned with our current and future business needs. Although we target a specific number of schools for on-campus visits and activities, we do not limit our interviewing and/or hiring to these targeted schools.

The Boeing Company

Boeing World Headquarters

100 N. Riverside

Chicago, IL 60606

www.boeing.com/employment/college

With a heritage that mirrors the first 100 years of flight, The Boeing Company provides products and services to customers in 145 countries. Boeing is a premier manufacturer of commercial jetliners and a global market leader in military aircraft, satellites, missile defense, human space flight, and launch systems and services. Total company revenues for 2003 were $50.5 billion. Boeing employs more than 156,000 people in 70 countries and 48 states within the United States, with major operations in the Puget Sound area of Washington state, Southern California, Wichita and St. Louis.

EOE statement: Boeing is an equal opportunity employer supporting diversity in the workplace.

Visit Vault at **www.vault.com** for insider company profiles, expert advice, career message boards, expert resume reviews, the Vault Job Board and more.

VAULT CAREER LIBRARY   233

3Com Corporation
350 Campus Dr.
Marlborough, MA 01752-3064
Phone: (508) 323-5000
Fax: (508) 323-1111
www.3com.com

Advanced Micro Devices, Inc.
1 AMD Place
Sunnyvale, CA 94088
Phone: (408) 749-4000
Fax: (408) 749-4291
www.amd.com

Analog Devices, Inc.
1 Technology Way
Norwood, MA 02062-9106
Phone: (781) 329-4700
Fax: (781) 461-3638
www.analog.com

Apple Computer, Inc.
1 Infinite Loop
Cupertino, CA 95014
Phone: (408) 996-1010
Fax: (408) 974-2113
www.apple.com

Applied Materials, Inc.
3050 Bowers Ave.
Santa Clara, CA 95054
Phone: (408) 727-5555
Fax: (408) 748-9943
www.appliedmaterials.com

Ariba, Inc.
807 11th Ave.
Sunnyvale, CA 94089
Phone: (650) 390-1000
Fax: (650) 390 1100
www.ariba.com

Atmel Corporation
2325 Orchard Pkwy.
San Jose, CA 95131
Phone: (408) 441-0311
Fax: (408) 436-4200
www.atmel.com

Cisco Systems, Inc.
170 W. Tasman Dr.
San Jose, CA 95134
Phone: (408) 526-4000
Fax: (408) 526-4100
www.cisco.com

Computer Associates International, Inc.
1 Computer Associates Plaza
Islandia, NY 11749
Phone: (631) 342-6000
Fax: (631) 342-5329
www.ca.com

Cypress Semiconductor Corporation
3901 N. 1st St.
San Jose, CA 95134-1599
Phone: (408) 943-2600
Fax: (408) 943-6841
www.cypress.com

Dell Computer
1 Dell Way
Round Rock, TX 78682-2222
Phone: (512) 338-4400
Fax: (512) 728-3653
Toll free: (800)-289-3355
www.dell.com

EMC Corporation
176 South St.
Hopkinton, MA 01748
Phone: (508) 435-1000
Fax: (508) 497-6912
www.emc.com

Gateway, Inc.
14303 Gateway Place
Poway, CA 9206
Phone: (858) 848-3401
Fax: (858) 848-3402
www.gateway.com

Hewlett-Packard
3000 Hanover St.
Palo Alto, CA 94304
Phone: (650) 857-1501
Fax: (650) 857-5518
www.hp.com

IBM
New Orchard Rd.
Armonk, NY 10504
Phone: (914) 499-1900
Fax: (914) 765-7382
Toll free: (800) 426-4968
www.ibm.com

Intel Corporation
2200 Mission College Blvd.
Santa Clara, CA 95052-8119
Phone: (408) 765-8080
Fax: (408) 765-9904
Toll free: (800) 628-8686
www.intel.com

Intuit Inc.
2535 Garcia Ave.
Mountain View, CA 94043
Phone: (650) 944-6000
Fax: (650) 944-3699
Toll free: (800) 446-8848
www.intuit.com

LSI Logic Corporation
1621 Barber Ln.
Milpitas, CA 95035
Phone: (408) 433-8000
Phone: (408) 954-3220
www.lsilogic.com

Microsoft Corporation
1 Microsoft Way
Redmond, WA 98052-6399
Phone: (425) 882-8080
Fax: (425) 936-7329
www.microsoft.com

Motorola, Inc.
1303 E. Algonquin Rd.
Schaumburg, IL 60196
Phone: (847) 576-5000
Fax: (847)-576-5372
www.motorola.com

Novell, Inc.
404 Wyman St., Ste. 500
Waltham, MA 02451
Phone: (781) 464-8000
Fax: (781) 464-8100
www.novell.com

Oracle Corporation
500 Oracle Pkwy.
Redwood City, CA 94065
Phone: (650) 506-7000
Fax: (650) 506-7200
Toll Free: (800) 672-2531
www.oracle.com

PeopleSoft, Inc.
4460 Hacienda Dr.
Pleasanton, CA 94588-8618
Phone: (925) 225-3000
Fax: (925) 694-4444
Toll Free: (800) 380-7638
www.peoplesoft.com

Red Hat, Inc.
1801 Varsity Dr.
Raleigh, NC 27606-2072
Phone: (919) 754-3700
Fax: (919) 754-3701

Visit Vault at **www.vault.com** for insider company profiles, expert advice,
career message boards, expert resume reviews, the Vault Job Board and more.

VAULT CAREER LIBRARY

235

Sun Microsystems
4150 Network Circle
Santa Clara, CA 950, Inc.54
Phone: (650) 960-1300
Fax: (408) 276-3804
Toll Free: (800) 555-9786
www.sun.com

Samsung Electronics
250, 2-ga, Taepyung-ro, Jung-gu
Seoul, 100-742, South Korea
Phone: +82-2-727-7114
www.samsung.com

SAP Aktiengesellschaft
Neurottstrasse 16
69190 Walldorf, Germany
Phone: +49-6227-74-7474
www.sap.com

Siebel Systems, Inc.
2207 Bridgepointe Pkwy.
San Mateo, CA
Phone: (650) 295-5000
Fax: (650) 295-5111
www.siebel.com

Siemens Corporation
153 E. 53rd St.
New York, NY 10022-4611
Phone: (212) 258-4000
Fax: (212) 767-0508
www.usa.siemens.com

Sony Corporation
7-35, Kitashinagawa, 6-chome,
Shinagawa-ku
Tokyo, 141-0001, Japan
Phone: +81-3-5448-2111
www.sony.net

Sybase, Inc.
1 Sybase Dr.
Dublin, CA 94568
Phone: (925) 236-5000
Fax: (925) 236-4321
www.sybase.com

Symantec Corporation
20330 Stevens Creek Blvd.
Cupertino, CA 95014-2132
Phone: (408) 517-8000
Fax: (408) 253-3968
www.symantec.com

Texas Instruments Incorporated
12500 TI Blvd.
Dallas, TX 75266-4136
Phone: (972) 995-2011
Fax: (972) 995-4360
www.ti.com

Xerox Corporation
800 Long Ridge Rd.
Stamford, CT 06904 (Map)
Phone: (203) 968-3000
Fax: (203) 968-3218
www.xerox.com

Hospitality and Tourism

The Industry of Fun

The hospitality and tourism industry

The hospitality and tourism industry is made up of a variety of interconnected sectors, including lodging (everything from luxury resorts to roadside motels), recreational activities (theme parks, cruises and the like), rental cars, and food services. All of these sectors work in tandem with the airline and transportation industries that bring consumers to the destinations where they'll spend money on these goods and services. In the industry, this is known as an "upstream" effect – the more likely travelers are to board a plane to get somewhere, for instance, the more in-demand the hospitality and tourism industry's services become. As a whole, the travel industry was a $552 billion business in 2004.

Because of the relationship between tourism, hospitality and transportation, the after-effects of September 11's domestic terrorist attacks, along with other terrorist activities overseas, had a chilling effect on the industry in 2001 and beyond. The subsequent dip in the economy also led to slashed budgets for business travel – the bread and butter of the lodging and rental car sectors. But recently, a variety of factors – including a perception that the economy is improving, increased confidence about security, and lower-cost plane fares – have led to a rebound in travel and tourism overall.

Travel experts forecast total travel spending in 2004 to hit $585 billion, up $33 billion from 2003. By 2005, this figure is expected to surpass the record set by the industry back in 2000. Leisure travel was expected to grow by 2.4 percent in 2004, compared with less than two percent during 2003. And certain sectors have been faring particularly well, like theme parks, which saw domestic attendance rise by 15 percent over 2003's figures. Hotel occupancy rates are at the highest level they've seen in years, with New York City bookings up nearly 10 percent in April 2004 over the same month a year earlier.

Checking into hotels

In 2002, nearly 61,000 establishments, including upscale hotels, RV parks, motels, resorts, casino hotels, bed-and-breakfasts, and boarding houses, provided overnight accommodation in America, employing 1.8 million wage and salary workers in 2002, according to the Bureau of Labor Statistics (BLS). Most of these workers – about 66 percent – worked in service occupations, like housekeeping, food prep, and linen-room attendants. Hotels are classified into five basic categories: commercial, resort, residential, extended-stay, and casino. Some commercial hotels are classified as conference facilities, featuring spaces designed to accommodate large-scale meetings and events. In recent years, the industry has seen the most growth in extended-stay properties, accommodating guests for visits of five nights or longer. By eliminating traditional hotel services including lobby facilities, 24-hour staff, and daily housekeeping, the sector has been able to reap profits. Average revenue per available room (known as RevPAR in the trade) is expected to increase 5.8 percent in 2004 to $52.03.

Visit Vault at **www.vault.com** for insider company profiles, expert advice, career message boards, expert resume reviews, the Vault Job Board and more.

VAULT CAREER LIBRARY   237

Top hotel corporations include Marriott International, Starwood Hotels and Resorts, and Intercontinental Hotels Group. Another hospitality giant is Cendant Corporation, considered the world's largest hotel franchiser, with Days Inn, Super 8 and other brands under its roof. Cendant also has a hefty stake in the rental car market (more on that below), holding the Avis and Budget Rent A Car brands. In addition, Cendant, with revenues topping $18 billion in 2003, owns top travel distribution engine Galileo International and e-commerce travel vendor Cheap Tickets.

Unhospitable climate

If you've had a bad customer service experience in the hospitality and tourism industry, you're not alone – and the industry itself is taking notice. The hospitality and tourism industry struggles with human resource issues, and "the current bad situation is worsening," worries the International Society of Hospitality Consultants (ISHC). The ISHC frets about the way the "spirit of hospitality is deteriorating," with guest services compromised by staff reductions, high turnover, and poorly trained workers. As hotels compete with other sectors like retail and fast food for unskilled and semi-skilled labor, costs are rising, and workers are becoming increasingly demanding of health benefits. In addition, for a sector that relied heavily on an immigrant labor population, post-September 11 border tightening has been a burden.

Another challenge for the lodging market in particular is a looming real estate crunch. Over the past decade, many hoteliers enjoyed a "forbearance honeymoon," with generous concessions from lenders. This phase is over, and more lenders are becoming owners, according to the ISHC. As a wave of refinancings are set to mature, the cash shortfall is exacerbated by deteriorating property conditions and values and lenders hesitant to invest in the sector.

The wired customer

Hotels, along with nearly every other portion of the hospitality and tourism industry, are adjusting to the increased presence of the Internet in travel planning and spending. An official with online travel retailer Expedia has predicted that online travel planning and purchasing will grow at a rate of 25 percent through 2008. Reportedly, 63 percent of leisure travelers and 69 percent of business travelers now use the Internet to plan some aspect of their trips. In the hotel sector, online reservations grew from an estimated $6 billion in 2002 to around $8 billion in 2003. The Internet has had the effect of empowering customers, allowing them to comparison shop for the best deals and go through so-called "e-mediaries" like Expedia, Orbitz and Travelocity, that sell rooms to consumers, often at discounted rates. The trend of "commoditizing the hotel buying experience" has created downward pressure on room rates, which will continue to impact hotels' profitability, according to the ISHC.

Global distribution

At the same time, hotels are becoming more reliant on electronic database systems and the Internet to book rooms. Indeed, across the hospitality and tourism industry, electronic distribution – an online means of allowing travel agencies, consolidators, consumers, and other bookers to access available rooms, rental cars, flights, and even golf course tee times – has become the norm. This trend stems from the Global

Distribution System (GDS) and Internet Distribution System (IDS) models that form the inner machinery of the travel industry. There are four main GDSs, or booking systems, in the world, allowing access to booking for airlines, car rentals, hotels and cruise reservations. Known by different names in various parts of the world, the GDSs are familiar to American travel bookers as Amadeus, Galileo (a subsidiary of Cendant Corporation), Sabre, and Worldspan.

The GDS sector arose in the 1960s as a means for airlines to keep track of their schedules, seat availability, and prices. Formed by airline leaders such as American (which founded Sabre), the GDSs were installed in travel agencies in the 1970s, marking one of the first successful business-to-business e-commerce ventures. A few decades later, e-commerce travel sites like Expedia and Travelocity, using Sabre and other GDS systems as their information engines, made travel booking available to the masses – at least those with a computer and decent Internet access. In addition, the more than 500,000 travel agents operating worldwide now have a wealth of electronic methods to plug into and shop from. This means that few entities that want to survive in hospitality and tourism can afford to be shut out of these systems. To be represented on a GDS, a hotel or hotel chain has to select a method of branding, as either a private label chain (the most attractive to consumers are therefore the most expensive option), part of a larger marketing brand, or as one of a collective group of similar properties. In any case, according to the Hotel Electronic Distribution Network Association (HEDNA), cost per booking for hotels through a GDS or IDS is cheaper than any other distribution method, including bookings made directly through the property.

De-commissioning agencies

Ironically, what started off as a tool to help travel agents access and sell travel to consumers has now led to the steady erosion of the travel agency sector of the tourism industry, as empowered consumers no longer need to rely on a middleman to purchase airline tickets and even travel packages. The agency industry is dominated by traditional retailers of travel like American Express, Carlson Wagonlit, and Navigant. But e-retailer Expedia's position at number four in 2003 illustrates the agencies' plight. Airlines – once a steady source of income for travel agencies – also have caught on to the diminishing agency trend. Beginning in the mid-1990s, major air carriers, after decades of providing at least a 10 percent commission to agents on sales, slashed or eliminated these commissions entirely. The loss of income drove some agencies out of business, while others consolidated. According to the BLS, the number of travel agents in the U.S. was about 104,000 in 2003. Associations such as the American Society of Travel Agents insist that the industry can continue to thrive by providing the extra attention to detail, insider knowledge, and customer service that consumers crave.

Feeding the masses

In the vast lodging and recreation territory, there has to be a way to deliver food and other sundries to guests cheaply and efficiently. That's where companies specializing in outsourcing come in. With more than $12 billion in revenues in 2003, French company Sodexho is a powerhouse in providing outsourced food and services to hospitality facilities (as well as a host of other institutions from nursing homes to elementary schools). It ranks fourth in market capitalization among all players in the restaurant industry, coming in behind McDonald's, Starbucks, and Yum! Brands. Another global contender is Aramark

Visit Vault at **www.vault.com** for insider company profiles, expert advice, career message boards, expert resume reviews, the Vault Job Board and more.

VAULT CAREER LIBRARY 239

Corporation, which in 2001 purchased ServiceMaster Management Services and boosted revenues to more than $9 billion. Aramark scored a huge contract in 2004 to provide food services for the Olympic Village at the Summer Games in Athens, its 13th time providing such services at the Olympics.

Motoring away

The rental car portion of the market shares close ties with the airline industry. After the Second World War, as leisure travel as well as travel for business became the norm, the rental car industry also took off. It's no surprise, then, that Orlando, Florida – with its convergence of theme parks, conference centers, and scores of tourist-oriented activities and accommodations – is the largest rental car market in the world. The car rental market in the U.S. is expected to grow by 27 percent by 2008, to $24 billion, according to research firm Euromonitor International. Hertz, which was acquired in 1994 by Ford Motor Company (appropriately, as the company got its start in 1918 when Hertz founded Walter Jacobs rented out a dozen Model Ts), holds a top spot in the market. Generally recognized as number one worldwide, Hertz enjoyed revenues of $5 billion in 2002, but its $150 million in losses that year put a damper on performance. Enterprise, with more than 5,500 offices worldwide, has become a powerful contender in recent years, taking the top spot in North America with annual revenues of more than $6.9 billion. Other big companies include Dollar Thrift Rental Group, which owns Dollar Rent A Car and Thrifty (with 2003 revenues of $1.3 billion), and Alamo.

Job prospects

There's always a job to be found in hospitality and tourism. Globally, the travel and tourism industry is expected to produce 3.3 million new jobs in 2004, constituting 2.8 percent of total world employment, according to the World Travel & Tourism Council. Jobs in accommodation and food services as a whole make up about 8 percent of total U.S. employment, the Bureau of Labor Statistics reports. Employment in leisure and hospitality in particular was at more than 12 million in 2003. In the American leisure and hospitality sector, employment is expected to increase 17.8 percent by 2012.

Hospitality Careers

It isn't easy working in the hospitality industry – guests can be rude, the holiday rush is nightmarish, and employees work seven days a week. Hotel workers must put the needs of their guests first and maintain a sunny and accommodating disposition at all times – not easy when you have been working for 12 hours on Christmas Day without a break. However, the perks in the business are such that hospitality workers put up with the disadvantages of the industry.

It takes a team

Every member of a hotel staff, from housekeeping to the hotel manager, is responsible for the seamless operation of the establishment. At smaller hotels and motels, the responsibility for overseeing rooms, food and beverage service, registration, and overall management can fall on the shoulders of a single manager.

Large hotels, such as The Plaza in New York, employ hundreds of workers. To start, the general manager may be aided by a staff of assistant managers, each with his or her own department to supervise. The hotel manager sets the establishment's standards of operation (within the owners' or executives' guidelines); it is the job of the assistant managers to see that these are executed adroitly. The general manager sets room rates, allocates funds to departments, approves expenditures, and establishes standards for service that employees in housekeeping, decor, food quality, and banquet operations must offer to guests. Many hotels have resident managers, who live in the hotel and are on hand 24 hours a day for guests and staff (though they usually work a standard eight-hour day).

The housekeeping staff is responsible for maintaining banquet, meeting and guest rooms – right down to the mints on the pillows – and ensuring that public areas are clean, orderly, and well-kept. Almost all hotels also have food and beverage managers on hand to supervise hotel restaurants, bars, banquet rooms, and room service. These employees plan menus and direct food presentation and preparation. Hotels employ a long list of support staff in various areas, including accountants, entertainers, maintenance workers, security officers, gardeners and everything in between. The behind-the-scenes services consist of sales, administration, and marketing personnel.

You're working late

Although hotel staff, managers in particular, officially work eight-hour days, the jobs almost invariably require overtime. And since hotels require 24-hour service, shifts can vary and sometimes be very hectic. In the hospitality industry, details are of the utmost importance and last-minute preparations and crisis aversion are par for the course. As compensation, however, hotel employees get paid sick leave and vacation, as well as full benefits (especially if they work for large corporations) and discounted or free food. Many hotels also offer free or cheap housing within the hotel itself to some employees, such as the resident manager.

Although in the past, most hotel managers have been hired from food and beverage, front desk, housekeeping, and sales positions without formal education, employers now give hiring preference to individuals with degrees in hotel and restaurant management. Internships and part-time jobs also give a step up when it comes to getting hired for a management-track position. Graduates of hotel or restaurant management programs usually start as trainee assistant managers or at least advance to such positions quickly. New hotels without formal on-the-job training programs often prefer experienced personnel for higher-level positions.

The majority of the jobs in the industry (more than 60 percent) are in service and administrative support. Large hotel and motel chains offer better opportunities for advancement than small, independently owned establishments and offer transfers to other hotels or motels in the chain. Hotel personnel are encouraged (and are in some cases required) to move around to different hotels several times in their careers.

Career path

Although in the past, most hotel managers have been hired from food and beverage, front desk, housekeeping, and sales positions without formal education, employers now give hiring preference to individu-

Visit Vault at **www.vault.com** for insider company profiles, expert advice, career message boards, expert resume reviews, the Vault Job Board and more.

V∧ULT CAREER LIBRARY 241

als with degrees in hotel and restaurant management. Internships and part-time jobs also give a step up when it comes to getting hired for a management-track position. Graduates of hotel or restaurant management programs usually start as trainee assistant managers or at least advance to such positions quickly. New hotels without formal on-the-job training programs often prefer experienced personnel for higher-level positions.

The majority of the jobs in the industry (more than 60 percent) are in service and administrative support. Large hotel and motel chains offer better opportunities for advancement than small, independently owned establishments and offer transfers to other hotels or motels in the chain. Hotel personnel are encouraged (and are in some cases required) to move around to different hotels several times in their careers.

Travel Agent

Overview

A travel agent is a harried traveler's best friend. Amateurs who have attempted to arrange their own airfare, hotel accommodations, or vacation schedule know that can be frustrating and fruitless without the insider savvy of a travel agent. But travel agents don't just book reservations. They give advice, weather forecasts and restaurant suggestions too.

The training required to become a travel agent is highly specialized; many agents have certifications from six- to 12-week college or continuing education courses. Even with their training and indispensability to their clients, travel agents aren't very well paid. Airlines have "capped" the commissions which they used to pay travel agents to a flat rate for fares over $500; previously an agent received 10 percent of the total fare, regardless of the price. It's not as if travel agents have a light work schedule, either. They often stay at their desks until at least 7 p.m., or later if a client should call with a missed flight or a lost passport. Travel agents generally choose their career path out of a love of travel and customer satisfaction, rather than expectations of fame and wealth.

There is, however, a wealth of job opportunities for travel agents – right now, anyway. This is something that is never stable for agents entering the job market, since the travel industry is easily upset by economic fluctuations and international political crises.

Career path

Some colleges offer four-year degrees in travel and tourism, while others have courses that relate to the industry. While a college degree is not required to become a travel agent, some employers prefer agents to have a background in computer science, geography, communications, or foreign languages. Courses in accounting and business management are also a wise investment, as many agents consider starting their own agencies. Six- to 12-week programs offered at community colleges and continuing education programs are comprehensive and are usually sufficient training for beginning travel agents. Some agents start as reservation clerks or receptionists in agencies, advance to office manager or other managerial positions, and eventually move on to become full-fledged agents. Agents in larger firms often specialize by type of travel (leisure vs. business), or by destination (The Galapogos Islands vs. Iceland).

Travel agents who wish to advance quickly can take advanced courses from the Institute of Certified Travel Agents. Upon completion of the courses, an agent becomes a Certified Travel Counselor. The American Society of Travel Agents (ASTA) offers a correspondence course as well. These certifications can be helpful for those wishing to start their own businesses, as is gaining formal supplier or corporation approval (airlines, ship lines, and rail lines), since approval is necessary before travel agents are authorized to receive commissions. Certain states also require some form of registration or certification of retail sellers of travel services.

Visit Vault at **www.vault.com** for insider company profiles, expert advice, career message boards, expert resume reviews, the Vault Job Board and more.

VAULT CAREER LIBRARY   243

Employer Directory

Sodexho
200 Continental Drive,
Suite 400
Newark, DE 19713
Phone: 302 738-9500 ext 5209
E-mail: John.lee@sodexhousa.com
www.sodexhousa.com

Sodexho is the leading provider of food and facilities management in the U.S. and Canada, with $4.9 billion in annual sales. Sodexho offers innovative outsourcing solutions in food service, housekeeping, grounds keeping, plant operations and maintenance, asset and materials management and laundry services to corporations, health care and long term care facilities, retirements centers, schools, college campuses, military and remote sites. Headquarters in Gaithersburg, MD, the company has more than 100,000 employees in 50 states and Canada.

Accor
2, rue de la Mare Neuve
91021 Évry Cedex, France
Phone: +33-1-69-36-80-80
www.accor.com

Aramark Corporation
ARAMARK Tower, 1101 Market St.
Philadelphia, PA 19107-2988
Phone: (215) 238-3000
Fax: (215) 238-3333
www.aramark.com

Budget Rent A Car System, Inc.
6 Sylvan Way
Parsippany, NJ 07054
Phone: (973) 496-3500
Fax:(973) 496-7999
www.budget.com

Carlson Companies, Inc.
701 Carlson Parkway
Minnetonka, MN 55305
Phone: (763) 212-1000
Fax: (763) 212-2219
www.carlson.com

Carnival Corporation
3655 N.W. 87th Ave.
Miami, FL 33178-2428
Phone: (305) 599-2600
Fax: (305) 406-4700
www.carnivalcorp.com

Cendant Corporation
9 W. 57th St.
New York, NY 10019
Phone: (212) 413-1800
Fax: (212) 413-1918
www.cendant.com

Cintas Corporation

6800 Cintas Blvd.

Cincinnati, OH 45262-5737

Phone: (513) 459-1200

Fax: (513) 573-4130

www.cintas-corp.com

Compass Group

Compass House, Guildford Street

Chertsey

Surrey KT16 9BQ, United Kingdom

Phone: +44-1932-573-000

www.compass-group.com

Enterprise Rent-A-Car Company

600 Corporate Park Dr.

St. Louis, MO 63105

Phone: (314) 512-5000

Fax: (314) 512-4706

www.enterprise.com

The Hertz Corporation

225 Brae Blvd.

Park Ridge, NJ 07656-0713

Phone: (201) 307-2000

Fax: (201) 307-2644

www.hertz.com

Hilton Hotels Corporation

9336 Civic Center Dr.

Beverly Hills, CA 90210

Phone: (310) 278-4321

Fax: (310) 205-7678

www.hilton.com

Hyatt Corporation

200 W. Madison St.

Chicago, IL 60606

Phone: (312) 750-1234

Fax: (312) 750-8550

www.hyatt.com

InterActiveCorp

152 W. 57th St.

New York, NY 10019

Phone: (212) 314-7300

Fax: (212) 314-7309

www.iac.com

InterContinental Hotels Group PLC

67 Alma Rd.

Windsor

SL4 3HD, United Kingdom

Phone: +44-1753-410-100

Fax: +44-1753-410-101

www.ihgplc.com

Kohler Co.

444 Highland Dr.

Kohler, WI 53044

Phone: (920) 457-4441

Fax: (920) 457 1271

www.kohlerco.com

Royal Caribbean Cruises Ltd.

1050 Caribbean Way

Miami, FL 33132

Phone: (305) 539-6000

Fax: (305) 374-7354

www.rccl.com

Starwood Hotels & Resorts Worldwide, Inc.

1111 Westchester Ave.

White Plains, NY 10604

Phone: (914) 640-8100

Fax:(914) 640-8310

wwwstarwood.com

Vanguard Car Rental USA, Inc.

200 S. Andrews Ave.

Fort Lauderdale, FL 33301

Phone: (954) 320-4000

Fax: (954) 320-4456

www.vanguardcar.com

Visit Vault at **www.vault.com** for insider company profiles, expert advice,
career message boards, expert resume reviews, the Vault Job Board and more.

VAULT CAREER LIBRARY   245

Investment Management

How many industries can you think of that impact households all over the world? Very few. That is one of the many exciting aspects of the asset management industry – more people than ever before are planning for their future financial needs, and as a result, the industry is more visible and important than ever. The asset management community seeks to preserve and grow capital for individuals and institutional investors alike.

Investment management vs. asset management

A quick note about the terms **investment management** and **asset management**: these terms are often used interchangeably. They refer to the same practice – the professional management of assets through investment. Investment management is used a bit more often when referring to the activity or career (i.e., "I'm an investment manager" or "That firm is gaining a lot of business in investment management"), whereas "asset management" is used more with reference to the industry itself (i.e., "The asset management industry").

More stability

Because of the stability of cash flows generated by the industry, investment management provides a relatively stable career when compared to some other financial services positions (most notably investment banking). Investment management firms are generally paid a set fee as a percentage of assets under management. (The fee structure varies, and sometimes is both an asset-centered fee plus a performance fee, especially for institutional investors.) Still, even when investment management fees involve a performance incentive, the business is much less cyclical than cousins like investment banking. Banking fees depend on transactions. When banking activities such as IPOs and M&A transactions dry up, so do fees for investment banks, which translates into layoffs of bankers. In contrast, assets are quite simply always being invested.

History

To better understand why asset management has become such a critical component of the broader financial services industry, we must first become acquainted with its formation and history.

The beginnings of a separate industry

While the informal process of managing money has been around since the beginning of the 20th century, the industry did not begin to mature until the early 1970's. Prior to that time, investment management was completely relationship-based. Assignments to manage assets grew out of relationships that banks and insurance companies already had with institutions – primarily companies or municipal organizations with employee pension funds – that had funds to invest. (A pension fund is set up as an employee benefit. Employers commit to a certain level of payment to retired employees each year and must manage their

Visit Vault at **www.vault.com** for insider company profiles, expert advice, career message boards, expert resume reviews, the Vault Job Board and more.

VAULT CAREER LIBRARY   247

funds to meet these obligations. Organizations with large pools of assets to invest are called institutional investors.)

These asset managers were chosen in an unstructured way – assignments grew organically out of pre-existing relationships, rather than through a formal request for proposal and bidding process. The actual practice of investment management was also unstructured. At the time, asset managers might simply pick 50 stocks they thought were good investments – there was not nearly as much analysis on managing risk or organizing a fund around a specific category or style. (Examples of different investment categories include small cap stocks and large cap stocks. We will explore the different investment categories and styles in a later chapter.) Finally, the assets that were managed at the time were primarily pension funds. Mutual funds had yet to become broadly popular.

ERISA, 401(k) plans and specialist firms

The two catalysts for change in the industry were: 1) the broad realization that demographic trends would cause the U.S. government's retirement system (Social Security) to be underfunded, which made individuals more concerned with their retirement savings, and 2) the creation of ERISA (the Employment Retirement Income Secruity Act) in 1974, which gave employees incentives to save for retirement privately through 401(k) plans. (401(k) plans allow employees to save pre-tax earnings for their retirement.) These elements prompted an increased focus on long-term savings by individual investors and the formation of what can be described as a private pension fund market.

These fundamental changes created the opportunity for professional groups of money managers to form "specialist" firms to manage individual and institutional assets. Throughout the 1970s and early 1980s, these small firms specialized in one or two investment styles (for example, core equities or fixed income investing).

During this period, the investment industry became fragmented and competitive. This competition added extra dimensions to the asset management industry. Investment skills, of course, remained critical. However, relationship building and the professional presentation of money management teams also began to become significant.

The rise of the mutual fund

In the early to mid 1980s, driven by the ERISA laws, the mutual fund came into vogue. While mutual funds had been around for decades, they were only used by financially sophisticated investors who paid a lot of attention to their investments. However, investor sophistication increased with the advent of modern portfolio theory (the set of tools developed to quantitatively analyze the management of a portfolio; see sidebar on next page). Asset management firms began heavily marketing mutual funds as a safe and smart investment tool, pitching to individual investors the virtues of diversification and other benefits of investing in mutual funds. With more and more employers shifting retirement savings responsibilities from pension funds to the employees themselves, the 401(k) market grew rapidly. Consequently, consumer demand for new mutual fund products exploded (mutual funds are the preferred choice in most

401(k) portfolios). Many specialists responded by expanding their product offerings and focusing more on the marketing of their new services and capabilities.

Modern Portfolio Theory

Modern Portfolio Theory (MPT) was born in 1952 when University of Chicago economics student Harry Markowitz published his doctoral thesis, "Portfolio Selection," in the *Journal of Finance*. Markowitz, who won the Nobel Prize in economics in 1990 for his research and its far-reaching effects, provided the framework for what is now known as Modern Portfolio Theory. MPT quantifies the benefits of diversification, looking at how investors create portfolios in order to optimize market risk against expected returns. Markowitz, assuming all investors are risk averse, proposed that investors, when choosing a security to add to their portfolio, should not base their decision on the amount of risk that an individual security has, but rather on how that security contributes to the overall risk of the portfolio. To do this, Markowitz considered how securities move in relation to one another under similar circumstances. This is called "correlation," which measures how much two securities fluctuate in price relative to each other. Taking all this into account, investors can create "efficient portfolios," ones with the highest expected returns for a given level of risk.

Consolidation and globalization

The dominant themes of the industry in the 1990s were consolidation and globalization. As many former specialists rapidly expanded, brand recognition and advanced distribution channels (through brokers or other sales vehicles) became key success factors for asset management companies. Massive global commercial and investment banks entered the industry, taking business away from many specialist firms. Also, mutual fund rating agencies such as Lipper (founded in 1973, now a part of Reuters) and Morningstar (founded in Chicago in 1984) increased investor awareness of portfolio performance. These rating agencies publish reports on fund performance and rate funds on scales such as Morningstar's 4-star rating system.

These factors led to a shakeout period of consolidation. From 1995 to 2001, approximately 150 mergers took place, creating well-established and formidable players such as Capital Group and Citigroup. As opposed to specialist firms, these large financial services firms provide asset management products that run the gamut: mutual funds, pension funds, management for high-net-worth individuals, etc. While many excellent specialist firms continue to operate today, they are not the driving force that they once were.

Visit Vault at **www.vault.com** for insider company profiles, expert advice, career message boards, expert resume reviews, the Vault Job Board and more.

VAULT CAREER LIBRARY   **249**

Buy-side vs. Sell-side

If you've ever spoken with investment professionals, you've probably heard them talk about the "buy-side" and the "sell-side." What do these terms mean and how do the two sides of the Street interact with one another?

What's the difference?

Simply stated, the buy-side refers to the asset managers who represent individual and institutional investors. The buy-side purchases investment products with the goal of increasing its assets. The sell-side refers to the functions of an investment bank. Specifically, this includes investment bankers, traders and research analysts. Sell-side professionals issue, recommend, trade and "sell" securities for the investors on the buy-side to "buy." The sell-side can be thought of primarily as a facilitator of buy-side investments – the sell-side makes money not through a growth in value of the investment, but through fees and commissions for these facilitating services. In this chapter, we'll take a brief look at the types of jobs on each "side." The rest of the book will look at the buy-side in detail.

Jobs on the Buy-side

Buy-side firms are structured in a far less formal manner than sell-side firms. Consequently, career paths are more flexible and job descriptions vary more from one firm to another. In general, buy-side firms have a three-segment professional staff consisting of:

• Portfolio managers who invest money on behalf of clients

• Research analysts who provide portfolio managers with potential investment recommendations

• Marketing and sales professionals who distribute the investment products to individual and institutional investors

When beginning your career on the buy-side, you typically will start as an assistant or associate in one of these three areas.

Professional Positions in Asset Management

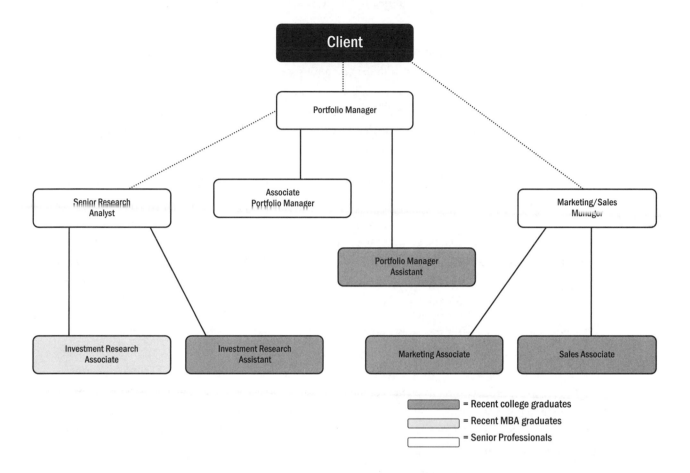

Portfolio Manager Assistant

In general, portfolio manager assistants screen for potential investments, monitor portfolio characteristics, and assist in client relations. Recent college graduates typically will spend 2 to 4 years in this role before returning to business school or migrating to a role in the investment research department.

This position varies among the firms in the industry, and the role itself differs depending on which segment of the firm you work in – mutual fund, institutional or high-net-worth. For instance, high-net-worth portfolio assistants spend more time working with clients, while institutional assistants spend more time monitoring and analyzing portfolios. Regardless, the general assignment focuses on supporting the portfolio manager.

Portfolio manager assistants are often instrumental in the process of screening for potential investments. Using the general strategy of the investment product – such as market-capitalization, earnings growth, valuation multiples or industry – the assistant screens all available stocks in the market (about 10,000) to identify the smaller list that meets the portfolio's criteria. The screened list for an active portfolio varies,

Visit Vault at **www.vault.com** for insider company profiles, expert advice, career message boards, expert resume reviews, the Vault Job Board and more.

VAULT CAREER LIBRARY 251

but typically ranges between 100 and 300 securities. Portfolio manager assistants then gather additional research for the portfolio manager to begin the process of fundamentally analyzing the potential investment.

Once investments are made, portfolio manager assistants are responsible for monitoring the reconciliation of the trades. In this role, they work with the operations staff to assure that the portfolio is properly updated and performance records are accurate. Most firms have separate operations departments that reconcile trades and produce monthly client reports. However, many of the smaller firms require their portfolio assistants to perform the operations function as well. You should be aware of this, and clarify the exact job responsibilities when applying and interviewing for the job.

Portfolio assistants also participate in the process of client service, although the proportion of time spent in this area depends on the type of client being served. For instance, an assistant to a mutual fund portfolio manager would spend very little time on client service. Institutional and high-net-worth portfolio managers have fewer clients and they meet with them once or twice a year. Intermittently, their clients require vast and detailed investment reports and market commentaries. While marketing helps prepare these formal presentations, the portfolio manager assistant plays a crucial role in collecting economic and market data for the investment commentary and portfolio analysis sections of the report.

The position requires a person who understands capital markets, is capable of meeting deadlines and enjoys working on multiple projects simultaneously. The downside is that the reporting and operational components of the job have a quick learning curve and then become repetitive. Furthermore, it is not the best place to learn how to really value companies. Rather, you are being exposed to the years of experience that the portfolio manager possesses. Most important, portfolio manager assistants receive the benefit of seeing a broad picture of investing money across several industries, whereas research assistants typically get exposure to one component or sector. All in all, in the right setting, the position is a great introduction to the industry and a worthwhile apprenticeship to pursue.

Portfolio Manager Assistant Uppers and Downers

Uppers	Downers
• Broad exposure to the industry	• Less formal training process
• Reasonable working hours	• Some operations work
• Direct exposure to portfolio managers	• Repetitive assignments

Investment Research Assistant

Investment research assistants work with senior research analysts to help in developing investment recommendations to portfolio managers. Recent college graduates will spend, on average, 2 to 4 years in this role before returning to business school. However, some of the most successful assistants are often promoted directly to research associate (most of these fast-trackers will have completed their CFA while working as an assistant).

The investment research assistant is responsible for helping to monitor the industry and changes within companies covered in the industry, and for updating financial models accordingly. Assistants collect data for industry data services, company conference calls and surveys. For instance, in the previous Apple Computer example, the assistant would be collecting data about consumer demand and input prices for semiconductors. Additionally, the assistant provides support to the senior analyst in the construction of recommendation reports sent out to the portfolio managers. Specifically, the assistant updates charts and modifies numerical sections of the report.

While some of the work is routine and the hours are long, assistants are sitting next to, and learning from, the intellectual capital of the firm. A good analyst will teach you the ropes, including the intangibles behind analyzing companies, financial valuation and industry knowledge.

The role of investment research assistant requires a high level of quantitative knowledge. Primarily, a basic working knowledge of accounting, financial markets, financial analysis and statistics is needed for this position. Aside from a strong quantitative background, research assistants need to be detail oriented, analytical problem solvers, diligent, and superior communicators. Generally, firms are looking for finance or accounting majors for these jobs, but engineers and science majors are also coveted for technology and health care related industries.

Investment Research Assistant Uppers and Downers

Uppers	Downers
• Great quantitative experience	• Long hours (60+ hours/week)
• Most portfolio managers were once in research	• Lots of independent time in front of the computer
• Gain industry expertise	• Repetitive assignments
• Pays well	
• Typically a collegial environment	

Visit Vault at **www.vault.com** for insider company profiles, expert advice, career message boards, expert resume reviews, the Vault Job Board and more.

VAULT CAREER LIBRARY   253

Marketing and Sales

Increasingly, as the industry grows and matures, investment management companies are focusing on professional marketing and sales as a point of differentiation – especially on the institutional side of the business.

Traditionally, marketing and sales have been more or less an afterthought: much of the marketing and sales work was performed by investment professionals. This is no longer the case, however, and firms are increasingly building teams of dedicated marketing and sales professionals.

Because sales and marketing professionals are typically required to be fluent in all of the investment products, these positions create a great opportunity to learn about the various investment styles that clients demand. This area is a great career opportunity for those who are interested in asset management but don't want to be the investment decision maker.

If your goal is to use sales and marketing as a stepping stone to the investment side, make it a point to network early on with investment professionals and prove yourself at your current job before making it known that you want to make the switch, and work toward developing the quantitative skills needed for the investment positions.

Below is a broad description of the positions that exist in the institutional marketing and sales segment.

Marketing or Sales Associates

Marketing and sales associates are typically recent college graduates. The positions are quite similar, although they are traditionally segmented by different types of organization.

Marketing associates assist in creating portfolio review presentations and in developing promotional presentations for potential new clients. They are traditionally segmented by investment product type such as equity or fixed income.

Sales associates assist in answering RFPs (request for proposals) issued by institutions seeking to hire new investment managers. Additionally, associates assist senior client servicing officials in maintaining and expanding client relationships. Sales associates are traditionally segmented by client type – public pension funds, corporate pension funds, endowments and foundations.

Marketing or Sales Associate Uppers and Downers

Uppers	Downers
• Broad knowledge of all of the investment products in the marketplace	• Difficult to jump to the investment side
• Great professional atmosphere for people that like the industry, but don't want to be the investment decision maker	• Limited focus on building quantitative skills
• Less hierarchical career path than the investment side	• Repetitive assignments
• More entry level jobs than the investment side	
• Lots of client interaction	

Visit Vault at **www.vault.com** for insider company profiles, expert advice, career message boards, expert resume reviews, the Vault Job Board and more.

VAULT CAREER LIBRARY   255

Employer Directory

Advest Group

90 State House Sq.

Hartford, CT 06103

Phone: (860) 509-1000

Fax: (860) 509-3849

www.advest.com

AIG Global Investment Group

175 Water St., 24th Fl.

New York, NY 10038

Phone: (212) 458-2000

Fax: (212) 458-2200

www.aiggig.com

AIM Investments

11 Greenway Plaza, Suite 100

Houston, TX 77046

Phone: (713) 626-1919;

Fax: (713) 993-9890

www.aiminvestments.com

Alliance Capital Management

1345 Avenue of the Americas

New York, NY 10105

Phone: (212) 969-1000

Fax: (212) 969-2229

www.alliancecapital.com

American Century Investments

4500 Main Street

Suite 1500

Kansas City, MO 64111

Phone: (816) 531-5575

Fax: (816) 340-7962

www.americancentury.com

BlackRock, Inc.

40 East 52nd Street

New York, NY 10022

Phone: (212) 754-5560

Fax: (212) 935-1370

www.blackrock.com

CalPERS

400 P Street

Lincoln Plaza

Sacramento, CA 95814

Phone: (916) 326-3000; (800) CalPERS

Fax: (916) 558-8400

www.calpers.ca.gov

Dreyfus Corporation

200 Park Ave.

New York, NY 10166

Phone: (212) 922-6000

Fax: (212) 922-7533

www.dreyfus.com

Federated Investors, Inc.

Federated Investors Tower

1001 Liberty Avenue

Pittsburgh, PA 15222-3779

Phone: (412) 288-1900

Fax: (412) 288-1171

www.federatedinvestors.com

Fidelity Investments

82 Devonshire St.

Boston, MA 02109

Phone: (617) 563-7000

Fax: (617) 476-6150

www.fidelity.com

Franklin Resources

One Franklin Parkway

San Mateo, CA 94404

Phone: (650) 312-2000

Fax: (650) 312-5606

www.franklintempleton.com

Gabelli Asset Management

1 Corporate Center

Rye, NY 10580

Phone: (914) 921-3700;

Fax: (914) 921-5392

www.gabelli.com

ING Americas

5780 Powers Ferry Road NW

Atlanta, GA 30327

Phone: (770) 980-3300

Fax: (770) 980-3301

www.ing-usa.com

Janus Capital Group Inc.

100 Filmore Street

Suite 300

Denver, CO 80206

Phone: (303) 333-3863

Fax: (303) 336-7497

www.janus.com

MFS Investment Management

500 Boylston St.

Boston, Ma 02116

Phone: (617) 954-5000

Fax: (617) 954-6620

www.mfs.com

Nuveen Investments, Inc.

333 W. Wacker Dr.

Chicago, IL 60606

Phone: (312) 917-7700;

Fax: (312) 917-8049

Toll Free: (800) 257-8787

www.nuveen.com

Pacific Investment Management Co.

840 Newport Center Dr., Ste. 300

Newport Beach, CA 92660

Phone: (949) 720-6000

Fax: (949) 720-1376

www.pimco.com

Pequot Capital Management

500 Nyala Farm Road

Westport, CT 06880

Phone: (203) 429-2200

Fax: (203) 429-2400

www.pequotcap.com

Putnam Investments

One Post Office Square

Boston, MA 02109

Phone: (617) 292-1000

Fax: (617) 482-3610

www.putnaminvestments.com

T. Rowe Price Group, Inc.

100 East Pratt Street

Baltimore, MD 21202

Phone: (410) 345-2000

Fax: (410) 345-2394

www.troweprice.com

TIAA-CREF

730 Third Ave.

New York, NY 10017-3206

Phone: (212) 490-9000

Fax: (212) 916-6231

www.tiaa-cref.org

The Vanguard Group Inc.

100 Vanguard Boulevard

Malvern, PA 19355

Phone: (610) 669-1000

Fax: (610) 669-6605

www.vanguard.com

Wellington Management Company, LLP

75 State Street

Boston, MA 02109

Phone: (617) 951-5000

Fax: (617) 951-5250

www.wellington.com

Visit Vault at **www.vault.com** for insider company profiles, expert advice, career message boards, expert resume reviews, the Vault Job Board and more.

VAULT CAREER LIBRARY 257

"A HAPPY BUNCH,
THOSE WINSTON ASSOCIATES ARE."

—Vault Guide to the Top 100 Law Firms, 6th Ed.

HAPPY THEN, HAPPY NOW

Ranked in the Top 3 in **"Best Firms to Work For"** for five consecutive years.

THIS YEAR, ALSO RANKED TOP 5 IN...

Satisfaction, Offices, Compensation, Mentoring, Diversity for Minorities,
Associate/Partner Relations, Pro Bono, and Overall Diversity.

Vault Guide to the Top 100 Law Firms, 7th Ed.

WINSTON & STRAWN LLP

CHICAGO   GENEVA   LONDON   LOS ANGELES   NEW YORK   PARIS   SAN FRANCISCO   WASHINGTON, D.C.

Law/Paralegal

Corporate Law Basics

What is corporate law?

Corporate law is the law of corporations. A corporation is an artificial legal entity, typically chartered by a state and formed in order to operate a business. Once chartered, the corporation is completely separate from its owners, is liable for its own debts and must pay its own taxes.

But many lawyers deal with corporations, and not all of them call themselves corporate lawyers. In fact, at this point, you might not have a clear idea of the differences among a litigator who works in-house for a corporation, a tax lawyer who advises corporations from the vantage point of a law firm and a corporate lawyer. If you watch too much television, you might believe that lawyers represent clients on deals one day and head to the courtroom for high-profile litigation the next. This is highly unusual in the real practice of law. While both litigators and corporate lawyers deal with corporations, they do so in very different ways.

Litigation vs. transactional law

One of the basic divisions in the practice of law is between litigation and corporate, or transactional, law. Litigation attorneys, or litigators, deal with the judicial process, with civil disputes or criminal cases that are headed to court. In the realm of criminal law, they are prosecutors, public defenders or private defense attorneys. Those attorneys who handle conflicts between individuals, whether over personal injuries, domestic disputes or other matters, are civil trial lawyers. Commercial litigators are trial attorneys whose clients include corporations and businesses.

Note that being a litigator doesn't automatically put you in a courtroom. Public defenders may indeed be in court every week. But litigators who work on corporate or commercial matters might never go to court. They serve their clients by filing motions and briefs and settling conflicts without actually going to trial.

It's a myth that everyone who wants to be a lawyer wants to spend time in a courtroom. Many people don't have any interest in criminal law or personal injury. Some would rather contribute to the creation of a business venture than participate in its breakdown. Some lawyers don't care to write the (many) documents that must be submitted to court. Attorneys who facilitate transactions in the fields of corporate or tax law, intellectual property or employee benefits are considered transactional lawyers. In the world of business, transactional lawyers try to set up deals in a way that will avoid litigation and make clear the rights and responsibilities of all parties in the event that something does go wrong.

The difference between corporate law and commercial litigation is simple. Corporate lawyers build transactions or deals, and litigators deal with transactions gone wrong, whether through the judicial system or through alternative methods of dispute resolution like mediation or arbitration.

Visit Vault at **www.vault.com** for insider company profiles, expert advice, career message boards, expert resume reviews, the Vault Job Board and more.

VAULT CAREER LIBRARY 259

Transactional law and corporate lawyers

So, what is a corporate lawyer? Basically, corporate lawyers advise businesses on their legal obligations, rights and responsibilities. People who call themselves corporate lawyers are usually corporate generalists, lawyers who provide advice on how to structure a business and evaluate ventures and who coordinate with specialists, like tax lawyers, employee benefits lawyers and real estate attorneys (who are all transactional lawyers), to serve the sophisticated needs of their corporate clients.

While corporate attorneys may provide day-to-day advice to their clients, most of their work, at least in larger law firms, is transactional in nature. In fact, some firms use the terms "transactional" and "corporate" interchangeably when describing areas of practice. Corporate lawyers structure transactions, draft documents, review other lawyers' agreements, negotiate deals, attend meetings and make calls toward those ends. A corporate lawyer ensures that the provisions of an agreement are clear, unambiguous and won't cause problems for their client in the future. Corporate attorneys also advise on the duties and responsibilities of corporate officers, directors and insiders.

There are many varieties of corporate law practice, and not all corporate lawyers do the same kind of work. Moreover, not all firms categorize corporate practice in the same way. For example, some firms might have separate practice groups for antitrust or mergers & acquisitions, while others include them within their corporate department. The following list, while not exhaustive, outlines some of the areas in which corporate attorneys might spend their time.

Areas of Corporate Practice

Corporate formation, governance and operation

A corporation is a legal entity created through the laws of its state of incorporation. Individual states make laws relating to the creation, organization and dissolution of corporations. The law treats a corporation as a legal "person" that has the standing to sue and be sued, and is distinct from its stockholders. The legal independence of a corporation prevents shareholders from being personally liable for corporate debts. The legal person status of corporations gives the business perpetual life; the death (or, in today's climate, discrediting) of an official or a major stockholder does not alter the corporation's structure, even if it affects the stock price.

A corporate lawyer can help a client create, organize or dissolve a business entity. To form a corporation, an attorney drafts articles of incorporation, which document the creation of the company and specify the management of internal affairs. Most states require a corporation to have bylaws defining the roles of officers of the company. Corporate lawyers also deal with business entities in the forms of partnerships, limited liability companies, limited liability partnerships and business trusts; each form has its own set of legal rights and responsibilities, organizational structure and tax burdens. Attorneys help their clients decide which of these legal forms is best suited for the business they want to run and the relationships the principals want to build with each other.

A corporate lawyer who helps a client form a company might later be called upon for other legal advice related to the start-up or management of the business, like reviewing a lease for office space or equipment, or drafting employment contracts, non-disclosure and non-compete agreements. Corporate lawyers might research aspects of employment law or environmental law or consult with another attorney who specializes in that field. Business executives also seek advice from corporate attorneys on the rights and responsibilities of corporate directors and officers.

Mergers & acquisitions

One major corporate practice area is mergers and acquisitions ("M&A"). Through acquiring (buying) or merging with another company, a business might add property, production facilities or a brand name. A merger or acquisition might also work to neutralize a competitor in the same field. Corporate attorneys provide legal counsel about proposed transactions. To help evaluate a proposed venture, a corporate lawyer (who typically relies on a team of corporate lawyers) reviews all of the company's key assets and liabilities, meaning financial statements, employment agreements, real estate holdings, intellectual property holdings and any current, pending or likely litigation. This is called due diligence. The corporate lawyer can then assess the situation and raise specific issues with the client – for example, who's responsible for the Environmental Protection Agency investigation of that piece of property the company owns? What happens to the employees of the target company or to the stock options of the company's directors?

Corporate lawyers consult with their clients about these questions and together lawyer and client determine which parties should accept current or potential liabilities. The lawyers then draft the merger or acquisition agreement and negotiate in detail the terms of each party's rights, responsibilities and liabilities.

Venture capital

In a venture capital practice, a lawyer works on private and public financings and day-to-day counseling. This means they help new businesses find money for their ventures, organize their operations and maintain their legal and business structures after formation. In venture capital, as in any corporate law position dealing with emerging companies, lawyers help build and expand businesses. Their responsibilities can include general corporate work, like drafting articles of incorporation and other documents, as well as technology licensing, financing, and mergers & acquisitions.

Some lawyers find this type of work less confrontational than M&A practice because the client is working with other parties toward a common goal. Sometimes, in mergers & acquisitions, the parties see the process as a zero-sum game in which each must get the best deal no matter how it may affect future relations with the other company. This is especially the case in hostile acquisitions.

Project finance

The development and construction of power plants, oil refineries, industrial plants, pipelines, mines, telecommunications networks and facilities and transportation systems involve the cooperation of many different entities, many different lawyers and extremely large sums of money. Project finance attorneys specialize in these deals. They form a project entity, a corporation, partnership or other legal entity that will exist for the term of the project, and they draft power purchase agreements and construction contracts and negotiate financial terms with lenders and investors.

Corporate securities

Some corporate lawyers specialize in corporate securities law. On a federal level, the Securities Act of 1933 requires companies who sell securities to the public to register with the federal government. Corporations must follow certain protocols regarding disclosure of information to shareholders and investors depending on the size of the corporation and the type of investor. If shares of a company's stock are traded on a public stock exchange, the company has to file detailed reports with the Securities and Exchange Commission and distribute parts of those reports (the prospectus) to shareholders. The Securities Act of 1934 addresses the obligations of companies traded on a national stock exchange.

To ensure the companies remain in accordance with these laws, corporate attorneys prepare reports for initial public offerings, yearly and quarterly disclosures, and special disclosures whenever something happens that might affect the price of the stock, like impending litigation, government investigation or disappointing financial results. Even if you don't specialize in corporate securities law, the issuance of stock and the creation and distribution of the reports are subject to a whole host of rules with which corporate lawyers must be familiar.

Visit Vault at **www.vault.com** for insider company profiles, expert advice, career message boards, expert resume reviews, the Vault Job Board and more.

V∧ULT CAREER LIBRARY 263

Intellectual property

Corporate lawyers often advise their clients on intellectual property matters. Intellectual property law can include research and analysis of trade secret issues, patent and trademark licensing and protection, software licensing and copyright law.

Non-legal roles

Business clients frequently look to their lawyers for advice directly related to the operation of their business but only tangentially related to the law, such as how to deal with special interest groups, how to respond to concerns about product safety, whether to fire an executive, how to plan for the possibility of adverse media coverage, how to create a business plan, how to cope with a serious ethical lapse, whether to close a factory and what kind of compensation plans should be offered to employees.

Lawyers think that all large firms are the same. Not true. There is a sense of camaraderie and "community" that I didn't experience in my last firm. And the typical barrier between partners and associates seems non-existent. Senior partners have me involved in developing our strategy for an important matter — and my opinions count. That's important to me. I don't want to be just a cog in a wheel.

I kissed a lot of frogs before deciding on Pillsbury Winthrop. A threshold issue for me was whether I liked the people — and whether my clients would get good service from the firm. I'm happy. My clients are happy.

I OFTEN GET CALLS FROM MY FRIENDS AT OTHER FIRMS ASKING ABOUT OUR BENEFITS — NEW BABY CARE LEAVE, TIME OFF TO DO COMMUNITY SERVICE, THAT SORT OF THING. THEY'RE IMPRESSED. WE WORK PRETTY HARD AROUND HERE, AND THAT'S OKAY — THE FIRM "WALKS THE TALK" WHEN IT COMES TO BALANCING WORK AND PERSONAL INTERESTS.

What will you say about your PW experience? www.pillsburywinthrop.com **PILLSBURY WINTHROP** LLP

(These are real comments from real PW people. Really.)

Day in the Life: Junior Corporate Associate

Here's a look at a day in the life of a junior corporate associate at a medium-sized firm.

8:30 am: Arrive at the office and proceed directly to an internal training session covering an aspect of the year-end reporting process. This training is part of a six-session series presented by the firm every year to prepare the associates for the upcoming reporting season.

10:00 am: Return to office to pick up file on a private biotechnology client and hurry to a meeting with a senior associate. At the meeting, discuss the list of names and addresses of the client's stockholders (mailing list), which I reviewed the day before in preparation for a Section 228 Notice of Action Taken mailing. Point out to the senior associate which addresses are missing and ask her to obtain these from the client. She also suggests where to look for additional information regarding stockholder addresses.

10:30 am: Discuss the upcoming Section 228 Notice of Action Taken with my assistant. This particular mailing will be to nearly one hundred stockholders. You have found that if you discuss upcoming large projects with your assistant in advance, she is more likely to clear her schedule of other work and help you complete the project in a timely manner.

10:35 am: Take a few minutes to check e-mails from the night before. Most of them discuss various due diligence issues that have been uncovered during document review for a merger. (I am working on a team with a mid-level associate and a partner on a merger of our client with and into another biotechnology company.)

10:50 am: Briefly review estimated corporate tax forms from California that need to be forwarded to another client. Draft a cover letter to the client to accompany the tax forms and instructions.

11:15 am: Meet with the mid-level associate to discuss various merger diligence issues and the "to-do" list for the day.

11:30 am: Proofread the cover letter to be sent with the tax forms and instructions and send the packet to the client.

11:40 am: At the request of the mid-level associate, call opposing counsel to discuss a new diligence question. Take notes of discussion. Copy a few documents from the master diligence file for the review of the mid-level associate and bring the copies to her office.

12:10 p.m.: Eat lunch in office. Organize e-mails from the previous day while eating. Moving e-mails from the Inbox into client-related folders helps you to locate relevant messages quickly.

1:00 p.m.: Revise the mailing list for the Section 228 mailing to incorporate new information provided by the senior associate. Find additional information in a closing binder that the senior associate provided during the morning meeting. Check the mailing list against the stock ledgers to ensure that all stockholders are accounted for. Give the list to assistant so that she can get an early start on preparing mailing labels.

FIND YOUR DIRECTION

With acclaimed practices in areas from finance to litigation to intellectual property, Orrick offers outstanding career opportunities for every interest. Our associates agree. Their reviews placed us in the *AmLaw 100* Top 10 for Associate Satisfaction, the *Vault Guide's* Best 20 firms to work for, and the *American Lawyer* Mid-Level Associates Survey Top 25. To start your career in the right direction, choose Orrick.

TO CONTACT ANY OF OUR RECRUITERS, PLEASE VISIT WWW.ORRICK.COM

ORRICK

LONDON   MILAN   PARIS   ROME   TOKYO

NEW YORK   SAN FRANCISCO   SILICON VALLEY   LOS ANGELES   WASHINGTON DC   SACRAMENTO   PACIFIC NORTHWEST   ORANGE COUNTY

ORRICK, HERRINGTON & SUTCLIFFE LLP

WWW.ORRICK.COM

Litigation Basics

What is litigation?

Litigation is always in the news – from the controversial landmark abortion case, Roe v. Wade, to the O.J. Simpson trials to the environmental class action lawsuits portrayed in the films Erin Brockovich and A Civil Action. A litigation is a legal proceeding between two or more parties. A litigator is a lawyer who represents a party in litigation. Because litigation is an adversarial proceeding between opposing parties, most of a litigator's job involves preparing for trial, even if a negotiated settlement is the ultimate goal.

In cases where parties have contracted to resolve their disputes out of court, a mediator can be hired to find an amicable compromise between the parties. This mediation (or, in some cases, arbitration) reduces the number of cases that go to trial so the already crowded courts are not completely overwhelmed.

Criminal proceedings

There are two kinds of litigation: civil and criminal. When someone breaks a state or federal law, he commits an offense against society. The government, on behalf of the community, begins a criminal proceeding to hold the offender responsible. A criminal litigation is therefore between the government and the accused, or defendant. The government is represented by a prosecutor, typically a district attorney (for state prosecutions) or a federal prosecutor (for federal crimes). The defendant is represented by either a private criminal attorney or a public defender appointed by the state. (Occasionally, usually against the advice of both his lawyer and the judge, a defendant chooses to represent himself, or acts pro se.)

Most states divide crimes into misdemeanors and felonies. A misdemeanor is any offense that results in less than one year of jail time. Petty theft, possession of a small amount of drugs, or breaking and entering is some examples of misdemeanors. Many misdemeanors can result in a fine or instead of jail time. Felonies are more serious offenses that virtually always result in prison terms of more than one year and may include a fine as well as incarceration. Murder, racketeering, rape and kidnapping are all felony offenses. In some states, serious felonies, such as the murder of a policeman or murder with premeditation, are capital offenses, in which cases a criminal defendant might face the death penalty. A person accused of a crime is presumed innocent until proven guilty beyond a reasonable doubt.

Civil actions

A civil action encompasses virtually any non-criminal court proceeding. It can be a private action between two citizens, a proceeding by one person against the state, a suit by an individual against a corporation or any combination thereof. The party bringing the suit, known as the plaintiff or petitioner, usually is seeking a sum of money (damages) from another party (the defendant or respondent) to compensate her for a claimed injury or loss. Sometimes the remedy sought involves not money but performance; one party wants the court to compel another either to do something he is obligated to do or to stop doing something that is injurious to one bringing suit. In a civil action, the case turns not on the defendant's guilt but on the issue of liability – a party is found either liable or not liable. The burden of proof required to establish liability in a civil suit is generally a lower threshold than the "guilt beyond a reasonable doubt" required in a criminal trial.

In the case of both criminal and civil litigation, the parties may never actually make it to court; they might come to a mutual compromise before the trial date. Parties to a civil suit might reach a financial agreement or other settlement, while the prosecution and defense in a criminal case might agree to a plea bargain, under which a prosecutor offers a reduced charge or sentence in exchange for the defendant's plea of guilt.

Lawsuits and Trials

A lawsuit is filed at the trial level. A trial might be in front of a jury or just a judge (known as a bench trial). In criminal actions, a defendant has the right to a speedy trial. There is no such right for parties in civil cases, and many civil actions go on for years. Most litigation will never even reach a courtroom – the parties might settle, one side might withdraw from the suit or a judge might dismiss the case before trial.

A trial entails everything you see on television: a judge, a jury, a variety of evidence, opposing lawyers and two parties. During the trial, the jury considers questions of fact: Did Mr. Hughes kill his wife? Was the car crash an accident? Was XYZ Company negligent in manufacturing faulty women's lingerie? Did the wire in the plaintiff's bra actually cause the injury she claims it did? The jury is there to decide these questions, using only the evidence presented in court. Before and during the course of the trial, there are also questions of law to be addressed by the judge: Should photos of Mr. Hughes' bedroom be allowed into evidence? Is the testimony of XYZ's chief designer admissible? Should the fact that juror number three slept through the testimony result in a mistrial?

The judge decides questions of law, usually after both parties have presented their arguments. In making her decision, the judge relies on previous case law and the relevant rules of civil and criminal procedure. (You can see questions of law being decided on Law & Order and The Practice when the lawyers meet the judge in chambers before trial, usually to request that she exclude a piece of the prosecutor's evidence for one reason or another. In real life, before making such a decision the judge would review lengthy written memoranda from all lawyers involved).

When the trial is over, the losing party often has the opportunity to appeal the decision to an appellate court. The role of the appeals court is not to second-guess the jury's or judge's rulings on the facts; at the appellate level, only questions of law can be reviewed. The appellate court hears from both sides to decide, essentially, if the trial was conducted properly. If the appeals court concludes that a question of law was not properly decided by the trial judge, it can reverse or overturn the lower court's decision – essentially negating it – or it can remand the case, asking the lower court to reconsider the case in light of the appellate court's opinion. A reversal is often followed by a remand. In the case of Mr. Hughes' murder trial, an appellate court would not decide whether or not Mr. Hughes killed his wife – the jury already concluded that he did – but it can find that the photos of his bedrrom were improperly admitted into evi-

Visit Vault at **www.vault.com** for insider company profiles, expert advice, career message boards, expert resume reviews, the Vault Job Board and more.

VAULT CAREER LIBRARY   269

dence. The court might then overturn the guilty verdict and remand the case back to the lower court for a new trial in which the jury will not be able to consider those photographs as evidence.

An appellate court is rarely seen on television, but the decisions of appeals courts are very important, not only to the parties involved but to future litigants in the same jurisdiction.

Day in the Life: Corporate Litigation Associate

9:30 a.m.: Arrive at work. Get coffee, make small talk with officemate, and check emails .and phone messages with secretary.

10:15 a.m.: Return phone calls and emails. Call senior associate with question regarding yesterday's research issue. Call duplicating to check on document review on white-collar crime case, and put them in contact with paralegal assigned to the case.

10:40 a.m.: Go down to document review room. There are 70 boxes of documents here, but some are out being copied. Review documents with fellow associates, looking for relevant issues.

12:30 p.m.: Associate Lunch in conference room. Lunch/training session is about witness interviews. Take notes and eat roast beef sandwiches. Schmooze with fellow associates about who's working for the most demanding partner.

1:50 p.m.: Return to office. Check emails and continue with yesterday's research issue about statute of limitations in federal court for securities fraud cases. Spend most of the time researching the issue on Westlaw and Lexis-Nexis.

4:00 p.m.: Take a break from the computer and go down to the document review room. Go through witness statements, expert testimony, product promotional materials, statistical data and internal memos to look for evidence of intent.

5:15 p.m.: Return to office and prepare for meeting with partner and rest of team.

5:30 p.m.: Meeting with partner and rest of team. Meeting goes long, but the focus of the research has now changed. Partner would like a memo in 48 hours on this new research issue. Update partner on document review and duplicating process.

6:30 p.m.: Speak with senior associate about organization and approach of new memo and how to research new issue. Check with document review room on duplications of documents. Plan out how much more needs to be done and talk with paralegal about organizing document review.

7:30 p.m.: If you're feeling really motivated, you can go back to the document review room. Otherwise, leave for home, knowing it will be waiting for you tomorrow!

Day in the Life: Assistant District Attorney

9:00 a.m.: Arrive at office, check emails and get files and paperwork for court.

10:00 a.m.: Arrive at court for multiple issues, including an arraignment for a burglary case, hearings for drug possession cases, money laundering case and attempted murder case. Speak with court clerks while clients arrive and judge hears various issues.

12:15 p.m.: Meet opposing counsel for plea bargain agreement for drug possession case.

1:00 p.m.: Quick lunch at desk, looking over emails and phone calls. Wait for witness to show up at 2:00.

2:00 p.m.: Witness doesn't show. Work on research for motion on attempted murder case involving Fourth Amendment right of seizure.

3:00 p.m.: Brief interview with police officers on felony assault case.

3:30 p.m.: Witness for 2:00 finally shows up with father and sister. Conduct fact-finding issue on domestic violence case. Witness recants some testimony and father pressures her not to testify against her husband, leaving ADA uncertain as to strength of case.

4:45 p.m.: Contact court clerks regarding hearing status of various cases.

5:10 p.m.: Review documents for money laundering and call witnesses and corporate officers for interviews in the next few days.

6:15 p.m.: Head home.

Visit Vault at **www.vault.com** for insider company profiles, expert advice, career message boards, expert resume reviews, the Vault Job Board and more.

VAULT CAREER LIBRARY 271

Paralegal

A mixed lot

From freshly graduated English BA's to document-drafting veterans with training and certification, paralegals are really something of a mixed lot. Some have formal training, while others do not. Some have one of many certifications, while others have none. Paralegals, or legal assistants as they are sometimes called, come from a great variety of backgrounds and perform a wide range of tasks. As a result, compensation and working conditions vary to a large degree. Further complicating matters is that, while some legal assistants find they enjoy their paralegal careers, many others aspire to law degrees.

Swimming in paper

Generally speaking, much of what paralegals do involves the large mounds of paperwork generated by legal work. Legal assistants may find themselves sifting through these documents, organizing them, analyzing them, or even drafting them. In addition, paralegals perform research and prepare reports based upon their findings. To do this, paralegals must have a good understanding of legal terminology and good research skills. When permitted by law, paralegals involved with community service sometimes even represent clients at administrative hearings. In short, paralegals can do everything a lawyer does, except the "practice of law": presenting cases in court, setting legal fees and giving legal advice. Paralegals are free to do just about anything else, which is good if it involves using the brain, but numbing if it involves rote clerical work.

Varying pay

Pay for legal assistants reflects the great variety of the work performed. Entry-level workers do not enjoy high salaries, but with increased experience and education, compensation becomes healthier. Paralegals in major metropolitan areas tend to earn more money than those in smaller locales. Similarly, working for a large law firm means higher pay. Major firms may also have perks in the way of bonuses, extra vacation time, and tickets to sports events and the like. At any rate, paralegals can almost always count on hefty overtime hours at the rate of time and a half to boost salaries.

Some feel that obtaining a certification or a degree in paralegal studies can lead to greater compensation and responsibility. Two certifications are available to those in the profession, the Certified Legal Assistant exam (CLA) and the Paralegal Advanced Competency Exam (PACE). The two-day CLA exam is offered by the National Association of Legal Assistants three times a year. The PACE exam is affiliated with the National Federation of Paralegal Associations and is administered throughout the year by an independent agency. Once either of these certifications has been obtained, a paralegal may use the title Registered Paralegal (PR).

Visit Vault at **www.vault.com** for insider company profiles, expert advice, career message boards, expert resume reviews, the Vault Job Board and more.

V∧ULT CAREER LIBRARY   273

In addition to certification exams, many paralegal training programs are available (some are run through colleges and universities, while others are independent). Most of these degrees are either two- or four-year programs. Correspondence courses, which have grown increasingly popular due to the Internet, are also an option. Degrees recognized by the American Bar Association and the American Association for Paralegal Education tend to be the most reputable.

Employer Directory

Arnold & Porter
555 12th Street, NW
Washington, DC 20004
Phone: (202) 942-5000
Fax: (202) 942-5999
www.arnoldporter.com

Cleary, Gottlieb, Steen & Hamilton
One Liberty Plaza
New York, NY 10006-1470
Phone: (212) 225-2000
Fax: (212) 225-3999
www.cgsh.com

Covington & Burling
1201 Pennsylvania Avenue, NW
Washington, DC 20004-2401
Phone: (202) 662-6000
Fax: (202) 662-6291
www.cov.com

Cravath, Swaine & Moore LLP
Worldwide Plaza
825 Eighth Avenue
New York, NY 10019
Phone: (212) 474-1000
Fax: (212) 474-3700
www.cravath.com

Davis Polk & Wardwell
450 Lexington Avenue
New York, NY 10017
Phone: (212) 450-4000
Fax: (212) 450-3800
www.dpw.com

Debevoise & Plimpton
919 Third Avenue
New York, NY 10022
Phone: (212) 909-6000
Fax: (212) 909-6836
www.debevoise.com

Gibson, Dunn & Crutcher LLP
333 South Grand Avenue
Los Angeles, CA 90071-3197
Phone: (213) 229-7000
Fax: (213) 229-7520
www.gibsondunn.com

Hale and Dorr LLP
60 State Street
Boston, MA 02109-1816
Phone: (617) 526-6000
www.haledorr.com

Jones Day
North Point – 901 Lakeside Avenue
Cleveland, OH 44114-1190
Phone: (216) 586-3939
Fax: (216) 579-0212
www.jonesday.com

Kirkland & Ellis
Aon Center
200 East Randolph Drive
Chicago, IL 60601-6636
Phone: (312) 861-2000
Fax: (312) 861-2200
www.kirkland.com

Latham & Watkins LLP
633 West Fifth Street
Suite 4000
Los Angeles, CA 90071-2007
Phone: (213) 485-1234
Fax: (213) 891-8763
www.lw.com

Milbank, Tweed, Hadley & McCloy LLP
One Chase Manhattan Plaza
New York, NY 10005
Phone: (212) 530-5000
Fax: (212) 530-5219
www.milbank.com

Visit Vault at **www.vault.com** for insider company profiles, expert advice,
career message boards, expert resume reviews, the Vault Job Board and more.

V∧ULT CAREER LIBRARY   **275**

O'Melveny & Myers LLP
400 South Hope Street
Los Angeles, CA 90071-2899
Phone: (213) 430-6000
Fax: (213) 430-6407
www.omm.com

Paul, Weiss, Rifkind, Wharton & Garrison LLP
1285 Avenue of the Americas
New York, NY 10019
Phone: (212) 373-3000
Fax: (212) 757-3990
www.paulweiss.com

Ropes & Gray LLP
One International Plaza
Boston, MA 02110-2624
Phone: (617) 951-7000
Fax: (617) 951-7050
www.ropesgray.com

Shearman & Sterling
599 Lexington Avenue
New York, NY 10022
Phone: (212) 848-4000
Fax: (212) 848-7179
www.shearman.com

Sidley Austin Brown & Wood LLP
Bank One Plaza
10 South Dearborn Street
Chicago, IL 60603
Phone: (312) 853-7000
Fax: (312) 853-7036

787 Seventh Avenue
New York, NY 10019
Phone: (212) 839-5300
Fax: (212) 839-5599
www.sidley.com

Simpson Thacher & Bartlett
425 Lexington Avenue
New York, NY 10017
Phone: (212) 455-2000
Fax: (212) 455-2505
www.simpsonthacher.com

**Skadden, Arps, Slate,
Meagher & Flom LLP & Affiliates**
4 Times Square
New York, NY 10036
Phone: (212) 735-3000
Fax: (212) 735-2000
www.skadden.com

Sullivan & Cromwell LLP
125 Broad Street
New York, NY 10004
Phone: (212) 558-4000
Fax: (212) 558-3588
www.sullcrom.com

Wachtell, Lipton, Rosen & Katz
51 West 52nd Street
New York, NY 10019-6150
Phone: (212) 403-1000
Fax: (212) 403-2000
www.wlrk.com

Weil, Gotshal & Manges LLP
767 Fifth Avenue
New York, NY 10153
Phone: (212) 310-8000
Fax: (212) 310-8007
www.weil.com

White & Case LLP
1155 Avenue of the Americas
New York, NY 10036-2787
Phone: (212) 819-8200
Fax: (212) 354-8113
www.whitecase.com

Williams & Connolly LLP

The Edward Bennett Williams Building

725 12th Street, NW

Washington, DC 20005

Phone: (202) 434-5000

Fax: (202) 434-5029

www.wc.com

Wilmer, Cutler & Pickering

2445 M Street, NW

Washington, DC 20037

Phone: (202) 663-6000

Fax: (203) 663-6363

www.wilmer.com

Visit Vault at **www.vault.com** for insider company profiles, expert advice, career message boards, expert resume reviews, the Vault Job Board and more.

V∧ULT CAREER LIBRARY   **277**

LIVE THE COLLABORATIVE BUSINESS EXPERIENCE.

Imagine working for a company that believes how you work is just as important as what you achieve. Picture yourself working alongside clients to create results that last. And think what it would be like to take your talent to another level by sharing and creating world-class knowledge. You could be part of a motivating environment with an open culture, where high performance is rewarded and freedom, innovation and trust are valued... Enjoy challenging work, personal growth and fun... Come live the Collaborative Business Experience.

www.us.capgemini.com

For more information on a career with Capgemini, please visit your school's career management office or visit us online at **http://us.capgemini.com/careers**

Capgemini
CONSULTING.TECHNOLOGY.OUTSOURCING

Management Consulting

What is Consulting?

A giant industry, a moving target

Consulting, in the business context, means the giving of advice for pay. Consultants offer their advice and skill in solving problems, and are hired by companies who need the expertise and outside perspective that consultants possess. Some consulting firms specialize in giving advice on management and strategy, while others are known as technology specialists. Some concentrate on a specific industry area, like financial services or retail, and still others are more like gigantic one-stop shops with divisions that dispense advice on everything from top-level strategy, to choosing training software, to saving money on paper clips.

But consulting firms have one thing in common: they run on the power of their people. The only product consulting firms ultimately have to offer is their ability to make problems go away. As a consultant, you are that problem-solver.

Not the kind of consulting we mean

As a standalone term, "consulting" lacks real meaning. In a sense, everyone's a consultant. Have you ever been asked by a friend, "Do I look good in orange?" Then you've been consulted about your color sense. There are thousands upon thousands of independent consultants who peddle their expertise and advice on everything from retrieving data from computers to cat astrology. There are also fashion consultants, image consultants, and wedding consultants. For the purposes of this section, we are going to use the term "consulting" to refer specifically to management consulting.

Management consulting firms sell business advisory services to the leaders of corporations, governments, and non-profit organizations. Typical concentrations in consulting include strategy, IT, HR, finance, and operations. Types of problems in consulting include pricing, marketing, new product strategy, IT implementation, or government policy. Finally, consulting firms sell services in virtually any industry, such as pharmaceuticals, consumer packaged goods, or energy.

Firms can be organized or broken up according to topic, type of problem, or industry. For example, a firm might focus on strategy problems only, but in virtually any industry. Bain & Company is an example of one such firm. Another firm might focus on a specific industry, but advise on nearly any type of issue. Oliver, Wyman and Company, which focuses on the financial services industry, is an example of this type of firm. Many of the larger firms have a "matrix" organization, with industry practice groups but also functional practice groups. And some firms are extremely specialized. For example, a firm might have only two employees, both focusing solely on competitive analysis in the telecommunications industry. All of these are examples of management consulting.

Visit Vault at **www.vault.com** for insider company profiles, expert advice, career message boards, expert resume reviews, the Vault Job Board and more.

VAULT CAREER LIBRARY   279

Caveats about consulting

All this might sound great, but before we go on, we should address some common misconceptions about consulting.

- **Implementation** – You might be thinking, "All consultants do is figure out problems at companies and explain them. Awesome. I'm going to be making great money for doing something really easy." Unfortunately, that's not true. Spotting a client's problems is a mere fraction of the battle. (Most people with a fair amount of common sense and an outsider's perspective can identify a client's problems. And in many cases, clients also understand where the problems lie.)

The job of the consultant, therefore, isn't just about knowing what's wrong. It's about figuring out how to make it right. Even finding the solution isn't the end of the story. Consultants must make sure the solution isn't too expensive or impractical to implement. (Many consulting firms have what's called an 80 percent rule: It's better to put in place a solution that takes care of 80 percent of the problem than to strive for a perfect solution that can't be put into place.) A corollary to this is the 80/20 rule: 80 percent of a problem can be solved in 20 percent of the time. Consultants must also get buy-in from the clients. Not only does bureaucracy often make implementation tough, but consultants must also convince individual client employees to help them make solutions work. It's tough to solve problems – and that's why clients hire consultants.

- **Glamour** – Consulting can indeed be exciting and high profile, but this is the exception, not the rule. Chances are, you won't be sitting across from the CEO at your next project kick-off, and you probably won't be staying in four-star hotels in the coolest cities in the world (though both are possible). Depending on the industry and location of your client's business, your environment might be a mid-range hotel in a small city, and you might be working with the senior vice president of one of the company's many business units.

- **Prestige** – Consulting is widely thought of as a prestigious career among business circles, particularly MBAs. But you should realize that in contrast to work in investment banking, your work in consulting will probably never get mentioned in *The Wall Street Journal*. Very few consulting firms are publicly recognized for the help they give.

As a result, few people outside of the industry really understand what consulting is. In fact, a running joke about consulting is that no one can explain it, no matter how hard or many times one tries. If you want a job you can explain to your grandmother, consulting isn't for you. Most "civilians" won't have heard of your firm – unless it has been involved in a scandal, that is.

- **Income** – The salary looks attractive on paper, but remember, it's not easy money. Divide your salary over the (large) number of hours, and the pay per hour isn't much better than other business careers.

So what does a consultant actually do, anyway?

Most "non-consultants" are mystified by the actual job and its day-to-day responsibilities. There are good reasons why this is so. While you're used to giving advice and solving problems, you may not understand how this translates into a career path. The problem is compounded because consultants tend to use a very distinctive vocabulary. You may not know what your skill set is, or how not to boil the ocean, or what the heck consultants mean when they talk about helicoptering. In addition, many consulting firms have their own specific philosophies and problem-attacking frameworks, which only raise the level of jargon.

The short answer is that you will be working on projects of varying lengths at varying sites for different clients. What you do will depend on your seniority, experience, phase of the project and your company. If you are a partner, you are selling work most of the time, whereas if you have a recent MBA degree, you are probably overseeing a couple of entry-level consultants doing research. For the most part, we'll describe the job that entry-level and mid-level (MBA or the equivalent) consultants do. Generally, projects follow the pitching/research/analysis/report writing cycle.

Depending where you are in the project lifecycle, here are some of the things you could be doing:

Pitching

- Helping to sell and market the firm (preparing documents and researching prospective clients in preparation for sales calls)

- Helping to write the proposal

- Presenting a sales pitch to a prospective client (usually with PowerPoint, Microsoft's presentation software)

Research

- Performing secondary research on the client and its industry using investment banking reports and other research sources (these include Bloomberg, OneSource, Hoover's Online, Yahoo! News and SEC filings)

- Interviewing the client's customers to gather viewpoints on the company

- Checking your firm's data banks for previous studies that it has done in the industry or with the client, and speaking to the project leads about their insights on the firm

- Facilitating a weekly client team discussion about the client company's business issues

Analysis

- Building Excel discounted cash flow (DCF) and/or other quantitative financial models

- Analyzing the gathered data and the model for insights

- Helping to generate recommendations

Reporting

- Preparing the final presentation (typically a "deck" of PowerPoint slides, though some firms write up longer reports in Microsoft Word format)

- Helping to present the findings and recommendations to the client

Visit Vault at **www.vault.com** for insider company profiles, expert advice, career message boards, expert resume reviews, the Vault Job Board and more.

VAULT CAREER LIBRARY 281

Implementation

- Acting as a project manager for the implementation of your strategy, if your firm is typically active during the implementation phase of a project

- Executing the coding, systems integration, and testing of the recommended system, if you work for an IT consulting practice

- Documenting the team's work after the project is over

Administration

- Working on internal company research when your firm has no projects for you. (Being unstaffed is referred to as being "on the beach," a pleasant name for what is often a tedious time.)

- Filling out weekly time tracking and expense reports

Keep in mind that the analysis phase — usually the most interesting part — is probably the shortest part of any assignment. Consultants staffed on projects typically do a lot of research, financial analysis, Excel model building and presentation. You will attend lots of meetings in your quest to find the data, create the process and meet the people who will help you resolve the issues you've been hired to address. And, when you're not staffed, you will spend time "on the beach" doing research on prospective clients and helping with marketing efforts. (It's called "on the beach" because the time when you're not staffed on a paid engagement is usually less frenetic – though not always so!) Consulting firms spend a lot of time acquiring the work, and depending on how the firm is structured or how the economy is doing, you could spend significant amounts of time working on proposals. For you, this usually means lots of research, which is then elucidated on the omnipresent PowerPoint slides.

To some extent, though, the boundaries of the job are virtually limitless. Each project carries with it a new task, a new spreadsheet configuration, a new type of sales conference, or an entirely new way of thinking about business. To top it all off, you often must travel to your work assignment and work long hours in a pressurized environment. It's not easy.

Consulting Skill Sets

Consultants focus their energies in a wide variety of practice areas and industries. Their individual jobs, from a macro level, are as different as one could imagine. While a supply chain consultant advises a client about lead times in their production facility, another consultant is creating a training protocol for a new software package. What could be more different?

Despite the big picture differences, however, consultants' day-to-day skill sets are, by necessity, very similar. (Before we go any further: by skill set, we mean "your desirable attributes and skills that contribute value as a consultant." Skill set is a handy, abbreviated way to refer to same.)

Before we talk about the skill sets, keep in mind that there is a big difference between the job now and the job six to eight years from now, if and when you are a partner. We are going to talk about whether you would like the job now, but you should think about whether this might be a good long-term career for you. Is your goal to see it through to partner? If you would rather have an interesting job for six years, you just have to know you have the qualities to be a good consultant and manager. To be a partner, you have to be a persuasive salesperson. You will spend nearly 100 percent of your time selling expensive services to companies who don't think they need help. Your pay and job security will depend on your ability to make those sales.

Do you have the following characteristics in your skill set?

- **Do you work well in teams?** Consultants don't work alone. Not only do they frequently brainstorm with other consultants, but they also often work with employees at the client company, or even with consultants from other companies hired by the client. Consultants also frequently attend meetings and interview potential information sources. If you're the sort of person who prefers to work alone in quiet environments, you will not enjoy being a consultant.

- **Do you multi-task well?** Not only can consulting assignments be frenetic, but consultants are often staffed on more than one assignment. Superior organizational skills and a good sense of prioritization are your friends. Would your friends describe you as a really busy person who's involved in a ton of activities, and still able to keep your personal life on track?

- **Speaking of friends, do you like talking to people?** Do you find yourself getting into interesting conversations over lunch and dinner? If you consider yourself a true introvert and find that speaking to people all day saps your energy, you will likely find consulting quite enervating. On the other hand, if you truly relish meetings, talking to experts, explaining your viewpoints, cajoling others to cooperate with you and making impromptu presentations, you've got some valuable talents in your consulting skill set.

- **Did you love school?** Did you really like going to class and doing your homework? There's a high correlation between academic curiosity and enjoyment of consulting.

- **Are you comfortable with math?** Consulting firms don't expect you to be a math professor, but you should be comfortable with figures, as well as commonly used programs like Excel, Access and PowerPoint. If you hate math, you will hate consulting. On a related note, you should also relish and be good at analysis and thinking creatively. Consultants have a term, now infiltrating popular culture, called "out of the box thinking." This means the ability to find solutions that are "outside the box" – not constrained by commonly accepted facts.

- **Are you willing to work 70, even 80 hours a week?** Consultants must fulfill client expectations. If you must work 80 hours a week to meet client expectations, then that will be your fate. If you have commitments outside work, for example, you may find consulting hours difficult. Even if you have no major commitments outside work, understand what such a schedule means to you. Try working from 8 a.m. to 10 p.m. one day. Now imagine doing so five days a week for months on end.

- **Last, but certainly not least, are you willing to travel frequently?** (See the next section for a discussion of travel in consulting.)

Be truthful. If you can't answer most of these points with a resounding "yes," consulting is most likely not for you. The point is not just to get the job, but also to know what you're getting into — and to truly want to be a consultant.

Visit Vault at **www.vault.com** for insider company profiles, expert advice, career message boards, expert resume reviews, the Vault Job Board and more.

 VAULT CAREER LIBRARY   **283**

The traveling salesman problem

A lot of people go into the consulting field with the notion that travel is fun. "Traveling four days a week? No problem! My last vacation to Italy was a blast!" However, many soon find the traveling consultant's life to be a nightmare. Many consultants leave the field solely because of travel requirements.

Here's what we mean by consulting travel. Different consulting firms have different travel models, but there are two basic ones:

- A number of consulting firms (the larger ones) spend four days on the client site. This means traveling to the destination city Monday morning, spending three nights in a hotel near the client site, and flying home late Thursday night. (This will, of course, vary, depending on client preference and flight times.) The same firms often try to staff "regionally" to reduce flying time for consultants.

- The other popular travel model is to go to the client site "as needed." This generally means traveling at the beginning of the project for a few days, at the end of the project for the presentation, and a couple of times during the project. There is less regularity and predictability with this travel model, but there is also less overall time on the road.

Here are some variations of these travel modes that pop up frequently:

- International projects involve a longer-term stay on the client site. (Flying consultants to and from the home country every week can get expensive.) For example, the consultant might stay two or three weeks on or near the client site (the client might put you up in a corporate apartment instead of a hotel to save costs) and then go home for a week, repeating the process until the end of the project.

- Then, there is the "local" project that is really a long commute into a suburb, sometimes involving up to two hours in a car. Examples of this include consulting to Motorola (based in not-so-convenient Schaumberg, IL) while living in Chicago, or consulting to a Silicon Valley client while living in San Francisco. In these cases, you might opt to stay at a local hotel after working late, instead of taking the long drive home. This is not very different from non-local travel, and it can be more grueling, due to the car commute.

You need to ask yourself a number of questions to see if you are travel-phobic. For example, when you pack to go on vacation, do you stress about it? Do you always underpack or overpack? Do you hate flying? Do you hate to drive? Do you mind sleeping in hotel rooms for long periods of time? Are you comfortable with the idea of traveling to remote cities and staying there for three or four nights every week for ten weeks? If you're married, do you mind being away from your spouse (and children if you have them) for up to three nights a week? Does your family mind? Will your spouse understand and not hold it against you if you have to cancel your anniversary dinner because the client wants you to stay a day later? If you and your spouse both travel for work, who will take care of the pets? Does the idea of managing your weekly finances and to-do lists from the road bother you?

If these questions make your stomach churn, look for consulting companies that promise a more stable work environment. For example, if you work in financial consulting and live in New York City, most of your clients may be local. But because consulting firms don't always have the luxury of choosing their clients, they can't guarantee that you won't travel. Moreover, many large companies build their corporate campus where they can find cost-effective space, often in the suburbs or large corporate parks. (If you absolutely can not travel, some of the largest consulting firms, such as Accenture, have certain business units that can guarantee a non-traveling schedule. Ask.)

Note that travel is common in the consulting field, but not all consultants travel. And not all clients expect you to be on site all the time. It absolutely depends on the firm's travel model, industry, your location, and most importantly, your project.

Who Hires Consultants, and Why?

Corporations, governments, and non-profit institutions hire consultants for a number of reasons. Every consulting project springs from a client's need for help, or at least the kind of help that short-term, internal hiring can't solve. Some clients, for example, need to overhaul their entire IT infrastructure, yet they're out of touch with the latest back-end systems or don't have the staff resources for such a large project. Other clients may be merging, but lack any experience with post-merger staffing procedures, and need a neutral party to mediate. Some clients may need an outsider's perspective on a plant shutdown. Perhaps a client wants to bring in extra industry knowledge.

Consultants get hired for political reasons too. Launching big projects can be very cumbersome, particularly at Fortune 500 companies,. In order for a single dollar to be spent on such a project, most companies require senior executive approval. And without a major consultancy's brand name attached to the project, approval can be hard to get. But once a consulting firm steps into the picture, everyone involved has plausible deniability in the event that the project fails. There is an old adage: "No one ever got fired for hiring McKinsey" (or a similarly prestigious consulting firm.) Some clients still adhere to this as a rule of thumb.

Second, even if a giant project gets the green light, there's no guaranteeing it will be implemented. The reason? Simple bureaucratic inertia. Senior executives lose interest. Direct reports move on to other issues. In short, companies lose their focus. (An insider at a large private global corporation reports that steps from a BCG report from 1996 have been approved but, as of September 2002, have not yet been implemented.) By bringing in consultants to oversee large projects, companies ensure that someone is always watching the ball. In many cases, the correct solution may be quite evident to many, but having it confirmed by an outside party makes implementing a plan easier politically.

In the era of downsizing, consultants have another political use. Companies with an itch to fire a percentage of their workforce often like to bring in consultants. When the consultants recommend a workforce reduction, the company can fire at will, blaming their hired guns for the downsizing.

For some types of consulting (particularly outsourcing or IT), consultants are actually a form of cost-effective labor. It costs the firm less money to hire some outsiders to help them with a project, rather than hire some folks full-time at the expense of a competitive salary and benefits package. Consultants may also get the job done faster, not because they are necessarily better, but because the company might not get away with forcing regular employees to adhere to a compressed time frame by staying late hours. By def-

Visit Vault at **www.vault.com** for insider company profiles, expert advice, career message boards, expert resume reviews, the Vault Job Board and more.

V\ULT CAREER LIBRARY **285**

inition, consultants are hired to work not at the pace of the corporation but at a differently prescribed pace. A contingency performance basis makes this an even better deal for the client.

Whatever the reasons for hiring consultants, they're bound to be compelling – because, even despite the cost-effectiveness argument in some cases, consultants are very costly on average. Given travel expenses, hotel bills, and actual project fees, hourly prices for consultants can easily climb into the $500 per hour range.

The worker behind the curtain

Consultants are a back-room breed of professional. In joint projects with their clients, they do much of the work and can expect none of the recognition. All consultants must deliver bottom-line value, and often spend countless hours huddled in cramped spaces to do just that. If you do a great job, chances are your client will thank you, but you may never hear about it again. In some cases, you will leave your project before its completion and may never know whether it succeeded or failed.

If you enjoy recognition and completion, you will want to consider the type of consulting firm you join. Does your firm have a history of repeat business? If so, you will have a better chance of seeing the client through different projects and business cycles; you may even work with the same client on different engagements. (Marakon Associates, for example, boasts that 90 percent of its work comes from engagements with previous clients.) Other firms might offer a methodology that isn't as repeatable. If your firm focuses solely on competitive analysis studies, chances are good that, if your client stays in the same industry, you won't need to sell that service to them again.

Economic consulting firms like Charles River Associates and the Brattle Group often help law firms with litigation support, including research, economic analysis, and testimonies. This can be very interesting work, and since you're supporting one side or the other of a public dispute, you will certainly know how the fruits of your labor will turn out. Depending on the size of the dispute, so might everyone else who follows the business news.

Another example is M&A consulting. Some firms, like L.E.K. Consulting, have practice areas specifically focused on due diligence, company analysis, and transaction support. The bad news is that on such projects, you are subject to the even longer and more erratic hours suffered by other M&A professionals. On the bright side, you will eventually read in *The Wall Street Journal* about any triumph enjoyed by your client. Your firm may not be mentioned, but at least you will be able to see the results of your hard work become a reality. (It'll also be easier for you to transition to other financial work in the future, if that is your wish.)

So, think about the level of recognition and completion you need for your work, and look for a firm that does the type of work that suits that level. If you find that you require higher levels of recognition and completion than any type of consulting can offer, then you may want to look into other professions.

Training for Consultants

A career in consulting is attractive for many reasons, but few of these are as important to jobseekers as the amount of training they will receive. Unlike industries such as consumer products or pharmaceuticals, where companies funnel investment dollars into product design and research & development, the consulting industry's largest expenditure (apart from staff salaries and overhead) is training. Every year, consulting firms allocate as much as 20 percent of their revenues to internal training programs, and consultants reap the benefits. It is not uncommon for a consultant to spend four to eight weeks per year attending firm-sponsored classes, taking computer-based training programs (CBTs), and studying industry-related literature to improve their performance on the job.

The training requirements in consulting are, by any measure, extensive, and employees who hail from top-ranked schools and prestigious firms find the ongoing skill development not only to be personally satisfying, but also valuable. Headhunters and recruiters for Fortune 500 companies realize how much training consultants receive, and they are willing to pay top dollar for people who have spent considerable time developing their skills.

Orientation training

Over the course of their careers, consultants will encounter two general categories of training: orientation and ongoing training. Orientation training begins soon after new hires walk in the door and greet their assigned human resource representatives. In large firms, most of the orientation training actually occurs in a distant location: after new hires fill out reams of paperwork at their home office, they board a plane and fly to the firm's massive training campus. Once they check into their assigned rooms, attend a welcome meeting, and spend some time getting to know their "classmates" from around the world, they begin a program that will last anywhere from one to four weeks, depending on the firm.

Orientation training is notoriously rigorous and exhausting. New hires spend most of their days working in teams, meeting with firm executives who pose as clients, attending lectures, learning computer code and completing CBTs. Consulting firms spend millions of dollars each year to prepare new hires for their first few projects and they make sure that, by the end of the training, employees understand just how strenuous consulting can be. Consulting firms do budget in time for rest and relaxation, but such time pales in comparison to the hard work and countless hours of team-based learning. Regardless, most new consultants, despite feeling worn out at the end of each day, find the experience very gratifying. Orientation training may be a rude awakening, but it offers many perks. Where else can recent college graduates work with people from around the world, build lasting friendships, and be paid large sums of money to attend class?

Ongoing training

Once consultants get acclimated to living in hotels and working with clients, training requirements re-emerge as part of their ongoing development. Every year experienced consultants complete a curriculum

Visit Vault at **www.vault.com** for insider company profiles, expert advice, career message boards, expert resume reviews, the Vault Job Board and more.

V∧ULT CAREER LIBRARY   **287**

of computer training, industry-specific seminars, management workshops and a host of other training programs designed to complement on-the-job learning.

Aside from making consultants better at what they do, ongoing training also functions as a tool to gauge how ready employees are for promotion. Indeed, many firms will not promote an employee unless he first completes the required curriculum for that particular year. Consultants, therefore, have a two-part incentive for completing their ongoing training requirements. Not only do they hope to become better consultants, but they want very much to rise through the ranks, make more money and have greater responsibility.

Employer Directory

Accenture

Offices in 48 countries

campusconnection.accenture.com

Accenture's the world's leading management consulting, technology services and outsourcing company. We deliver cutting-edge technologies and solutions to companies around the world to help them become high-performance businesses. By improving their operations or reducing their costs, our innovative solutions help clients transform the way they do business, making them more competitive in their market.

Whether you want to develop deep technical skills, build business and industry expertise, develop leadership qualities or extend your personal development, Accenture offers a variety of career opportunities to help you achieve your goals. Visit campusconnection.accenture.com to learn more about the exciting opportunities with Accenture.

Schools Accenture recruits from

Duke University; Northwestern; Penn State; Texas A&M; University of CA-Berkeley; University of Michigan; University of Norte Dame; University of Georgia; University of Pennsylvania; University of Texas-Austin; Virginia Tech Univ; Cornell University; RPI; U of Illinois; U of Virginia; Georgia Tech; Purdue University; Ohio State University; Columbia University; UCLA

Bain & Company, Inc.

BAIN & COMPANY

131 Dartmouth Street

Boston, MA 02118

Phone: 617-572-2000

www.bain.com

Bain & Company's business is helping to make companies more valuable. We work collaboratively with top management teams on their most critical business issues. Our focus is on helping our clients beat their competitors and generate substantial, lasting financial impact. We provide practical insights, customized recommendations, and we work with our clients on implementation. Our focus is on driving change within an organization and achieving real results. We have a diversified client base – across industries, geographies and client types. In all, we are 2,800 employees from a diverse set of backgrounds working in 30 offices across 19 countries worldwide.

Schools Bain & Company recruits from

Brown; Georgetown; Princeton; Yale; Harvard; MIT; Williams; Amherst; Dartmouth; Columbia; Cornell; Duke; UVA; Stanford; U. Michigan; UPenn; UCLA; UC Berkley; Northwestern; Emory; BYU; Rice; U North Carolina; Wake Forest; U Southern Cal; SMU; Notre Dame; Illinois; Indiana; Oxford; Cambridge

Capgemini

Five Times Square
New York, NY 10036
www.us.capgemini.com/careers

In providing innovative consulting solutions, we offer management and IT consulting services, systems integration, technology development, design and outsourcing capabilities on a global scale to help businesses continue to implement growth strategies and leverage technology in the new economy. Our goal is to help our clients realize significant improvement in revenue growth, operating efficiency and the management of capital by solving mission-critical problems. We assist global companies by identifying, designing, and implementing value added changes in their strategies and operations. The organization employs about 50,000 people worldwide and reported 2002 global revenues of about 5.754 billion euros.

Schools Capgemini recruits from

Columbia University Graduate School of Business; Duke University Fuqua School of Business; Georgia Institute of Technology Dupree college of School of Management; University of Florida; University of Michigan @ Ann Arbor School of Business; New York University Stern School of Business; University of California @ Los Angeles Anderson School of Management; University of California @ Berkeley Haas School of Business; University of Texas @ Austin McComb School of Business; Cornell University Johnson School of Business; University of North Carolina @ Chapel Hill Kenan-Flagler School of Business; University of Pennsylvania Wharton School of Business; Northwestern University Kellogg school of Management; University of Chicago Graduate school of Business; Michigan State University Eli Broad School of Business

Deloitte

Deloitte.

1633 Broadway
New York, New York 10013-6754

All candidate are to submit to opportunities via our career website located at www.deloitte.com/careers

Deloitte, one of the nation's leading professional services firms, provides audit, tax, consulting, and financial advisory services through nearly 30,000 people in more than 80 U.S. cities. Known as an employer of choice for innovative human resources programs, the firm is dedicated to helping its clients and its people excel. "Deloitte" refers to the associated partnerships of Deloitte & Touche USA LLP (Deloitte & Touche LLP and Deloitte Consulting LLP) and subsidiaries. Deloitte is the U.S. member firm of Deloitte Touche Tohmatsu.

Visit Vault at **www.vault.com** for insider company profiles, expert advice, career message boards, expert resume reviews, the Vault Job Board and more.

V∧ULT CAREER LIBRARY   291

The Advisory Board
The Watergate
600 New Hampshire, N.W.
Washington, DC 20037
Phone: (202) 672-5600
Fax: (202) 672-5700
www.advisoryboardcompany.com

Arthur D. Little
68 Fargo Street
Boston, MA 02210
Phone: (617) 443-0309
Fax: (617) 443-0166
www.adlittle-us.com

A.T. Kearney
222 West Adams Street
Chicago, IL 60606
Phone: (312) 648-0111
www.atkearney.com

BearingPoint
1676 International Drive
McLean, VA 22102
Phone: (703) 747-3000
Fax: (703) 747-8500
www.bearingpoint.com

Boston Consulting Group
Exchange Place
31st Floor
Boston, MA 02109
Phone: (617) 973-1200
Fax: (617) 973-1339
www.bcg.com

Cambridge Associates
100 Summer Street
Boston, MA 02110-2112
Phone: (617) 457-7500
Fax: (617) 457-7501
www.cambridgeassociates.com

Charles River Associates
John Hancock Tower
200 Clarendon Street, T-33
Boston, MA 02116-5092
Phone: (617) 425-3000
Fax: (617) 425-3132
www.crai.com

DiamondCluster International
Suite 3000
John Hancock Center
875 N. Michigan Avenue
Chicago, IL 60611
Phone: (312) 255-5000
Fax: (312) 255-6000
www.diamondcluster.com

The Gallup Organization
901 F Street, NW
Washington, D.C. 20004
Phone: (877) 242-5587
or (202) 715-3030
Fax: (202) 715-3041
www.gallup.com

Gartner
56 Top Gallant Road
Stamford, CT 06904
Phone: (203) 964-0096
www.gartner.com

Hewitt Associates
100 Half Day Road
Lincolnshire, IL 60069
Phone: (847) 295-5000
Fax: (847) 295-7634
www.hewitt.com

IBM Business Consulting Services
Route 100
Somers, NY 10589
www-1.ibm.com/services/bcs/index.html

L.E.K. Consulting
28 State Street
16th Floor
Boston, MA 02109
Phone: (617) 951-9500
Fax: (617) 951-9392
www.lek.com

Marakon Associates
245 Park Avenue
44th Floor
New York, NY 10167
Phone: (212) 377-5000
Fax: (212) 377-6000
www.marakon.com

McKinsey & Company
55 East 52nd Street
New York, NY 10022
Phone: (212) 446-7000
Fax: (212) 446-8575
www.mckinsey.com

Mercer Human Resource Consulting
1166 Avenue of the Americas
New York, NY 10036
Phone: (212) 345-7000
Fax: (212) 345-7414
www.mercerHR.com

Mercer Management Consulting
1166 Avenue of the Americas
32nd Floor
New York, NY 10036
Phone: (212) 345-8000
Fax: (212) 345-8075
www.mercermc.com

Mercer Oliver Wyman
99 Park Avenue
Fifth Floor
New York, NY 10016
Phone: (212) 541-8100
Fax: (212) 541-8957
www.merceroliverwyman.com

Monitor Group
Two Canal Park
Cambridge, MA 02141
Phone: (617) 252-2000
Fax: (617) 252-2100
www.monitor.com

NERA
50 Main Street
White Plains, NY 10606
Phone: (914) 448-4000
Fax: (914) 448-4040
www.nera.com

Stern Stewart & Company
135 East 57th Street
New York, NY 10022
Phone: (212) 261-0600
Fax: (212) 581-6420
www.sternstewart.com

Visit Vault at **www.vault.com** for insider company profiles, expert advice,
career message boards, expert resume reviews, the Vault Job Board and more.

VAULT CAREER LIBRARY   293

The Parthenon Group
200 State Street
Boston, MA 02109
Phone: (617) 478-2550
Fax: (617) 478-2555
www.parthenon.com

Towers Perrin
One Stamford Plaza
263 Tresser Blvd.
Stamford, CT 06089
Phone: (203) 326-5400
Fax: (203) 326-5499
www.towersperrin.com

Watson Wyatt Worldwide
1717 H Street, NW
Washington, DC 20006
Phone: (202) 715-7000
Fax: (202) 715-7700

Visit Vault at **www.vault.com** for insider company profiles, expert advice,
career message boards, expert resume reviews, the Vault Job Board and more.

VAULT CAREER LIBRARY   295

Manufacturing

The Engine Driving the Economy

The manufacturing industry

America's manufacturing industry is a powerful engine driving the nation's economy, making up roughly one-fifth of all U.S. economic activity. Between 1992 and 2000, the industry contributed 22 percent of the country's economic growth, or 28 percent with the addition of software production. It's a major force in employment, as well, comprising 12 percent of all jobs. Through its "multiplier effect," manufacturing actually creates economic output in other industries by using intermediate goods and services in its production process – so that every $1 of a manufacturing product sold to a final user creates an additional $1.43 in intermediate economic output, according to the Department of Commerce. The U.S. continues to lead the world in many manufacturing sectors, including automobiles, aerospace, steel, telecommunications and consumer goods, and it also maintains the lead in exports of manufactured products. It's no wonder economists pay such close attention to U.S. manufacturing stats and figures – and no wonder that the pronounced slump in the sector since 2000 has been cause for concern.

The big slump

Beginning in 2000, following a boom that spanned most of the 20th century, manufacturing was hit by a recession that eventually led to the loss of more than 2.7 million jobs, or about 17 percent of the sector's workforce. A number of circumstances led to the slump, including high interest rates, increased natural gas prices, and a strong U.S. dollar that weakened the export trade, according to the National Association of Manufacturers (NAM). Recovery began in 2003, though at the slowest pace recorded since the Federal Reserve started keeping track of such things in 1919. And though overall hiring came back, the industry, which had seen job losses each month for more than three years in a row, was still on shaky ground.

More efficiency, fewer jobs

Like many industries, manufacturing has seen a steady push toward technologies that promise greater efficiency and productivity – while reducing the need for manpower. So even as employment figures edged up in early 2004, manufacturing giants like 3M continued to make cuts. The Bureau of Labor Statistics (BLS) predicts total manufacturing employment will decrease by 1 percent through 2012. It's likely that many of the factory jobs lost since the beginning of the century will never return, signaling a fundamental shift in the industry as a whole.

A shift also has taken place in the makeup of the industry. According to the NAM, chemicals, industrial machinery and equipment, and electronics are the three largest manufacturing sectors today, making up a third of the industry's gross domestic product. Fifty years ago, the three largest sectors in manufacturing were food, primary metals and motor vehicles.

Visit Vault at **www.vault.com** for insider company profiles, expert advice, career message boards, expert resume reviews, the Vault Job Board and more.

VAULT CAREER LIBRARY   297

The auto sector

Still, manufacturing is closely tied to the production of automobiles – indeed, an assembly line in Michigan may be what many people think of when they hear the term "manufacturing." In 2002, the latest year for which BLS data is available, the auto sector accounted for about 1.2 million jobs. For the most part, the U.S. was able to ward off the competitive threat from Japanese companies that surfaced in the early 1990s by improving their quality and product lines domestically (a bullish environment on Wall Street and economic weakness in Asia also helped). The so-called "Big Three" automakers – General Motors, DaimlerChrysler and Ford – had about 57 percent of the domestic passenger car market in 2000. But since big-ticket purchases like cars are closely tied to consumer confidence, the terrorist attacks of September 11 and the resulting economic turmoil forced car makers to offer customers heavy discounts (such as the zero-percent financing campaign initiated by GM) and cash-back incentives to keep inventory moving. Capacity also needed to be slashed to bring inventories in line with reduced demand, leading to an unhealthy combination of diminished productivity and weak prices. All of this has led to major job cuts, as well as negative ripple effects for related sectors like steel companies.

Though the auto industry has attempted to rebound by revamping cars to meet consumer demand for items like SUVs and, in contrast, fuel-efficient hybrid vehicles, analysts warn that U.S. companies need to look to the east again as the Asian markets improve and manufacturers like Toyota (currently number four in terms of sales) pick up the pace.

Steely resolve

Steel is another traditional mainstay in U.S. manufacturing. Like its manufacturing counterparts, the steel sector recently experienced its worst days since the Depression, with more than 30 U.S. steel companies, including giants like Bethlehem Steel and National Steel, filing for bankruptcy since 2000. But more recently, steel has rebounded, largely due to the lifting of tariffs on steel imports to avoid reprisals from Europe. With efficiency in line, steel producers raised prices by 20 percent in late 2003, and have continued to post strong orders. The sector isn't slowing down – in fact, the U.S. is actually producing 50 percent more steel today than it did in the early 1980s.

Flying the friendly skies

Aerospace also contributes significantly to U.S. manufacturing. In the commercial sphere, aerospace manufacturing is dominated by Boeing and European rival Airbus. These companies and others, like Lockheed Martin, Northrop Grumman, and Raytheon, also are involved in the production of military aircraft, missiles, and equipment for space. But following 2001's domestic terrorist attacks, civilian air travel plummeted, and major airlines like United were driven into bankruptcy. Fewer planes were being ordered, leading to massive layoffs in the sector. Though the industry has been bolstered a bit by innovations such as Boeing's new 7E7 Dreamliner, a fuel-efficient passenger jet that should take to the skies by 2008, total sales for civilian and military planes in 2004 were expected to grow by less than one percent, to $148 billion – down $7 billion from 2002, according to the Aerospace Industries Association.

All about chemicals

In the chemical manufacturing sector, high-profile names like BASF, DuPont, and Dow Chemical lead the market. The chemical giants have struggled in recent years, since they're dependent on materials like natural gas and petroleum, which have seen sharp increases in prices. And when prices for energy increase, the chemical manufacturers' customers – such as automakers – cut back on production, weakening demand for chemicals. This all has added up to decreased revenues during the first years of the century, along with an increased drive toward mergers and acquisitions. Notable deals recently have included Dow Chemical's purchase of Union Carbide and Valspar's purchase of Lilly Industries.

Other manufacturing sectors include the forest products industry, estimated at around 7 percent of U.S. manufacturing output. Here again, employment figures have plummeted in recent years due to a convergence of unfavorable economic conditions and changes in demand due to the new "paperless" business environment. Additional heavy manufacturing sectors include plastics, textiles, apparel, rubber and minerals.

Visit Vault at **www.vault.com** for insider company profiles, expert advice, career message boards, expert resume reviews, the Vault Job Board and more.

VAULT CAREER LIBRARY   299

Employer Directory

International Paper

6400 Poplar Avenue
Memphis, TN 38197
www.careers-ipaper.com
www.internationalpaper.com

At International Paper we're looking for new ideas and perspectives. If you are preparing to graduate and are ready to make a contribution to a company's goals and direction, IP may just be the place for you to begin your career. At IP, we'll provide you with an environment that encourages you to do your best work and reach your full potential. Through diverse opportunities, each employee is challenged to increase their skills, knowledge, experience and leadership. Our carefully structured career development programs provide the framework for your professional development, including a combination of hands-on responsibility, formal training, coaching and teamwork that will help you to excel.

Schools International Paper recruits from:

University of Alabama; University of Arkansas; Auburn University; Clemson University; Florida A&M University; Georgia Institute of Technology; Howard University; University of Illinois; Louisiana State University; Louisiana Tech University; University of Maine; Michigan State University; University of Mississippi; Mississippi State University; North Carolina State University; Ohio State University; Penn State University; Purdue University; Rensselaer Polytechnic Institute; University of South Carolina; University of Tennessee (Knoxville); University of Texas (Austin); Virginia Polytechnic Institute; University of Wisconsin (Madison); University of Wisconsin (Stevens Point).

3M Company
3M Center
St. Paul, MN 55144
Phone: (651) 733-1110
Fax: (651) 736-2133
www.mmm.com

Alcoa
201 Isabella St.
Pittsburgh, PA 15212-5858
Phone: (412) 553-4545
Fax: (412) 553-4498
www.alcoa.com

Applied Materials
3050 Bowers Ave.
Santa Clara, CA 95054
Phone: (408) 727-5555
FAx: (408)-748-9943
www.appliedmaterials.com

The Boeing Company
100 N. Riverside Plaza
Chicago, IL 60606-2609
Phone: (312) 544-2000
Fax: (312) 544-2082
www.boeing.com

BMW Manufacturing Corporation
1400 Hwy. 101 S.
1400 Hwy. 101 S.
Greer, SC 29651-6731
Phone: (864) 968-6000
Fax: (864) 968-6050
www.bmwebcam.com

Caterpillar Inc.
100 NE Adams St.
Peoria, IL 61629
Phone: (309) 675-1000
Fax: (309) 675-1182
www.cat.com

Daimler-Chrysler Corporation

1000 Chrysler Dr.

Auburn Hills, MI 48326-2766

Phone: (248) 576-5741

Fax: (248) 576-4742

www.daimlerchrysler.com

Dana Corporation

4500 Dorr St.

Toledo, OH 43615

Phone: (419) 535-4500

Fax: (419) 535-4643

www.dana.com

Deere & Company

1 John Deere Place

Moline, IL 61265

Phone: (309) 765-8000

Fax: (309) 765-5671

www.deere.com

Eaton Corporation

Eaton Center, 1111 Superior Ave.

Cleveland, OH 44114-2584

Phone: (216) 523-5000

Fax: (216) 523-4787

www.eaton.com

E. I. du Pont de Nemours and Company

1007 Market St.

Wilmington, DE 19898

Phone: (302) 774-1000

Fax: (302) 999-4399

www.dupont.com

Federal-Mogul Corporation

26555 Northwestern Hwy.

Southfield, MI 48034

Phone: (248) 354-7700

Fax: (248) 354-8950

www.Federal-Mogul.com

Ford Motor Company

1 American Rd.

Dearborn, MI 48126-2798

Phone: (313) 322-3000

Fax: (313) 845-6073

www.ford.com

GE Advanced Materials

One Plastics Ave.

Pittsfield, MA 01201

Phone : (413) 448-7110

Fax: (413) 448-7465

www.geadvancedmaterials.com

Georgia-Pacific Corporation

133 Peachtree St., NE

Atlanta, GA 30303

Phone: (404) 652-4000

Fax: (404) 230-1674

www.gp.com

General Motors Corporation

300 Renaissance Center

Detroit, MI 48265-3000

Phone: (313) 556-5000

Fax: (248) 696-7300

www.gm.com

Honeywell Electronic Materials

1349 Moffett Park Dr.

Sunnyvale, CA 94089

Phone: (408) 962-2000

Fax: (408) 962-2257

www.honeywell.com/sites/sm/em

Ingersoll-Rand Industrial Solutions

200 Chestnut Ridge Rd.

Woodcliff Lake, NJ 07675

Phone: (201) 573-0123

Fax: (201) 573-4041

www.irco.com/business/industrial.html

Visit Vault at **www.vault.com** for insider company profiles, expert advice,
career message boards, expert resume reviews, the Vault Job Board and more.

VAULT CAREER LIBRARY   **301**

ITT Industries, Inc.
4 W. Red Oak Ln.
White Plains, NY 10604
Phone: (914) 641-2000
Fax: (914) 696-2950
www.ittind.com

Johnson Controls, Inc.
5757 N. Green Bay Ave.
Milwaukee, WI 53209
Phone: (414) 524-1200
Fax: (414) 524-2077
www.johnsoncontrols.com

Lockheed Martin Corporation
6801 Rockledge Dr.
Bethesda, MD 20817-1877
Phone: (301) 897-6000
Fax: (301) 897-6704
www.lockheedmartin.com

Newell Rubbermaid Inc.
10 B Glenlake Pkwy., Ste. 600
Atlanta, GA 30328
Phone: (770) 407-3800
Fax: (770) 407-3970
www.newellrubbermaid.com

Northrop Grumman Corporation
1840 Century Park East
Los Angeles, CA 90067-2199
Phone: (310) 553-6262
www.northgrum.com

PPG Industries, Inc.
1 PPG Place
Pittsburgh, PA 15272
Phone: (412) 434-3131
Fax: (412) 434-2448
www.ppg.com

Raytheon Company
870 Winter St.
Waltham, MA 02451-1449
Phone: (781) 522-3000
Fax: (781) 522-3001
www.raytheon.com

Thermo Electron Corporation
81 Wyman St.
Waltham, MA 02454-9046
Phone: (781) 622-1000
Fax: (781) 622-1207
www.thermo.com

Toyota Motor North America, Inc.
9 W. 57th St., Ste. 4900
New York, NY 10019-2701
Phone: (212) 223-0303
Fax: (212) 759-7670

United Technologies Corporation
One Financial Plaza
Hartford, CT 06103
Phone: (860) 728-7000
Fax: (860) 728-7979
www.utc.com

U.S. Steel Corporation
600 Grant St.
Pittsburgh, PA 15219-2800
Phone: (412) 433-1121
Fax: (412) 433-5733
www.ussteel.com

Weyerhaeuser Company
33663 Weyerhaeuser Way South
Federal Way, WA 98063-9777
Phone: (253) 924-2345
Fax: (253) 924-2685
www.weyerhaeuser.com

Media and Entertainment

The Industry

The media universe is dotted with veritable galaxies of companies – from multi-billion dollar diversified conglomerates to small, independent movie studios and production facilities. High school dropouts and PhDs in philosophy, MBAs and computer programmers, septuagenarians and twentysomethings, all work cheek by jowl to bring to life creative endeavors, to grow sustainable billion-dollar franchises like Batman and Harry Potter, and to create new ways to keep the American public entertained and spending money on leisure.

There are two broad subcategories within media and entertainment: creative and business. The creative side actually makes the products or content and has four major areas: motion pictures, television, publishing and music. The business side sells the content, ensures that everything is legal and helps the business grow. The business encompasses the corporate high-level strategy groups, the divisions (a.k.a. business units) that work in the trenches of a specific operation and the standard overarching business functions evident in every company (e.g. accounting, legal, human resources, IT).

First and foremost, entertainment and media industries start with creative content. Everything else stems from this.

Motion pictures

Movies are by far the biggest segment of the media and entertainment industry, not only because of their prominence within the American cultural landscape, but also because of a successful motion picture's ability to sell products in other enormously profitable places as well (also known as ancillary revenue streams) – home video, international distribution, TV rights and so on. Each of the eight major film studios releases about 20 to 30 films each year, with the average studio release costing about $30 million. Studios are typically broken down into two functional components, the business side and the creative side.

The creative side is the where the movies are actually made. There are a few key divisions on the creative side of the movie business:

- **Development:** The key players in the development stage are producers, screenwriters, agents and studio executives. Production companies, the "homes" of producers, start with a script. Every year, these companies are delivered hundreds of scripts (mostly unsolicited) from famous, semi-famous and unknown writers. The executives at each of the production companies then sort through the scripts (written by both new and established screenwriters), negotiate with agents to purchase interesting ones, and then bring together key players (e.g. a director, lead actors, other producers) who will commit to starring in or making the film if a studio finances it. A studio is then "pitched" the idea and if the film is approved, the film then gets a "green light" to go into production. The latter stage of development is also often called pre-production.

Visit Vault at **www.vault.com** for insider company profiles, expert advice, career message boards, expert resume reviews, the Vault Job Board and more.

VAULT CAREER LIBRARY 303

- **Pre-production:** This is everything that happens to get a movie rolling just before filming starts – location scouting, and the casting and hiring of the crew, for instance.

- **Production:** Once a movie is "green lit," production starts. To use an analogy, if the screenplay is the blueprint, production is when the movie is built by the cast and crew. Filming sometimes happens on a soundstage on a film studio's property, but often it occurs "on location," at an out-of-studio venue.

- **Post-Production:** After all the raw footage has been filmed, it is taken to an editing studio, where professional film editors and the director work together with sound effects artists and special effects wizards (if necessary) to pull a movie together. This is also the stage when music, titles and credits are added and when the film preview (called a "trailer" in industry-speak) is created and sent to movie theaters.

Top Studios

- Disney
- Dreamworks SKG
- MGM/UA
- Paramount
- Sony/Columbia
- Universal
- Warner Brothers
- 20th Century Fox

Top "Indy" Studios

- Artisan
- Fine Line/New Line
- Fox Searchlight
- Miramax
- Sony Pictures Classics
- USA Films

Vital in the movie business is the relationship that studios have with movie theaters, or exhibitors, as they are called in the industry. Exhibitors decide which movies they will show and often split marketing costs with theaters. Because of the 1948 antitrust ruling that divorced theaters from studios, the power of studios weakened. Multiplexes (cinema theaters with multiple screens) then came into the picture, taking advantage of the separation from studios to release many different types of movies, contributing to the proliferation of movie niches and independent films produced on small budgets.

The other side of filmmaking is the business side, which deals with ancillary revenue streams and creative vehicles (e.g., theme parks, licensed products, home video) that come after the filmmaking process. These are often completely separate businesses that employ different media for dissemination (e.g., stores, third party distributors like McDonald's, the Internet). Because many of the most successful movies of all time are franchises (Star Wars, Indiana Jones, Lord of the Rings), the business side works to exploit the enormous revenue opportunities that come with leveraging those properties. As the business side has come to generate billions of dollars in recent years, movie studios have grown into diversified conglomerates with many different business arms. The main divisions are:

- **Home video:** Tapes and DVDs are the second phase of a movie's life cycle, bringing films into the homes of consumers after its life in the box office has run its course.

- **Consumer products:** All filmed properties and characters with commercial appeal are further exploited by other companies that pay licensing fees for the rights to use images and names.

- **Retail:** Virtually all major film studios sell customized items directly to customers either through stores, catalogs or direct mail, some in larger endeavors than others (e.g. The Disney Stores, Warner Brothers Studio Stores).

- **Theme parks:** Large destination parks (e.g. Disneyland, Universal Studios) provide the opportunity to further leverage a film's appeal to consumers in an exciting, live-action setting.

Television

With televisions in the homes of over 99% of the U.S. population, TV is arguably the most powerful media vehicle in the entertainment industry. Deregulation of cable companies and increased bandwidth in distribution (with digital cable) has further increased the options of television networks. This has resulted in a glut of channels targeting ever-narrower niches (e.g. golf, cooking, independent movies).

This growth, however, has resulted in the popularity of several successful cable channels eroding the once dominant share of the networks (ABC, CBS, NBC). Success stories include ESPN, E!, Lifetime, USA and MTV. One result of all this change is the growth in career opportunities for people considering television careers.

Top TV Networks	
ABC	USA
NBC	ESPN
CBS	A&E
Fox	CNN
PBS	TNT
TBS	Nickelodeon
Discovery	Lifetime

The TV industry is structured somewhat differently from film. One of the key difference is that TV is full of sales and marketing positions, since most networks make money on advertising. (If a show is particularly successful, it can make even more money by being sold into syndication (e.g., Law & Order), by being made into a movie (e.g., The X-Files) or by launching spin-offs (e.g., Cheers launching Frasier). Typically, the network does not make much money from these types of deals; the winners are usually the creators of the show and the production company that originally produced the show. Advertising, therefore, is all the more critical for networks.

Here are some key divisions of television networks:

- **Development:** The television industry parallels the film industry in that scripts for new television shows are constantly sought out and studied in the hopes of creating the next Friends or ER. Job positions within TV development are typically divided into the different types of programming that appears on TV – sitcoms, dramas, miniseries, specials and daytime. Network executives are "pitched" ideas by production companies and writers. If the executive likes an idea, a "green light" is given for the show's pilot, the introductory episode. If the pilot is successful, it then becomes a series.

- **Production:** Because television typically calls for shorter production cycles, television studios are often fully equipped soundstages where TV shows are filmed and edited and where final cuts are put into post-production.

- **Programming:** Once a show is on the air, it is watched carefully to see how it performs. Programming executives closely monitor Nielsen ratings, provide comments on scripts to develop shows with the most promising audience appeal, reconfigure schedules to improve performances and cut shows when they fail to build a loyal audience. Shows may be kept when their ratings are low but they attract the desirable 18- to 34-year-old audience.

Visit Vault at **www.vault.com** for insider company profiles, expert advice, career message boards, expert resume reviews, the Vault Job Board and more.

V∧ULT CAREER LIBRARY   **305**

- **Network affiliates:** While the bulk of ad revenues come in at the national level, the major networks have bodies of network affiliates throughout the country that have individual sales forces that sell local advertising, which comprises most of the remaining portion of overall company revenues. In addition to ad sales, affiliates also manage some content creation, primarily local news production.

Music

The music industry has several components – there are divisions that discover new artists, there are those that develop and produce music with mass appeal, and there are the promoters and marketers. And now, in the age of the Internet, there are lots of people hired to make sure that the record labels do not get fleeced by music freeloaders who find ways to acquire and disseminate the product for free, or to figure out how to create profitable businesses distributing or marketing music through the Internet.

While the music industry is enormous, and one of the most globally-significant parts of the entertainment industry because music is so universal and ubiquitous, the threat of its erosion due to Internet piracy concerns poses a serious threat to the growth of new artists and revenue opportunities.

That said, for job seekers, the most promising opportunities continue to be in A&R, distribution and marketing.

> **Big 5 Record Labels**
> - BMG (Arista, Jive Records, RCA)
> - EMI-Capitol (Virgin)
> - Sony (Columbia, Epic)
> - Universal (MCA, Polygram)
> - Warner (Warner Brothers, Elektra, Atlantic)

- **A&R:** These are the talent scouts that listen to demo tapes, attend shows, travel and keep their ear to the ground to understand new trends and to uncover fresh voices that best bring those trends to life.

- **Production:** Once an act has been signed onto a record label, the producers perfect the music to make it commercially palatable for radio stations, critics and consumers. The packaging of the CD and creation of the artist image is also finalized in this stage.

- **PR/Marketing:** This is the group that toils to get airplay on radio stations, gets the music video shot and hopefully aired, leverages television and press coverage and puts the artist in the public eye. Arbitron ratings, essentially Nielsen ratings for radio, let both radio stations and record labels know what consumers are listening to, what is working and what is most popular.

- **Distribution:** This group specifically deals with getting the CDs into record stores and venues where consumers can purchase them.

- **Concerts:** Concerts and live performances that are able to attract large numbers of consumers are increasingly underwritten by large corporate sponsors to defray expenses (e.g., Pepsi sponsoring a Britney Spears concert tour).

The biggest media companies (i.e. AOL Time Warner, Viacom, The Walt Disney Company, Viacom) span across all of these industries (and then some). The chart on the next page shows roughly how these large organizations are structured.

Media Conglomerate Relationships

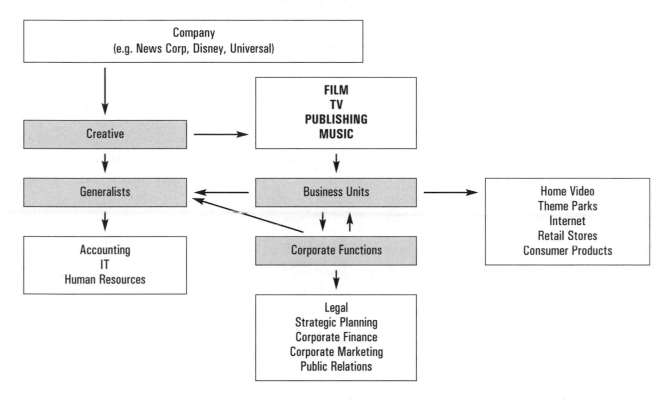

The Big Conundrums

In choosing to enter the entertainment industry, there are several personal decisions that you need to carefully consider. There are no "right" answers. Starting a career in entertainment often calls for steadfast commitment and patience. Some of these decisions involve location, others involve education, still others involve the line of business one can pursue.

New York or Los Angeles?

Most entertainment companies are situated on either the East or West Coast, and that is, by and large, where most newcomers end up. "You definitely want to start in New York or Los Angeles – it's where all the action is," were the words of one record label executive at Virgin. Los Angeles has the development and distribution arms of all the major film and television studios as well as many of the top offices of music labels as well. New York has the balance of the music business, as well as some television (MTV and Nickelodeon for example) and almost 90 percent of all the publishing powerhouses.

Increasingly though, the media and entertainment industry offers opportunities beyond New York and L.A. There are now far more businesses located in other parts of the United States and the world, especially as production costs soar in New York and L.A. Canada is increasingly popular with movie studios, and

Visit Vault at **www.vault.com** for insider company profiles, expert advice,
career message boards, expert resume reviews, the Vault Job Board and more.

V/\ULT CAREER LIBRARY **307**

Vancouver and Toronto both have thriving arts communities. Likewise, the concentration of software engineers in Silicon Valley makes it the home of many special effects companies. Cable networks are increasingly located away from major cities, and shows are often shot in studios in smaller cities like Atlanta and New Orleans. In fact, the most music production outside of New York and Los Angeles occurs in Nashville, the home of the ever-popular country music genre.

Creative or business?

While the creative side of the entertainment business is often considered more interesting because it is what encourages creativity (and because it is the side that holds the best parties with all the famous celebrities), the compensation is lower, the career trajectory is less certain and the work, especially initially, can be demeaning. Assistants often work 12 hours a day, endure being yelled at regularly and must often trek around town every morning to fetch their boss' coffee, dry-cleaned clothes and children.

The business side, on the other hand, is generally regarded as less exciting. There is a fair amount of showmanship even in this part of the business (there was one such businessman who was legendary for keeping his "director-level" business card after being promoted to VP in the hopes that others would believe him to be a film director), but for the most part the path is more predictable, performance is rewarded and the pay is more generous. The tradeoff is, of course, that the positions are not glamorous and the hours are often just as long. "You always feel like you are on the periphery of where the action really is," laments one executive who works in a studio's home video division.

The choice is certainly a difficult one. Success is often not transferable. There are occasionally tales of the studio accountant who transitioned to be a TV producer, but in general, very few make lateral moves, especially since the work required to build up a creative resume is very different than for a business resume, and vice versa.

The role of education

The role of education in the success of Hollywood players remains an enigma. Insiders often say that their degree was worthless in landing their job. In general, the creative side does not reward MBAs. On the business side, however, a graduate degree is often a critical success factor. Furthermore, entrée into the business side of entertainment comes to many only because of an MBA – there are executive training programs at many top media companies (e.g. Bertelsmann, Sony, Disney, Random House) that recruit at many leading business schools. While these are competitive and coveted positions, there is enough to go around for the truly committed. One recent MBA graduate from a top program said, "I just moved to Los Angeles without a job and had interviews with everyone I knew for a month straight – informationals, job interviews, anyone who would talk to me." She eventually landed a promising manager-level position in television distribution.

On the creative side, there are a slew of hot directors and other moviemakers that hail from the ranks of the film school elite – New York University, the American Film Institute, UCLA, USC and others. While these schools offer strong alumni networks and thorough training, there are costly investments. In addition to the annual tuition of the program, there is the additional expense of creating one's final project – a film that will likely cost at least $20,000. There are many success stories of talented people who saved money by taking classes at local community colleges, rented cheap equipment and made their way to festivals like Sundance.

Choosing an industry

The decision on what industry to pursue depends on one's interests and passions. The industries are all similar – personalities drive the business, egos are enormous, attitudes are bad and expectations are high. There are important differences, however. Film and TV generally allow more transition between the two (writers, actors, directors, even producers switch between the two media), but for the most part, it is much harder to transition out of music or publishing.

The key questions to ask yourself:

- What medium do you prefer? Do you really love music? Are you a big film buff? Do you read 20 magazines a month?

- Do you enjoy the artistic or business dimension of a project?

- Can you handle working on a project for several years (as is common in the film and music industries) or do you prefer projects that have shorter production cycles (which you will find in television and magazine publishing)?

- Would you enjoy working with a set team (the creative department of a film studio) or setting up projects with new people (as on the production side of filmmaking)?

- Where do you know more people? Where could you leverage a personal or alumni network?

- Where do you want to live? Do you like city living? Do you mind driving or do you prefer walking?

Remember that there are the inevitable sub-specializations, much like a lawyer who focuses on criminal litigation or a doctor who is a radiologist. Music executives, for instance, are known for the genre of music they produce, and film producers are normally associated with a certain type of film.

Creative Assistants

While widely regarded as the bottom, the legendary dregs of the pool, the creative assistant (CA) position is the starting point for any career launch into the creative side of the industry. Cynics say assistants are there to feed the egos of self-important creative executives, but others assert that it is a rite of passage to the brotherhood (and sisterhood) of entertainment, not to mention a good training ground for the next generation of creative executives.

The typical job of a creative assistant is to do everything from fetching coffee to kids from one's boss' day care, answering hundreds of calls on a daily basis and making dinner reservations for one's manager, to occasionally, if there is time, reading scripts and writing coverage.

Visit Vault at **www.vault.com** for insider company profiles, expert advice, career message boards, expert resume reviews, the Vault Job Board and more.

V∧ULT CAREER LIBRARY   **309**

Survival Skills for Assistants

Being an assistant is the first rung up the entertainment ladder. Here are some tips for getting and keeping these jobs – and setting yourself up to move up beyond the assistant level.

Getting in

While assistants are the proverbial low men on the creative totem pole, they are nonetheless difficult positions to land because there are a fixed number of spots and openings are rare. A position becomes available only when people are promoted, fired or quit. Furthermore, it is the starting place for everyone, so the competition is quite tough. Even experienced business executives with MBAs who want to transition to the creative side are unable to avoid becoming a CA. Throughout the media and entertainment world are countless former attorneys, accountants and other aspiring professionals.

The most popular way of breaking into an assistant position is through referrals. Others break in through cold calls. Still others penetrate the ranks by making friends with other assistants and then patiently trolling for the next job opening. Some CAs migrate from a low-status boss to a higher-status boss, remaining in the assistant ranks for many years.

The interview

The interview for an assistant position is usually intended to assess one's humility, modesty and overall industriousness. There will be the inevitable questions that inquire into one's general tolerance in gruntwork. Often, it takes the form of the following question: "But you're overqualified for this job – won't you get bored?" Beware. The point of the question is to question your dedication to tiring, detailed work. A good answer will showcase your intelligence while pointing out that you are not only capable, but eager, willing and very able to execute even the most menial of tasks with alacrity and aplomb. Typical tasks that are the domain of assistants are answering phones, running errands and accepting a less-than-ideal lifestyle.   You need to persuade your interviewer, who is unlikely to be the person you will work for (Hollywood types often prefer to forego meeting with the "little people"), that you will do anything and everything that's asked and required of you, and then some. You will be told about your benefits (few to none) and your pay. Do not flinch or waver in any way. It will be construed as a sign of weakness!

Occasionally, an interviewer will ask you for your "coverage," which is essentially a synopsis and analysis of a script. Assistants are sometimes entrusted with the responsibility of writing coverage on scripts, and any previous experience writing such coverage can prove to one's advantage. If you don't have any coverage experience, an interviewer will sometimes give you a script and ask that you provide your written comments on it.

Managing your boss

The position of assistant encompasses such duties as secretary, butler, chauffer, mother and confidante. For all the books ever written on management skills, they are all but irrelevant in the entertainment industry. Rarely will you aggregate a larger group of individuals who care less about developing others. One executive described the junior ranks as "suckling on the teats of wolves."

The most important traits of successful assistants are:

- *Flexibility.* Many assistants are required to juggle and reprioritize their own lives in order to accommodate their managers. One assistant tells of missing a flight out for a vacation because the manager called inquiring about some small bit of information that the assistant was supposed to have had.

- *Patience.* Many assistants report countless evenings of waiting around in the office long after the boss had left to a leisure dinner with "business partners." Many managers often tell their underlings to wait until they they are told to go home. Usually the request is legitimized by the (flimsy) guise of receiving a phone call that must be immediately patched through.

- *Resourcefulness.* Often, it is the assistant's responsibility to unearth obscure tidbits of information or to seek out some difficult-to-find object. Whether it reservations at 8 p.m. on a Friday night for the most popular restaurant in town or a rare edition, out-of-print book, assistants are often expected to find ways to make difficult things happen.

- *Indulgence.* The assistant is also expected to be kind and proactive – remembering birthdays and special occasions, congratulating successes and commiserating failures. The best assistants are known for anticipating special requests, accommodating the quirks of their managers, before the manager asks. "I'll try to get my boss his favorite latte every morning if he's unable to pick one up for himself," says one assistant at a prominent Hollywood talent agency.

- *Eagerness.* Cheerfulness and a positive attitude, even in the face of adversity, is vital in the profession. The grumpy are quickly replaced with those more eager and willing.

Making the most of low wages

Assistants make anywhere from $20,000 per year to above $45,000. Usually, the higher paid assistants are in the coveted positions of working at a studio in a unionized position. The majority of assistants earn a salary near the lower end of the spectrum. In order to sustain a viable lifestyle, most assistants resort to the usual manners of making ends meet – sharing living expenses with roommates in modest neighborhoods, limiting indulgences on food (ordering in on the company's dime whenever possible), cutting back expenses on clothing and entertainment, investing in modest transport, borrowing funds from parents. Despite the low salaries, there are often perks to the profession that should not be overlooked. Many assistants manage to allay some of their expenses on staples like dry cleaning by leveraging the generous expense accounts of their managers. Others engage in supplementary income sources, such as teaching on weekends, in order to increase their cash flow.

Getting promoted

If you stick it out long enough in a CA job, you'll probably move up The hard part is waiting it out, often over the course of several years, sacrificing late nights, while making the right connections and waiting

Visit Vault at **www.vault.com** for insider company profiles, expert advice, career message boards, expert resume reviews, the Vault Job Board and more.

V/\ULT CAREER LIBRARY   **311**

for a lucky break. While there are things that can be done – meeting lots of people, keeping your ears and eyes open to opportunities, jumping to a lesser-known company in order to make a transition out of the assistant ranks – promotion ultimately boils down to timing, persistence and good fortune. Good assistants quickly learn to build networks with other assistants, to share information on what's hot in order to give their bosses the extra edge, to religiously listen in on phone calls and to constantly look out for their own best interests.

The information in this section was excerpted from the *Vault Career Guide to Media & Entertainment Careers*. Get the inside scoop on media careers with Vault:

- **Vault Guides:** *Vault Career Guide to Media & Entertainment Careers, Vault Career Guide to Book Publishing*

- **Employer Research:** Online Media and Entertainment Employer Profiles, Employee Surveys and more

- **Message Boards:** Vault Media and Entertainment Career Advice Message Board

- **Career Services:** Vault Resume and Cover Letter Reviews, rated the "Top Choice" by *The Wall Street Journal* for resume makeovers

Go to www.vault.com
or ask your bookstore or librarian for other Vault titles.

Employer Directory

Reed Business Information

360 Park Avenue South

New York, NY 10010

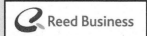

www.reedbusiness.com/employment

nycjobs@reedbusiness.com

Reed Business Information, the largest business-to-business publisher in the U.S., offers business professionals in the media, manufacturing, electronics, construction and retail industries more than 100 market-leading business-to-business publications, 75 Webzines and Web portals, custom publishing, directories, research and direct-marketing lists. RBI is a member of the Reed Elsevier Group plc (NYSE: RUK and ENL) – a world-leading publisher and information provider operating in the science and medical, legal, education and business-to-business industry sectors.

AMC Entertainment Inc.

920 Main St.

Kansas City, MO 64105

Phone: (816) 221-4000

Fax: (816) 480-4617

www.amctheatres.com

Bertelsmann AG

Carl-Bertelsmann-Strasse 270

D-33311 Gütersloh, Germany

Phone: +49-5241-80-0

Fax: +49-5241-80-9662

www.bertelsmann.de

Black Entertainment Television, Inc.

1900 W. Place Northeast

Washington, DC 20018

Phone: (202) 608-2000

Fax: (202) 608-2589

www.bet.com

Clear Channel Communications, Inc.

200 E. Basse Rd.

San Antonio, TX 78209 (Map)

Phone: (210) 822-2828

Fax: (210) 822-2299

www.clearchannel.com

CNN News Group

One CNN Center, Box 105366

Atlanta, GA 30348-5366

Phone: (404) 827-1500

Fax: (404) 827-2437

Cox Communications, Inc.

1400 Lake Hearn Drive, NE

Atlanta, GA 30319

Phone: (404) 843-5000

Fax: (404) 843-5975

Visit Vault at **www.vault.com** for insider company profiles, expert advice, career message boards, expert resume reviews, the Vault Job Board and more.

VAULT CAREER LIBRARY 313

Discovery Communications, Inc.

1 Discovery Place

Silver Spring, MD 20910

Phone: (240) 662-2000

Fax: (240) 662-1868

www.discovery.com

Dreamworks L.L.C.

100 Universal Plaza, Bldg. 10

Universal City, CA 91608

Phone: (818) 733-7700

Fax: (818) 695-7574

Home Box Office, Inc.

1100 Avenue of the Americas

New York, NY 10036

Phone: (212) 512-1000

Fax: (212) 512-1182

Liberty Media Corporation

12300 Liberty Blvd.

Englewood, CO 80112

Phone: (720) 875-5400

Fax: (720) 875-7469

www.libertymedia.com

Metro-Goldwyn Mayer (MGM)

10250 Constellation Blvd.

Los Angeles, CA 90067

Phone: (310) 449-3000

Fax: (310) 449-8857

www.mgm.com

NBC Universal, Inc.

30 Rockefeller Plaza

New York, NY 10112

Phone: (212) 664-4444

Fax: (212) 664-4085

www.nbcuni.com

Public Broadcasting Service

1320 Braddock Place

Alexandria , VA 22314

Phone: (703) 739-5000

Phone: (703) 739-0775

www.pbs.org

Pixar Animation Studios

1200 Park Avenue

Emeryville, CA 94608

Phone: (510) 752-3000

Fax: (510) 752-3151

Time Warner Inc.

1 Time Warner Center

New York, NY 10019

Phone: (212) 484-8000

Fax: (212) 489-6183

www.timewarner.com

Tribune Company

435 N. Michigan Ave.

Chicago, IL 60611 (Map)

Phone: (312) 222-9100

Fax: (312) 222-1573

www.tribune.com

Viacom Inc.

1515 Broadway

New York, NY 10036 (Map)

Phone: (212) 258-6000

Fax: (212) 258-6464

www.viacom.com

The Walt Disney Company

500 S. Buena Vista St.

Burbank, CA 91521-9722 (Map)

Phone: (818) 560-1000

Fax: (818) 560-1930

http://disney.go.com

Nonprofit

Imagine what it might be like to say:

"Today at work I helped to provide a safe place for 100 teens in my community to go after school to receive tutoring and homework assistance."

"This year at work I raised a million and a half dollars to fund a program that promotes better early education for young children."

"Throughout the course of my career I helped to clean up my city's most depressed neighborhoods and developed hundreds of new affordable homes for disadvantaged families."

If being able to do this type of work in the course of your career appeals to you, you may want to consider a career in the nonprofit/philanthropy world. It won't be easy going, though. In recent years, and especially since the September 11 terrorist attacks, the U.S. has seen a recent extraordinary jump in its number of registered charitable organizations. All of these organizations are in need of strong leaders as many in the sector are concerned that our country is not prepared to financially support this recent influx of newly registered charities. It is clear that only the strongest and savviest organizations are certain to survive.

This need for more and better trained nonprofit administrators is fueling the development of many well respected degree programs at universities and colleges nationwide. At the same time, more people, particularly college age and recent graduates are showing an interest in pursuing a career in nonprofit administration.

The rewards can be quite satisfying for professionals who succeed. Such positions come with, at times, a tremendous amount of prestige and respect, interactions with a broad array of people from all class levels and at executive levels, a satisfying salary. Many organizations represent the lifeblood of their communities and are in the daily eye of the local, sometimes national, public and media.

Nonprofit Uppers and Downers

Uppers

Many of the positive aspects of working in a nonprofit/philanthropy career apply to many different organizations.

- The work a nonprofit staff member goes beyond simply executing a role in the general pursuit of making someone more money, or as much money as possible. The job that a staff member does can positively impact the lives of sometimes thousands of people, or change or improve some negative aspect of our society for future generations, or create new, affordable homes for disadvantaged families, or teach a mentally disabled person a trade and help him achieve financial independence. Nothing can measure up to the feeling at the end of the day when you realize that every call you made, letter you

Visit Vault at **www.vault.com** for insider company profiles, expert advice, career message boards, expert resume reviews, the Vault Job Board and more.

VAULT CAREER LIBRARY   315

wrote, bill you reconciled, staff meeting you sat through, paper you filed, or decision you made could benefit someone who needs your organization's help.

- Non-profits are generally more family-friendly than the corporate world. Many are more casual, offer better vacation and work hours, and have a more liberal approach to lifestyle choices. However this is not universal – so check before making the assumption.

- Because there are never enough people to do the work, working in a non-profit can give you the opportunity to perform a variety of tasks outside your job description.

Downers

Downers in nonprofit careers tend to depend on the organization. Common negatives include:

- Staff members often do the equivalent of more than one person's job for often lower salaries (overstaffed and underpaid)

- There are few, if any, company perks of the sort offered by employers in the corporate world (gym memberships, entertainment tickets, etc.). Perhaps more importantly, in recent years, standard benefit packages (health care plans, etc.) have also been shrinking.

- Success is often difficult to determine. For example, say a local advocacy organization implements a community education campaign promoting parents to read more to their children. Is it possible to truly achieve an accurate determination of the campaign's success and to what degree parent behavior changed? Quite possibly, there is simply not enough funding that would be needed to design a community survey, or, at best, conduct adequate focus groups.

- Success is often tied to bringing in money/fundraising. While you may reap greater satisfaction from working at an organization whose overriding goal is not to make money, don't think that you're escaping the importance of money altogether.

- Working at certain nonprofits can mean continually seeing unhappy, indigent people – or worse. For example, employees at women's domestic abuse shelters see a steady daily stream of battered women and their children. The shelter's staff often faces depression and burnout.

- High academic standards – many nonprofits require a Master's degree, and some require PhDs for senior positions. Many also require hands on experience with target beneficiaries before being taken seriously.

Many Choices

While work in the nonprofit world includes can be characterized in certain general ways such as the ones above, the sector is hugely diverse, both in terms of types of organizations, and types of positions available. Nonprofits can be huge organizations, employing thousands of paid workers coordinated through a well-defined organizational structure (for example, regional chapters). They can just as easily be tiny – many nonprofits are comprised of only a paid executive director coordinating volunteers.

Moreover, the missions of nonprofits vary widely. The type of organization most commonly associated with the term "nonprofit" is the community-based organization, frequently referred to as a "CBO." CBOs represent a tremendously important group of service providers, implementing their programs on the "front lines" of direct service. These organizations are seen as diligent, tireless workers, often responding to very basic, unmet needs that exist within a community. Typical examples of CBOs would be homeless shelters, "meals-on-wheels" programs and job placement nonprofits.

CBOs aren't the only type of nonprofit, of course. Other types include nonprofit arts/culture organizations (e.g., the Whitney Museum of Art, the Goodman Theater in Chicago), advocacy/social policy research organizations (e.g., Children's Defense Fund, Mothers Against Drunk Driving), scientific research organizations (RAND and the CATO Institute), international (e.g., Save the Children, UNICEF), and foundations that fund the nonprofit world (e.g., Pew Charitable Trust, the Ford Foundation).

Finally, there are many different roles within the nonprofit world. The way to best understand these is to understand the executives who head up these functions. The most prominent include the executive director (basically, the CEO of a nonprofit), the director of development (who oversees fundraising), the director of programming/project director (who has hands-on responsibility for designing the nonprofits programs and services), the director of public relations & marketing/communications (who oversees relationships with the press and reports to donors). Working with these executives are staff workers and volunteers, as well as employees of different organizations working with the nonprofit, usually as a source of funding. (For example, employees of philanthropic foundations or government agencies work with nonprofits their organizations help fund.)

Nonprofit Doesn't Mean Money Doesn't Matter

Today's nonprofit organization is a very different institution than it was only a decade ago. In a nutshell, the nonprofit corporate culture has become savvier. Many years of lessons learned have improved the sector's approach to program implementation or problem solving (including the problems without an absolute solution) by developing better, more cost-effective strategies for providing services. Just as importantly, nonprofit organizations have also greatly improved their approach to cultivating and accessing stronger financial support. Many unpredictable variables impact our national economy and subsequently philanthropic donations to nonprofits. The nonprofit/philanthropy field is learning how to protect itself from the roller coaster ride that our country's economy can be.

One common approach to this challenge is to diversify funding sources. An extreme example of this is a church in Jamaica, NY that is running and staffing its own charter bus company, essentially running its own for-profit venture and "donating" the income to the church's operational funds. More commonly, however, nonprofits are branching out into other areas of service in hopes of attracting new donors. This is programmatically justified as a way of making a more comprehensive impact on a single area of service or issue.

Other nonprofits are developing entirely new competencies in hopes of introducing the organization to an entirely new pool of supporters. One example of this is an early education advocacy group, Child Care

Visit Vault at **www.vault.com** for insider company profiles, expert advice, career message boards, expert resume reviews, the Vault Job Board and more.

VAULT CAREER LIBRARY   **317**

Action Campaign, which has served as a facilitator and communicator of research and best practices for 20 years. Recently, however, it developed and implemented an early literacy childcare provider training program, sending trainers out into neighborhoods to teach providers how to encourage literacy with the young children in their care. This decision was responsible for nearly $300,000 in new support from donors who only fund "direct service" programs (nonprofits that work directly with those it seeks to serve, rather than just training workers who work with them or conducting research), essentially opening a door to a new revenue stream. In this instance, the organization jumped into community or direct service while continuing its work in advocacy and research.

The Board of Directors

At the top of a nonprofit's administrative structure is the Board of Directors. The only similarity that nonprofit Boards have with for-profit corporate Boards of Directors is the name – the purpose and duties of the nonprofit Board are very different.

In the eyes of the IRS and the Federal Government, a nonprofit organization's existence is solely based on the presence of an active Board of Directors, from its is inception to its maintenance to its ultimate decision to close. In theory, a nonprofit is to have evolved out of a community's identification of a need for its existence and the organization is conceived of to administer the service that will meet the stated need. Because the work that the organization is to perform will either solve a problem or benefit the community in some way, the IRS assigns a tax-exempt status to the entity for any revenue it brings in to pay for the costs of running the business. The status is granted on the stipulation that a group of volunteer community representatives will oversee the organization's well being, particularly to insure that the finances are appropriately maintained, that the organization adheres to the programmatic purpose it was originally founded on, and that the organization is able to raise the funds it needs to be successful. For organizations that employ paid administrative staff, the Board is responsible hiring and firing the most senior staff position.

As a first step in pursuing tax-exempt status, the Board of Directors, before raising any money or implementing any programs, drafts and adopts organizational bylaws that set the parameters for what the organization is does and how it will function, such as stating that the Board members all agree to meet four or six times a year to review the entity's activities and progress. The bi-laws, similar to a constitution, are submitted and approved by the IRS as the key step in the granting of the tax-exempt status. From that point forward, the Board uses the document as a road map for how the organization proceeds and decisions are made.

The most important part of the bylaws is the organization's Mission Statement, the specific description of what the organization will accomplish. Should the organization decide to develelope program areas that fall outside the stated mission, the board is responsible for ultimately making the decision to do so, rewriting the mission statement so that it encompasses the new program areas, and resubmitting the Mission Statement to the IRS.

As basic duties, Boards are required by law to perform those tasks. Every other way that Boards and individual Board Members choose to involve themselves in the organization's activities varies greatly from one organization to another.

Development Work and Organizations

From large development organizations and banks such as the IMF and the World Bank funding giant multi-decade projects, to small NGOs (non-governmental organizations) organizing grass-roots projects, to volunteer agencies providing everything from fence builders to business consultants, global development has become a huge industry.

There is a wide range of opportunities under the "development" umbrella, and just as wide a variety of people working in this industry. Development gurus range from top-level senior executives to junior volunteers straight out of college. Opportunities run from micro-finance to building bridges, from environmental work to helping democracy take hold in remote corners of the world. Many development organizations focus on economic development and financial skills. While there are certainly still opportunities to help villagers build houses, more and more opportunities focus on small business development, nurturing local entrepreneurship and providing sustainable business skills.

Types of "development" organizations

Development is such a broad term, but the following groups of organizations are generally included under this umbrella:

- Public multinationals: Huge organizations like the UN, the World Bank, and the ADB (Asian Development Bank).

- Multinational NGOs: Large non-government organizations, such as Amnesty International, CARE, Doctors without Borders and the World Wildlife Fund (WWF)

- Smaller NGOs: Hundreds of locally based, often grassroots organizations devoted often to one particular issue or problem, be it women's health, micro-finance or political education.

- Volunteer organizations: Organizations that rely on volunteers, though they may pay a stipend.

There are also private companies involved in development work and branches of private companies that work as a non-profit on development-related issues. For example, many of the major consulting and tax consulting companies have arms dedicated to the issues of development, privatization and economic development. Their clients are mainly governments and the public multinationals.

Volunteering for development work

Volunteering is often the first step for many people to get involved in development work, though volunteering can be an attractive option even if you don't envision a long-term career in development.

Visit Vault at **www.vault.com** for insider company profiles, expert advice, career message boards, expert resume reviews, the Vault Job Board and more.

VAULT CAREER LIBRARY 319

Volunteering, either on a long-term (up to two years) or short-term (a few months) basis is a great way to experience another culture while making a difference.

There are thousands of volunteer opportunities out there, offering you the chance to get involved in whatever your particular passion or geographic preference is. The most famous organization for Americans is the Peace Corps, but there are numerous other organizations and agencies that offer opportunities for committed volunteers.

Most volunteer assignments are just that: volunteer, meaning you won't be drawing a salary. In some cases, though, you may draw a stipend. A stipend is a living allowance to cover basic necessities, so that while you might not be saving any money, you won't be out of pocket either. Some programs will cover airfare and housing. When evaluating whether or not volunteering is feasible for you, consider loan-forgiveness – many universities have loan-forgiveness programs for graduates who choose to work in the nonprofit sector.

Many volunteer opportunities require you to pay the organization for the opportunity to volunteer. Think seriously about these types of opportunities, especially for "volunteer" programs that are for teaching English. While it is great to have the support these programs offer, you could easily be paid for doing the same work.

Day in the Life: Peace Corps Volunteer, Senegal

Mark is a Peace Corps Volunteer in Senegal, West Africa.

6:30 a.m.: Thwunk! Thwunk! The sound has been creeping into my sleep for about an hour now, and I finally wake up and acknowledge it. Outside my hut, the women of the village have been up since pounding millet.

7:15 a.m.: I dress – no shower now, but one later. With no electricity or running water, a shower in the morning would be a luxury. Plus, I know I'm going to get dirty today, so what's the point?

7:45 a.m.: Time for a leisurely breakfast in the family compound. We all sleep in our own huts, and meet in the middle for meals and socializing. I sit on a raised dais and drink the local coffee – bitter but good. As I drink, I think about what I have to do today: the upcoming meeting, the state of my motorcycle – do I have enough gas?

8:00 a.m.: I wave goodbye to my host family – the men are heading out to the fields and the women are cooking or going out on water runs. I hop on my motorcycle with 50 villages in my area of responsibility, good, reliable transport is a major concern. Luckily this little guy hasn't let me down yet.

8:30 a.m.: I drive along the dusty roads and wave to the occasional villager I see. After two years here, they all know me, and I know most of them.

9:15 a.m.: I arrive at my target village, dusty and hot. Even though it's still relatively early, the sun seems impossibly high in the sky, like it's been every day. Senegal is one of the hottest places on earth. Sometimes, I feel like I spend every day just sweating.

9:30 a.m.: The women of the village are slowly gathering in one of the central compounds around me. Today is our fifth meeting, and we're actually going to get started on the project we've been talking about for two months now: planting a fruit orchard. The women will use the fruit to supplement their family's diets, or to sell for some surplus cash at the market.

10:00 a.m.: All the women have finally arrived. Time is a different concept here: having everyone together an hour after the meeting was scheduled is actually great. Heck, I was even 10 minutes late! I explain what we're going to be doing today, and then we all head down to the field that's designated to be the orchard.

10:45 a.m.: We're hard at work in the future orchard, carefully preparing the fruit seedlings in little bags of soil and lining them up in the ground. As we work, the women chatter and tease me. They all want to know when I'm going to bring my girlfriend to live in the compound. The fact that I don't have a girlfriend doesn't seem to stop them! They also ask about my family, and tell me about theirs.

12:00 p.m.: A good morning's work, and time to get out of the sun. I have lunch at one of the compounds and share news with the men of my host family. Then a short nap, a quick play with some of the smaller kids, and then it's time to be off. I'll be back next month when the seedlings start to sprout.

1:30 p.m.: I head towards the nearest town, realizing I've actually got a free afternoon. This is a rarity – with the number of villages I'm responsible for, I usually have two or even three meetings in a given day. This is good – I've got some shopping to do, not to mention getting some more gas for the motorcycle...

2:30 p.m.: Fuda is the central town around here, a hub for all the villages in the area. I wander through the market, picking out some vegetables for my family. They don't receive a stipend for hosting me, so I try to help out in other ways. Buying some vegetables to add to the family's cooking budget and (I've got to admit – bring some changes in my diet!) is a good way to help out.

3:30 p.m.: Potatoes, tomatoes, onions, a couple of delicious looking oranges, gas for my motorcycle and a new shirt for myself. All in order. I've still got time and some energy, so I stop by a local bar. I hope to see one or both of the other Peace Corps volunteers that serve in the area, but I'm out of luck.

4:00 p.m.: I down a local beer – like the coffee it's bitter but good! I chat with the owners of the bar and a couple of men who have sought refuge on the cool patio. They all know me by now, and after studying the local language fairly intensively during my first year I'm now comfortable enough to talk bout anything.

4:30 p.m.: No more beer, I have a long drive ahead of me back to my village. I leave a note for the other PCs, telling them I'll be back on Saturday, and telling them to look for me. Then it's back on the motorcycle and the dusty roads.

6:00 p.m.: My favorite time of the day. The work is over, I've had my shower, and the heat is slipping away as the sun starts to set. All around the village people are drifting between compounds, talking and catching up on the news of the day. We have plenty of visitors over at our house. I relax on our dais in the middle of the compound, trying to forget about the busy day I have ahead of me tomorrow. It'll take care of itself.

Visit Vault at **www.vault.com** for insider company profiles, expert advice, career message boards, expert resume reviews, the Vault Job Board and more.

V\ULT CAREER LIBRARY   321

8:00 p.m.: Supper is prepared by my 8 year old "niece," who is just learning to cook. Tonight it's chicken and a rice mixture we eat with our hands. The sun is setting now, and after eating we lie back on the dais, staring up at the sky. We talk about astronomy and the stars, then listen to the BBC on the radio for a while. After, we discuss international politics and the state of the world. The villagers are very interested in the world outside, and since I've come to live here I've become much more aware of world events too. Funny to think that in a tiny village on the edge of Africa the people are more informed than in some of the biggest cities back home.

10:00 p.m.: My host dad wakes me gently. I've drifted off to sleep outside on the dais, and now it's time to go to my hut and my real bed.

Employer Directory

American Cancer Society
1599 Clifton Rd. NE
Atlanta, GA 30345
Phone: (404) 320-3333
Fax: (404) 982-3677
www.cancer.org

American Civil Liberties Union
125 Broad St., 18th Fl.
New York, NY 10004-2400
Phone: (212) 549-2500
Fax: (212) 549-2646
www.aclu.org

AmeriCorps
16000 Dallas Pkwy., Ste. 400
Dallas, TX 75248
Phone: (972) 490-1776
www.americorp.com

American Red Cross
430 17th St., NW
Washington, DC 20006-5307
Phone: (202) 737-8300
Fax: (202) 942-2024
www.redcross.org

American Heart Association
7272 Greenville Ave.
Dallas, TX 75231-4596
Phone: (800) 242-8721
Fax: (214) 706-1191
www.americanheart.org

Big Brothers Big Sisters
230 N. 13th St.
Philadelphia, PA 19107
Phone: (215) 567-7000
Fax: (215) 567-0394
www.bbbsa.org

The Ford Foundation
320 E. 43rd St.
New York, NY 10017
Phone: (212) 573-5000
Fax: (212) 351-3677
www.fordfound.org

Habitat for Humanity
121 Habitat St.
Americus, GA 31709-3498
Phone: (229) 924-6935
Fax: (229) 924-4157
www.habitat.org

Human Rights Watch
350 5th Ave., 34th Fl.
New York, NY 10118-3299
Phone: (212) 290-4700
Fax: (212) 736-1300
www.hrw.org

National Women's Law Center
11 Dupont Circle, NW
Suite 800
Washington, DC 20036
Phone: (202) 588-5180
www.nwlc.org

Open Society Institute
400 W. 59th St.
New York, NY 10019
Phone: (212) 548-0600
Fax: (212) 548-4679
www.soros.org

Visit Vault at **www.vault.com** for insider company profiles, expert advice,
career message boards, expert resume reviews, the Vault Job Board and more.

VAULT CAREER LIBRARY   323

Peace Corps
1111 20th St. NW
Washington, DC 20526
Phone: (202) 692-2230
Fax: (202) 692-2901
www.peacecorps.gov

RAND
2200 Rand Bldg.
Buffalo, NY 14203
Phone: (716) 853-0802
Fax: (716) 854-8480
www.randcapital.com

Rotary International
1 Rotary Center, 1560 Sherman Ave.
Evanston, IL 60201-3698
Phone: (847) 866-3000
Fax: (847) 328-8281
www.rotary.org

The Salvation Army National Corporation
615 Slaters Ln.
Alexandria, VA 22313
Phone: (703) 684-5500
Fax: (703) 684-3478
www.salvationarmyusa.org

UNICEF
3 United Nations Plaza
New York, NY 10017
Phone: (212) 326-7000
Fax: (212) 887-7465
www.unicef.com

United Way of America
701 N. Fairfax St.
Alexandria, VA 22314-2045
Phone: (703) 836-7112
Fax: (703) 683-7840
http://national.unitedway.org

Public Relations

What is PR?

It's hard to give an all-encompassing definition of public relations because it is practiced in so many different ways for different people and organizations. PR includes publicity, press agentry, book publicity, propaganda (for the government), corporate communications, crisis management, and advertising.

Like advertising, the concept of "public relations" existed long before the 20th century. Socrates is said to have remarked that "the way to a good reputation is to endeavor to be what you desire to appear." In Ecclesiastes, the Bible says, "Have regard for your name, since it will remain for you longer than a great store of gold." And Greenland was given its name because the Danish government wanted to encourage settlement there – even though "Iceland" may have been more appropriate. But the business as we know it today was born at the end of World War I. In a nutshell, PR is chiefly concerned with image management, and it is intended to help individuals, corporations, governments, and other organizations communicate effectively with the public.

The term "public" can suggest many different groups. For a corporation, it can mean employees, shareholders, environmental groups, or the government. For an individual, it could mean voters, fans, or an entire community. PR professionals deal with perception, representation, and effective communication. For example, they help employers communicate with employees, customers to understand the companies that serve them, and citizens to understand the politicians who serve their communities. At the same time, PR agents analyze trends – they study existing social attitudes and advise their clients about how they can win the support of the "publics" they answer to. In some cases, the PR agent tries to shape the attitudes of the general population so that they will respond in a positive way. At its best, PR presents a true image of reality to the public, and facilitates an effective, honest dialogue. But at the core of it all, their job is to present their clients to the public in a favorable light, which is why people tend to associate PR with "spin."

Public Relations History

A little background

Though publicity and press agentry (essentially getting clients' names into newspapers) were common in the 19th century, PR as we know it is generally considered to be a 20th century phenomenon. It was born during a period of increasing hostility toward big business. Early in the century, investigative reporters – disparagingly referred to as muckrakers – began exposing the rampant corruption of corporate America. Among the most popular of these exposes were Ida Tarbell's History of the Standard Oil Company and Upton Sinclair's The Jungle. The latter sparked the creation of the Federal Food and Drugs Act in 1906. In response to the scrutiny, corporations began taking steps to improve their reputations. Several railroad companies retained ex-journalists and ex-press agents to handle publicity issues. The Publicity Bureau, founded in 1900, was retained by railroad companies and other businesses who feared they were next in

Visit Vault at **www.vault.com** for insider company profiles, expert advice, career message boards, expert resume reviews, the Vault Job Board and more.

VAULT CAREER LIBRARY 325

line for legislation. Soon thereafter, a few other publicity agencies popped up, and several organizations, including the United States Marine Corps and the University of Pennsylvania, set up their own publicity offices.

During World War I, the government began using PR extensively. In 1917, President Wilson endorsed the creation of the Committee on Public Information. Led by George Creel, the CPI was staffed by several budding architects of the PR industry, including Edward Bernays and Carl Byoir. There they learned, according to the Museum of Public Relations, that "words could be used as weapons." To gain public support for the war effort, encourage enlistment, and sell Liberty Bonds, the CPI organized public rallies, reached out to non-English speaking men eligible for the draft, and created newsreel announcements to urge people to contribute to the war effort.

The "Father of Spin"

Many of today's major PR firms were founded in the period directly following the war, and the basic groundwork of the industry was laid by the founders of those firms. The business as we know it was largely the brainchild of Edward Bernays, the fabled "Father of Spin." The nephew of Sigmund Freud, Bernays is said to have inherited the famed psychoanalyst's knack for understanding human behavior. He also possessed a trait critical to the PR business – the ability to anticipate changes in public opinion. Early in his career, he worked as a press agent for the theatre. As a member of the CPI, he helped sell the war as an effort to "Make the World Safe for Democracy." In 1919, Bernays set up shop in New York, calling himself a "public relations counselor," and handled communications and marketing-related "persuasion projects" for clients including the U.S. War Department and the American Tobacco Company. For the former, he convinced businesses to hire returning war veterans. For the latter, he created a campaign to convince women that smoking helped them to stay slim. He claimed smoking also disinfected the mouth, and went on to paint cigarettes as figurative "torches of freedom" for women, encouraging them to contest the taboo against female smoking in public by marching down Fifth Avenue on Easter Day in 1929, cigarettes in hand.

Bernays published the first book on the PR profession, Crystallizing Public Opinion, in 1922. He felt that the average man is an intellectually limited, conformist creature, so it was up to the intellectual elite to mold public opinion. He felt that the so-called "intelligent few" were essentially social scientists who could guide the masses and influence history by applying the theories of mass psychology to corporate and political agendas. Not surprisingly, Bernays was approached for counsel by both Adolf Hitler and Spain's Francisco Franco (he turned both down). An Austrian-born Jew, Bernays reportedly lamented the fact that Joseph Goebbels, the notorious Nazi, kept a copy of Crystallizing Public Opinion on his desk.

Bernays pioneered the practice of promoting corporate agendas through social causes. In his own words, he helped his clients "create events and circumstances from which favorable publicity would stem." To that end, he developed "public service" agendas for unnamed corporate sponsors. After WWI, for example, he was called upon to help an ailing hair net company. Bernays urged labor commissioners to require women who worked with machinery to wear hair nets for their safety and waitresses to wear them in the interests of hygiene. He never named the hair net company, but sales improved. To help sell one client's bacon, he published a survey of 5,000 doctors who agreed that Americans should eat big breakfasts. He later orchestrated "Light's Golden Jubilee," a global media event in celebration of the invention of the light bulb, which was ghost-sponsored by General Electric.

Further growth

After WWI and throughout the Depression, the PR industry continued to grow. The National Association of Public Relations Counsel was founded in 1936, and the American Council on Public Relations formed in 1939. In 1948, the NAPC and ACPR were merged to form the Public Relations Society of America, which still exists today. Just as it did during WWI, PR grew considerably during WWII. The federal government created the Office of War Information in 1942 and used PR to develop support and distribute information. The division was later renamed the United States Information Agency and continues to disseminate news across the globe.

In the 1940s and '50s, Bernays continued to help political leaders use mass persuasion to their advantage. During this period he wrote the famous "Engineering of Consent" in which he explained, among other things, the particular usefulness of visual symbols to influence the masses. And while universities and journalism schools had been offering PR courses since 1920 (the first to offer a PR curriculum was the University of Illinois), Boston University created the first school wholly dedicated to public relations in 1947.

Few people outside the industry have every heard of Bernays, largely because he was a staunch believer in the hidden yet omnipresent PR professional. For him, the PR counselor is ever the strategist, never the voice. This attitude underlies another of Bernays' innovations – the front organization. For example, in the late 1940s and early 1950s, a newly elected government in Guatemala threatened to take over some of the plantations owned by the United Fruit Company and divide them among the peasants. When Bernays was called in, he set up the Middle America Information Bureau, which was financed by – you guessed it – United Fruit. The Bureau disseminated information to American newspapers about communist influences in Guatemala, and soon the Guatemalan government was overthrown in a CIA-backed rebellion. If you think that such tactics are a thing of the past, think again. In the early 1990s, several PR firms became embroiled in ethics controversies for taking on questionable accounts. For example, Hill and Knowlton drummed up support for the war against Iraq by creating a group called "Citizens for a Free Kuwait." What became clear later was that the $11 million account was more than 99 percent funded by the exiled Kuwaiti Government. Another classic example is Burson-Marsteller's work to develop a National Smokers Alliance, funded by members of the tobacco industry.

Entertainment PR

Henry Rogers, known as the master of entertainment PR, entered the industry by launching his own publicity firm in 1936. Rogers is credited with setting many ethical and creative standards for the PR profession, and is often credited for bringing respect to the industry. In 1939, he helped make the then-unknown Rita Hayworth a household name by convincing a magazine editor to do a story on her. In 1945, Rogers launched the first full-scale Oscar publicity blitz, which helped Joan Crawford win the award for Best Actress. That campaign set a standard followed by studios and actors to this day. Within five years,

Visit Vault at **www.vault.com** for insider company profiles, expert advice, career message boards, expert resume reviews, the Vault Job Board and more.

V∧ULT CAREER LIBRARY   **327**

Rogers became one of the most successful independent PR agents in Hollywood. In 1950, he teamed up with Warren Cowan to create Rogers and Cowan, the largest entertainment PR agency in the world. Now a division of Shandwick, R&C later expanded to serve corporate clients as well as motion picture, television, and recording stars.

Creating an industry

From the 1950s on, PR has built upon the foundation laid by Bernays, Rogers, and a few other PR notables. Daniel Edelman founded his eponymous Chicago-based firm in the 1950s, as did Harold Burson and Bill Marsteller (today their firm is one of the largest in the business). By the late 1980s, there were more than 2,000 PR agencies in the U.S. alone, and many more around the world. All of the major U.S. agencies have foreign outposts, most of which are staffed and run by local residents. Today, the strategy aspect of PR has become one of its most important components, and the agency end of the business has begun to edge in on the territory once reserved for consulting firms.

PR has essentially created a distinction between reality and what is presented by the media. Most people don't realize that many of the stories presented in newspapers, magazines, and on TV are essentially planted by PR people. Reporters don't just go out every day and look for the news – they find much of their information in press releases prepared by PR professionals. PR agents spend a lot of time brainstorming story ideas that relate to their clients and then call up journalists to pitch them. And usually, when journalists review products, it's because publicity agents send them samples and hope to get a story or a mention.

Ironically enough, the image-making industry has a negative reputation of its own. Even though many PR professionals are ex-journalists, press releases are considered the stepchildren of journalism. This may change, however, as more journalism and communications graduates choose to pass on paltry newspaper and magazine salaries in favor of more varied, better-paid gigs in PR. Additionally, PR offers greater management potential, the chance to learn business skills, and the opportunity to apply those skills to other industries.

While PR professionals uphold the fact that their major objective is to merge the client's interest with the public interest, it's important to remember that in the end, the clients are writing the checks. Even Bernays, by the end of his life, believed that the PR business had taken a turn for the worse. And PR professionals constantly cite the need to uphold ethical standards within the industry. Still PR gaffles from none other than the leading figures in the industry have caused the industry to continue to suffer from image problems. In 1996, Rich Edelman, heir to Edelman Worldwide and now its president and CEO, said, "In this era of exploding media technologies, there is no truth except the truth you create yourself." When Esquire used that quote in an exposé of the industry that December, many PR professionals spoke out in defense of their business, noting that while spin is an essential part of PR, the term indicates "putting one's best foot forward," not manipulation. In the end, they claim that they simply want to enable an honest dialogue between their clients and the public.

Outlook

The PR industry has doubled in size over the past 15 years, and in 1999, the Bureau of Labor Statistics identified PR as one of the three fastest growing industries in the U.S. Within the PR industry, high tech has become the fastest growing specialty. Along with that growth, PR professionals expect to see a lot of changes in the business over the coming years. Because PR is too often associated with "hucksters" and "spin," many think the term PR will be phased out by agencies and some corporations. Terms such as "corporate communications" and "reputation management" (Shandwick's preferred term) will likely grow popular. PR agents also plan to improve the perception of the industry by collaborating to create a set of rules and a code of ethics to abide by. The PR Society of America has been pushing such a code for several years. There has also been talk of establishing an official education requirement for the industry.

The 1990s have been an unparalleled time for corporate mergers and acquisitions, making it a prime time for PR professionals, who have proven indispensable to the integration process. Because communications issues are so integral to a company's performance, the need for PR extends far beyond a product launch or a crisis. It is believed that the industry's reputation will improve as more executives invite PR agents to help create their management strategies, facilitate internal and external communications, and keep investors informed.

Publicist

Any publicity is good publicity

Publicists are the vanguard for high-profile clients and the cheerleaders for obscure companies. Though publicity and press agentry (essentially getting clients' names into newspapers) were common in the 19th century, PR as we know it is generally considered to be a 20th century phenomenon. It was born out of a period when people were becoming increasingly hostile towards the violations of big business. Early in the century, investigative reporters – disparagingly referred to as muckrakers – began exposing the rampant corruption of corporate America. Among the most popular of these exposes were Ida Tarbell's History of the Standard Oil Company and Upton Sinclair's The Jungle. The latter sparked the creation of the Federal Food and Drugs Act in 1906. In response to the scrutiny, corporations began taking steps to improve their reputations. Several railroad companies retained ex-journalists and ex-press agents to handle publicity issues. The Publicity Bureau, founded in 1900, was retained by railroad companies and other businesses who feared they were next in line for legislation. Soon thereafter, a few other publicity agencies popped up, and several organizations, including the United States Marine Corps and the University of Pennsylvania, set up their own publicity offices.

Publicists understand the way the media are perceived by the public and target certain demographic groups to get their clients' image across. They must also be chummy with journalists to ensure that the media will be receptive to their pitches. Radio and television special reports and magazine feature articles can often be traced back to a public relations firm or an independent publicist. PR specialists also plan events and programs such as speaking engagements, and often write speeches for politicians and business executives.

Visit Vault at **www.vault.com** for insider company profiles, expert advice, career message boards, expert resume reviews, the Vault Job Board and more.

V∧ULT CAREER LIBRARY   **329**

Hobnobbing with celebrities is one of the draws of the PR industry, but most entry-level publicists soon find out that before they can be exposed to such perks, they have to wade through grunt work and long hours. Though the pay is not high compared to other industries, the fast pace and interesting work are stimulating. Publicists are courted by the press and by their clients, and the pros enjoy a degree of celebrity themselves.

Different type of publicity employers

Work in a PR firm is one of the most popular ways to get into the business. Most major firms have departments that serve different industries, and many small to mid-size firms specialize in a few related businesses. Agencies can specialize in functions such as consumer relations, corporate communications, brand marketing, business to business relations, crisis management, event marketing, media relations, public affairs, product placement, or reputation management. Agencies also specialize in industries, such as financial services, health care, high tech and the Internet, and sports. PR agencies tend to pay pretty well – more than book publishing and nonprofits – and tend to invest the most in employee development. In addition, agency life offers the promise of structured learning and a clearly defined career path.

If you know you're interested in a specific company, or hope to move from PR to another area of a business, working for an in-house corporate communications, investor relations, or publicity department can be an exciting and fulfilling job. Though PR by definition is a behind-the-scenes job, you get a different kind of satisfaction working inside the company you are promoting. Working in publicity for a publishing house is a perfect job for people who love books and reading. Book publicists schedule book tours, work to get authors' books reviewed, and think up ways to get authors and their work featured in as many media outlets as possible.

Employer Directory

Burson-Marsteller
230 Park Ave. South
New York, NY 10003
Phone: (212) 614-4000
Fax: (212) 598-6914
www.bm.com

Edelman Worldwide
200 E. Randolph Dr., 63rd Fl.
Chicago, IL 60601
Phone: (312) 240-3000
Fax: (312) 240-2900
www.edelman.com

Hill & Knowlton
466 Lexington Ave., 3rd Fl.
New York, NY 10017
Phone: (212) 885-0300
Fax: (212) 885-0570
www.hillandknowlton.com

Ketchum
711 3rd Ave.
New York, NY 10017
Phone: (646) 935-3900
Fax: (646) 935-4499
www.ketchum.com

Waggener Edstrom Inc.
3 Centerpointe, Ste. 300
Lake Oswego, OR 97035
Phone: (503) 443-7000
Fax: (503) 443-7001
www.wagged.com

Fleishman-Hillard Inc.
200 N. Broadway
St. Louis, MO 63102
Phone: (314) 982-1700
Fax: (314) 231-2313

Weber Shandwick Worldwide
640 5th Ave.
New York, NY 10019
Phone: (212) 445-8000
Fax: (212) 445-8001
www.webershandwick.com

Visit Vault at **www.vault.com** for insider company profiles, expert advice,
career message boards, expert resume reviews, the Vault Job Board and more.

VAULT CAREER LIBRARY   **331**

Use the Internet's
MOST TARGETED
job search tools.

Vault Job Board

Target your search by industry, function, and experience level, and find the job openings that you want.

VaultMatch Resume Database

Vault takes match-making to the next level: post your resume and customize your search by industry, function, experience and more. We'll match job listings with your interests and criteria and e-mail them directly to your in-box.

> the most trusted name in career information™

Publishing

The Book Publishing Industry

By most standards book publishing is a modestly sized industry. According to the U.S. Department of Labor's U.S. Industrial Outlook, the publishing business generates over $25 billion in annual revenue, which, compared to the income of a single company like Microsoft ($32 billion in 2003) doesn't seem like much. In fact, many people would probably hesitate to call book publishing an "industry" at all since the product is "intellectual property" and publishers generally lack manufacturing operations.

Whatever you call it though, there are over 85,000 employees at book publishing companies in the U.S. busily writing, editing, designing, marketing, and selling an extremely diverse array of products for both business and consumer markets. The content of these publications runs the gamut from romance novels to children's books, tenth-grade math textbooks to bibles, and timeless literary fiction to cookbooks. In all, over two billion books are sold in the United States every year (Communications Industry Forecast, 2002) 60,000 of which are wholly new titles.

The companies that drive the publishing industry are themselves a disparate bunch, comprised of multi-national media conglomerates and smaller independent presses.

Publishing operations are an eclectic mix of multinational conglomerates, private firms, associations, and educational institutions. Below is a list of the industry's largest book publishing employers in the U.S.

As you can see, ownership is heavily international, with European, Australian, and Canadian firms controlling the majority of the well-known American publishing companies.

Trade Books	Size (Revs/Growth)	Employees	Parent Co. (HQ)
Random House	$2.1 Billion (+18.3%)	6,100	Bertelsmann (Germany)
The Penguin Group	$1.4 Billion (+13.5%)	4,362	Pearson (UK)
HarperCollins Publishers	$1.1 Billion (+10.5%)	3,000	News Corp. (Australia)
Simon & Schuster	$649 Million (+8.8%)	1,518	Viacom (US)
Time Warner Books	Not available	Not available	Time Warner (US)
FSG/St. Martin's/Macmillan	$2.4 Billion (+6.8%)*	12,600	Holtzbrinck (Germany)

Visit Vault at **www.vault.com** for insider company profiles, expert advice, career message boards, expert resume reviews, the Vault Job Board and more.

VAULT CAREER LIBRARY   333

Educational/Professional			
Thomson Corporation	$7.8 Billion (+7.2%)	43,000	(Canada)
Reed Elsevier	$6.6 Billion (+17.6%)	34,600	(UK)
McGraw-Hill	$4.8 Billion (+3.1%)	16,500	(US)
Pearson Education	$4.4 Billion (+17.6%)	20,035	Pearson (UK)
Wolters Kluwer	$3.4 Billion (-1.5%)	19,766	(Netherlands)
Houghton Mifflin	$1 Billion (+0%)	4,400	(US)
John Wiley & Sons	$734 Million (+19.6%)	3,100	(US)
Children's			
Scholastic	$1.9 Billion (-2.3%)	3,000	(US)

Sources: Hoover's Inc.; corporate web sites
* Includes newspaper and other non-book publishing holdings

As you can see, the largest U.S. publishing operations are often units of even larger multinational media conglomerates. Each of these firms has many divisions, and within each of these divisions, there are a number of imprints (sometimes called 'lines' or 'lists'), which are the publicly used "brand" names for groups of books in a given market, format, and/or genre.

No matter what types of books they produce, however, you'll see the same types of publishing professionals at all of these organizations – editors, marketers, salespeople, and production specialists – performing very similar tasks.

Operating units/imprints

The operating units or divisions of book publishing companies are typically organized around their "imprints" – the brand names given to particular product lines. Often imprints specialize in certain genres or areas of interest and have names that reflect their focus. Other times the imprints are the names of companies that were acquired and have a publishing reputation that the acquiring company wishes to keep alive.

Here are some examples of the nation's largest trade book publishers and the imprints within them.

Trade Book Publishers	Imprints
Random House	Bantam, Doubleday, Dell; Pantheon; Knopf; Ballantine; Fodor's
The Penguin Group	Putnam; Viking; Dutton; Puffin; Dorling Kindersley; Rough Guides
HarperCollins Publishers	HarperCollins; Avon; Perennial; ReganBooks; Quill; Zondervan
Simon & Schuster	Pocket Books; The Free Press; Scribner
Time Warner Books	Little, Brown; Warner Books

Departments at a Book Publisher

Within each imprint or operating unit is a departmental organization structured along these lines:

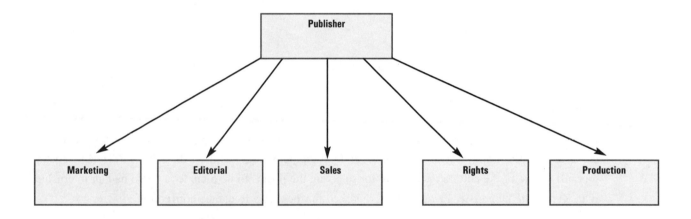

While this structure may seem fairly flat, with equally important departments reporting to a single publisher, the sales and editorial groups make the crucial business recommendations to the publisher and are responsible for delivering the most important things the company needs: quality manuscripts and sales revenue. The head of book publishing units are traditionally drawn from the editorial department, given the group's emphasis on creating compelling editorial products, although the ever-increasing emphasis on sales has meant that more top executives now come from that department.

The publisher decides which titles will be published and, of these, which titles will be pushed the hardest by the sales and marketing folks. This pecking order will be determine where the lion's share of budgeted marketing and production monies will go.

Visit Vault at **www.vault.com** for insider company profiles, expert advice, career message boards, expert resume reviews, the Vault Job Board and more.

V/\ULT CAREER LIBRARY   335

Product teams

Each title usually has a team comprised of an editor, copyeditor, proofreader, and a production staffer. Each member will handle many titles at any given time and team members will be mixed and matched throughout the operating unit. Often freelancers assist the members of the team with editing, indexing, layout, and/or graphic design.

The product teams report to their respective senior managers (developmental editors, production managers) and these senior managers work with the sales and marketing managers on things like cover art, cover copy, catalog copy, etc. The product team gets the opportunity to review and comment on everything related to the book in their particular domain (e.g., the copy editor is free to nitpick about the grammar of the marketing copy on the cover) but the senior editor responsible for the title generally gets the final say.

Day in the Life: Book Editorial Assistant

Name: Susan Hutner
Title: Editorial Assistant
Company: The Princeton Review
Age: 22

Education

BA from Hiram College. Major in English with a minor in creative writing. I worked on the college newspaper as a contributing writer, copy editor, and photography editor and on the *Hiram Review* (a poetry journal) as one of the editors responsible for selecting the poems to be included. I also had an internship with Kent State University Press, and later worked for them as a freelance copyeditor.

Professional history

After I graduated college, I wanted to do something exciting, interesting, and vastly different from anything I'd done before. Unfortunately, the circus wouldn't have me, so I decided to look for jobs in New York City. Although I loved working at a university press, I thought that working for a commercial press would give me experience in working in a faster-paced environment. I also wanted to work on more titles and different types of books so I could gain the kind of experience that would open up more professional opportunities for me. An alumna of my college who works for The Princeton Review sent me a description of a job opening there, and I applied. I've been working for The Princeton Review for two months now.

Job description

I act as a copy editor, proofreader, and, occasionally, a content editor for the K-12 division, which produces educational and test preparation titles for children and high school kids. I assist the content and production editors by entering in changes made by editors, copy editing, proofreading bluelines, editing online content, and otherwise assisting the editorial staff.

One of my first projects here was editing a book designed to teach test preparation skills to third-graders in Florida who will be taking the FCAT test. This involved making sure the language was very simple and understandable, which is actually pretty hard to do. (Try explaining to an eight-year-old how to answer multiple choice questions and you'll see what I mean.) Other titles are designed for high school kids, and those are easier to edit to grade level.

Typical day

I get in around 9:00 a.m. and spend the first part of my day doing administrative types of things like photocopying, processing invoices, making travel plans for other members of the editorial team, and following up on technical support issues for the department. After this administrative work, I get to work on copy editing and proofreading tasks until lunchtime. Among the projects I'm working on now is a new title where I am taking online content and repurposing it for print.

I take an hour for lunch, which is great because we're located in SoHo and it's a very exciting neighborhood. After lunch I go back to editorial tasks and typically attend one or more meetings. Sometimes I sit in for people who can't make the meetings and I take notes on their behalf. If the meeting is related to titles on which I am working, administrative issues for which I have some responsibility, or about general production schedules, I actively participate. In either case, these meetings are a great opportunity for me to learn about new books and to better understand how the publishing operation works. I generally get to leave at 6:00 p.m., but many of the senior editors stay until 7:00 or later.

Favorite part of job

Any chance I get to work on improving a manuscript or an online product, whether it's proofreading, copy editing, content editing, or even making sure content is consistently formatted, is great. All the seemingly minor changes I make contribute to the overall accuracy and quality of the product, which is very satisfying. The best projects are ones where I get to do some significant copy editing or content editing.

Least favorite part of job

Preparing invoices and photocopying is not much fun. I understand that I'm just starting my career, though, and I've got to pay my dues with this kind of administrative work.

Advice

Intern, intern, intern. My internship with the Kent State University Press opened so many doors for me, both personally and professionally. In addition to learning editorial skills, I also learned about how a professional office works. I had great mentors there, and I'm still very close to many of them. Because I had two years of background in publishing, it was also much easier for me to find a job once I graduated. My work there was proof that I had the skills an employer needed to do the job well. My transition from col-

Visit Vault at **www.vault.com** for insider company profiles, expert advice, career message boards, expert resume reviews, the Vault Job Board and more.

V∧ULT CAREER LIBRARY   **337**

lege to professional life also went much smoother because I knew what sort of work I would be doing and was comfortable in an office.

Day in the Life: Book Publicity

Name: Amy Ehrenreich
Title: Senior Publicist
Company: Random House Children's Books (New York, NY)
Age: 27

Education

B.A. in journalism; University of Florida. While at college I interned for a regional student-oriented entertainment publication. As an intern, I wrote a monthly food column and worked on public relations for the college swimsuit calendar. The calendar hosted an annual fashion show in South Beach, and I was responsible for pitching the event to the media, coordinating travel arrangements, and assisting during photo shoots. The internship was an invaluable experience that improved my writing skills and taught me how to multi-task and liaise with the media.

Professional history

As a self-proclaimed "book nerd" my dream occupation was in the book publishing industry and since publishing opportunities were in New York City, that's where I went. However, since I've always been an outgoing "people person" I wasn't sure that the lifestyle of writing and editing positions would be the right fit for me, so I looked for a promotional position. My first job was as an assistant to the marketing director at Promotions, Inc., an events-oriented firm that did both web and traditional promotions. I helped marketing managers run consumer outreach campaigns and my big project was the "Shot of a Lifetime" sweepstakes (where the winner of a half-court basketball shot would win a million dollars) to take place on NBC's *Today Show*. That promotion generated tons of free media and its success meant that I was assigned to more PR-oriented projects. After a year and a half of this type of work, I realized I loved working with the media, but I still wanted to work in the book publishing industry.

A friend led me to Golden Books, where I was hired as an assistant marketing manager assigned to grow their in-store event marketing programs. I wrote and produced several different "event kits" for Golden that gave bookstores costumes (e.g., *The Poky Little Puppy*), event ideas, and promo materials so they could attract large groups of children and parents to their stores. I also managed Golden's outside PR agency, and ultimately decided it would be best to handle our PR from in-house. By the time Golden Books was purchased by Random House, I was promoted to marketing manager and was ready to move into more of a PR role. In my new position, I was responsible for publicity on licensed properties and trade titles (new, author-driven books), which was very new and challenging, considering the many well-known authors published by Random House.

Job description

The main goal of my job is to generate an "advance buzz" in the trade and with consumers. I create demand and build momentum for our books to assure there will be a strong reader interest in our titles. Judging the return on investment in terms of revenue is difficult for publicity, so we judge most of our successes on the quality of impact and the amount of impressions achieved. The "pie in the sky" goals are getting media with big impressions, like *The Today Show* or *TV Guide*.

Specifically, my responsibilities are to create and implement publicity strategies for our children's titles and product lines. I am assigned books several months ahead of their pub date and I create a publicity campaign for each one. These involve proposing a budget and laying out a schedule of actions and events to promote the title. Among the many components of each campaign are: sending out galleys and books; setting up author tours; creating promotional materials (stationary, custom press kits, flyers, etc.); and setting up a promotional mailing schedule.

All of these tasks require intense logistical planning. For instance, planning an author tour involves working with the author's schedule, arranging appearances, determining the number of appearances per day, making transportation and lodging arrangements, and setting up face-to-face interviews. Knowing the media is equally important so leaving enough "lead time" and tailoring pitches to media outlets is imperative for a successful pitch. Magazines, for example, are "long-lead" media, needing galleys four to five months in advance to adhere to their press schedules. Short-lead media (local and regional TV, radio, and newspapers) can be pitched anywhere from two to four weeks beforehand.

Describe your day today

Usually I'm in the office by 8:45 a.m. and out around 7:30 p.m. The first thing I do each day is to write up a list of my top four or five goals for the day. This allows me to focus on the important tasks one at a time and still allows time for meetings and putting out the fires that pop up every day (like tracking down a missing review copy release or setting up a last-minute car service for a stranded author). Throughout the day, I'm in constant motion working on my many campaigns. This can be very challenging, but it's always rewarding, and, fortunately, I have the help of our department's two publicity assistants, one of which works very closely with me. Occasionally I travel with my touring authors.

Favorite part of job

Without a doubt my favorite part of my job is working closely with our authors. Some really amazing and incredibly intelligent people write and illustrate these books, and it's truly an honor to know them, and often astounding that they depend on me to a certain degree to ensure their books' success. Every day I am inspired by them.

Least favorite part of job

The relentless pace of a publicist's job can be challenging. It is difficult to even walk away from your desk, and especially my phone, when so many things need to be accomplished in a day. Often, just going

Visit Vault at **www.vault.com** for insider company profiles, expert advice, career message boards, expert resume reviews, the Vault Job Board and more.

VAULT CAREER LIBRARY 339

to a meeting can throw me off schedule when things pile up so quickly. But it definitely keeps you on your toes!

Advice

Five things. 1) Be creative, assertive, and be prepared. This is not a job for the meek. Outgoing people and "out-of-the-box" thinkers make the best publicists. Try not to take rejection personally if an editor or producer is not interested in your book. Remember that the reviewers and editors need you as much as you need them. 2) Create realistic goals and hit them. 3) Keep your authors happy. 4) Make contacts and network. 5). Read!!!!

Magazine Careers: Working Your Up

Every magazine has a different number of people on staff. Some features-focused magazines (like *Vanity Fair* and *Conde Nast Traveler*) have mostly copy, features and research editors; fashion publications have large fashion, photo and art departments; and so on. What follows is a general list of entry level editorial, fashion, and art department positions, plus the scoop on getting promoted to the next level.

Editorial assistants – an introduction

An unspoken rule here is that the level at which you assist has a great bearing on how far you will go and how quickly you will get there. Assisting lower level associate editors, some of which have just been promoted and given their first-ever assistant, may include more menial tasks and doesn't allow for the direct experience you'd get assisting someone on an executive level.

With most assistant level positions, salaries are usually in the same, low range. Executive assistants (usually for an editor in chief, who has both editorial and executive assistants), however, get paid almost as much as the assistant editors, in some cases more. But you aren't in it for the money, remember?

Generally, you could be an assistant for anywhere from one to five years before you are promoted from within. It all depends on how much you learn, how fast you master your menial tasks and what kind of changes may be happening within the magazine. If you are given extra editorial writing and editing responsibilities, or if you work for an executive editor or director for one or two years, you may be able to score an assistant editor's post by moving to another magazine.

The department you choose to work in will have direct bearing on how you move within the magazine. Switching directions just wastes time, so choose wisely. Select something you have a personal interest in and can dedicate yourself to for the long-term.

General responsibilities of all editorial assistants

You will do grunt work and love it. Filing, opening and sorting mail, faxing, scheduling, expense reports, typing, research, making appointments, copying and anything else that will make the editors' lives easier. You'll need excellent organizational and phone skills, and be responsible for maintaining updated contact lists, juggling the phone, faxing and figuring out which tasks are most important and which you can hold off on in an emergency. When you get promoted to a higher position, your success will depend on just how organized you are and how successful you've been in these areas.

This phase seems never-ending at times, but it prepares you for the mania to come. You definitely need to know Excel, Word and all Microsoft Office suite programs thoroughly. It's a plus if you are familiar with Desktop Publishing software like Quark. You'll also need to know how to draft letters, make charts, etc. Even though you may think that personal requests such as dry cleaning, shopping and dinner reservations are not part of your job responsibility, you'll need to realize that attitude is everything. How badly do you want to make your boss' life easier, and how much will you appreciate it when someone does it for you later on?

Salaries start at $23,000 per year plus benefits, and most large magazines pay overtime. There will be a great deal of overtime, so most months it will feel like you're making $30,000 or more.

Breakdown of Magazine Assistant Positions

Editorial assistant, features

Responsibilities

Support one or more editors with daily administrative work. After all that is done, depending on what level editor you work for, you may also: keep contacts with freelance editors, preview and open manuscripts and story proposals, answer reader mail, contribute to small news sections 100-200 word articles in the magazine, research for feature stories, write headlines and decks and keep track of story ideas and editorial planning.

Getting hired

Experience at a school newspaper, magazine or freelance contributions to other smaller local publications are a plus. A journalism and/or English education is also attractive. Also consider the topics covered at the magazine of your choice, news, economics, psychology, fashion, and so on. Any education or background that could help you come up with relevant topics and ideas is essential. This may even help you specialize in a section – such as interior design or business news.

Getting promoted

If you handle your administrative duties well and balance any writing or editing assignments, you could be promoted to assistant editor level in a year. It also depends on whom you work for. If it is an executive-level editor who allows you to take on larger responsibilities, the experience will be invaluable and essential to your promotion within or at another magazine.

Visit Vault at **www.vault.com** for insider company profiles, expert advice, career message boards, expert resume reviews, the Vault Job Board and more.

VAULT CAREER LIBRARY   341

Fashion editor/writer's assistant

Responsibilities

The fashion editors and writers conceive and compose stories. For an assistant, duties include administrative work as mentioned, but may include some editing, proofreading, research, caption and headline writing. You may also be able to write small stories and reporting for the Front of Book. (All the pages that come before the main feature stories and photo shoots in the middle to back of book. The Front of Book (FOB) usually contains short report-style stories.)

Getting hired

The requirements here are much the same as a features assistant's. A genuine interest in the magazine you are working for, and knowledge of the reader is essential as well. Some editors may ask you to make a list of ideas you'd have for certain FOB sections, just to see how you think. But, the main concern is whether or not you will be patient enough to put in the time, do the administrative work and learn slowly. There may also be times when you are called upon to write a larger story, so any clips you have from school publications, or writing samples from essays and reports you've written, would be helpful. An internship is also a plus, as is knowledge of fashion history.

Getting promoted

Some assistants wait two years, just to be passed over for a position for someone from the outside. Be sure to ask what your prospective employer's policy is on promoting from within. Others are gradually given more reports to write and pages to edit. It all depends on how quickly you work and how well you handle each responsibility, as well as how willing you are to learn the craft. The concern here is not to move up in title, but to accumulate clips and bylines. If you are an assistant who is allowed to write in every issue, and consistently given larger assignments, it is beneficial for you to remain where you are until the right opportunity arrives.

Fashion market editor's assistant

Responsibilities

There are also fashion market editors' assistants. Here you'll be doing all of the administrative work, including: calling in all the clothes for your editor's markets and assigned shoots (sometimes that means five or six shoots at once), returning all the clothes, keeping track of the items needed and there is a tremendous amount of follow-through involved, you have to be meticulous. Most of your time will be spent sitting at your desk and returning clothes or accessories from the fashion closet, which means long hours. You will not be going on any appointments unless you have built a solid relationship with your editor and she is willing to let you cover some smaller markets (like sunglasses or lingerie). This usually happens after one year. There will be long hours and tremendous amounts of scheduling. If you love clothes and would love to be a market editor, then this is the job for you.

Getting hired

Market editors look for people who are interested in becoming market editors. Previous work as an executive assistant in fashion will get you in, as will an internship at a major magazine working in the fashion market department. Be professional and polished in attitude and appearance. Market editors are representatives for their magazines and always look the part. A fashion education is not essential. Organization, computer skills and ability to juggle tasks are a plus.

Getting promoted

Countless assistants have become frustrated with the grunt work and long hours associated with this position. It is all about your boss' attitude and trust. You may start off with small markets like swimwear and lingerie or sunglasses and depending on how well you handle these responsibilities, is how long it will take to climb. It is a very competitive ladder and contacts generated are the keys, which many editors guard fiercely. It's always wise to ask up front what the chances are for increased responsibilities.

Fashion editor/stylist's assistant

Responsibilities

If you work for a fashion editor who styles shoots, you will be making travel arrangements, packing trunks of clothes, hauling them everywhere you go and keeping track of every last item you take with you. You will also be responsible for returning the items, calling the designers to get items in (although sometimes this is up to the market editors), and keeping track of ideas and ideas boards. You'll also be going on every shoot with the editor. Warning: This is very exciting and attractive to many young aspiring editors because of the glamorous veneer. It wears off very quickly and unless you have a genuine interest in photography, models, and the visual aspect of the craft, then this is not a wise choice. You are working every day of the week (weekends too), traveling at a moments notice, waking up at 5am and going to bed past 12 midnight at times. You have to love it, and realize that you are an assistant and most assistants are treated that way on and off shoots. If you have a large ego and aren't willing to do anything and everything your editor tells you, then this is best left alone.

Getting hired

Stylists look for proficient, humble, hard-working assistants. You'll be keeping longer hours then they do, and they work long hours, so you need to be dedicated. You will also be working with difficult cranky photographers and models with major egos at times. To succeed, you must have a calm, patient and diplomatic manner, no matter what is going on around you. It has also common for stylists to request assistants that can commit to the job for more than a year. Usually two to three years is essential. Your background should include some work with photographers (perhaps assisting) or with another stylist. Fashion design and photography education are most desirable.

Getting promoted

After two to three years working with a top-notch stylist at a major fashion publication or a cutting edge magazine, you can go to a smaller publication and style your own shoots. Usually most assistants begin to freelance on the side for lesser-known publications in order to build a portfolio. Without a portfolio it will take you longer. Please be advised that this is tricky – most major companies do not allow employees to freelance (there may be an intellectual property laws stipulated in your contract). You could also look for an opportunity to style style smaller shoots for your

Visit Vault at **www.vault.com** for insider company profiles, expert advice, career message boards, expert resume reviews, the Vault Job Board and more.

V∆ULT CAREER LIBRARY   **343**

employer – perhaps still life styling – and if you have the right eye for your magazine, you may be promoted.

Photo Assistant

Responsibilities

Administrative responsibilities abound here as well. But you'll also log in and return film and portfolios, correspond with photographers, assist with travel arrangements for shoots, order prints, prepare expense reports, invoices and budgets, send issues to contributing photographers, and organize countless files for the department.

Getting hired

An interest in photography, especially the type used in the magazine you've chosen, is a must. Knowledge of and an educational background in photography are also beneficial. Being good with numbers and budgets is essential, as are follow-through skills. You may also have to be diplomatic when faced with irate requests from photographers and other editors.

Getting promoted

After 1 year you should be able to move up to assistant or associate level, where you'll have direct relationships with photographers, organize shoots, and have developed a good eye for the kind of look your magazine prefers. This takes time, however, and it all depends on how quickly you learn your craft.

Art Assistant

Responsibilities

You'll probably be doing more administrative follow-up and page proof trafficking here than anything else. There will also be photo research and art research, where you will find pictures and photographs from agencies for relevant pages. Computer knowledge and use is essential, since you will be using scanners, Quark and Photoshop.

Getting hired

A BFA and folio of past layouts or design projects you've worked on in school is needed, in addition to extensive knowledge of Desktop Publishing programs.

Getting promoted

To get promoted, you will have to master the look of the magazine you work for, and after work under somcone who allows you added responsibilities with pages. This usually comes after two years. It is an enormous responsibility to manage the total look of a magazine and many places require you to have added education in mastering copy fitting as well as visuals.

Production Assistant

Responsibilities

You'll be responsible for maintaining the deadline schedules of the magazine and following up on all internal delays, in addition to the typical administrative duties. This department focuses on all stages of editorial production, from beginning concepts, page numbers and budgets to final approvals by editors and editors-in-chief. Your job will be to learn this and master it, eventually taking some of the pressure off your superior.

Getting hired

A genuine interest in management and production is essential. Don't take this job as a back door to another department. You have to be extremely organized, willing to work long hours, and able to work well under pressure and when things go wrong. Knowledge of Quark and Photoshop is also a plus.

Getting promoted

After a solid year at this job, you may be able to demonstrate the responsibility and attention to warrant a promotion. It really depends on how much your supervisor thinks you're capable of.

Copy Assistant

Responsibilities

In addition to administrative duties, usually for the copy chief, you will be responsible for maintaining records of what pages and projects have gone through the departments as part of the production process. You may be asked to line edit short copy and fact-check on credits as well.

Getting hired

An interest in the written word, familiarity with the *Chicago Manual of Style* and a journalism or English background is key. Experience at a newspaper or internship is also a plus. Attention to detail and the ability to work long-hours under deadline to get the job done are required.

Getting promoted

Pitching in to lighten the load wherever you can here is the fastest way to a promotion; familiarity with your magazine's writing style and effective line editing will also give you a leg up in a year.

Research Assistant

Responsibilities

This is also called fact checking. You'll be responsible for the department's administrative duties as well as any research requests that come in from other editors. This department's responsibility is to be certain that every fact it publishes is correct. Your job will be to help them do that. This is great for someone who loves research and fact-finding.

Visit Vault at **www.vault.com** for insider company profiles, expert advice, career message boards, expert resume reviews, the Vault Job Board and more.

VAULT CAREER LIBRARY 345

Getting hired

This is also not a back door position into another department and there is careful screening for that. A two-year commitment is usually preferred. Attention to detail and a great deal of follow-through are essential. Also have knowledge of Lexis-Nexis, Baseline and other research sources.

Getting promoted

Being dedicated to tackling anything, from the longest features to the smallest reports, will help you rise quickly. Promotion is more an issue of being in the right place at the right time – i.e., whenever an opening comes up.

Employer Directory

Reed Business Information

360 Park Avenue South

New York, NY 10010

www.reedbusiness.com/employment

nycjobs@reedbusiness.com

Reed Business Information, the largest business-to-business publisher in the U.S., offers business professionals in the media, manufacturing, electronics, construction and retail industries more than 100 market-leading business-to-business publications, 75 Webzines and Web portals, custom publishing, directories, research and direct-marketing lists. RBI is a member of the Reed Elsevier Group plc (NYSE: RUK and ENL) – a world-leading publisher and information provider operating in the science and medical, legal, education and business-to-business industry sectors.

Bantam Doubleday Dell

(part of Bertelsmann AG)

1540 Broadway

New York, NY 10036

Phone: (212) 354-6500

Conde Nast Publications Inc.

4 Times Square, 17th Fl.

New York, NY 10036

Phone: (212) 286-2860

Fax: (212) 286-5960

www.condenast.com

Harcourt Brace

15 E. 26th Street

New York, NY 10010

Phone: (212) 614-7850

HarperCollins Publishers, Inc.

10 E. 53rd St.

New York, NY 10022

Phone: (212) 207-7000

Fax: (212) 207-7145

www.harpercollins.com

Hearst Magazines

959 8th Ave.

New York, NY 10019

Phone: (212) 649-2000

Fax: (212) 765-3528

www.hearstcorp.com

Houghton Mifflin

Houghton Mifflin Company

222 Berkeley St.

Boston, MA 02116-3764

Phone: (617) 351-5000

Fax: (617) 351-1105

www.hmco.com

Visit Vault at **www.vault.com** for insider company profiles, expert advice, career message boards, expert resume reviews, the Vault Job Board and more.

VAULT CAREER LIBRARY   **347**

John Wiley & Sons, Inc.
111 River St.
Hoboken, NJ 07030
Phone: (201) 748-6000
Fax: (201) 748-6008
www.wiley.com

The McGraw-Hill Companies, Inc.
1221 Avenue of the Americas
New York, NY 10020
Phone: (212) 512-2000
Fax: (212) 512-3840
www.mcgraw-hill.com

Pearson Education, Inc.
1 Lake St.
Upper Saddle River, NJ 07458
Phone: (201) 236-7000
Fax: (201) 236-3290
www.pearsoned.com

The Penguin Group
80 Strand
London
WC2R ORL, United Kingdom
Phone: +44-2070103396
Fax: +44-2070106642
www.penguin.com

Random House, Inc.
1745 Broadway
New York, NY 10019
Phone: (212) 782-9000
Fax: (212) 302-7985
www.randomhouse.com

Scholastic Corporation
557 Broadway
New York, NY 10012
Phone: (212) 343-6100
Fax: (212) 343-6934
www.scholastic.com

Simon & Schuster, Inc.
1230 Avenue of the Americas
New York, NY 10020
Phone: (212)-698-7000
Fax: (212) 698-7099
www.simonsays.com

The Thomson Corporation
Toronto-Dominion Bank Tower,
66 Wellington Street West
Toronto, Ontario M5K 1A1, Canada
Phone: (416) 360-8700
Fax: (416) 360-8812
www.thomson.com

Time, Inc.
1271 Avenue of the Americas
New York, NY 10020-1393
Phone: (212) 522-1212
Fax: (212) 522-0602

Time, Warner Books
1271 Avenue of the Americas
New York, NY 10020-1393
Phone: (212) 522-7200
Fax: (212) 522-7989
www.twbookmark.com

W.W. Norton & Company
500 Fifth Ave.
New York, NY 10110
Phone: (212) 354-5500
Fax: (212) 869-0865
www.wwnorton.com

Real Estate

History of the Real Estate Industry in the United States

Real estate is tangible. It's a piece of land and any building or structures on it, as well as the air above and the ground below. Everyone comes into direct contact with real estate. The places we live, work, go to school, vacation, shop and exercise, are all assets to be bought, sold and rented. And it's always been an important element of the economy. .

Real estate has always been big business in the United States. Shortly after the signing of the Constitution, the federal government began transferring one billion acres of land to private owners through land sales and land grants. In the 1830s, for example, the government sold 20 million acres at roughly $1.25 per acre. This sounds like a bargain to us today, but at the time the vast majority of citizens couldn't afford that price. Consequently, a grassroots group called the Free Soil Movement formed and lobbied the government for an alternate method of distributing land.

The Homestead Act of 1862 was Congress' answer to the appeal. Settlers who did not already own what was considered a "judicious" amount of land were given title to 160 acres for each adult in the family. There was no cash exchange. Instead, the understanding was that the settlers would live on and improve the land for a period of at least five years. This program was very successful and similar federal land distribution programs followed until the later part of the nineteenth century. In total, the U.S. government distributed more than 300 million acres of public property to private landowners through the Homestead Act, creating the basis for the real estate market.

For the first time in the history of the young country, there was a system in place by which one landowner could transfer property rights to another through sale, lease or trade. This led to a tremendous amount of speculation. Some investors accumulated a tremendous amount of wealth, while others lost everything.

At the end of the 19th century, America was transitioning from an agricultural society to a manufacturing economy. Citizens flocked to urban areas to work at the burgeoning factories. For example, as the Midwest's industrial center, Chicago reached a population of one million people more rapidly than any other city in history. Settled in the 1830s, the city grew from less than 1,000 inhabitants to become the fifth largest city in the world by 1900.

The values of urban properties skyrocketed. By 1920, 50 percent of America's population lived in cities. This urban density created opportunities for real estate development as housing, office buildings, industrial facilities, hotels and retail centers were constructed to meet the demands of city dwellers.

Skyrocketing property values and associated costs began pushing people and businesses outside the city, just as advances in transportation made living outside the city easier. Suburbs, communities just outside urban centers, began to spread. Developers made these planned communities attractive by building along the transportation routes so people could easily commute to their jobs in the cities.

Technological advances influenced the building boom of the 1920s. Communities were wired for electricity, new machines such as elevators helped meet additional demand for space and allowed the construc-

Visit Vault at **www.vault.com** for insider company profiles, expert advice,
career message boards, expert resume reviews, the Vault Job Board and more.

VAULT CAREER LIBRARY   349

tion of ever-taller buildings. Planned communities began taking shape in the suburbs, while skyscrapers changed the way the cities looked. One hundred buildings higher than 25 stories were constructed in this decade, most of them in New York City, with Chicago a distant second.

The Great Depression crippled most industries – including real estate. Values dipped below debt levels, causing a collapse. The federal government put the domestic financial markets through a major overhaul and was shrewd enough to include real estate financing as part of the New Deal programs. The Federal Housing Administration (FHA) was created in 1930 to provide mortgage insurance, lowering the risk on real estate loans and making lending more palatable for savings and loans and banks. The government also created the Federal Home Loan Bank System (FHLB) to supervise and regulate local banks. In 1938, the Federal National Mortgage Association (FNMA or Fannie Mae) was created to provide a secondary mortgage market as well as to lure investment capital in the mortgage market, and continues to play a very important role in supplying capital to the mortgage market today. These New Deal programs ultimately made the real estate finance market more sophisticated and secure.

America and the real estate industry slowly climbed out of the Depression only to fall headlong into the Second World War. Development was put on hold during the war, but once the GIs returned from overseas, another era of prosperity began. A tremendous amount of demand for housing emerged virtually overnight. By 1946, new housing construction quadrupled to over 500,000 homes. In the postwar period, a white picket fence and peaceful green lawn proved very appealing. Two-thirds of the 15 million homes built in the 1950s were in the suburbs.

The decade was also a period of expansion for the highways, which provided access to more areas by car and truck. This enabled all types of real estate (e.g., hotels, industrial and retail centers) to be located further outside the city. Hotel chains like Holiday Inn started popping up along roadways across the country. The suburban shopping mall also became popular in this era.

As the suburbs grew, the cities slumped. By 1960, many urban centers hadn't seen new office building development in 30 years. The decay of America's urban areas didn't go unnoticed. Community activism and political pressure led to the creation of a cabinet position in 1965 focused on improving urban housing – what today is known as the Department of Housing and Urban Development (HUD). The central business districts of America's urban centers saw a number of new buildings (both commercial and retail) constructed during the last three decades of the twentieth century, spurred by growth in the service industry, increased access to financing and municipal incentives.

Today, the real estate industry is considered one of the most dynamic and healthy sectors in the American economy – people may divest their stocks, but they always need a place to live, work and shop. (To read more about the history of real estate, read *Real Estate Development* by Miles, Berns and Weiss.)

Industry Trends

As of 2003, the real estate business employed close to five million people. Opportunities abound for candidates to earn staggering income levels. Those who work in this sector often enjoy greater flexibility in job responsibilities than in other industries.

There can be drawbacks, though, in the form of low paying entry-level positions, competitive co-workers and long hours when starting out. Furthermore, once you're established relocation can be detrimental to your career, as this industry is often geography-specific.

The real estate sector is largely dependent on the economy; small shifts can impact trends significantly. For example, the technology industry boom certainly helped the real estate industry in the 1990s. There was more demand for space-both commercial and residential-and asset values skyrocketed. The subsequent technology bust had a dramatic effect on some parts of the sector. Commercial firms that focused on office and retail development projects now find the market glutted with available space.

The residential real estate market is also affected by economic swings. Unemployment and interest rates impact both consumer confidence and buying power. Although the U.S. economy was mired in recession for the first several years of the 21st century, the residential real estate market was one of the few bright spots. In 2002, home sales shot up 8 percent and housing starts grew by 7 percent.

There are many reasons for the current residential housing boom. The aging United States population and the influx of immigrants has increased the demand for households. The rockiness of the stock market makes investing in real estate look very appealing. The Federal Reserve is playing a big part as well. Lower mortgage rates and minimal inflations meant that in 2003, a 30-year home mortgage could be had at a 5 percent rate. The drop in mortgage rates meant that homeowners could refinance, freeing up more cash for them – and in the process making real estate look like an even more attractive investment.

The wealth isn't spread equally. Residential real estate values continue to soar on the coasts. During the real estate boom that began after the end of the 1991 recession, homes and apartments in the Boston-to-Washington corridor and California have doubled, tripled or quadrupled in value. Even in fast-growing areas in other parts of the country, such as Las Vegas, gains have been more modest because there is more land on which to build houses and apartments.

The remarkable gains in the residential real estate market have provoked fears among some economists and homeowners that the real estate market is a bubble about to burst. The prices of homes, especially on the West and East Coast, have outpaced the ability of many prospective first-time buyers to purchase a place to live. A jump in mortgage rates would stop the current trend of refinancing in its tracks and make it more difficult for many homeowners to make mortgage payments. A revival in the economy could cause investors to stop investing in real estate and start investing in stocks. (Such a revival would, on the other hand, help the commercial and industrial real estate markets.) In the meantime, however, the residential real estate market continues to be an engine of the economy – and of the real estate job market.

Visit Vault at **www.vault.com** for insider company profiles, expert advice, career message boards, expert resume reviews, the Vault Job Board and more.

V/\ULT CAREER LIBRARY **351**

Residential Real Estate Brokers

Residential real estate agents help buyers and sellers in the process of selling or renting residential property. Some agents work with buyers, helping them find places to live and negotiating with sellers. Other agents work with the sellers. Agents rarely represent both buyers and sellers since this is perceived as a conflict of interest. For property rentals, almost all agents represent property owners. There are close to 500,000 real estate brokers and agents in the United States.

Agents are usually independent sales professionals who contract their services to sponsoring real estate brokers in exchange for a commission-sharing agreement. The commission on a home sale varies by market but is roughly five to six percent of the sale price. This commission is split four ways among the seller's agent, buyer's agent and the sponsoring brokers with whom each agent is associated. Many agents work solely on commission and don't get much in the way of benefits. Agents are expected to cover most of the overhead necessary to perform their jobs.

In order to sell real estate services, you must be a licensed professional in the state where you do business. To become a realtor, all states require that you pass a written exam focused on real estate law and transactions and be affiliated with a broker. Most states require you to be at least 18 years old and a high school graduate, and to have completed a minimum number of classroom hours. Some states waive the classroom requirements for active attorneys or offer correspondence course credit options in lieu of the classroom hour requirement. The license fee depends on the state, but expect to pay around $100 for the exam and $400 for the classes.

Although there are different organizations through which you can receive your classroom instruction, the state government issues and oversees licenses. If you visit the National Association of Realtor's web site at www.realtor.org, you can find information about residential real estate as well as licensing requirements for each state and locations of authorized real estate classes.

This industry attracts all types of personalities. There's a potpourri of career switchers, from lawyers to housewives, who end up in residential real estate. If you like being your own boss and interacting with people, being a realtor can be very rewarding.

Tenant Representation

A tenant representation agent, commonly known as a "tenant rep," represents companies and other corporate clients looking to lease or buy either a portion of a property or an entire real estate asset. A large part of this job involves business development. Since tenant reps are often responsible for building their own book of business, prospecting for new clients is a big part of the job. Like residential agents, tenant reps are left to their own devices to find prospects. Although there's some direction by the broker and senior tenant reps in the office, for the most part you're cold-calling tenants or companies. First, you need to give the person on the other end of the phone a compelling reason to meet with you, then you must pitch the business. It's a tough sell.

Tenant representation is very competitive, even cutthroat. You're not only competing against outside reps but those inside your office. In fact, some tenant rep brokers think the competition inside is worse than outside the shops. Often there are disputes about who is entitled to chase what business. Ultimately, the senior brokers tend to win. Deal protocol is important to consider when you're selecting brokers because often there are disputes are common among tenant reps.

When the time comes for one of his or her clients to buy, sell or lease, the tenant rep finds a list of choices in the market, then handles the accompanying negotiations. Tenant reps usually work in teams to spread the work. Often the team is composed of one senior and one junior broker. The junior broker will make the cold calls and set up meetings with prospective clients. At the meetings the senior broker will take the lead and try to win the business. Once the process begins, the junior broker will do the legwork for market alternatives and examine options with the senior broker. All possible alternatives are presented to the client for review. The senior broker generally handles the lease or sale negotiations. This mutually beneficial system gives the senior broker a "cold caller" and provides a training platform for the junior broker. Junior brokers should expect to work at least 50 to 60 hours per week; senior brokers' hours fluctuate based on deal flow.

Once junior brokers have surpassed certain earning requirements, they're promoted to senior brokers. They still make cold calls to get leads, though not nearly as often as junior brokers. The company relies on its senior brokers to win business and handle transactions from start to finish. Sometimes senior brokers help create and execute management policy and even have equity at smaller firms.

Property Management

Real estate owners commonly employ professional property managers – either directly or through third-party management firms. Property managers are charged with the day-to-day management of real estate assets. They ensure that tenants are satisfied, the building is in good condition, rent is paid and that rents reflect market conditions. Property management provides a general introduction to real estate. As a property manager you'll learn how to efficiently operate a real estate asset in this capacity. Property managers deal with issues relating to leasing, construction, tenant relations and market analysis.

A good manager can save an owner a great deal of money by operating the asset efficiently and keeping the tenants happy. The property manager plays a crucial role in expense control; the owner relies on him to manage any and all operating expenses at the building. For instance, if there is construction work at the building, the property manager supervises the project, keeps close tabs on the progress and makes sure it doesn't go over budget. Property management also requires good interpersonal and analytical skills because tenants sometimes can be difficult and expect things to be resolved immediately. While leasing agents do much of the lease negotiations, property managers are involved in the process as well. A salesperson's license is therefore required for the position.

Visit Vault at **www.vault.com** for insider company profiles, expert advice, career message boards, expert resume reviews, the Vault Job Board and more.

VAULT CAREER LIBRARY   **353**

Employer Directory

AMB Property Corporation
Pier 1 Bay 1
San Francisco, CA 94111
Phone: (415) 394-9000
Fax: (415) 394-9001
www.amb.com

Boston Properties, Inc.
111 Huntington Avenue
Boston, MA 02199-7602
Phone: (617) 236-3300
Fax: (617) 536-5087
www.bostonproperties.com

CB Richard Ellis Group, Inc.
865 South Figueroa Street
34th Floor
Los Angeles, CA 90017
Phone: 213.438.4880
Fax: 213.438.4820
www.cbre.com

Century 21 Real Estate Corporation
1 Campus Drive
Parsippany, NJ 07054
Phone: (877) 221-2765
Fax: (973) 496-7564
www.century21.com

Cushman & Wakefield, Inc.
51 West 52nd Street
New York, NY 10019-6178
Phone: (212) 841-7500
Fax: (212) 841-7767
www.cushwake.com

Duke Realty Corporation
600 East 96th Street
Suite 100
Indianapolis, IN 46240
Phone: (317) 808-6000
Fax (317) 808.6794
www.dukerealty.com

Equity Office Properties Trust
Two North Riverside Plaza
Chicago, IL 60606
Phone: (312) 466-3300
Fax: (312) 454-0332
www.equityoffice.com

General Growth Properties, Inc.
110 North Wacker Drive
Chicago, IL 60606
Phone: (312) 960-5000
Fax: (312) 960-5475
www.generalgrowth.com

Hines Interests L.P.
Williams Tower
2800 Post Oak Boulevard
Houston, TX 77056
Phone: (713) 621-8000
Fax: (713) 966-2053
www.hines.com

HomeServices of America
6800 France Ave. South, Ste. 710
Edina, MN 55435
Phone: (952) 928-5900
Fax: (952) 928-5590
www.homeservices.com

Jones Lang LaSalle Incorporated

200 E. Randolph Drive

Chicago, IL 60601

Phone: (312) 782-5800

Fax: (312) 782-4339

www.joneslanglasalle.com

Julien J. Studley, Inc.

300 Park Ave.

New York, N.Y. 10022

Phone: (212) 326-1000

Fax: (212) 326-1034

www.studley.com

Lend Lease Corporation Limited

Level 46, Tower Building

Australia Square

Sydney, 2000 Australia

Phone: +61-2-9236-6111

www.lendlease.com.au

RE/Max International, Inc.

8390 E. Crescent Parkway, Suite 500/600

Greenwood Village, CO 80111-2800

Phone: (303) 770-5531

Fax: (303) 796-3599

www.remax.com

RREEF Funds L.L.C.

101 California Street

26th Floor

San Francisco, CA 94111

Phone: (415) 781-3300

Fax: (415) 391-9015

www.rreef.com

Trammell Crow Company

2001 Ross Avenue

Suite 3400

Dallas, TX 75201

Phone: (214) 863-3000

Fax: (214) 863-3138

www.trammellcrow.com

Visit Vault at **www.vault.com** for insider company profiles, expert advice, career message boards, expert resume reviews, the Vault Job Board and more.

VAULT CAREER LIBRARY   355

Retail

Retail Industry Overview

Chances are good that you've had at least one interaction with the retail industry today. From the corner drugstore to the online bookstore, retail is an ubiquitous presence in American life – the U.S. boasts more than 1.4 million retail establishments, which racked up sales of $3.8 trillion in 2003 alone, according to the National Retail Federation (NRF).

Rolling back the competition

One can't talk about retail without mentioning Wal-Mart, which looms large both as a sales leader (raking in more than $258 billion in 2003) and as a chain that has rendered the playing field much harder to compete on for many smaller retail establishments. Placing second in sales for 2003, according to NRF, was Home Depot (trailing far behind Wal-Mart at $64 billion); grocery giant Kroger came in third. Other top retail contenders are Target, Costco, Sears, and Safeway.

Branding the multi-brand retailer

In this competitive sector, marketing makes all the difference. Despite Wal-Mart's dominance, "multi-brand" retailers, like department stores and discounters, which sell a range of other companies' brands, have a tougher battle when it comes to establishing a national brand identity of their own, according to analysis by consulting firm McKinsey & Co. But multi-brand chains are catching onto the concept of aggressive self-promotion. Target is a notable example – in summer 2004, the chain spent more than $1 million on a massive billboard campaign in Times Square, where there's not a Target to be found for miles. McKinsey notes that Target has been an innovator in marketing for the sector. Its distinctive "bullseye" logo, featured in early campaigns with no products on display, "places the brand and the promise of the store ahead of its merchandise," a trend expected to grow ever more common in the sector, according to McKinsey.

Blue light bankruptcy

Other multi-brand retailers, like Kmart, haven't been so lucky – saddled with a sinking financial profile, the company was forced to declare bankruptcy in early 2002. In March of that year, it announced plans to close 283 stores and eliminate more than 20,000 jobs (a figure that would grow by another 40,000 or so by the end of the year, with a total of 600 out of 2,100 stores closing). The company eventually revealed that it had lost more than $2 billion in 2001, and had to restate its earnings for the previous three years. Investigations soon uncovered a host of financial shenanigans. Later in 2002, two former Kmart VPs were indicted for their part in the company's fall. Top Kmart exec Chuck Conway, however, walked away from his position relatively unscathed, with a $9 million package. Emerging from Chapter 11 in May 2003, the retailer took a leaner approach, trying to boost its image with a fresh marketing campaign. In June 2004, the company agreed to sell up to 54 stores to rival retailer Sears, to the tune of $621 million.

Visit Vault at **www.vault.com** for insider company profiles, expert advice, career message boards, expert resume reviews, the Vault Job Board and more.

VAULT CAREER LIBRARY 357

Managing customers

Once retailers have made a customer out of a shopper, the trick is to keep her coming back for more, not running to the next competitor that holds a sale. In the age of IT, this process is facilitated by customer relationship management (CRM), which applies software, Internet capabilities and other resources to help companies manage information about their clients. For instance, using a CRM database, a company might be able to access a customer's past purchases at the store and gear special offers toward him, or alert him when a product matching his interests becomes available. From the retailer's perspective, CRM can help integrate business functions to increase efficiency and manage supply chains better According to Forrester Research, the CRM market is expected to grow annually by 11.5 percent between now and 2007. This market includes software and applications as well as the consulting services many companies adopt to get their CRM systems up and running.

Going online

As in many other industries, technology has revolutionized retail. While "alternative retail outlets" like mail-order companies, home shopping and the Internet have taken some business from traditional stores, the change hasn't been dramatic as some had anticipated. In fact, studies indicate that while consumers are more frequently visiting the Internet to compare prices and research products, many still go to the store to make the final purchase. Still, online sales surpassed all industry expectations in 2003, totaling $114 billion, or more than 5 percent of all retail sales, according to a Forrester Research study. This figure represented a 51 percent jump over the previous year. Not only are consumers becoming less nervous about the security issues associated with online transactions, they're also expanding their horizons in terms of the types of products they're willing to shop for and purchase online. Online sales have been particularly strong in the health and beauty and apparel categories.

Radio, radio

Another technology that promises to change the face of retail in coming years is Radio Frequency Identification (RFID, to those in the know). According to research firm IDC, retail spending on this new technology will grow to more than $1 billion per year by 2008. What's all the fuss about? Basically, RFID allows manufacturers to tag each piece of merchandise with a microchip and tiny antenna containing information that can be tracked by reading devices equipped with radio signals. The Electronic Product Code (EPC) residing in the chip allows anyone with such a reader to track the item from conception all the way to delivery. While consumer advocacy groups fret about the privacy implications such technology raises (presumably, your late-night splurge on that extra-large bag of Ranch-flavored Doritos will reside in a database somewhere), retailers point to the technology's obvious benefits – including inventory management, loss prevention, and faster and more reliable product recalls, to name a few.

In fact, much of the rush toward RFID has been spurred by retail behemoth Wal-Mart, which has instituted a program mandating RFID tags on crates and pallets of goods coming from its major suppliers by 2005. Since none can afford to be left out of the Wal-Mart game, manufacturers are scrambling to catch up. Target announced similar plans in early 2004. So far, both retailers are sticking to the "case and pallet level" for their tagging, rather than insisting that individual items be tagged – though as RFID becomes cheaper and more efficient, the technology is likely to reach the product level in the next few years.

Life in retail

In 2003, about 14.9 million people were employed in retail, according to the Bureau of Labor Statistics (BLS). Of these workers more than 50 percent are employed as retail salespersons; other positions include stock clerks and order fillers and customer service representatives. The agency projects that employment in the sector will grow by 13.8 percent by 2012 – on a par with anticipated growth for all other industries. Because turnover is relatively high, the sector offers an abundance of job opportunities for people of all ages and educational levels, making it the leading creator of entry-level jobs among all industries. A list of colleges and universities offering degrees in retail can be found on the National Retail Federation's website, www.nrf.com.

Pursuing a career in retail

The role of technology in retail makes it necessary for job seekers to acquire and maintain good technological skills, in addition to communication, customer service and analytical skills. Those pursuing a career in retail will benefit by taking business courses, too. Entry-level jobs can be acquired with or without a college education in retail, but a college degree can make it possible to enter retailing at a higher level, such as through an executive training program. A list of colleges and universities offering degrees in retail can be found on the National Retail Federation's website, www.nrf.com.

Ideal qualities for the retail job seeker:

Good customer service skills: an understanding of the customer's wants and needs, serving them well and enthusiastically;

Good interpersonal skills: get along with customers and fellow employees;

Flexible: able to adjust in an ever-changing global retail marketplace, interacting with many people on different levels, performing a wide variety of tasks during the work day, being resourceful;

Decisive: self-motivated and self-starting, able to make quick calculated decisions, follow through with tasks and accept responsibility for their results;

Analytical: capable of problem-solving, analyzing data and predicting trends, establishing priorities, familiarity with technologically advanced tools for managing infrastructure;

Stamina: perform well under pressure, maintain professional standards under varied work conditions

Visit Vault at **www.vault.com** for insider company profiles, expert advice, career message boards, expert resume reviews, the Vault Job Board and more.

VAULT CAREER LIBRARY

359

Retail Careers in Fashion

Retail covers the sale of apparel and related goods and services in small quantities directly to consumers. In the rush for fashion jobs, the retail sector has emerged as a promising contender. Sears, Roebuck and Co., for example, has created the "Retail Executive Development Training Program" to recruit promising new professionals. Considered a retail milestone by many, the program targets 60 undergraduate campuses. After an eight- to 10-month training program, "executive trainees" handle up to $3 million in profit/loss responsibility. Some trainees have as many as 30 people reporting to them. Retailers such as Sears, Neiman Marcus, Federated and Meryvn's offer candidates a nice deal – signficant management responsibility in a relatively short amount of time.

Some larger retail programs have established training programs. The Gap hires recent college graduates for its Retail Management Program. The program is based in San Francisco over a seven-month period. New hires gain experience in merchandising, planning and production. After successfully completing the program, the graduates have an opportunity to work full-time in the brand (i.e., Old Navy, Banana Republic, Gap Baby, etc.) in which they trained – and are placed based on Gap's needs, as well as each graduate's skills and interests.

Jobs

Retail clerk: Assists the consumer in the purchase of products and services.

Store manager: Manages the store operations and supervises the clerks.

Marketing: Works on store advertisements and catalogs.

Inventory planner: Sets monetary limits on the retail buyers' purchasing power based on historical and market analysis.

Asset protection: Minimizes store losses and track fraud and theft.

Logistics: Works with stores and buyers to optimize supply-chain.

Real estate: Manages stores that vary in size, location, and layout to keep stores new. Responsibilities may include construction and building services management.

The Scoop

Many people have a less-than-positive view of retailing. "I didn't spend four years in college to work in a store!" is a frequent gripe. This negative reaction belies the fact that retail is a good place to start or build a fashion career. Because jobs selling fine design can be extremely lucrative, retail is becoming more attractive to college graduates. Larger stores are often the best places to start since some offer standardized training programs. Comments an insider: "One of retail's biggest problems is that there is no standard training pattern. Many retailers wait for people to get on the-job-training elsewhere and then cannibalize their competitors." Despite the problem of unstructured training, retail has one indisputably stellar element: almost anyone is eligible. "We look for employees with bachelor's degrees," says an industry source. "School isn't very important. Major isn't very important. Many people who specialized in business, finance or liberal arts will do just fine."

On the corporate side of fashion, opportunities exist in retail buying, planning, merchandising and product development. College grads typically start out as trainees and work their way up, following established or somewhat meandering career paths. Talented and dedicated new hires, especially in large companies or department stores, can expect regular promotions – up to divisional management roles. There are also opportunities in store management, finance and human resources. More creative jobs in retail include catalog production (graphics and copywriting) and window and display design.

Image

While some insiders laud department stores, others attest to the value of small designer companies. "Department stores are out," declares one adamant source. "Smaller, more prestigious retailers – CK, Armani, Tommy Hilfiger – are the way to go. Department stores are stuffy and they convey a feeling of being 'average.' The people I know working on the selling floor of department stores want to get out." Underlying this comment are issues of prestige and class, two prominent – although seldom discussed – aspects of retail. Fashion, and retail in particular, is an image-conscious sector in which an attractive appearance, up-to-date style, impeccable grooming and an air of affluence are important. "High-end retail is a glamour job," says an insider. "The positions are high-profile and low-paying. The people who work in retail are often highly educated and parentally subsidized. The job becomes a lifestyle of fashionable wardrobes, cocktail parties, elite crowds and making the right friends." If you detect an edge of superficiality, insiders confirm it. "High-end retail jobs are often aimed at high-class young women," says a source. "They deal with a wealthy and prominent clientele. Some of the girls are old school – out to find a rich husband."

Employees may have to invest thousands of dollars on a wardrobe to wear to work. In fact, most high-end retailers require their employees to wear only their label. One contact at Ralph Lauren says she must have her work apparel approved by the company, a cumbersome and expensive process. "For a job that pays by the hour," explains a contact, "you may have to invest quite a bit of money." This dress can be very expensive, even though employees receive discounts and supplementary commissions.

Fortunately, selling takes on new meaning when employees are dealing with celebrities and high-powered execs with money to burn. Those who excel in retail know how to build relationships with their customers – "setting aside" new arrivals or sending cards and little gifts (paid for by the company, of course). Wealthy clients may need pampering, but the insiders say the money compensates for the labor. "We're talking about people who walk into a store and buy the same outfit in five different colors," says an insider.

Visit Vault at **www.vault.com** for insider company profiles, expert advice, career message boards, expert resume reviews, the Vault Job Board and more.

VAULT CAREER LIBRARY 361

Employer Directory

JC Penney Company

PO Box 10001

Dallas, TX 75301-8115

Phone: (972) 431-1000

JCPenney.com

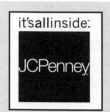

Company Description:

Communication Subcommittee Mission Statement

Improve communications by enhancing the sensitivity level surrounding diversity & work-life impacting customer service and associate satisfaction/productivity.

Personnel Relations Subcommittee Mission Statement

To foster the upward mobility of women and minorities into all levels of management, including senior management positions, by enhancing our current recruitment programs and implementing career development plans that allow the Company to retain, train and promote qualified women and minority associates.

Work-Life Issues Subcommittee Mission Statement

Identify Work-Life Issues that affect each associate's ability to perform to full potential. Encourage a supportive work environment that allows associates to maximize their contributions towards company objectives.

Schools JCPenney recruits from

Open to all accredited colleges and universities

Amazon.com, Inc.

1200 12th Ave. South, Ste. 1200

Seattle, WA 98144-2734

Phone: (206) 266-1000

Fax: (206) 266-1821

www.amazon.com

AutoZone, Inc.

123 S. Front St.

Memphis, TN 38103

Phone: (901) 495-6500

Fax: (901) 495-8300

www.autozone.com

Barnes & Noble, Inc.

122 Fifth Ave.

New York, NY 10011

Phone: (212) 633-3300

Fax: (212) 675-0413

www.barnesandnobleinc.com

Best Buy Co., Inc.

7601 Penn Ave. South

Richfield, MN 55423

Phone: (612) 291-1000

Fax: (612) 292-4001

www.bestbuy.com

Borders Group Inc.

100 Phoenix Dr.

Ann Arbor, MI 48108 (Map)

Phone: (734) 477-1100

Fax: (734) 477-1965

Circuit City Stores, Inc.

9950 Mayland Dr.

Richmond, VA 23233

Phone: (804) 527-4000

Fax: (804) -527-4164

www.circuitcity.com

Costco Wholesale Corporation

999 Lake Dr.

Issaquah, WA 98027

Phone: (425) -313-8100

Fax: (425) 313-8103

www.costco.com

Federated Department Stores, Inc.

7 W. 7th St.

Cincinnati, OH 45202

Phone: (513) 579-7000

Fax: (513) 579-7555

Toll Free: (800) 261-5385

www.federated-fds.com

Gap Inc

2 Folsom St.

San Francisco, CA 94105

Phone: (650) 952-4400

Fax: (415) 427-2553

Toll Free: (800) 333-7899

www.gap.com

Hallmark Cards, Inc.

2501 McGee St.

Kansas City, MO 64108

Phone: (816) 274-5111

Fax: (816) 274-5061

www.hallmark.com

The Home Depot, Inc.

2455 Paces Ferry Rd., Northwest

Atlanta, GA 30339-4024

Phone: (770) 433-8211

Fax: (770) 384-2356

Toll Free: (800) 430-3376

www.homedepot.com

Kmart Corporation

3100 W. Big Beaver Rd.

Troy, MI 48084

Phone: (248) 463-1000

Fax: (248) 463-5636

www.kmart.com

Kohl's Corporation

N56 W17000 Ridgewood Dr.

Menomonee Falls, WI 53051

Phone: (262) 703-7000

Fax: (262) 703-6143

www.kohls.com

Lowe's Companies, Inc.

1000 Lowe's Blvd.

Mooresville, NC 28117

Phone: (704) 758-1000

Fax: (336) 658-4766

Toll Free: (800) 445-6937

www.lowes.com

The Neiman Marcus Group, Inc.

1 Marcus Sq., 1618 Main St.

Dallas, TX 75201

Phone: (214) 741-6911

Fax: (214) 573-5320

www.neimanmarcus.com

Nordstrom, Inc.

1617 Sixth Ave.

Seattle, WA 98101-1742

Phone: (206) 628-2111

Fax: (206) 628-1795

www.nordstrom.com

Office Depot, Inc.

2200 Old Germantown Rd.

Delray Beach, FL 33445

Phone: (561) 438-4800

Fax: (561) 438-4001

www.officedepot.com

Saks Incorporated

750 Lakeshore Pkwy.

Birmingham, AL 35211

Phone: (205) 940-4000

Fax: (205) 940-4987

www.saksincorporated.com

Visit Vault at **www.vault.com** for insider company profiles, expert advice,
career message boards, expert resume reviews, the Vault Job Board and more.

VAULT CAREER LIBRARY

363

Sears, Roebuck and Co.
222 Jarvis St.
Toronto, Ontario M5B 2B8, Canada
Phone: (416) 362-1711
Fax: (416) 941-2501
Toll Free: (800) 747-0644

Staples, Inc.
500 Staples Dr.
Framingham, MA 01702
Phone: (508) 253-5000
Fax: (508) 253-8989
Toll Free: (800) 378-2753
www.staples.com

Target Corporation
1000 Nicollet Mall
Minneapolis, MN 55403
Phone: (612) 304-6073
Fax: (612) 696-3731
www.target.com

Tiffany & Co.
727 Fifth Ave.
New York, NY 10022
Phone: (212) 755-8000
Fax: (212) 230-6633
Toll Free: (800) 526-0649
www.tiffany.com

The TJX Companies, Inc.
770 Cochituate Rd.
Framingham, MA 01701
Phone: (508) 390-1000
Fax: (508) 390-2828
www.tjx.com

Toys "R" Us, Inc.
1 Geoffrey Way
Wayne, NJ 07470-2030
Phone: (973) 617-3500
Fax: (973) 617-4006
www7.toysrus.com

Technology Consulting

The State of Technology Consulting

IT consulting traces its roots from several parents. Traditional management and strategy consultants found their clients wanted more than just advice and reorganization; forward-thinking CEOs wanted their computers and electronics to be more than just a convenience. Another dollop of DNA comes from the engineers and Web heads who facilitated the rise of the Internet in the late 1980s and early 1990s. As technology became more complex, these Silicon Alley gurus scaled up their offerings to keep pace. Thirdly, traditional technology firms, like IBM, have moved strongly into the consulting field over the past 20 years as sales of their mainstay hardware have stagnated.

The technology consulting industry arose in response to the growing availability of computer technology in the workplace. Businesses realized that effective technology and technological processes were essential to maintaining competitive footing in the workplace. However, many companies found themselves without the internal capability to update their tech. The solution? Technology consulting companies. Outdated internal tech departments (or the absence of such a department altogether) prompted companies to employ computer savvy offered by IT consulting firms. The growth in governmental outsourcing of technology needs" both from the United States and other nations – has also been a boon to technology consulting firms.

The Big Five ... er, Four

Five firms (Andersen, Deloitte & Touche, KPMG, PricewaterhouseCoopers and Cap Gemini Ernst & Young) rose to dominate professional services, including both accounting and consulting. These so-called Big Five developed noteworthy technology consulting practices in the 20th century. Unfortunately, they also developed some noteworthy conflicts of interest; the highly-publicized accounting scandals of the late 1990s and early 21st century came from these sources. Ethical lapses at Andersen, in particular, led to its dissolution and sale to its rivals. Another result was the passage of the Sarbanes-Oxley Act, which established rules and penalties for professional services firms. The act made it less practical and more difficult for a firm to provide both accounting and advisory services; of the remaining Big Four (or, more popularly, Final Four), only Deloitte has maintained a unified practice.

Blue skies?

Like many businesses, technology consulting firms have suffered in recent years as the United States economy fell into a recession. Corporations cut back on technology spending and outside hiring during the slump, forcing the technology firms that depended on their business to endure falling profits and layoffs. (Technology firms that rely on government contracts, however, suffered a lighter downturn, especially with the increase in defense and security technology work contracts after the September 11 attacks and reconstruction efforts in Afghanistan and Iraq.) However, the beginning of 2004 is bringing brighter times to the industry. The United States economy is apparently in recovery, and companies are beginning to turn an eye to deferred technology upgrades. The cost-saving measure known as business process outsourcing

Visit Vault at **www.vault.com** for insider company profiles, expert advice, career message boards, expert resume reviews, the Vault Job Board and more.

VAULT CAREER LIBRARY   365

(BPO) continues to grow in popularity. Revenue growth outside the United States has been a plus for many technology consulting firms – BearingPoint, for example, grew its business by just 1 percent in the United States in 2002, but 33 percent overall.

The internationalization of technology consulting

One of the most noteworthy trends in technology consulting has been outsourcing engagements outside North America and Europe. India, China and a number of other countries (including Singapore, the Philippines and Pakistan) have benefited from the outsourcing of development and tech support to those countries. According to US Banker, a Forrester Research report projects that 3.3 million service- and knowledge-based jobs will migrate to other countries by 2015. Market research firm Gartner predicts that up to 40 percent of U.S. companies will develop or test software, provide tech support, or provide storage functions overseas by 2004. The loss of American jobs to foreign corporations is a hot campaign issue; Democratic presidential candidates Howard Dean and John Edwards have both made this a plank in their platforms. There has been some talk among legislators as well of action to limit the practice of " off-shoring," as it is also called, but so far it's just talk.

Outsourcing started in India, as U.S. consultancies, financial firms and other businesses tried to take advantage (literally) of a large pool of technical personnel who were willing to work for less. Alok Aggarwal, head of outsourcing-expediter Evalueserve, estimated in a Business Standard article that new consultants in India earn about a fifth what their U.S. counterparts do. The smarter firms also used their Asian locations as a selling point; Sapient Corp. instituted a " global distributed delivery" model, passing engagements across time zones to speed completion. Other firms have either independently developed similar models or copied Sapient's.

What goes around, comes around

Now, however, the influx of work has created offshore powerhouses that compete with the very companies who provided the work. The Indian government has worked to create a business-friendly environment by instituting economic incentives and infrastructure investments. In addition to India holding 70 to 80 percent of the outsourcing market, India-based firms such as Infosys Technologies and Tata Consultancy Services have become major players in their own right. As a result, wages are on the rise among Indian technicians, and their firms may in turn begin to outsource as well, perhaps to China. Stefan Spohr, a principal with EDS's A.T. Kearney, predicts that new outsourcing hot spots will include Mexico, South Africa and Hungary, to name a few candidates.

Mergers and acquisitions

IBM made big news when it acquired PricewaterhouseCoopers Consulting in October 2002. Big Blue saw its revenue surge as a result; IBM Global Services and IBM Business Consulting Services account for half of IBM's revenue today. Since that merger, there have been a large number of acquisitions in the tech consulting industry. Announcements of firms buying rivals, software developers and just about anybody else they think will improve and increase their business occur almost daily. Details of the more significant mergers may be found in this book's profiles, but many more are in the works. For example, SchlumbergerSema would have been ranked in this guide – but the company was acquired by Atos Origin in 2003.

Harvesting the tech consulting crop

Recently, there's been a blurring of the lines between management and technology consulting. Big strategy firms such as McKinsey and Booz Allen Hamilton have been beefing up their technology capabilities (Booz Allen Hamilton is especially prominent in the government consulting sector) while some IT firms look to make a name in management consulting (EDS, for example, acquired A.T. Kearney).

A major reason for this is inherent to the sort of work consultants do. A lot of engagements don't fit neatly into one category or the other; revamping a company's business strategy might very well involve nuts-and-bolts changes to the infrastructure. Similarly, a " simple" technology implementation might spark a client to change its organization to take full advantage of the new tech resources. The result of a management process audit might show the client can work more efficiently by outsourcing some of its business processes, and all of a sudden a management project is an operations job.

Less concrete, but still important, is the matter of image and perception. Consultants are problem solvers by nature and profession. To succeed, a firm must either own a niche or have a reputation for being able to do it all. Though most firms have specialties, competition makes niche ownership difficult to achieve, so a full-service image is often the solution.

There's also a perception, erroneous but driven by potential clients' cost-cutting efforts, that strategy consultants don't deliver anything that the company's own personnel couldn't come up with in time. Management firms have always had to overcome that prejudice, whereas technology specialists tend to work with deliverables a client can see and touch – hardware, software and personnel.

Engagements

Security

The world is still coping with the effects of the September 11 terrorist attacks and trying to prevent backlash from military expeditions. IT businesses have realized there's money to be made in designing and implementing better security and identification methods. Strides have been made in biometrics (the science of identifying a person via retina patterns, voice, fingerprints and other unique biological characteristics), contraband detection and secure communications. SchlumbergerSema, acquired by Atos Origin in September 2003, devotes its DeXa suite of services to firewalls, security badges and disaster recovery.

Research and development

Some consultants spend their time in the lab creating new hardware and software. Often, this work is geared toward creating new products (servers, analysis software and the like) that will help the consultancy sell work or accomplish the engagements is undertakes. In other cases, the consultants must create something entirely new for a client's use; for example, this is the realm of military contractors like Raytheon.

Visit Vault at **www.vault.com** for insider company profiles, expert advice, career message boards, expert resume reviews, the Vault Job Board and more.

VAULT CAREER LIBRARY   **367**

System Integration

This is one of the traditional jobs of the IT consultant. When two companies merge, or a single company wants to implement new hardware or software, they turn to consultants to make all the technology compatible. Sometimes, this is a simple matter of installing upgrades or changing settings. More often, it's a long and arduous process of writing new code to force all the machines to play nicely together.

Outsourcing

Another long-time area of tech consulting expertise, business process outsourcing (BPO) is the bread and butter of many firms. Some companies find it easier and more cost-effective to pay somebody else to manage their technology for them. The consultants, in effect, become the client's IT department. They handle everything from help desk and call center operations to server maintenance to passkey and ID tag issuance. Even governments and their armies outsource nowadays; CIBER has a number of contracts with the U.S. Army Reserve's Regional Support Commands and the U. S. Army Civil Affairs and Psychological Operations Command, while Computer Sciences Corporation has outsourcing deals with the U.K., Germany's armed forces and Australia.

Web services

Long the domain of design and hosting companies based in Silicon Alley (New York's tech center), Web services include e-commerce implementation and other secure-transaction work, though consultancies do some page design and site hosting as part of their overall deliverables as well. This specialty is receiving a lot of attention from major technology players like IBM, Hewlett-Packard and Accenture. Gartner predicts Web services spending will reach $14.3 billion by 2006, and a 2003 article in ConsultingCentral's Global IT Services Report claims, " Each week acquisitions and business alliances are announced, with dozens of firms jostling for position in the space." Clearly, this is an emerging business that bears watching.

Day in the Life: IT Consultant

Kristine is a consultant at a major consulting firm with many IT consulting engagements. Her role is Team Lead of the design and developer for eight Web-based training modules. She has five analysts on her team.

4:30 a.m.: It's Monday morning. Time to wake up. There's time for a shower this Monday morning – such luxury!

5:30 a.m.: I am in a cab on the way to the airport, making a mental list of anything that could have been forgotten. I ask the cabbie to tune the radio to NPR.

6:10 a.m.: At the airport I go up to the self check-in kiosk. I take the boarding pass and head down to the security line, laptop and small carry-on in hand.

6:25 a.m.: At security, I remove my laptop from my bag and place it on the tray. I move through security quickly. No alarms beep.

6:35 a.m.: After a quick stop at Starbucks, I arrive at the gate. I say hello to three other members of my project and check out the other passengers I see every week on this Monday morning flight. I board early along with the other premier fliers – one of the perks of being a frequent traveler.

7:00 a.m.: The flight departs on time. Yay! I relish my window seat close to the front of the airplane.

8:00 a.m.: The beverage cart wakes me up. I ask for coffee and scan the Wall Street Journal as I drink.

9:30 a.m.: I arrive at my destination and share a ride with my fellow consultants to the project site.

10:30 a.m.: At the project site. As I crawl underneath my desk to hook my laptop to the client LAN connection, one of my team members informs me that he still hasn't received feedback from his client reviewer. That's not good news.

11:00 a.m.: After checking and responding to e-mail, I call my team member's client reviewer. The reviewer agrees to send me the team member feedback on the training material by noon tomorrow.

11:15 a.m.: I remind the team of the 1 p.m. status meeting. I've got to start it on time – I have a meeting downtown at 3:15 p.m. I start to review the content outlines for the training modules.

12:00 p.m.: I scurry, along with two teammates, to get sandwiches at a nearby eatery. Mine is turkey and cheddar.

12:20 p.m.: Back at my desk, I get a call from the project manager, who is working at a client site in another state. He tells me that clients in the training department are nervous about their job security and asks that the entire team be sensitive to how the training changes may affect the training positions in the organization.

1:00 p.m.: The team holds a status meeting. I pass on the message from the project manager. Each member discusses what has been completed and what he or she expects to complete that week. Two other team members are having difficulty obtaining feedback from their client reviewers. We all brainstorm ideas on how to obtain the feedback.

2:00 p.m.: I finish up the meeting and get directions to my meeting downtown.

2:40 p.m.: Off to the 3:15 p.m. meeting.

3:15 p.m.: I meet the head of the training department to discuss the training courses. He calls in a close associate who has opinions on how the courses should be organized. The associate wants to add several more Web-based training modules. I politely suggest that part of the additional subject matter could be covered in the modules that have been agreed to in the scope of the project. We all sketch out the course structure on a white board.

4:45 p.m.: Back at the project site. I check in with my team members via e-mail.

5:45 p.m.: I complete a draft of the course flow in PowerPoint and send it to the client and my manager for review.

7:00 p.m.: I have reviewed 50 percent of the course outlines. It's time to head back to the hotel. I stop by a local diner for a quick dinner.

Visit Vault at **www.vault.com** for insider company profiles, expert advice, career message boards, expert resume reviews, the Vault Job Board and more.

VAULT CAREER LIBRARY   369

8:30 p.m.: Time for a workout in the hotel gym.

9:15 p.m.: I'm ready for bed. Clothes for the next day are hanging in the closet. The alarm clock is set to 6:30 a.m.

10:30 p.m.: I go to sleep.

Employer Directory

Accenture

Offices in 48 countries

campusconnection.accenture.com

Company Description:

Accenture's the world's leading management consulting, technology services and outsourcing company. We deliver cutting-edge technologies and solutions to companies around the world to help them become high-performance businesses. By improving their operations or reducing their costs, our innovative solutions help clients transform the way they do business, making them more competitive in their market.

Whether you want to develop deep technical skills, build business and industry expertise, develop leadership qualities or extend your personal development, Accenture offers a variety of career opportunities to help you achieve your goals. Visit campusconnection.accenture.com to learn more about the exciting opportunities with Accenture.

Schools Accenture recruits from

Duke University; Northwestern; Penn State; Texas A&M; University of CA-Berkeley; University of Michigan; University of Norte Dame; University of Georgia; University of Pennsylvania; University of Texas-Austin; Virginia Tech Univ; Cornell University; RPI; U of Illinois; U of Virginia; Georgia Tech; Purdue University; Ohio State University; Columbia University; UCLA

Capgemini

Five Times Square

New York, NY 10036

www.us.capgemini.com/careers

In providing innovative consulting solutions, we offer management and IT consulting services, systems integration, technology development, design and outsourcing capabilities on a global scale to help businesses continue to implement growth strategies and leverage technology in the new economy. Our goal is to help our clients realize significant improvement in revenue growth, operating efficiency and the management of capital by solving mission-critical problems. We assist global companies by identifying, designing, and implementing value added changes in their strategies and operations. The organization employs about 50,000 people worldwide and reported 2002 global revenues of about 5.754 billion euros.

Schools Capgemini recruits from

Columbia University Graduate School of Business; Duke University Fuqua School of Business; Georgia Institute of Technology Dupree college of School of Management; University of Florida; University of Michigan @ Ann Arbor School of Business; New York University Stern School of Business; University of California @ Los Angeles Anderson School of Management; University of California @ Berkeley Haas School of Business; University of Texas @ Austin McComb School of Business; Cornell University Johnson School of Business; University of North Carolina @ Chapel Hill Kenan-Flagler School of Business; University of Pennsylvania Wharton School of Business; Northwestern University Kellogg school of Management; University of Chicago Graduate school of Business; Michigan State University Eli Broad School of Business

Visit Vault at **www.vault.com** for insider company profiles, expert advice, career message boards, expert resume reviews, the Vault Job Board and more.

VAULT CAREER LIBRARY　371

Deloitte

Deloitte.

1633 Broadway
New York, New York 10013-6754

All candidate are to submit to opportunities via our career website located at www.deloitte.com/careers

Deloitte, one of the nation's leading professional services firms, provides audit, tax, consulting, and financial advisory services through nearly 30,000 people in more than 80 U.S. cities. Known as an employer of choice for innovative human resources programs, the firm is dedicated to helping its clients and its people excel. "Deloitte" refers to the associated partnerships of Deloitte & Touche USA LLP (Deloitte & Touche LLP and Deloitte Consulting LLP) and subsidiaries. Deloitte is the U.S. member firm of Deloitte Touche Tohmatsu.

Atos Origin
Immeuble Ile-de-France
3, place de la Pyramide
92067 Paris La Défense Cedex, France
Phone: +33 1-49-00-90-00
Fax: +33 1-47-73-07-63

American Management Systems
4050 Legato Road
Fairfax, VA 22033
Phone: (703) 267-8000
Fax: (703) 267-5073
www.ams.com

BearingPoint, Inc.
1676 International Drive
McLean, VA 22102
Phone: (703) 747-3000
Fax: (703) 747-8500
www.bearingpoint.com

Capgemini

Five Times Square
New York, NY 10036
Phone: (917) 934-8000
Fax: (917) 934-8001
www.us.capgemini.com

Computer Sciences Corporation
2100 East Grand Avenue
El Segundo, CA 90245
Phone: (310) 615-0311
Fax: (310) 322-9768
www.csc.com

DiamondCluster International
Suite 3000
John Hancock Center
875 N. Michigan Avenue
Chicago, IL 60611
Phone: (312) 255-5000
Fax: (312) 255-6000
www.diamondcluster.com

Electronic Data Systems Corporation (EDS)
5400 Legacy Drive
Plano, TX 75024-3199
Phone: (972) 604-6000
Fax: (972) 605-2643
www.eds.com
info@eds.com

Fujitsu Consulting
333 Thornall Street
Edison, NJ 08837
Phone: (732) 549-4100
Fax: (732) 632-1826
us.fujitsu.com

IBM Global Services
New Orchard Road
Armonk, NY 10504
Phone: (914) 499-1900
Fax: (914) 765-7382
www.ibm.com/services

Infosys Technologies Ltd.
Plot No. 44 & 97A, Electronics City
Hosur Road, Bangalore
561 229
India
Phone: (080) 8520261
Fax: (080) 8520362
www.infosys.com

Keane, Inc.
100 City Square
Boston, MA 02129
Phone: (617) 241-9200
Fax: (617) 241-9507
www.keane.com

LogicaCMG plc
Stephenson House
75 Hampstead Road
London, UK NW1 2PL
Phone: +44 20 7637 9111
Fax: +44 20 7468 7006
www.logicacmg.com

META Group, Inc.
208 Harbor Drive
Stamford, CT 06912-0061
Phone: (203) 973-6700
Fax: (203) 359-8066
www.metagroup.com

PA Consulting Group, Ltd.
123 Buckingham Palace Road
London, UK SW1W 9SR
Phone: +44 20 7730 9000
Fax: +44 20 7333 5050
www.paconsulting.com

Perot Systems Corporation
2300 W. Plano Pkwy.
Plano, TX 75075
Phone: (972) 577-0000
Fax: (972) 340-6100
www.perotsystems.com

Sapient Corporation
One Memorial Drive
Cambridge, MA 02142
Phone: (617) 621-0200
Fax: (617) 621-1300
www.sapient.com

SBI Group Inc.
2823 E. Cottonwood, Suite 480
Salt Lake City, UT 84121
Phone: (800) 294-0090
Fax: (801) 733-3201
www.sbiandcompany.com

Syntegra
Guidion House
Harvest Crescent
Ancells Business Park
Fleet, Hants GU51 2QP
United Kingdom
Phone: +44(0) 1252 777 000
Fax: +44(0) 1252 777 111
www.syntegra.com

Visit Vault at **www.vault.com** for insider company profiles, expert advice,
career message boards, expert resume reviews, the Vault Job Board and more.

V∧ULT CAREER LIBRARY   **373**

T-Systems International
Hahnstrabe 43 d
60528 Frankfurt, Germany
Phone: 49-69-6-65-31-0
Fax: 49-69-6-65-31-4-99
www.t-systems.com

Tata Consulting Services
Air India Building
11th Floor
Nariman Point, Mumbai 400021
India
Phone: +91 22 5668 9999
Fax: +91 22 2204 0711
www.tcs.com

Telcordia Technologies
One Telcordia Drive
Piscataway, NJ 08854-4157
Phone: (732) 699-2000
www.telcordia.com

The Titan Corporation
3033 Science Park Road
San Diego, CA 92121-1199
Phone: (858) 552-9500
Fax: (858) 552-9645
www.titan.com

Wipro Ltd.
Doddakannelli, Sarjapur Road
Bangalore, Karnataka 560035
India
Phone: +91(80) 844 0011
Fax: +91(80) 844 0056
www.wipro.com

Telecommunications

Telecom Calling

In simpler times, the word "telecommunications" might conjure an image of a telephone – and not much else. These days, telecom is an industry encompassing everything from local and long-distance phone services to wireless communication, Internet access, and cable and digital television. In the U.S., total spending for telecom services reached more than $720 billion in 2004, and is expected to hit the $1 trillion mark in 2007, according to the Telecommunications Industry Association (TIA). Internationally, the TIA predicts telecom spending, estimated at $1.5 trillion in 2004, to top $2 trillion by 2007.

For whom the bell tolls

Established in 1877 as American Bell, AT&T enjoyed the largest share of the industry pie for nearly a century, thanks to the government's belief that the utility constituted a "natural" monopoly. That monopoly crumbled in 1969, when the Federal Communications Commission (FCC) allowed other companies to play in Ma Bell's sandbox. Companies like MCI were quick to get in the game. But monopolies don't disappear overnight – to encourage competition in the long-distance market, the Department of Justice followed up with an antitrust suit against AT&T in 1974, resulting in the division of AT&T into a long-distance retailer and seven regional Bell operating companies (RBOCs), which would compete in the local call market as independent local exchange carriers (LECs). The final breakup took place in 1984.

The industry thrived under the breakup, exploding into hundreds of smaller competitors, lowering the cost of long-distance calling dramatically. While AT&T held about 70 percent of the market in 1984, it holds about a third today, according to Hoover's. Still, it's these so-called "Tier 1" carriers – AT&T, Sprint, and WorldCom – that make up the bulk of the long-distance market.

Untangling the wires

As the long distance market diversified, the local exchange market remained relatively homogenous. The Telecommunications Act of 1996 aimed to change that, deregulating entry into local markets and requiring that the so-called Baby Bells, or incumbent local phone companies (ILECs), retail their network elements to smaller competitors. The incumbents were required to unbundle their networks for reasonable prices, with the goal of decentralization of the system into a "network of networks." The act also temporarily blocked an RBOC from entering the long-distance market until it could prove that there was sufficient competition in its local territory.

Another provision of the Telecom Act, allowing RBOCs the right to sell cable television services and phone equipment, proved to be a boon for the strongest RBOCs. Thanks to those services and the entry of the Babies into long distance, the Telecom Act actually had the opposite of its intended effect, allowing a few RBOCs to solidify their positions and dominate the market through mergers and acquisitions. Today, there are just four RBOCs – Verizon Communications, BellSouth, SBC Communications, and

Visit Vault at **www.vault.com** for insider company profiles, expert advice, career message boards, expert resume reviews, the Vault Job Board and more.

VAULT CAREER LIBRARY   375

Qwest Communications International – dominating both local phone service access and the burgeoning DSL (digital subscriber line) markets.

Still, sniping among the RBOCs and long distance giants like MCI and AT&T over network-access rights continues. As late as May 2004, the FCC was engaged in a dispute between the Baby Bells and the long distance carriers, as the LD companies argued for increased access to local calling networks.

Merger mania

The Telecom Act ushered in an era of merger fever among telecom companies. In 1997, Bell Atlantic purchased little sib NYNEX for $25.6 billion, and SBC bought Pacific Telesis. The following year, SBC acquired local and long-distance provider Southern New England Telecommunications, entering the LD market through this Telecom Act loophole. SBC also acquired Baby Bell Ameritech for $68.8 billion, and Bell Atlantic merged with GTE to form Verizon. Also in 1998, Qwest Communications International bought long-distance company LCI International, entering the struggle between the big three of long distance, AT&T, Sprint, and MCI. The next year, Qwest's bid to acquire US West (the smallest of the Baby Bells) defeated that of fiber optics leader Global Crossing of Bermuda. Also in 1999, AT&T acquired cable operator Tele-Communications, Inc. and merged with MediaOne Group in a $44-billion deal. Meanwhile, MCI was folded into WorldCom for $47 billion, (more on this later) becoming the world's leading Internet carrier and a full-fledged global telecom company, boasting a 25 percent share of the U.S. long-distance market after the deal.

The activity wasn't limited to America's shores. Telecom became truly global in 1997, when 70 members of the World Trade Organization agreed to open up their telecom markets to each other at the start of the following year. Those 70 countries control 90 percent of worldwide telecom sales. Nearly all telecom companies around the world had privatized in anticipation of this expanded level of competition. The accord led to a rush of international deals, especially in the world's second-largest telecom market, Japan. In 1999, British Telecommunications and AT&T partnered to acquire a 30 percent stake in LD operator Japan Telecom, combining their Japanese ventures under JT. Britain's Cable & Wireless bought Japan's No. 6 carrier, IDC, a few months later. Also in 1999, Global Crossing teamed up with Marubeni to build an entirely new network, called Global Access, to service Japan.

Wall Street highs and lows

As M&A activity heated up, Wall Street took notice – investors poured $1.3 trillion into telecom industry companies in the five years following the Telecom Act's passage, according to *Forbes* magazine. But with this activity came increased scrutiny and risk. Ultimately, the industry was subject to the same meltdown that hit the rest of the tech sector beginning in late 2000. According to *Forbes*, the industry's market value plummeted by $1 trillion after the Dow Jones took its dive. Mergers also fell by the wayside. In July 2000, a proposed deal between Sprint and WorldCom fell through when the Justice Department filed a lawsuit that attempted to block the deal. The prospect of a lengthy DOJ suit effectively killed the merger, and it may similarly discourage future unions.

Compounding the gloom in the industry, some major telecoms had high-profile problems in their accounting departments. The two biggest offenders were WorldCom and Global Crossing, both of which ran afoul of the feds in 2002. WorldCom filed for the largest bankruptcy in U.S. history in July 2002, racking up $41 billion in debts and an estimated $11 billion in fraudulent expenses – leading to a $100 billion loss to shareholders. Even as the company attempted a rebound, emerging from bankruptcy in April 2004 with a lighter debt load, a moderately healthy outlook, and a less tarnished name (the company reverted to the MCI brand), it had to contend with scores of class action lawsuits; former chief executive Bernard J. Ebbers also faced a growing list of federal fraud and conspiracy charges as late as Spring 2004. Accounting firm Citigroup announced in May 2004 that it would pay $2.65 billion to investors for its role in the scandal. The turmoil has led some industry analysts to speculate about a possible sale of MCI to one of its Baby Bell competitors.

A debt burden of $12.4 billion, along with an oversupply of high-speed network capacity, led to Global Crossing's Chapter 11 filing in January 2002. The outcome was predictable in this era of accounting scandals, including a Justice Department probe into the company's accounting practices, and lawyers rounding up plaintiffs. In April 2004, investors again had reason to worry as Global Crossing announced it would need to review and restate its financial statements for all of 2002 and 2003 thanks to a $50 million to $80 million understatement of liability costs.

In addition to WorldCom and Global Crossing, about a half-dozen other providers of telecom services began Chapter 11 bankruptcy proceedings in 2002, dumping customers and employees as they went. In September 2003, Sprint reported a reorganization into business and consumer lines in an effort to save $1 billion.

Wireless wins the day

Thanks to the booming wireless market, however, Sprint, which offers wireless service under the Sprint PCS name, faces less market risk, analysts say. The same holds true for other major telecoms that have devoted resources to wireless services. In fact, the wireless market, with $89 billion in spending in 2003, outpaced long distance for the first time that year, according to TIA research (LD posted $78 billion in spending). The number of wireless users was estimated at above 1 billion in 2003.

The boom in wireless may herald renewed business activity in telecom. One notable example is Cingular's $41 billion purchase of rival AT&T Wireless, announced in February 2004, following a fierce bidding battle with rival Vodafone. As an example of how complicated the industry's family ties are, consider this: Cingular happens to be owned by rival Baby Bells BellSouth and SBC; competitor Verizon Wireless is a joint venture of Verizon and the Vodafone Group. Competition began to sizzle in late 2003, as the first phase of a federal law allowing "portability" – the ability of consumers to retain their phone numbers when switching carriers – took effect. While the media emphasized a sudden boom in carrier-hopping among consumers, industry watchers like the Gartner Group pointed out

Visit Vault at **www.vault.com** for insider company profiles, expert advice, career message boards, expert resume reviews, the Vault Job Board and more.

VAULT CAREER LIBRARY   **377**

An end-run around the phone

Cell phones aren't the only way consumers are making calls these days – Voice over Internet Protocol (VoIP), offered by companies like Vonage, allows users to turn their personal computers into telephones by sending voice "data" over a broadband connection in the same way other data is sent online. Bypassing questions of local and long distance networks entirely, VOIP services allow complete number portability – users in Iowa can maintain Manhattan area codes. The technology also has an advantage in terms of cost – thanks to the FCC, VoIP is exempt from taxes and regulations regular phone carriers are saddled with. Of course, the major telecoms are busy on Capitol Hill, trying to level the playing field – meanwhile, most experts say the technology has a way to go in terms of reliability and simplicity for the average consumer.

But it isn't a simple question of phone companies competing with the Internet – indeed, telecom providers, seeing the Internet revolution early on, began expanding their data communication networks, constructing more than 90 million miles of fiber-optic cables alone. Cable lines, which are hooked up to 90 percent of American residences, have considerably greater bandwidth than current phone lines and appear to be the least painful replacement for the outdated phone lines connecting homes today. With AT&T currently gobbling up miles of cable wire, there's little mystery as to what its medium in the next few years will be.

A job market roller coaster

The numbers are intimidating: By some estimates, the telecom industry slashed 300,000 jobs during the troubled period beginning in late 2000. As recently as May 2004, MCI announced plans to lay off 7,500 workers – on top of 4,500 in cuts it had announced a few months prior to that. But outplacement firm Challenger Gray & Christmas sees the layoffs fading a bit – while more than 12,000 telecom workers lost their jobs in December 2002, that number was just over 8,700 in December of the following year. While employment prospects are expected to be limited in telecom for the time being, the U.S. Department of Labor's Bureau of Labor Statistics (BLS) says that rising demand for services will eventually boost hiring.

According to the BLS, telecom provided 1.2 million wage and salary jobs in 2002, the latest year for which statistics are available. Of these employees, just over half work in office and administrative support or in installation, maintenance and repair. Other positions in the industry include sales and IT-related functions like computer support, engineering and administration. Keeping job skills up-to-date is crucial in this rapidly changing industry, the BLS insists – many major employers offer training through Web sites and other resources.

Employer Directory

AT&T

One AT&T Way
Bedminster, NJ 07921
www.att.com/careers/mba

AT&T is among the world's leading voice and data communications companies. We are at the leading edge of today's technology and you can be part of that exciting, ever-changing environment. As a member of the AT&T Team, you will experience a culture that respects individuals and values diversity; an environment of open communications, teamwork, continuous improvement, innovation, and growth; and an opportunity to develop a challenging and rewarding career with competitive benefits.

We have career opportunities across the country for talented, energized professionals who are ready to join the AT&T tradition of excellence.

Sprint

6500 Sprint Parkway
KSOPHL0302-3B654
Overland Park, KS 66251-6108
Phone: 800-673-3656
E-mail: sprint.urr@mail.sprint.com
www.sprint.com/hr

Sprint is a global integrated communications provider serving more than 26 million customers in over 100 countries. With approximately 65,000 employees worldwide and over $26 billion in annual revenues in 2003, Sprint is widely recognized for developing, engineering and deploying state-of-the-art network technologies, including the United States' first nationwide all-digital, fiber-optic network and an award-winning Tier 1 Internet backbone. Sprint provides local communications services in 39 states and the District of Columbia and operates the largest 100-percent digital, nationwide PCS wireless network in the United States.

Visit Vault at **www.vault.com** for insider company profiles, expert advice, career message boards, expert resume reviews, the Vault Job Board and more.

VAULT CAREER LIBRARY   **379**

ALLTEL Corporation
1 Allied Dr.
Little Rock, AR 72202
Phone: (501) 905-8000
Fax: (501) 905-5444
www.alltel.com

BellSouth Corporation
1155 Peachtree St. NE
Atlanta, GA 30309-3610
Phone: (404) 249-2000
Phone: (404) 249-2071
www.bellsouth.com

Cingular Wireless LLC
Glenridge Highlands Two
5565 Glenridge Connector
Atlanta, GA 30342
Phone: (404) 236-6000
Fax: (404) 236-6005
www.cingular.com

Charter Communications, Inc.
12405 Powerscourt Dr., Ste. 100
St. Louis, MO 63131-3660
Phone: (314) 965-0555
Fax: (314) 965-9745
www.charter.com

Cisco Systems, Inc.
170 W. Tasman Dr.
San Jose, CA 95134
Phone: (408) 526-4000
Phone: (408) 526-4100
www.cisco.com

Comcast Corporation
1500 Market St.
Philadelphia, PA 19102-2148
Phone: (215) 665-1700
Fax: (215) 981-7790
www.comcast.com

Corning Incorporated
1 Riverfront Plaza
Corning, NY 14831-0001
Phone: (607) 974-9000
Fax: (607) 974-5927
www.corning.com

Cox Communications, Inc.
1400 Lake Hearn Dr.
Atlanta, GA 30319
Phone: (404) 843-5000
Fax: (404) 843-5975
www.cox.com

Echostar Communications Corporation
9601 South Meridian Blvd.
Englewood, CO 80112
Phone: (303) 723-1000
Fax: (303) 723-1379
www.dishnetwork.com

Lucent Technologies, Inc.
600 Mountain Ave.
Murray Hill, NJ 07974
Phone: (908) 582-8500
Phone: (908) 508-2576
www.lucent.com

MCI, Inc.
22001 Loudoun County Pkwy.
Ashburn, VA 20147
Phone: (877) 624-1000
Phone: (212) 885-0570
www.mci.com

Motorola, Inc.
1303 E. Algonquin Rd.
Schaumburg, IL 60196
Phone: (847) 576-5000
Fax: (847) 576-5372
www.motorola.com

Nextel Communications, Inc.
2001 Edmund Halley Dr.
Reston, VA 20191
Phone: (703) 433-4000
Phone: (703) 433-4343
www.nextel.com

Nortel Networks Corporation
8700 Dixie Rd., Ste. 100
Brampton, Ontario L6T 5P6, Canada
Phone: (905) 863-0000
Phone: (905) 863-8408
www.nortelnetworks.com

QUALCOMM Incorporated
5775 Morehouse Dr.
San Diego, CA 92121-1714
Phone: (858) 587-1121
www.qualcomm.com

Qwest Communications International Inc.
1801 California St.
Denver, CO 80202
Phone: (303) 992-1400
Phone: (303) 992-1724
www.qwest.com

SBC Communications Inc.
175 E. Houston
San Antonio, TX 78205-2233
Phone: (210) 821-4105
Phone: (210) 351-2071
www.sbc.com

Verizon Communications Inc.
1095 Avenue of the Americas
New York, NY 10036
Phone: (212) 395-2121
Fax: (212) 869-3265
www.verizon.com

Visit Vault at **www.vault.com** for insider company profiles, expert advice, career message boards, expert resume reviews, the Vault Job Board and more.

VAULT CAREER LIBRARY   **381**

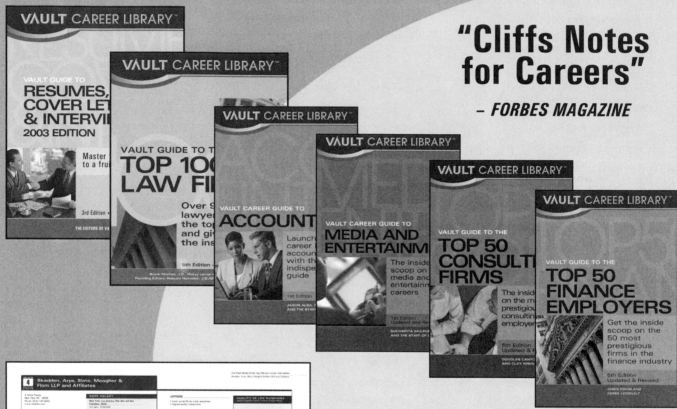

Transportation and Airlines

The vast transportation sector is charged with carrying people and products (safely and on-time, of course) to destinations around the globe – no small feat. The industry can be broken into a handful of sectors: airlines; air cargo and express delivery carriers; trucks; railroads; and buses.

Turbulent Skies for Airlines

It's an understatement to say that airlines are struggling these days. The nearly $25 billion lost by the airline industry from 2001 through the first quarter of 2004 is greater than the total of the profits it earned during the six years between 1995 and 2000. The aftermath of the September 11 terrorist attacks in the U.S. is an obvious factor in this downturn, but the industry has been weakened by other factors, as well, including unprecedented competition both within the sector and from other forms of transportation; skyrocketing fuel prices; online technologies empowering travel consumers; the SARS epidemic; increased liability insurance premiums; and unsustainable labor and operating costs. Still, the mammoth industry managed to post revenues of approximately $80 billion last year.

For the airline sector, turbulence is nothing new – since the early days of flight at the start of the last century, it's always been tough for air carriers to turn a profit. Major airline swan-dives took place long before the travel and economic crisis spurred by the increased attention to global terrorism – do the names Pan Am, Braniff, and Eastern ring a bell? They're among the approximately 100 airlines estimated by the Air Transport Association to have gone bankrupt since deregulation of the industry in 1978. In fact, industry analysts say that the number of airlines that have gone out of business since the dawn of the air travel industry outweighs those that have managed to survive.

Airline aid

Since the September 11 tragedies, Congress has given well over $20 billion to the industry, in the form of reimbursements for losses incurred while planes were grounded following the attacks, help with new passenger and plane security requirements, and pension funding relief. But many of the industry's major players were forced to shoulder massive debt loads to continue operating, on top of debt they had begun accumulating even before the terrorist attacks. This led a number of carriers to seek bankruptcy protection – since 2001, Great Plains, Hawaiian, Midway, National, Sun Country, TWA, Vanguard, United, and US Airways all have shown up in bankruptcy court.

While most of the majors managed to emerge with lighter debt burdens, United's parent company, UAL Corporation, remained in bankruptcy through early 2004, and observers worried that other troubled carriers might have to make a second trip through Chapter 11. Though passenger confidence continued to grow in the years following the attacks, and an improved economy bodes well for the travel industry as a whole, the industry's red ink continues to flow – according to a June 2004 Senate report, the industry carried combined debts of more than $100 billion as of that year, with much of it due by 2006. So major carriers continue to lobby the feds for financial support, in the form of subsidies and loans.

Visit Vault at www.vault.com for insider company profiles, expert advice, career message boards, expert resume reviews, the Vault Job Board and more.

VAULT CAREER LIBRARY   383

A global network

Around the world, many airlines still are heavily subsidized – or owned outright – by their home nations. While this has been a successful set-up for many, others haven't been so lucky – Swissair and Belgium's airline, Sabena, both crumbled when their respective governments couldn't keep up with demands for subsidies. Global alliances have been formed between subsidized international and U.S. carriers to avoid some regulatory issues and to maximize profits by sharing resources, including routes and marketing strategies. Well-known alliances include Oneworld, an alliance between American Airlines and British Airways, and SkyTeam, a partnership made up of Delta Air Lines, Air France, and AeroMexico. Such partnerships aren't always successful – an alliance between Dutch carrier KLM and AlItalia fell apart, for instance, after AlItalia had trouble securing funding from its government patrons.

But partnerships aside, the airline industry remains remarkably competitive, and in today's tough climate, it's everyone for themselves. The only major merger between top airlines in the past few years was the early 2004 acquisition of KLM by Air France (a deal expected to create one of the world's largest airlines). Tight regulatory controls in the U.S. make it tough for major domestic carriers to even consider merging; a plan to join United Airlines and U.S. Airways was the last such proposal to be floated, and it has since fallen to earth.

Going regional

Regional airlines, which benefit from smaller, newer jets and lower operating costs than the domestic giants, have gained ground in recent years, becoming the fastest-growing segment of the airline market. Approximately 25 to 30 regional, or commuter, carriers operate in the industry today, and one out of every eight passengers uses such a carrier for at least a portion of a trip, according to the BLS. The big carriers have taken notice, and many now have controlling interests in newer regional airlines – Delta controls Delta Express, Atlantic Southeast, and Comair, for instance, while American has American Eagle. The trend is reflected in Europe, too. Both globally and domestically, regional airlines benefit from such partnerships as alliances with major carriers allow the upstart regionals access to major airport hubs. In some cases, however, regional and low-budget airlines have skirted the hub question altogether by choosing to operate out of slightly out-of-the-way airports – Southwest's use of Islip airport, in the New York area, and JetBlue's adoption of Long Beach, near Los Angeles, are two examples.

And in other cases, regional airlines have decided to spread their wings and join the burgeoning low-cost boom. Independence Air is a prime example – once a regional carrier called Atlantic Coast Airlines, it relied on United for 85 percent of its revenue. Going independent, the carrier re-branded, changed its looks, and began marketing itself with rock-bottom rates, using Washington's Dulles airport as a hub, in the summer of 2004.

The budget boom

The budget airline sector – consisting of top performers like Southwest Airlines and JetBlue, plus a growing number of upstarts, has gotten a good deal of attention lately. But budget flight isn't a new phenomenon in the industry – in fact, Southwest has been around since 1971. The difference is in the branding, and public acceptance, of these carriers, fueled in part by Southwest's customer-centric approach, and partly by customers' reduced service expectations post-September 11. Expanded routes have helped, too – where once low-budget carriers limited their flights to relatively short hauls in regional markets, today's top discount airlines regularly offer cross-country, and even international, flights. The budget carrier phenomenon has rocked Europe, too, where more than 50 low-cost carriers were in operation in 2004, compared to just four in 1999. In fact, low-cost carrier Ryanair, operating out of Ireland, is one of the top performers in the industry worldwide, second in market capitalization only to Southwest as of mid-2004, according to Yahoo! Finance.

Around the world, carriers have come to realize that there just aren't as many passengers willing to pay for five-star air travel these days – at least, not enough to make these services profitable for most carriers. The demise of the luxury liner the Concorde, in 2003, was seen by many analysts as yet another indication of this trend.

Cutting costs

But above all, cost-savings are seen as key to the success of low-budget carriers. One way air carriers measure their fiscal health is through cost per available seat mile (or CASM), a complex formula involving airplane capacity, operating costs, route lengths, and other factors. Whereas American Airlines spends about 9.4 cents for each seat on each mile flown, budget competitors like Southwest and JetBlue lighten their loads with CASMs of 7.6 cents and 6.4 cents, respectively, according to an MSNBC article from December 2003. Those pennies add up over time, and so-called "legacy" carriers are under pressure to pinch them ever harder. But with more liberal work rules and a less-senior workforce overall, low-cost carriers beat their established rivals in terms of labor costs. Making matters worse for the legacy airlines, they're now under pressure to match the rock-bottom ticket prices issued by upstarts like JetBlue (founded in 2000) and seasoned discounters like Southwest. Combine that pressure with the growing presence of those once-fringe carriers at major domestic airport hubs, and the stage is set for all-out price wars. One way in which legacy carriers have begun to compete is by spinning off their own low-cost subsidiaries – Delta's Song took to the skies in April 2003, followed by United's Ted in early 2004. Where legacy carriers once competed with low-cost rivals, now the low-cost carriers are waging wars amongst themselves – Southwest, feeling the burn of higher labor and fuel costs, posted a 54 percent lower profit in the second quarter of 2004.

If budget airlines represent the great hope of major passenger carriers, corporate jets are the bright light on the business travel horizon. Fractional jet firms like NetJet, which allow the sharing of jets between multiple partners for charter use, are flying high, and even industry skeptics like Warren Buffett are backing the idea, MSNBC has noted.

Investing in a dream(liner)

Major carriers hope to save money in the future by investing in new planes that offer a lower cost of ownership and operation. In early 2004, Boeing got the go-ahead from Japan's Al Nippon Airlines to begin work on a new 7E7 Dreamliner passenger jet, which promises fuel savings of up to 20 percent – other car-

Visit Vault at **www.vault.com** for insider company profiles, expert advice, career message boards, expert resume reviews, the Vault Job Board and more.

VAULT CAREER LIBRARY   **385**

riers' orders are expected to follow. Boeing's rival manufacturer, Airbus, is also working on a new offering, the A380, which is touted as the largest passenger jet the industry has seen. Other cost-cutting measures in the airline industry overall include the streamlining of fleets and the retirement of older planes; the cancellation of unprofitable routes; greater efficiency in procurement processes involving suppliers; and the slashing of commissions once paid regularly to middlemen such as travel agencies. Many see technological advancements as their great hope – according to a January 2004 *BusinessWeek* article, Continental hopes to save $500 million annually in coming years partly by investing in Web-based check-in systems and wireless bag tracking.

Through these and other measures, legacy carriers have slashed annual operating expenses by $13.4 billion and annual capital expenditures by $8.1 billion since 2001, according to the Air Transport Association. The belt-tightening was beginning to pay off as of mid-2004: While industry capacity (a measure of per-seat miles flown) contracted by 8 percent in the three years following mid-2001, capacity was expected to expand by nearly 7 percent.

Labor pains

According to the BLS, labor costs make up roughly 38 percent of many airlines' operating costs – that's around 40 cents for every dollar spent by an air carrier. Passenger safety regulations, a workforce made up of highly specialized – and rarely cross-trained – professionals, and a strong union presence in the industry make it tough for airlines to trim costs from their labor budgets. One way they've done this is by cutting workforces to the bare bones. Following September 11, Continental Airlines and US Airways were the first to make dramatic cuts, laying off about 20 percent of their respective workforces and paring flight schedules. Most other carriers followed suit. With well over 110,000 jobs lost since mid-2001, the U.S. airline industry's workforce is at its lowest level since 1996. These trends were reflected in Europe, too, where carriers like British Airways and Lufthansa also made cuts in staff and services.

Carrying the Load

Amidst all this choppy air, the air cargo business remains comparatively stable, with major cargo carriers posting profits even in the dark days of 2001 and 2002. Worldwide revenues for the air freight and express delivery market were $75 billion in 2003, and the market has doubled every 10 years, according to the Air Line Pilots Association (ALPA). Still, a few air cargo carriers, including Arrow Air and Atlas Air, were forced into bankruptcy court alongside their passenger-carrier counterparts. Arrow emerged from Chapter 11 in June 2004, and Atlas Express (one of the world's largest cargo carriers) was expected to re-emerge shortly thereafter.

Express-delivery giants like United Parcel Service, FedEx, and DHL dominate the sector, both operating their own modes of transportation and leasing space and services on other cargo haulers' vehicles. Many of the challenges the sector faces, including tighter security requirements, high fuel costs, and the need to replace an aging fleet of planes, mirror those on the passenger side. Others are specific to the air cargo industry – for instance, the ALPA worries that international shippers may begin routing cargo through Canada and Mexico in response to the new security restrictions, meaning reduced activity in the domestic market. In addition, the ALPA notes that the need for hard copies of documents and other items has diminishes with the rise of e-signatures and other digital technologies, leading to load reductions. And air cargo services also have to contend with other forms of transport, like ships and trucks.

The Germans are coming

Run by German postal entity Deutsche Post, express delivery company DHL made aggressive steps to solidify its position in the U.S. market in 2003. In August of that year, DHL acquired Airborne Inc. for $1.1 billion, securing its American rival's number-three place domestically and further strengthening its dominance in the world market for express delivery services overall. As of September 2003, according to *BusinessWeek*, FedEx held 44 percent of the market, with UPS coming in at 34 percent and Airborne trailing at 13 percent. Meanwhile, FedEx and UPS have attempted to beat back the upstart by challenging DHL on regulatory grounds, particularly citing a restriction barring foreign companies from controlling U.S. airlines (DHL's airline was spun off from the company in 2003). But DHL has forged ahead, pulling out all the marketing stops in a $150 million PR campaign beginning in the summer of 2004.

In the fiercely competitive delivery market, where the leaders vie for massive corporate contracts as well as business from average consumers, marketing has become a hardball game. In 2003, the employee-controlled UPS, with a fleet of about 88,000 ground vehicles and 575 planes, branded itself as the "brown" company. FedEx has strengthened its market position by diversifying. The company, with approximately 42,000 ground vehicles and an air fleet of 643 planes, operates different Express, Ground, and Freight units. In early 2004, the firm further diversified by acquiring document services provider Kinko's, which now goes by "FedEx Kinko's" and incorporates its parent company's mailing services into its copy shops in the U.S.

Greening Brown

As for their ground services, both UPS and FedEx have taken steps recently to "green" their fleets, replacing diesel vehicles with environmentally friendlier options like compressed natural gas and electricity-powered vans. In March 2002, FedEx announced plans to eventually replace its entire 30,000-van fleet with hybrid electric vehicles over a number of years. While the companies get PR points for their efforts, what's really driving the green movement is, well, the green – cash, that is. An August 2003 *BusinessWeek* article notes that hybrid electric vehicles can cut operators' fuel costs in half. And as big companies like FedEx continue to place orders for the lower-emissions, fuel-friendly vehicles, prices of these vehicles will go down too, benefiting the entire sector over time.

Keep on truckin'

Express-delivery services also share ties – and in some cases overlap – with the trucking sector. Dominated by bulk truckers like Quality Distribution Inc., JB Hunt Transport Services, and Yellow Roadway Corporation the industry is seeing increased demand for its hauling services, with sales of $254 billion expected for 2004, according to Global Insight, Inc.

Visit Vault at **www.vault.com** for insider company profiles, expert advice, career message boards, expert resume reviews, the Vault Job Board and more.

VAULT CAREER LIBRARY   **387**

The trucking sector also overlaps with the railroad world, with giants like JB Hunt and Schneider International teaming up with old hands on the rails such as Union Pacific, Norfolk Southern, and Burlington Northern Santa Fe. With new technologies allowing real-time cargo tracking and time-specific delivery, this sector of the transportation industry is expected to grow increasingly integrated. Both road and train shippers started adding jobs in 2004, keeping truck fleets and rail lines running at maximum capacity.

Road and Track

While the shipping portion of the rail sector has continued to chug along, the passenger-train sector has contracted dramatically in previous decades. In fact, the rail sector has been in decline since the dawn of the automobile; in the 1960s, it was dealt a heavy blow when the U.S. Postal Service turned to trucks and airplanes for its first-class shipping needs. Amtrak took over the majority of U.S. passenger trains under its National Railroad Passenger Corporation umbrella following legislation in the 1970s intended to prop up the flagging sector, but the operator has had trouble turning any sort of profit. Though still a top draw for commuter travel, particularly in the Northeast, Amtrak's fares usually can't compete with the rock-bottom rates and speed offered by airlines. Following September 11, 2001 and the deadly Madrid train bombing in March 2004, security has become a primary focus. With these requirements, dwindling passenger rolls, and increased operating costs, Amtrak has become increasingly subsidized – the organization requested $1.8 billion from Congress in 2004 to help it stay on track.

On the bus

For long-haul passenger travel, about the only thing cheaper than a bus is sticking out your thumb. Intercity buses, also known as motorcoaches, provide regular service to more than 42,000 U.S. communities. According to the American Bus Association (ABA), more passengers travel by motorcoach in the U.S. than on any other commercial mode of transportation. The bus sector is unique in its composition – unlike the heavily subsidized rail and airline sectors, motorcoach companies are more likely to go it alone (though the industry received about $25 million in grant funding for security following September 11).

There are more than 4,000 bus companies on the roads in the U.S., many of which are small, entrepreneurial operators – 90 percent operate fewer than 25 buses, the ABA reports. Major operators include Trailways, which has been around for nearly 70 years and operates a group of 65 member companies, and Greyhound, founded in 1914 and acquired in 1999 by Laidlaw Inc. As insurance rates have increased tenfold in recent years, access to affordable coverage is a key challenge faced by the industry. Unaffordable rates have priced some operators out of the market.

A Life in Transportation

As a whole, the transportation industry offers a range of employment options for highly skilled professionals and newcomers alike.

The friendly skies

Even the most phobic of flyers can find a career working in the airline industry. In fact, the majority of the approximately 559,000 workers (as of 2002) in the U.S. airline industry are employed in ground occupations, as mechanics, reservation agents, and customer service representatives and the like. Flight crew members make up another large portion (around 31 percent) of the workforce – they include pilots and flight attendants. The size of the airline workforce depends in large part on the fluctuations of the market, but other factors are more predictable – for instance, the BLS notes, the ranks of reservation and ticket agents will continue to thin as these positions are phased out by paperless tickets, Internet travel purchases, and online check-ins.

Trucking along

In the truck sector, drivers hold about 44 percent of approximately 1.9 million jobs, with the remainder consisting of warehouse workers, dispatchers, and clerks. The number of wage and salary jobs in the sector is expected to grow 23 percent by 2012, according to the BLS, with opportunities opening up at all levels, particularly for drivers, service technicians and mechanics.

As of 2002, rail transportation workers held 101,000 jobs in the U.S., the BLS reports; this figure is expected to decline over the next decade. Occupations in the sector include conductors and yardmasters, engineers, brake, signal, and switch operators, and subway and streetcar operators.

Visit Vault at **www.vault.com** for insider company profiles, expert advice, career message boards, expert resume reviews, the Vault Job Board and more.

V/\ULT CAREER LIBRARY 389

Employer Directory

AMR Corporation (American Airlines)
4333 Amon Carter Blvd.
Fort Worth, TX 76155
Phone: 817-963-1234
www.amrcorp.com

Canadian National Railway Company (CN)
935 de la Gauchetière St. West
Montreal, Quebec H3B 2M9, Canada
Phone: 514-399-5430
Fax: 204-987-9310
www.cn.ca

Continental Airlines, Inc.
1600 Smith St., Dept. HQSEO
Houston, TX 77002
Phone: (713) 324-2950
Fax: (713) 324-2637

CSX Corporation
500 Water St., 15th Fl.
Jacksonville, FL 32202
Phone: (904) 359-3200
www.csx.com

Delta Air Lines, Inc.
Hartsfield Atlanta International Airport
1030 Delta Blvd.
Atlanta, GA 30320-6001
Phone: (404) 715-2600
Fax: (404) 715-5042
www.delta.com

DHL Worldwide Network
De Kleetlaan 1
B-1831 Diegem, Belgium
Phone: +32-2-713-4000
www.dhl.com

FedEx Corporation
942 S. Shady Grove Rd.
Memphis, TN 38120
Phone: (901) 369-3600
Fax: (901) 395-2000
www.fedex.com

Greyhound Lines, Inc.
15110 N. Dallas Pkwy., Ste. 600
Dallas, TX 75248
Phone: (972) 789-7000
Phone: (972) 387-1874
www.greyhound.com

JetBlue Airways Corporation
118-29 Queens Blvd.
Forest Hills, NY 11415
Phone: (718) 286-7900
Phone: (718) 709-3621
www.jetblue.com

Norfolk Southern Corporation
3 Commercial Place
Norfolk, VA 23510-2191
Phone: (757) 629-2600
Phone: (757) 664-5069
www.nscorp.com

Northwest Airlines Corporation
2700 Lone Oak Pkwy.
Eagan, MN 55121
Phone: (612) 726-2111
Phone: (612) 726-7123
www.nwa.com

Southwest Airlines Co.
2702 Love Field Dr.
Dallas, TX 75235
Phone: (214) 792-4000
Phone: (214) 792-5015
www.southwest.com

Trailways Transportation System, Inc.
3554 Chain Bridge Rd., Ste. 301
Fairfax, VA 22030-2709
Phone: (703) 691-3052
Phone: (703) 691-9047
www.trailways.com

UAL Corporation (United Airlines)
1200 E. Algonquin Rd.
Elk Grove Township, IL 60007
Phone: (847) 700-4000
Phone: (847) 700-4081
www.united.com

Union Pacific Corporation
1416 Dodge St.
Omaha, NE 68179
Phone: (402) 271-5777
Phone: (402) 271-6408
www.up.com

United Parcel Service, Inc. (UPS)
55 Glenlake Pkwy., NE
Atlanta, GA 30328
Phone: (404) 828-6000
Fax: (404) 928-6562
www.ups.com

Visit Vault at **www.vault.com** for insider company profiles, expert advice,
career message boards, expert resume reviews, the Vault Job Board and more.

VAULT CAREER LIBRARY 391

APPENDIX

Employer Directory Index

Accounting

Deloitte 87
BDO Seidman LLP. 87
BKD LLP 87
Clifton Gunderson LLP. 87
Crowe Chizek and Company LLC 87
Deloitte & Touche LLP 87
Ernst & Young LLP 87
Grant Thornton LLP 88
KPMG LLP. 88
McGladrey & Pullen LLP 88
Moss Adams LLP 88
Plante & Moran PLLC 88
PricewaterhouseCoopers LLP 88

Advertising

Arnold Worldwide. 95
BBDO Worldwide 95
Cliff Freeman and Partners. 95
DDB Worldwide 95
Dentsu 95
FCB Worldwide 95
Grey Worldwide 95
J. Walter Thompson Co. 95
Leo Burnett Co. 95
Mad Dogs & Englishmen 95
McCann World Group 95
Ogilvy & Mather. 95
Saatchi & Saatchi. 96
Young & Rubicam (Y&R Advertising) 96

Aerospace and Defense

The Boeing Company 101
BAE Systems 101
General Dynamics Corporation 101
General Electric Company 101
Honeywell International Inc.. 101
L-3 Communications Holdings 101
Lockheed Martin. 101
Northrop Grumman Corporation 101
Parker Hannifin Corporation 101
Raytheon Company. 102
Textron Inc.. 102
United Technologies Corporation 102

Banking

Citigroup global corporate and investment bank 118
Goldman Sachs 118
Lehman Brothers. 118
Merrill Lynch 118
SG Cowen & Co., LLC 118
Banc of America Securities LLC 121
Bank of America. 121
Bank One. 121
Barclays Capital 121

Bear, Stearns & Co., Inc.. 121
The Blackstone Group 121
CIBC World Markets 121
Credit Suisse First Boston 121
Deutsche Bank. 121
Dresdner Kleinwort Wassderstein. 121
FleetBoston Financial. 121
Houlihan Lokey Howard & Zukin. 121
HSBC Bank USA. 121
ING Group 121
Jefferies & Co.. 122
J.P. Morgan Chase 122
Lazard 122
Lehman Brothers. 122
Morgan Stanley 122
Piper Jaffray & Co.. 122
Rothschild North America 122
Thomas Weisel Partners 122
UBS Investment Bank 122
Wachovia 122
Wells Fargo & Company 122

Biotech and Pharmaceuticals

Roche 136
Abbott Laboratories 136
Amgen Inc. 136
AstraZeneca plc 136
Aventis 136
Bayer Corporation. 136
Becton, Dickinson and Company 136
Eli Lilly and Company 137
Genentech, Inc. 137
Genzyme Corporation 137
GlaxoSmithKline plc 137
Johnson & Johnson 137
McKesson 137
Merck & Co., Inc.. 137
Novartis AG 137
Pfizer Inc. 137
Schering-Plough Corporation 137
Wyeth Pharmaceuticals 137

Consumer Products/Marketing

Procter & Gamble. 148
Avon Products 148
The Black & Decker Corporation. 148
Campbell Soup Company. 148
The Coca-Cola Company 148
The Clorox Company. 148
Colgate-Palmolive Company 148
The Dial Corporation 149
Eastman Kodak Company 149
General Mills, Inc.. 149
The Gillette Company 149
Hallmark Cards, Inc. 149
Hasbro, Inc.. 149
Hershey Foods Corporation 149

H.J. Heinz Corporation 149
Johnson & Johnson 149
Kimberly-Clark Corporation. 149
Kraft Foods Inc. 149
Liz Claiborne, Inc. 149
Mattel, Inc. 150
Nestle USA, Inc.. 150
Newell Rubbermaid, Inc. 150
Nike, Inc.. 150
PepsiCo, Inc. 150
Sara Lee Corporation. 150
Unilever. 150

Energy

ConocoPhillips 166
Alliant Energy Corporation 166
Amerada Hess Corporation 166
American Electric Power Company, Inc. 166
Anadarko Petroleum Corporation . . . . , , 166
Baker Hughes Incorporated 166
BP plc 167
ChevronTexaco 167
Consolidated Edison, Inc.. 167
Duke Energy Corporation 167
Exelon Corporation 167
ExxonMobil Corporation. 167
FirstEnergy Corporation 167
GE Energy 167
Halliburton Company. 167
Marathon Oil Corporation 167
Occidental Petroleum Corporation 167
Pacific Gas and Electric Company. 168
Schlumberger Limited 168
Shell Oil Company 168
Sunoco, Inc. 168
TXU Corp.. 168
Unocal Corporation 168
Valero Energy Corporation 168
The Williams Companies, Inc.. 168

Fashion

Abercrombie & Fitch Co.. 177
Ann Taylor Stores Corporation 177
The Body Shop International PLC 177
Chanel S.A. 177
Dolce & Gabbana SPA. 177
Donna Karan International Inc. 177
Eddie Bauer, Inc. 177
Estee Lauder Companies Inc. 177
Federated Department Stores. 177
Gap Inc. 177
Guess?, Inc.. 177
J. Crew Group Inc.. 177
Tommy Hilfiger. 178
Kenneth Cole Productions, Inc.. 178
L'Oreal USA. 178
Levi Strauss & Co. 178
Limited Brands 178
Nike, Inc.. 178

Nordstrom, Inc. 178
Pacific Sunwear of California, Inc. 178
OshKosh b'Gosh, Inc. 178
Polo Ralph Lauren Corporation 178
Reebok International Ltd.. 178
Revlon, Inc. 178

Financial Services and Insurance

Nationwide Insurance 195
Naval Financial Management Career (NAVY) 195
Northwestern Mutual 196
Standard & Poor's 196
The Advest Group, Inc.. 197
AFLAC Incorporated 197
A.G. Edwards, Inc. 197
The Allstate Corporation 197
American Express Company. 197
American International Group, Inc. (AIG) 197
Bank of America Corporation 197
Bank One. 197
Berkshire Hathaway, Inc.. 197
Capital One Financial Corporation 197
The Chubb Corporation 197
Discover Financial Services 197
Edward Jones & Co.. 198
Fitch Ratings 198
GE Consumer Finance 198
Guardian Life Insurance Company of America 198
Hartford Financial Services Group, Inc. 198
HSBC Bank USA. 198
MasterCard International 198
MBNA Corporation 198
MetLife, Inc. 198
Moody's Corporation. 198
The Mutual of Omaha Companies 198
New York Life Insurance Company 198
Principal Financial Group, Inc. 199
Prudential Financial, Inc. 199
Standard & Poor's 199
State Farm Insurance Companies 199
Visa International 199

Government and Politics

Naval Financial Management Career (NAVY) . . 212
U.S. Secret Service 212
Central Intelligence Agency. 212
Democratic National Committee 212
Democratic Senatorial Campaign Committee. . 212
Federal Bureau of Investigation 213
National Republican Senatorial Committee . . . 213
National Republican Congressional Committee. 213
Office of Management and Budget. 213
Republican National Committee 213
Small Business Administration. 213
U.S. Department of Commerce. 213
U.S. Department of Education. 213
U.S. Department of Health and
Human Services 213
U.S. Department of Justice. 213

Visit Vault at **www.vault.com** for insider company profiles, expert advice,
career message boards, expert resume reviews, the Vault Job Board and more.

VAULT CAREER LIBRARY   **395**

U.S. Department of Labor 213
U.S. Department of State 213
U.S. Environmental Protection Agency 213

Health Care

Aetna, Inc. 223
Oxford Health Plans 223
AdvancePCS, Inc. 224
Anthem, Inc. 224
Baxter International Inc. 224
Becton, Dickinson and Company 224
Boston Scientific Corporation 224
Caremark Rx 224
CIGNA Corporation 224
Express Scripts, Inc. 224
Guidant Corporation 224
HCA, Inc. 224
Health Net Inc. 224
Humana Inc. 224
Kaiser Foundation Health Plan, Inc. 225
MedTronic, Inc. 225
PacifiCare Health Systems, Inc. 225
Quest Diagnostics Incorporated 225
Tenet Healthcare Corporation 225
UnitedHealth Group Incorporated 225
WellChoice, Inc. 225
WellPoint Health Networks Inc. 225

High Tech

Agilent Technologies 233
The Boeing Company 233
3Com Corporation 234
Advanced Micro Devices, Inc. 234
Analog Devices, Inc. 234
Apple Computer, Inc. 234
Applied Materials, Inc. 234
Ariba, Inc. 234
Atmel Corporation. 234
Cisco Systems, Inc. 234
Computer Associates International, Inc. 234
Cypress Semiconductor Corporation 234
Dell Computer 234
EMC Corporation 234
Gateway, Inc. 235
Hewlett-Packard 235
IBM 235
Intel Corporation 235
Intuit Inc. 235
LSI Logic Corporation 235
Microsoft Corporation 235
Motorola, Inc. 235
Novell, Inc. 235
Oracle Corporation 235
PeopleSoft, Inc. 235
Red Hat, Inc. 235
Sun Microsystems 236
Samsung Electronics 236
SAP Aktiengesellschaft 236
Siebel Systems, Inc. 236
Siemens Corporation 236

Sony Corporation 236
Sybase, Inc. 236
Symantec Corporation 236
Texas Instruments Incorporated 236
Xerox Corporation 236

Hospitality and Tourism

Sodexho 244
Accor 244
Aramark Corporation 244
Budget Rent A Car System, Inc. 244
Carlson Companies, Inc. 244
Carnival Corporation 244
Cendant Corporation 244
Cintas Corporation 245
Compass Group 245
Enterprise Rent-A-Car Company 245
The Hertz Corporation 245
Hilton Hotels Corporation 245
Hyatt Corporation 245
InterActiveCorp 245
InterContinental Hotels Group PLC 245
Kohler Co. 245
Royal Caribbean Cruises Ltd. 245
Starwood Hotels & Resorts Worldwide, Inc. 245
Vanguard Car Rental USA, Inc. 245

Investment Management

Advest Group 256
AIG Global Investment Group 256
AIM Investments 256
Alliance Capital Management 256
American Century Investments 256
BlackRock, Inc. 256
CalPERS 256
Dreyfus Corporation 256
Federated Investors, Inc. 256
Fidelity Investments 256
Franklin Resources 256
Gabelli Asset Management 257
ING Americas 257
Janus Capital Group Inc. 257
MFS Investment Management 257
Nuveen Investments, Inc. 257
Pacific Investment Management Co. 257
Pequot Capital Management 257
Putnam Investments 257
T. Rowe Price Group, Inc. 257
TIAA-CREF 257
The Vanguard Group Inc. 257
Wellington Management Company, LLP 257

Law/Paralegal

Arnold & Porter 275
Cleary, Gottlieb, Steen & Hamilton 275
Covington & Burling 275
Cravath, Swaine & Moore LLP 275
Davis Polk & Wardwell 275
Debevoise & Plimpton 275

Gibson, Dunn & Crutcher LLP. 275
Hale and Dorr LLP. 275
Jones Day 275
Kirkland & Ellis 275
Latham & Watkins LLP 275
Milbank, Tweed, Hadley & McCloy LLP. 275
O'Melveny & Myers LLP 276
Paul, Weiss, Rifkind, Wharton & Garrison LLP 276
Ropes & Gray LLP. 276
Shearman & Sterling 276
Sidley Austin Brown & Wood LLP. 276
Simpson Thacher & Bartlett 276
Skadden, Arps, Slate, Meagher & Flom LLP & Affiliates 276
Sullivan & Cromwell LLP 276
Wachtell, Lipton, Rosen & Katz 276
Weil, Gotshal & Manges LLP 276
White & Case LLP. 276
Williams & Connolly LLP 277
Wilmer, Cutler & Pickering 277

Management Consulting

Accenture 290
Bain & Company, Inc. 290
Booz Allen Hamilton 291
Capgemini 291
Deloitte 292
The Advisory Board 292
Arthur D. Little 292
A.T. Kearney 292
BearingPoint. 292
Boston Consulting Group 292
Cambridge Associates 292
Charles River Associates 293
DiamondCluster International 293
The Gallup Organization. 293
Gartner 293
Hewitt Associates. 293
IBM Business Consulting Services. 293
L.E.K. Consulting 293
Marakon Associates 293
McKinsey & Company. 293
Mercer Human Resource Consulting 293
Mercer Management Consulting 293
Mercer Oliver Wyman 293
Monitor Group 294
NERA 294
Stern Stewart & Company. 294
The Parthenon Group 294
Towers Perrin. 294
Watson Wyatt Worldwide 294

Manufacturing

International Paper 300
3M Company. 300
Alcoa 300
Applied Materials 300
The Boeing Company 300
BMW Manufacturing Corporation 300
Caterpillar Inc. 300
Daimler-Chrysler Corporation 301

Dana Corporation 301
Deere & Company 301
Eaton Corporation. 301
E. I. du Pont de Nemours and Company 301
Federal-Mogul Corporation 301
Ford Motor Company 301
GE Advanced Materials 301
Georgia-Pacific Corporation 301
General Motors Corporation 301
Honeywell Electronic Materials 301
Ingersoll-Rand Industrial Solutions 301
ITT Industries, Inc. 302
Johnson Controls, Inc. 302
Lockheed Martin Corporation 302
Newell Rubbermaid Inc. 302
Northrop Grumman Corporation 302
PPG Industries, Inc.. 302
Raytheon Company. 302
Thermo Electron Corporation 302
Toyota Motor North America, Inc. 302
United Technologies Corporation 302
U.S. Steel Corporation. 302
Weyerhaeuser Company 302

Media and Entertainment

Reed Business 313
AMC Entertainment Inc. 313
Bertelsmann AG 313
Black Entertainment Television, Inc. 313
Clear Channel Communications, Inc. 313
CNN News Group 313
Cox Communications, Inc. 313
Discovery Communications, Inc. 314
Dreamworks L.L.C. 314
Home Box Office, Inc. 314
Liberty Media Corporation 314
Metro-Goldwyn Mayer (MGM) 314
NBC Universal, Inc. 314
Public Broadcasting Service 314
Pixar Animation Studios. 314
Time Warner Inc. 314
Tribune Company 314
Viacom Inc. 314
The Walt Disney Company. 314

Nonprofit

American Cancer Society. 323
American Civil Liberties Union 323
AmeriCorps. 323
American Red Cross 323
American Heart Association 323
Big Brothers Big Sisters 323
The Ford Foundation 323
Habitat for Humanity. 323
Human Rights Watch 323
National Women's Law Center 323
Open Society Institute. 323
Peace Corps. 324
RAND 324
Rotary International. 324

Visit Vault at **www.vault.com** for insider company profiles, expert advice,
career message boards, expert resume reviews, the Vault Job Board and more.

VAULT CAREER LIBRARY   397

The Salvation Army National Corporation 324
UNICEF 324
United Way of America 324

Public Relations

Burson-Marsteller 331
Edelman Worldwide 331
Hill & Knowlton 331
Ketchum 331
Waggener Edstrom Inc. 331
Fleishman-Hillard Inc. 331
Weber Shandwick Worldwide 331

Publishing

Reed Business 347
Bantam Doubleday Dell 347
Conde Nast Publications Inc. 347
Harcourt Brace 347
HarperCollins Publishers, Inc. 347
Hearst Magazines 347
Houghton Mifflin. 347
John Wiley & Sons, Inc. 348
The McGraw-Hill Companies, Inc. 348
Pearson Education, Inc. 348
The Penguin Group 348
Random House, Inc. 348
Scholastic Corporation. 348
Simon & Schuster, Inc. 348
The Thomson Corporation 348
Time, Inc. 348
Time, Warner Books 348
W.W. Norton & Company 348

Real Estate

AMB Property Corporation 354
Boston Properties, Inc. 354
CB Richard Ellis Group, Inc. 354
Century 21 Real Estate Corporation 354
Cushman & Wakefield, Inc. 354
Duke Realty Corporation 354
Equity Office Properties Trust. 354
General Growth Properties, Inc. 354
Hines Interests L.P. 354
HomeServices of America 354
Jones Lang LaSalle Incorporated. 355
Julien J. Studley, Inc. 355
Lend Lease Corporation Limited 355
RE/Max International, Inc. 355
RREEF Funds L.L.C. 355
Trammell Crow Company 355

Retail

JCPenney 362
Wal-Mart 362
Amazon.com, Inc. 362
AutoZone, Inc. 362
Barnes & Noble, Inc. 362

Best Buy Co., Inc. 362
Borders Group Inc. 362
Circuit City Stores, Inc. 362
Costco Wholesale Corporation 363
Federated Department Stores, Inc. 363
Gap Inc. 363
Hallmark Cards, Inc. 363
The Home Depot, Inc. 363
Kmart Corporation 363
Kohl's Corporation 363
Lowe's Companies, Inc. 363
The Neiman Marcus Group, Inc. 363
Nordstrom, Inc. 363
Office Depot, Inc. 363
Saks Incorporated 363
Sears, Roebuck and Co. 364
Staples, Inc. 364
Target Corporation 364
Tiffany & Co. 364
The TJX Companies, Inc. 364
Toys "R" Us, Inc. 364

Technology Consulting

Accenture 371
Deloitte 371
Atos Origin 372
American Management Systems 372
BearingPoint, Inc. 372
Capgemini 372
Computer Sciences Corporation 372
DiamondCluster International 372
Electronic Data Systems Corporation (EDS) 372
Fujitsu Consulting 372
IBM Global Services 372
Infosys Technologies Ltd. 372
Keane, Inc. 372
LogicaCMG plc. 372
META Group, Inc. 373
PA Consulting Group, Ltd. 373
Perot Systems Corporation 373
Sapient Corporation 373
SBI Group Inc. 373
Syntegra 373
T-Systems International 373
Tata Consulting Services 373
Telcordia Technologies 373
The Titan Corporation 373
Wipro Ltd. 373

Telecommunications

AT&T Corp. 379
Sprint Corporation. 379
ALLTEL Corporation 380
BellSouth Corporation 380
Cingular Wireless LLC 380
Charter Communications, Inc. 380
Cisco Systems, Inc. 380
Comcast Corporation. 380
Corning Incorporated. 380
Cox Communications, Inc. 380

Echostar Communications Corporation 380
Lucent Technologies, Inc. 380
MCI, Inc.. 380
Motorola, Inc.. 381
Nextel Communications, Inc. 381
Nortel Networks Corporation 381
QUALCOMM Incorporated 381
Qwest Communications International Inc. 381
SBC Communications Inc. 381
Verizon Communications Inc.. 381

Transportation and Airlines

AMR Corporation (American Airlines) 390
Canadian National Railway Company (CN) 390
Continental Airlines, Inc. 390
CSX Corporation. 390
Delta Air Lines, Inc. 390
DHL Worldwide Network 390
FedEx Corporation 390
Greyhound Lines, Inc, , ... 390
JetBlue Airways Corporation 390
Norfolk Southern Corporation. 390
Northwest Airlines Corporation. 390
Southwest Airlines Co. 391
Trailways Transportation System, Inc. 391
UAL Corporation (United Airlines) 391
Union Pacific Corporation 391
United Parcel Service, Inc. (UPS) 391

Visit Vault at **www.vault.com** for insider company profiles, expert advice, career message boards, expert resume reviews, the Vault Job Board and more.

VAULT CAREER LIBRARY

399

About the Author

Vault Editors

Vault is the leading media company for career information. Our team of industry-focused editors takes a journalistic approach in covering news, employment trends and specific employers in their industries. We annually survey 10,000s of employees to bring readers the inside scoop on industries and specific employers.

Much of the material in The College Career Bible is excerpted from Vault titles to specific industries or career titles. Vault publishes more than 80 titles for job seekers and professionals. To see a complete list of Vault titles, go to www.vault.com.